TABLE SETTINGS

The Material Culture and Social Context of Dining
AD 1700–1900

edited by

James Symonds

Oxbow Books
Oxford and Oakville

Published by
Oxbow Books, Oxford UK

ISBN 978 1 84217 298 8

A CIP record for this book is available from the British Library

This book is available direct from

Oxbow Books, Oxford UK
(Phone: 01865-241249; Fax: 01865-794449)

and

The David Brown Book Company
PO Box 511, Oakville, CT 06779, USA
(Phone: 860-945-9329; Fax: 860-945-9468)

or from our website

www.oxbowbooks.com

Library of Congress Cataloging-in-Publication Data

Table settings : the material culture and social context of dining, AD 1700-1900 / edited by James Symonds.
   p. cm.
  Includes papers presented at conference entitled "The table : the material culture and social context of dining in the historical periods," held at University of Sheffield, April 23-25, 2004.
  Includes bibliographical references.
  ISBN 978-1-84217-298-8 (hbk.)
  1. Food habits--History--18th century--Congresses. 2. Food habits--History--19th century--Congresses. 3. Dinners and dining--Social aspects--History--18th century--Congresses. 4. Dinners and dining--Social aspects--History--19th century--Congresses. 5. Material culture--History--18th century--Congresses. 6. Material culture--History--19th century--Congresses. 7. Archaeology and history--Congresses. 8. Social archaeology--Congresses. 9. Social history--18th century--Congresses. 10. Social history--19th century--Congresses. I. Symonds, Jim.
  GT2850.T316 2010
  641.3009'033--dc22

2010029592

Printed in Great Britain by
Short Run Press, Exeter

Contents

Acknowledgements

This volume has been many years in preparation, and I must first of all thank the contributors, and Oxbow Books, for their patience and unfailing good humour over this extended period of time. Many of the papers within this volume were presented at a conference organized by the editor and entitled 'The Table: the material culture and social context of dining in the historical periods'. This took place at the University of Sheffield between 23rd to 25th April 2004. I thank the British Academy for support in the form of a conference grant which enabled overseas delegates to travel to the conference. Anna Badcock, Mark Edmonds, Jenny Moore, Ian Mayes, Naomi Nathan all offered help and much appreciated support during the conference, and in the slow passage to publication. My greatest debt, as ever, is to Victoria Parsons, and it is to her that I dedicate this book.

List of Contributors

JAMES SYMONDS
Department of Archaeology
University of York, UK

DAVID BARKER
Freelance Ceramic Researcher
Newcastle-under-Lyme, UK

CHRISTINE BALL
Ken Hawley Collection Trust
Sheffield, UK

ANNIE GRAY
Freelance Researcher & Heritage Interpreter
Ely, UK

JOAN UNWIN
The Company of Cutlers in Hallamshire
Sheffield, UK

JULIE BANHAM
Humanities Research Institute
University of Sheffield, UK

MARY C BEAUDRY
Department of Archaeology
Boston University, USA

DIANA DI ZEREGA WALL
PhD Program in Anthropology
City University of New York, USA

HAROLD MYTUM
Centre for Manx Studies
University of Liverpool, UK

DARREN GRIFFIN
Wurundjeri Tribe Land & Compensation Cultural Heritage
Council Incorporated
Abbotsford, Australia

ELEANOR CONLIN CASELLA
School of Arts, Histories and Cultures
University of Manchester, UK

GAVIN LUCAS
Institute of Archaeology
Reykjavik, Iceland

LINDA YOUNG
School of History Heritage and Society
Deakin University, Australia

SUSAN LAWRENCE
Archaeology Program
La Trobe University, Australia

ALASDAIR BROOKES
School of Archaeology and Ancient History
University of Leicester, UK

ALEXY SIMMONS
Simmons & Associates Ltd
Hamilton, New Zealand

1

Introduction

James Symonds

Fernand Braudel famously observed that the 'mere smell of cooking can evoke a whole civilization' (Braudel 1973, 123). The way that food is prepared, served, and eaten also reveals a great deal about the structure and workings of any society. It is therefore not surprising that food, and the culturally specific etiquettes and equipment that surround the act of eating have been studied by scholars from a wide range of disciplines. Indeed, one might be forgiven for thinking that this pot has been on the hob rather too long to yield anything new of substance. Nevertheless, as in the Portuguese fable of the *sopa de pedra*, the flavour and nourishment in this particular stone soup has been created by the inclusion of fresh ingredients, and an adventurous use of seasoning.

The papers in this volume consider the changes that occurred in Old and New World dining and related culinary activities between the 17th century and the early 20th century. This period saw the widespread acceptance of the fork in dining and the adoption of routinized etiquettes to govern eating. In the 18th century the rise of individualism ushered in new forms of segmented dining based upon symmetrically arranged tables and individual place settings. Against this backdrop of manufactured uniformity, made possible by advances in industrial production, highly stylized dining rituals and *haute cuisine* which had previously been the exclusive domain of European courtly elites entered the homes and routines of the 'middling sort'. Henceforth, material expressions of status and social identity became commonplace at the table, and an integral part of dining in all but the humblest homes.

Historians have traced changes in dining and the use of eating implements and table settings from cookbooks, guides to etiquette, trade catalogues, and probate inventories, as well as descriptions contained in contemporary fiction, and diaries. The unique contribution of this volume lies in the way in which a distinguished group of international historical archaeologists have combined the richness of primary archaeological evidence with a wealth of documentary

evidence to create insightful new material histories of dining. The new light which this throws upon manufacturing processes, feasting rituals, the rise of respectability, the inter-continental spread of the Victorian cult of domesticity, and foodways among peripheral agricultural communities will be of interest to scholars beyond archaeology, in the cognate fields of anthropology, social and economic history, cultural geography, and material culture studies.

The intentional focus upon mundane materiality within this volume should not be taken to suggest that the contributors are simply content to catalogue the minutiae of daily life, or that their findings should used to embellish larger historically-constructed pictures. Much of the early 20th century interest in table settings, be they ceramic, glass, silver, pewter, or of some other material, came from antique collectors and connoisseurs, who naturally prized high value and rare items. Items selected for acquisition into museum collections also tended to be high value items, or entire sets of a certain product, such as a dinner plates and bowls.

Archaeology has the capacity to broaden our understanding of tablewares of all kinds by recovering evidence of their production, use, and discard. Often this can shed new light on supposedly familiar objects, such as the knives, forks, and spoons produced by the Sheffield metals trades (Symonds 2002). Archaeology can also, as already mentioned, recover items from a wide social spectrum, offering material evidence for the eating arrangements of the poorer elements of society, in addition to the better documented practices of the well-to-do, and elite.

Historical archaeologists have approached the study of tablewares and other household materials in a variety of ways. In the UK, the Society for Post-Medieval Archaeology (Barton 1967) developed out of the earlier Post-Medieval Ceramic Research Group, and many of its early publications were concerned with 16th and 17th century coarse ware industries and their products (for an overview, see Barker and Majewski 2006, 206–209). In the US, archaeologists on the eastern seaboard seized upon the temporal variation in tableware forms to create detailed typologies that allowed early European settler sites to be more closely dated (Noël Hume 1969; Miller 1980, 1991). Others wrapped up in the promise of the New Archaeology, devised functional catalogues in an effort to locate behavioural patterns in artefactual assemblages (South 1977).

The connection between race and poverty has led some North Americans to search for evidence of status differences on African American plantation sites (Orser 1988; Otto 1977, 1984). Social identities and subaltern strategies have also been explored through the evidence of consumer choices (Groover 2003; Klein and LeeDecker 1991; Spencer Wood 1987) or ethnically distinct food ways and their associated tablewares (Deagan 1983; Fitts 2002; Griggs 1999; Loren 1999; Praetzellis and Praetzellis 1998). Similar work in Australasia has produced intriguing material evidence for early life in a dependent British colony (Staniforth 2003), demonstrating how individuals jostled with their plates and cups for social status and respectability in a diverse range of settings from the country estate, urban block, mining camp, and whaling station (Brookes and Connah 2007; Karskens 1997; Murray 2003; Lawrence 2000, 2006).

One of the most famous examples of how historical archaeology can be used to move beyond supposedly mute and passive objects or features to expose the hidden workings of ideology is Mark Leone's study of William Paca's 18th century garden in Annapolis (Leone 1984). In this ground-breaking study Leone moved beyond simple horticultural questions to expose the Georgian world view of a Chesapeake merchant capitalist, concluding that Paca had created his formal garden to naturalize and safeguard his social position and that it was therefore 'a garden about power, not plants' (Leone 2005, 67). A similar observation can be made about dining tables in the homes of the 18th century well-to-do (Shackel 1993). Here the geometry of carefully placed settings and the delicately choreographed succession of courses to the table spoke more about aspiration than appetite. Rituals of formal dining were eagerly embraced as a way of reinforcing a sense of familial cohesion. The transformative power of dinner parties allowed hosts and their guests to partake in an imagined community of gentility and style.

The consumption of table wares and other goods continues to play a central role in the construction of individual and collective identities in the modern world, but quite how consumer society actually works is open to interpretation. Thorstein Veblen identified the emergence of 'conspicuous consumption' and suggested that individuals emulated the consumption patterns of higher status members of society (Veblen [1899] 1994). In contrast, Pierre Bourdieu has claimed that consumption is motivated more by a desire for *differentiation* than emulation, 'where each class strives

to distinguish itself from others' (Bourdieu 1984). More recently, Elizabeth Kowaleski-Wallace has argued that porcelain can be regarded as a 'defining trope for femininity' (Kowaleski-Wallace 1996) and Moira Vincentelli has stressed the importance of gender to the consumption of ceramics in domestic settings (Vincentelli 2000).

The economic historian Neil McKendrick coined the phrase 'consumer revolution' to describe the heightened desire for mass produced goods which he claimed accompanied industrialization in 18th century England. McKendrick pinpointed this so called revolution to the third quarter of the 18th century, and famously commented that at this time "Men, and in particular women, bought as never before" (McKendrick 1982, 9). Much of the activity which Kendrick describes centred on the purchase of mass-produced ceramics for the table, created by the Staffordshire entrepreneurial giant Josiah Wedgwood. In McKendrick's view modern mass consumption emerged in the late-18th century as the new wealth generated by industrialization and the commercialization of manufacturing triggered an explosion in competitive and emulative behaviour, of the kind described by Veblen. The new upwardly mobile middle classes emulated the tastes of the aristocracy, and their behaviour trickled down, and was in turn emulated by poorer members of society, especially servants.

McKendrick's co-authored book, *The Birth of a Consumer Society* (McKendrick, Brewer, and Plumb 1982) brought an interest in fashion and the material world to the fore in historical debates and made a seminal contribution to the emerging field of consumption studies. In Chapter 2 of this volume David Baker examines the ways in which north Staffordshire potters responded to the growth in demand for factory-made table wares in the eighteenth century, relating the appearance of new wares and vessel types to technical developments within the industry. Barker identifies a 'Ceramic Revolution' in north Staffordshire in the three decades between *c.*1720–50, arguing that the wider availability of tea and coffee served as a catalyst that encouraged the production of specialist tea and coffee making and drinking equipage. The momentum created by the need to service the growing taste for hot beverages was added to from the mid 18th century by the elaboration of Georgian dining rituals. Here the introduction of individual and symmetrical place settings, and a desire for uniformity in vessel form and decoration, was more readily achieved through the use of factory-made ceramics.

A century earlier, another exotic beverage, hot chocolate, had excited the taste-buds of the well-to-do in the Coffee houses of Oxford and London. The foodstuff *Chocolatada*, was first encountered by Europeans when the Spanish Conquistadors made inroads into South America in the early 16th century. Although initially disliked, the foodstuff became popular among the Spanish when the bitter beans were crushed and mixed with spices to create a hot drink.

In Chapter 3, Annie Gray describes the early use of chocolate in Europe, and uses experimental archaeology to re-create a chocolate and cinnamon drink based upon a 17th century Spanish recipe. Her exercise in experiential archaeology, which included a memorable live demonstration and tasting session at the conference, allowed the elaborate and time-consuming nature of early chocolate making to be appreciated, and enabled the unfamiliar and spicy taste of the 17th century beverage to be compared to modern-day chocolate products.

The next three chapters concentrate on aspects of the late 18th and 19th century metals trades, and the British industrialists and firms that prospered by manufacturing goods for the table. Christine Ball discusses the catalogues of the cutlery, flatware, and hollow-ware trades, principally in Sheffield, but with reference to Birmingham, and London, and demonstrates how the early 18th century trade card, which served as a simple schedule of goods and prices, evolved to become an elaborate illustrated catalogue. In the 19th century trade catalogues projected the real and virtual capabilities of the company in an effort to capture the expanding global markets, and ultimately became a metaphor for the company itself.

The organization and regulation of the Sheffield metals trades and the performative and self-congratulatory role of elite feasting in the promotion of industrial culture is explored by Joan Unwin. Taking the example of the Company of Cutlers of Hallamshire, incorporated in 1624, Unwin shows how a simple dinner in a local tavern to celebrate a successful year of trading grew to become an ostentatious display of corporate dining that attracted a mix of nobility, landed gentry, merchants, clergymen, and cutlers, in the splendour of a purpose-built banqueting hall.

The theme of the Sheffield 19th century manufacturing elite is continued by Julie Banham, who explores the building and furnishing of Endcliffe Hall in the 1860s by one of Sheffield's pre-eminent Victorian industrialists, Sir John Brown. In an effort to counter the impression that Sheffield was an essentially plebeian society of craft-workers, and labourers, Brown created Endcliffe Hall as a showpiece not only for himself, but also for his town and its skills. Brown's apparently altruistic promotion of the industrial workforce of Sheffield is qualified by a carefully observed study of Brown's relationship with his leading industrial rival, the steel master Mark Firth, in which Banham shows how the personal rivalry between the two men even permeated into their domestic dining arrangements.

In Chapter 7, Mary C. Beaudry examines the role that food and lavish hospitality played in bolstering the reputation of North American elites, with a diachronic study of the three merchant families who successively occupied the Spencer-Pierce-Little Farm in Newburyport, Massachusetts. Beaudry's fine-grained analysis combines family histories with archaeological evidence and demonstrates how the vicissitudes of personal fortune in the early American republic impacted upon the retention and transmission of dynastic wealth, and how this is manifest in the material residues of feasting and dining rituals that have been recovered by her excavations within and around the farmhouse.

Diana diZerega Wall considers the transformation of domestic life in 18th and early 19th century New York in Chapter 8. Taking the suggestion that has been made by historians that the affluent families divided their homelife and workplace into 'separate spheres' of male and female influence after the American Revolutionary War as her starting point, Wall scrutinises the changing styles of teawares and tablewares in 11 excavated household assemblages from New York City. She concludes that far from being the passive victims of an industrializing society, middle class women were actively selecting their tea sets and dinner services, and had devised a range of secular tea and dining rituals to reinforce family ties and the moral values of home life by the late 1820s.

Section three of the volume contains five chapters that are concerned with the routines for preparing, serving, and consuming food among less privileged families.

Harold Mytum draws upon his long term research project in south-west Wales to discuss the performance of domestic practices in 19th century Pembrokeshire. Mytum combines information from folk life, architectural history, and archaeological work on buildings, deposits, and artefacts, to highlight the central importance of the dresser, an item of furniture used to store food and display ceramics, in daily life. Mytum argues that the maintenance and display of ceramics on dressers materialized the authority of women within the home, and also served as a didactic devise. The rituals of eating allowed mothers to teach their children language and social skills, and the transfer-printed plates and other items that women chose to display on the dresser for their colours and imagery often symbolized the aesthetic and cultural values of Welsh rural life.

In Chapter 10, Darren Griffin and Eleanor Conlin Casella offer a parallel study of the everyday material worlds of working-class households in the 19th and 20th century English countryside. Seizing upon the power of historical archaeology to challenge and subvert received historical narratives Griffin and Casella combine excavated evidence from the Hagg Cottages at Alderley Edge with oral testimonies from some of the elderly former inhabitants of the cottages. The picture that emerges challenges conventional models of rural society and offers significant insights into the community scale of social life, and the material dimensions of class aspiration.

The final chapters in this section were commissioned from two leading historical archaeologists who were unable to attend the conference in Sheffield. The papers have been included in the volume as they add geographical depth to the coverage of the North Atlantic world, and also contribute new and exciting theoretical approaches to the inter-disciplinary study of food and foodways.

Stephen A. Brighton explores the material evidence for cultural continuity and transition among 19th century Irish immigrants to America and makes the important point that the Irish diaspora needs to be viewed as a process that linked people and attitudes towards possessions in the donor and recipient cultures. Brighton develops this position by comparing excavated assemblages of teawares and table wares from two abandoned famine period cabins in County Roscommon, Ireland, with finds from the Irish immigrant sites in Five Points, New York, and Patterson, New Jersey. The case studies offer an important transnational and transatlantic approach to material culture, and show how transgenerational changes led, by the end of the 19th century, to the adoption of a new Irish-American identity and culture of consumption.

The ceramic revolution in Iceland, 1850–1950, is considered by Gavin Lucas in Chapter 12. Up until the mid-19th century Iceland was effectively aceramic. Food preparation was undertaken in wooden or metal vessels, and consumed from personalized wooden vessels, held in the lap. This pattern of eating was transformed in the late 19th and early 20th century by the mass importation of English and Scottish industrial whitewares. Lucas uses documentary evidence and excavated ceramic assemblages from sites at Eyri, and Kúvíkur, to explore this transition, and concludes that the high incidence of repairs noted on ceramic vessels may indicate that the pre-modern attachment to personalized wooden eating vessels was carried over onto ceramics as they were incorporated into Icelandic culture.

The final section of the book extends the exploration of food and dining rituals to the southern hemisphere, with chapters about etiquette and consumption in 19th century Australia and New Zealand. Three of these chapters originated as papers given at the conference, and the fourth, by Alasdair Brookes, was commissioned later.

Linda Young draws upon research for her book *Middle Class Culture in the Nineteenth Century: America, Australia, and Britain* (Young 2003) to discuss the material culture of the table in the 'long 19th century', 1780–1915. She identifies the concept of gentility, which she defines as the pursuit of private refinement and public respectability, as being central to the values of the Victorian middle classes. Moving beyond conventional analyses of class that use economics or politics, Young employs Bourdieu's notion of habitus to show how this form of highly mannered behaviour was enacted within a framework of lived practice in Britain and the colonies of settlement.

Susan Lawrence reminds us, in Chapter 14, that most settlers in Australia between *c*.1788–1840 were workers, be they convicts, soldiers, farmers, or maritime workers.

Lawrence investigates the shore whaling industry, which accounted for the bulk of exports from Australia before being overtaken by wool in the 1840s. Much Australian historical archaeology has concentrated upon the lifestyles of the British ruling elite, or conversely, that of convicts. Lawrence breaks new ground by combining documentary evidence with artefactual and faunal analysis from two whaling stations in Tasmania to show that rather than being deficient, the diet of the free and highly skilled workers who manned these outposts was actually more varied, more abundant, and more nutritious, including a large amount of beef, than the food consumed by contemporary workers in Britain.

Alasdair Brooks focuses on transfer-printed ceramics, a British technological innovation that became a global phenomenon in 19th century. The Australian market rarely exceeded 2% of British ceramic exports, and yet brightly coloured transfer prints are commonly found in excavations of all classes of sites in southern Australian. Brooks constructs an interpretive framework that allows transfer prints to be assessed in terms of the information they hold on economy, status, function, meaning, and the inter-relationship between all of these issues. Intriguingly, Brooks suggests that the ubiquity of transfer prints in southern Australian contexts is evidence that mass produced transfer prints, which were more expensive than plain ceramics, and designed to appeal to more genteel tastes, were widely appropriated and used by the lower strata of colonial society.

The concluding chapter of the book, by Alexy Simmons, investigates eating and drinking among the British troops that served in the New Zealand War campaigns of 1863–1872. Using archaeological findings from redoubts and other military sites in the Waikato and Bay of Plenty area, supplemented by evidence from diaries, journals, letters, and military records, Simmons constructs a detailed picture of the provisioning of daily life in the field. The complexity of feeding a standing army while at the same time attempting to reinforce differences of rank and social class are discussed in detail, and the eagerness of the troops to supplement their rations by pillaging fresh fruit, vegetables, and meat, from abandoned Maori villages is highlighted.

References

Barker, D. and Majewski, T. (2006) Ceramic studies in historical archaeology, in Hicks, D. and Beaudry, M. C. (eds.) *Historical Archaeology*, Cambridge, Cambridge University Press, 205–231.

Barton, K. J. (1967) The origins of the Society for Post-Medieval Archaeology, *Post-Medieval Archaeology* 1:1–3.

Bourdieu, P. (1984) *Distinction: A Social Critique of the Judgement of Taste*, London, Routledge.

Braudel, F. (1973) *Capitalism and Material Life 1400–1800*, New York, Harper and Row.

Brookes, A. and Connah, G. (2007) A hierarchy of servitude: ceramics at Lake Innes Estate, New South Wales, *Antiquity*, 81:3, 133–147.

Deagan, K. A. (ed.) (1983) *Spanish St. Augustine: the Archaeology of a Colonial Creole Community*, New York, Academic Press.

Fitts, R. K. (2002) Becoming American: the archaeology of an Italian immigrant, *Historical Archaeology* 36:2, 1–17.

Griggs, H. J. (1999) *Go gCuire Dia Rath Blath Ort* (God Grant that You Prosper and Flourish): Social and Economic Mobility Among the Irish in Nineteenth-Century New York, *Historical Archaeology* 33, 1, 87–101.

Groover, M. D. (2003) *An Archaeological Study of Rural Capitalism and Material Life: The Gibbs Farmstead in Southern Appalachia*, New York, Plenum Press.

Karskens, G. (1997) *The Rocks: Life in Early Sydney*, Parkville, Melbourne University Press.

Klein, T. H. and LeeDecker. C. H. (eds.) (1991) Models for the study of consumer behaviour, *Historical Archaeology* 25: 2, 1–91.

Kowaleski-Wallace, E. (1996) *Consuming Subjects, Women, Shopping and Business in the Eighteenth Century*, New York, Columbia University Press.

Lawrence, S. (2000) *Dolly's Creek: An Archaeology of a Victorian Goldfields Community*, Melbourne, Melbourne University Press.

Lawrence, S. (2006) *Whalers and Free Men: Life on Tasmania's Colonial Whaling Stations*, Melbourne, Australian Scholarly Publishing.

Leone, M. P. (1984) Interpreting ideology in historical archaeology: using the rules of perspective in the William Paca garden, Annapolis, Maryland, in Miller, D. and Tilley, C. (eds.) *Ideology, Power, and Prehistory*, Cambridge, Cambridge University Press, 25–35.

Leone, M. P. (2005) *The Archaeology of Liberty in an American Capital*, Berkeley, Los Angeles, University of California Press.

Loren, D. D. (1999) *Creating Social Distinction: Articulating Colonial policies and Practices along the 18th Century Louisiana/Texas Frontier*, PhD dissertation, Department of Anthropology, State University of New York, Binghampton.

McKendrick, N. (1982) The Consumer Revolution of Eighteenth-century England, in McKendrick, N. Brewer, J. and Plumb, J. H. (eds.) *The Birth of a Consumer Society: The Commercialization of Eighteenth-century England*, London, Europa Publications Ltd, 9–33.

Miller, G. L. (1980) Classification and economic scaling of 19th century ceramics, *Historical Archaeology*, 14, 1–40.

Miller, G. L. (1991) A revised set of CC index values for classification and economic scaling of English ceramics from 1787 to 1880, *Historical Archaeology* 25:1, 1–25.

Murray, T. (ed.) (2003) *Exploring the Modern City: Recent Approaches to Urban History and Archaeology*, Sydney, Historic Houses Trust of New South Wales.

Noël Hume, I. (1969) *A Guide to the Artifacts of Colonial America*, New York, Knoph.

Orser, C. E. (1988) Towards a theory of power for historical archaeology: plantations and space, in Leone, M. P. and Potter, P. B. (eds.) *The Recovery of Meaning: Historical Archaeology in the Eastern United States*, Washington DC, Smithsonian Institution Press.

Otto, J. S. (1977) Artifacts and status differences: a comparison of ceramics from planter, overseer, and slave sites on antebellum plantations, in South, S. (ed.) *Research Strategies in Historical Archaeology*, New York, Academic Press, 91–118.

Otto, J. S. (1984) *Cannon's Point Plantation, 1794–1860: Living Conditions and Status Patterns in the Old South*, Orlando, Academic Press.

Praetzellis, M. and Praetzellis, A. (1998) Further tales of the Vasco. *Historical Archaeology* 32:1, 55–65.

Shackel, P. (1993) *Personal Discipline and Material Culture: An Archaeology of Annapolis, Maryland 1695–1870*, Knoxville, University of Tennessee Press.

South. S. (1977) *Method and Theory in Historical Archaeology*, New York, Academic Press.

Spencer-Wood, S. (1987) *Consumer-choice in Historical Archaeology*, New York, Plenum Press.

Staniforth, M. (2003) *Material Culture and Consumer Society; Dependent Colonies in Colonial Australia*, New York, Kluwer Academic, Plenum Press.

Symonds, J. (ed.) (2002) *The Historical Archaeology of the Sheffield Cutlery and Tableware Industry 1750–1900*, Sheffield, ARCUS Studies in Historical Archaeology.

Veblen, T. [1899] (1994) *Theory of the Leisure Class*, London, Harmondsworth, Penguin Classics.

Vincentelli, M. (2000) *Women and Ceramics, Gendered Vessels*, Manchester, Manchester University Press.

Young, L. (2003) *Middle Class Culture in the Nineteenth Century: America, Australia, and Britain*, London, Palgrave.

2

Producing for the Table: A View from the Staffordshire Potteries

David Barker

Ceramics are closely connected with two of the best things in life – food and drink – and are intimately bound up with the preparation, consumption and storage of these. Ceramic table wares have been part of the picture for as long as people have sat at tables to eat their meals, and even today their role in food consumption is assured, even in those households in which the table has been replaced by tray and the knee.

Of course, the way in which ceramics have been used at, and beyond, the table has changed over time, and the range of ceramic table wares has evolved to keep pace with changing practices and fashions. This paper briefly examines the manner in which the north Staffordshire pottery manufacturers responded to a growing demand for ceramic table wares in the mid 18th century, considering particularly the relationship between the new types of ware and the technical developments within the industry which made their manufacture possible.

Lorna Weatherill (1996, 38–41) has identified the decade 1705–1715 as that in which probate inventories show a marked increase in all kinds of material goods. It is also the period when imports of tea and coffee increased rapidly. This, together with a corresponding decrease in their price, brought these new drinks within the reach of a significantly greater number of potential consumers, something which was radically to change the fortunes of ceramic manufacture in Britain. Hitherto, vessels of imported Chinese porcelain were just about all that was available for the consumption of these increasingly popular hot drinks, leaving a gap in the market for more affordable alternatives of home-produced earthenware and stoneware. The north Staffordshire pottery manufacturers capitalised upon this situation and within a short time the ceramics industry of that area had been completely transformed. The period from *c*.1720–1750 witnessed what was, without doubt, a 'Ceramic Revolution' in north Staffordshire (Barker 1999), a revolution for which the catalyst was tea and coffee.

These hot beverages required that north Staffordshire manufacturers develop a completely new range of wares for both serving and consumption which was unlike anything produced in that area hitherto. They in turn necessitated the introduction of new, improved manufacturing methods, including lathe turning, and separate biscuit and glost firings for earthenwares, which involved the use of new raw materials and their improved preparation (Barker 2004, 204–208). While refined red earthenwares were produced from local red-firing clays, albeit considerably better prepared than those used for the unrefined wares, the introduction by *c*.1720 of white salt-glazed stonewares stimulated the consumer's preference for white-bodied wares which has been predominant since that time.

The impact upon north Staffordshire manufacture of the new beverages is clearly in evidence in a small number of production assemblages of the period *c*.1720–1745. Waster groups from Broad Street, Shelton (Mountford 1975a), Shelton Farm (Barker & Klemperer 1992), Fen Park Road (Boothroyd 1998) and Lower Street, Newcastle-under-Lyme (Bemrose 1975), are all entirely dominated by tea wares – teapots, tea bowls, saucers, sugar boxes, milk jugs, kettles, slop bowls and spoon trays – and coffee wares – coffee pots and handled coffee cups (which in a set would have shared saucers with the tea bowls). However, some of these early groups include a small number of vessels, in a limited range of forms, which can be considered to be table wares; typically these include mustards, salts, and occasional dishes of indeterminate function. By the 1750s, though, the composition of production assemblages in north Staffordshire had changed. Just as the ritualisation of tea drinking (with all its necessary equipment) had provided a new market opportunity for manufacturers from the 1720s, so the elaboration of Georgian dining, with multiple dishes and courses, provided opportunities for factories to enter into the table ware market in the middle years of the 18th century.

Evidence of ceramic manufacturers' growing interest in developing ceramic table wares can be seen amongst the products of some of the earliest English porcelain factories. Although tea wares remained the dominant items in these

Figure 2.1 (above left). Moulded white salt-glazed stoneware soup tureen with the star, dot, diaper decoration typical of such mid 18th-century table wares. (The Potteries Museum & Art Gallery)

Figure 2.2 (above right). White salt-glazed stoneware plate with a standard moulded 'barleycorn' edge pattern.

Figure 2.3 (right). Cream-coloured earthenware plate of a typical mid 18th-century octagonal form with a rilled edge and under-glaze tortoiseshell decoration. (The Potteries Museum & Art Gallery)

factories, wasters from excavations on the site of the short-lived (1745–1748) Limehouse porcelain factory in London attest to the production of large numbers of sauce boats, pickle dishes, dishes and other moulded forms (Tyler & Stevenson 2000). At the north Staffordshire Longton Hall porcelain factory, which operated from 1750 until 1760, table ware forms included plates, sauce boats, tureens, dishes, baskets and a range of figures, some of which were probably intended to be table ornaments, as well as the full range of tea and coffee wares (Watney 1993). The mid 18th century porcelain factories by no means typified ceramic manufacture in England, with expensive wares aimed at the well-to-do customer, but they do mirror the changes that were occurring, or were about to occur in other sectors of the ceramics industry.

By the 1750s, the majority of north Staffordshire manufacturers of refined earthenware and stoneware were to some extent engaged in the production of table wares, but predominantly in white bodies. Sauce boats, tureens (Figure 2.1), plates of all types and sizes (Figure 2.2), and a variety of dishes and baskets were by that time typical products in both white salt-glazed stoneware and cream-coloured earthenware, or creamware, although the cream-white colour of the latter was frequently disguised by the application of under-glaze metallic oxide colours to produce a tortoiseshell effect (Figure 2.3). Exactly why manufacturers

did not develop more extensive ranges of table wares in redware, agate ware or the other contemporary coloured-bodied earthenwares is not known, but it is clear that the consumers of north Staffordshire ceramics preferred the new table ware forms in white-bodied ware to the exclusion of almost every other ceramic type.

The introduction of a wider range of table wares in the mid 18th century necessitated some major technical developments within the industry, the most important of which was the use of moulding for forming wares, and specifically the use of moulds of plaster of Paris. This was a significant innovation in the industrial-scale production of fine ceramics, making possible the manufacture of an infinite number of identical wares which, for the first time, could be made in elaborate shapes or with relief-moulded decoration. The occurrence together of this new (or, at least, greatly improved) manufacturing process and a new range of wares was no coincidence, for the north Staffordshire manufacturers drew the inspiration for their table wares not

Figure 2.4. Case mould for a plate with a floral edge pattern; c.1760. Plates with this edge pattern are known in white salt-glazed stoneware. (The Potteries Museum & Art Gallery)

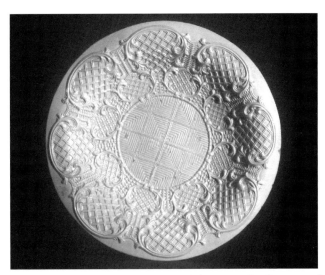

Figure 2.5. Case mould for a pierced dish; c.1760. This type of dish occurs in both white salt-glazed stoneware and in tortoiseshell coloured creamware. (The Potteries Museum & Art Gallery)

from the simple thrown forms of contemporary delftware or Chinese porcelain, but from a combination of metalware forms and the rococo-style European porcelains which were beginning to be imitated in England during the 1740s. Both metalwares and porcelains of the mid 18th century were capable of being elaborate, fanciful creations with extensive surface ornamentation. Such wares could not be produced on a wheel and moulding was therefore a necessity.

Moulded slipwares and other wares had been made in England since the early 17th century, when the typical products were dishes pressed over a fired clay mould into which decoration (if any) had been incised, stamped or rouletted. The production of press-moulded dishes in this way continued into the 19th century for a range of domestic uses. Moulding in this manner is perfectly adequate, but has its limitations. Chief amongst these is the use of the original mould in the actual making process. The increased use of moulding as a method of manufacture in an industrial situation necessitated the removal of the original from the making process, and the provision of numerous identical copies of this mould for the purposes of mass production, which could be replaced from a master mould should the need arise. A complex solution to the problem resulted in the establishment of an entirely new branch of the pottery business, that of modeller and 'block cutter'. The impact of this upon the industry and its products was significant and lasting, resulting in the wares of most factories rapidly becoming quite standardised in form and decoration, to the point where they were effectively interchangeable. This situation continued for the next two centuries.

In order to produce even the most simple moulded form, several processes were required before the flatware (plates, dishes, saucers, etc.) or hollow ware (cups, bowls, jugs,

teapots, etc.) presser could commence work. These are described in more detail by Goodby (2000), but are summarised here. The first stage involved the creation of the model, the original for the moulded form from which all subsequent moulds were taken. This was skilled work which involved creative talent. Once the modeller had completed his work, the 'block cutter' or 'block maker', who was often the same person as the modeller, performed the subsequent stages of the process. First, a 'master block' mould would be made from the model, which was a negative of the original in two or more pieces, possibly in plaster of Paris, and from this would be made a second positive, the 'master case' mould. The model, being in a fragile material, often wax, would be unlikely to survive long, and may indeed have been destroyed during mould-making. Consequently, the master block and case moulds were precious items which were used sparingly, if at all. Two further stages in the process were therefore required to produce moulded wares. First, a 'working block', a negative, was taken from the master case, and from this was made the 'working case' mould, both of which were most likely to have been made of stoneware with a thin salt-glaze which would protect the surface while not affecting the definition of the details (Figures 2.4 and 2.5).

From this positive working case mould were taken the factory's working moulds which were of plaster of Paris (Figure 2.6). Plaster of Paris is an ideal material for this last stage of the process. It is easily and cheaply cast around a master mould; it absorbs water readily from clay pressed into it; and, unlike clay which required firing, it does not shrink. The date at which plaster of Paris was introduced into ceramic manufacture in Britain is uncertain. Traditionally this is said to have been at some time around 1740 (Shaw 1829, 163), although it seems inconceivable that that north

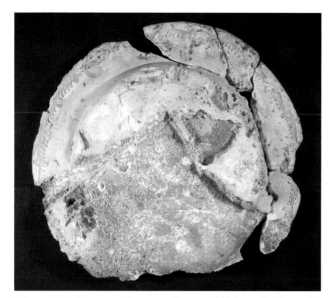

Figure 2.6. Plaster of Paris working mould for a feather-edge dinner plate, excavated on the waste tip of William Greatbatch's factory, Fenton, Stoke-on-Trent; 1770–1782. (The Potteries Museum & Art Gallery)

Staffordshire potters were unaware of it and its potential, given that its use in the manufacture of pottery dates back to at least the mid 16th century on the Continent of Europe, where it was also being used in the metal-working trades since the 17th century. The Dutchmen John Philip and David Elers almost certainly used moulds of plaster of Paris during their short-lived production of slip-cast red stonewares at Bradwell in north Staffordshire, and at Vauxhall (Elliott 1998, 18), but there is no evidence that other Staffordshire potters made use of plaster of Paris in the years following the Elers' removal from Bradwell in 1697 or 1698. Limited archaeological evidence from production sites, together with the evidence of extant wares, seems broadly to support a date of *c.*1740 to 1745, if not for reintroduction of plaster of Paris, at least for its more general use by manufacturers. From this time, a small, but growing demand for tea and,

especially, table wares in elaborate forms revived the need for vessels to be produced by moulding, rather than by throwing alone. Evidence for the date at which moulded forms were first reintroduced by north Staffordshire manufacturers, and by which, it follows, plaster of Paris was probably being used, will most probably come from the excavation of closely dated domestic assemblages or from shipwrecks or similar 'time capsules', but dated moulds confirm that by 1748, at least, moulds were in use in north Staffordshire for the production of new types of table ware (as well as wares for hot drinks) in complex forms and styles not seen before.

The disadvantage of plaster of Paris is that it has a short working life and wears quickly with use. New casts need to be taken from the working case moulds on a fairly regular basis, and consequently factories need to have easy access to these. In most factories the case moulds would not have been made on site, but would have been bought in from specialist suppliers.

The introduction of manufacture by moulding involved very high start-up costs. These would have been beyond the means of all but the most successful factories, with few being able to afford the luxury of employing a full-time modeller and block cutter. Consequently, from the late 1740s north Staffordshire industry seems largely to have relied upon a small number of freelance modellers and block makers who supplied the working case moulds to any factory which needed them and could afford them. The best documented of these modellers is Aaron Wood who, having worked for several major manufacturers during his early career, is said to have been 'modeller to all the potters in Staffordshire' from the mid 1750s until his death in 1785 (Goodby 2000, 224–225). Aaron's brother Ralph also worked as a modeller from *c.*1748 until 1772 (*ibid.*, 222–223), but at the Burslem factory of John and Thomas Wedgwood, the most successful north Staffordshire manufacturers and businessmen of their day (Barker 2004, 212–214). Ralph's work is well-known from a large collection of moulds, many of which are initialled, dated and sometimes signed, which survive in the

Figure 2.7. Case moulds for two sauce boats. That on the left is in the standard star, dot, diaper pattern, while that on the right is of a more unusual design and is inscribed 'R W / 1756'. (The Potteries Museum & Art Gallery).

collection of the Potteries Museum & Art Gallery in Stoke-on-Trent (Figure 2.7). These moulds are for a range of tea and table wares, but most are unexceptional. They are for the types of wares which were being made by a majority of manufacturers in north Staffordshire, and show clearly that the industry's modellers were largely responsible for the high degree of standardisation which is evident in its products, although arguably they were making moulds in the common styles of the day, for which there was a demand, rather than setting trends. That manufacturers could, and regularly did, purchase working case moulds for the latest styles of ware only served to increase this standardisation, with moulds originating from a very limited number of possible block cutters' workshops. This should in no way be regarded as a situation which was undesirable to manufacturers, for most factories depended upon on their products being inter-changeable with those of their neighbours, from whom they were likely to buy-in wares to fill orders on a regular basis. This was, and has always been a striking aspect of the ceramics business.

Working case moulds were, by their nature, expensive items. In 1764, for example, Josiah Wedgwood paid William Greatbatch 10s 6d for '1 Chinese Teapot' (Barker 1991, 93) and twelve shillings for a pair of cornucopiae, or wall vases (*ibid.*, 95). They represented a financial asset for factories to be sold upon closure or at bankruptcy sales. In this way, working case moulds could have very long lives, as they were passed down from manufacturer to manufacturer at prices which were less than buying new. This practice has enhanced the standardisation of the industry's products and has also contributed to the conservative approach of most factories to the design of their wares. One such auction of equipment is that from John Gilbert's Burslem factory, in 1803, an advertisement for which survives in the Enoch Wood Scrap Book (The Potteries Museum & Art Gallery). Amongst the items offered were:

Block Moulds in good Condition
Table Service, Bath Pattern
Dessert ditto, ditto
Dessert Shell Service
Eye Pattern, Shell Edge Service
Twig Baskets and Stands
Fine Shell Table Service
Royal Table Service

Working Moulds,
CONSIST OF
Fine Shell Edge Service
Bath Pattern
Eye Pattern Shell Edge
Royal Pattern, and a great variety of Dish, Plate, Twiffler, Muffin,
and other Moulds

It should be stressed that the majority of table wares produced from the mid 18th century were press-moulded, not slip-cast. Slip-casting was not to become a viable process for the mass-production of wares until the early 20th century when chemical deflocculents became available to reduce the amount of water needed in casting with slip. Without deflocculents, casting resulted in the saturation of moulds, which could not then be used again without a lengthy period of drying out, which would have been a great inconvenience in a factory situation in which the rapid mass-production of wares was essential.

This, then, is the manufacturing context for the production of new table ware forms. The physical evidence is to be found in both present-day ceramic collections and in archaeological assemblages. Neither are without problems for interpretation.

Museum and private collections can highlight the exceptional variety of moulded table ware forms, but inevitably emphasise the finest, the most elaborate and most expertly decorated wares, giving the viewer the impression that such items are representative of the products of most early factories. These collections tell us more about the tastes of curators and fashions of collecting than they do about the early ceramics industry and its products. Such bias is absent from archaeological assemblages, whether production groups or domestic groups, and from these it is possible to form a clearer picture of those wares which were widely produced and used. There is an inevitable tendency for archaeological groups to under-represent the better quality or more elaborate wares, which were likely to have been made in smaller quantities and with greater care, used sparingly, and retained when other less expensive wares were discarded. Archaeological assemblages also suggest that manufacturers moved into table ware production only gradually. From the outset, plates were the dominant form, an inevitability, of course, given the number of these required for use at the table in contrast to sauces boats, sauce tureens, soup tureens, and other forms. They were being produced in both white salt-glazed stoneware and tortoiseshell throughout the 1750s, but not initially in overwhelming quantities. The key north Staffordshire production groups of the period, those at Shelton Farm, and Town Road, Hanley, include a modest range of table ware forms, but it is still tea wares which dominate these assemblages.

By contrast, the wares recovered from excavations on the site of Thomas Whieldon's factory in Fenton include a wide variety of table ware forms in both earthenware and stoneware (Mountford 1972; Halfpenny 1997). As well as plates, there is an abundance of moulded dishes, baskets, tureens, pickle leaves, butter dishes and cutlery hafts in a variety of bodies and finishes. Unfortunately, the material has its interpretive limitations as the finds are not all from good contexts and appear to be a mixture of both pre- and post-1760 wares. The heavily moulded cream-coloured wares with coloured glazes in a rococo style, which are present in some quantity, are certainly typical of the decade

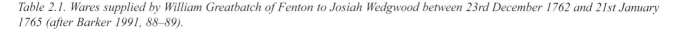

Table 2.1. Wares supplied by William Greatbatch of Fenton to Josiah Wedgwood between 23rd December 1762 and 21st January 1765 (after Barker 1991, 88–89).

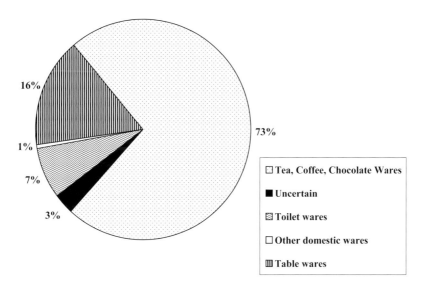

Table 2.2. Table ware forms produced by William Greatbatch and supplied to Josiah Wedgwood between 23rd December 1762 and 21st January 1765, as recorded in surviving invoices (after Barker 1991, 88–89).

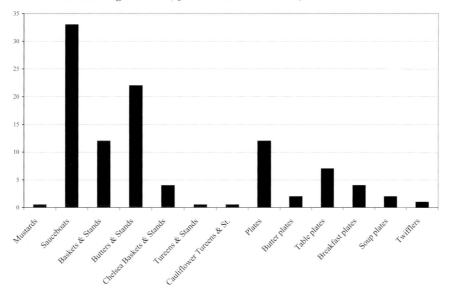

1760 to 1770, if not a little later, but precise dating is not possible. The ceramics do not, therefore, provide a clear snapshot of developments at a given time, but rather represent the range of wares and moulded forms made by Whieldon over an undefined period which may span two decades or more.

A body of better dated, and quantifiable data relates to another Fenton potter, William Greatbatch, whose business was, from the outset, devoted primarily to producing cream-coloured earthenwares, or creamwares, in the latest styles (Barker 1991). Surviving invoices for the period between December 1762 and January 1765 show that Greatbatch

sold approximately 220,000 pieces of ware to Josiah Wedgwood at Burslem. These are itemised in thirty-six surviving invoices for 250 crates of ware, out of an original total of 563 supplied during this period, and the picture is clear (Table 2.1). Tea wares appear to have formed the majority of Greatbatch's production at this time, or at least Wedgwood had a particular need for tea wares over this two-year period, which constituted 73% of the wares supplied. Of the remainder, 7% were toilet wares and 16% table wares. The table ware forms and the percentages supplied are shown in Table 2.2 and, perhaps surprisingly, sauceboats were the most numerous of these, exceeding in

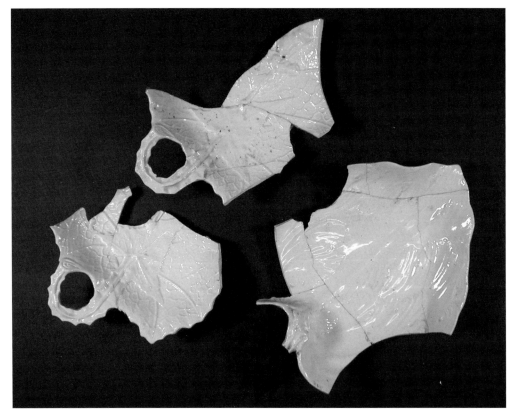

Figure 2.8. Creamware pickle dishes moulded in the form of leaves, excavated on the waste tip of William Greatbatch's factory, Fenton, Stoke-on-Trent; 1770–1782. (The Potteries Museum & Art Gallery)

quantity all of the various plate forms combined. The precise form of the curiously-named 'Chelsea baskets' can only be guessed at, but the other forms listed are all standard table ware types which require no explanation.

The practice of manufacturers buying-in wares from neighbouring factories is well-documented in the 18th century and later and it is therefore clear that this is not a definitive picture of Greatbatch's production. What we are seeing in the invoices are only those wares supplied to Josiah Wedgwood and there is no unambiguous documentary evidence for other wares produced by Greatbatch, if any, which might have been destined for other customers at this time. Nevertheless, the low proportion of table wares in these invoices accords well with the archaeological evidence. The complete excavation of Greatbatch's factory waste tip revealed a similarly modest proportion of table ware forms during the first eight to ten years of dumping on the site. So, both the documentary and the archaeological evidence show conclusively that table wares were very much subordinate to tea wares amongst the products of Greatbatch's factory during the 1760s.

A different picture emerges during the years from *c.*1770 to early 1782, represented by the final phase of dumping on Greatbatch's waste tip. The is no supporting documentary evidence for this period, but the excavation of this site has

shown that by the 1770s Greatbatch's output included a greatly increased proportion of table wares, especially plates of all sizes, soup plates, and the oval forms which we might today describe as platters, but which in their day were generally described as dishes, except when they served as stands for, for example, tureens. Other table ware forms which were recovered from this phase in quantity include salts, pickle dishes (Figure 2.8), salad dishes, covered vegetable dishes, baskets, covered mustard pots, egg cups, pepper castors, bottle coolers, candlesticks, and a variety of other forms. The variety of Greatbatch's table wares is striking. He produced plates with almost thirty different moulded edge patterns (Barker 1991, 180–181), which included all of the popular contemporary types and a few which may have been peculiar to this one factory.

One aspect of table ware production is particularly evident on the Greatbatch site. This is the way in which the increase in the volume of plates produced coincided with the appearance of specialist types of kiln furniture used for placing the wares within their saggars for the glost (or glaze) firing. This relatively minor innovation vastly increased this manufacturer's ability to produce large quantities of plates with a greatly reduced risk of damage at this stage of manufacture and only minimal scarring from contact with the kiln furniture. The new kiln furniture supports were a development of the saggar pins which were used in delftware production. These are, in effect, thin ceramic bars which were arranged within the saggar in groups of three to support the underside of a plate's rim; the groups of bars were then arranged one above another either by being inserted into pre-formed holes in the saggar wall, or by being fixed into strips of clay which were run vertically up the saggar wall (Barker 1991, 137–138). The result was that several plates could be placed within a saggar, one on top of another, without coming into contact with each other. That this simple method of placing was not used at the Greatbatch factory during the 1760s suggests that the volume of plate production at that time did not necessitate special measures being introduced, for the method would surely have been known to most north Staffordshire manufacturers.

The output of this one manufacturer strongly suggests that consumer demand for ceramic table wares, already a factor during the 1760s, had increased considerably by *c*.1770, a picture which appears to be supported by the limited evidence from a small number of north Staffordshire waster deposits of a similar date. The reasons for this increase in demand are several but impossible to identify from a study of production groups alone.

In the mid 18th century north Staffordshire fine earthenwares and stonewares were competing with table wares of delftware, Chinese porcelain, and pewter. The north Staffordshire ceramics had obvious advantages over delftware, in that they were durable and hard-wearing, and not subject to glaze loss during use. In terms of serving as a vehicle for decoration Chinese porcelain had a clear advantage, and was a material ideally suited for plates, platters and dishes, but at a significantly higher cost. Pewter, too, was durable, well-established and more or less ubiquitous on mid 18th-century tables, but involved a major initial financial outlay, even if some of this could eventually be recouped through pewter's scrap value. Pewter table wares were certainly copied by north Staffordshire manufacturers, suggesting that the customers for pewter wares were very much in their sights for an expansion of their business. While it is difficult to determine the impact of changing tastes and fashions for table wares upon a consumer's preference for one material over another, it would appear that the new north Staffordshire wares were extremely versatile, easily and cheaply made in matching sets, could be decorated if required, were durable, and, perhaps most important, were comparatively inexpensive. The Swedish industrial spy Reinhold Rücker Angerstein does not list the wholesale prices of table wares following his visit to Burslem and Hanley in 1754, noting only that tortoiseshell plates sold at 4s per dozen (Berg & Berg 2001, 340). He does, however, give the prices of tea wares of different types, and it can be seen that the cost of white salt-glazed stoneware teapots was one-third that of tortoise-shell teapots, and one quarter that of 'cream-colour' teapots (*ibid.*, 340–342). A similar differential between plates in these different wares would seem likely, the higher cost of the earthenwares being due to the additional firing required for their manufacture.

From the mid 1760s, the appeal of earthenwares at the dinner table received a significant boost following Josiah Wedgwood's success in securing, in 1765, the patronage of Queen Charlotte for his wares. Thereafter, Wedgwood's creamwares were marketed under the name 'Queen's Ware', a name which rapidly came to be widely used by manufacturers and customers alike. Wedgwood's relentless promotion of his wares amongst the nobility, gentry and the affluent classes achieved considerable success (McKendrick 1982), to the extent that creamware became the table ware of choice at the expense of Chinese porcelain which had hitherto dominated the higher end of the market for ceramics. In many respects, the time was right for refined English-made ceramics to achieve a more prominent position at the dinner table.

As food preparation increasingly became separated from its consumption during the 18th century, so separate dining rooms were set aside for that purpose in middle class households, introducing a degree of intimacy and refinement into mealtimes (Richards 1999, 161–163). In elite households formal dining came to be used as a demonstration of wealth, rank and taste. Elaborate meals with many courses required elaborate table settings and a wide range of table wares, many with specialised uses. These were available in silver or silver-plated metalwares, but the versatility of fine earthenware made it suitable for moulding into the wide range of elaborate forms which were needed at the dinner table. The full extent of these elaborate, specialised forms can be seen in, for example, the 1798 Whitehead Catalogue (below) and other early factory shape books. Not only were different vessels required for different courses, but entirely separate sets of ware were used for different meals. The appearance of elaboration in serving was the greater as it was common practice until the middle of the 19th century to lay out all the courses together, with many 18th-century household manuals and cookery books prescribing the manner in which courses should be arranged on the table (e.g. *ibid*, 159–161). It was not until the mid 19th century that dinners took on a more modern appearance with the introduction of service *à la Russe*, in which separate courses were brought to the table in succession and upon completion of the previous course.

Mealtimes for the less affluent involved little of the conspicuous consumption enjoyed by the elite members of society, although elements of the formality of dining clearly spread widely throughout the social classes. Archaeological assemblages from domestic sites suggest that there was a gradual increase in the use of ceramic table wares at all social levels during the third quarter of the 18th century.

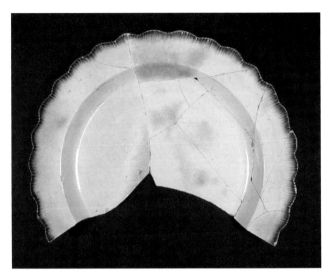

Figure 2.9. Creamware plate with a moulded feather edge from a clearance group excavated in St Mary's Grove, Stafford; c.1770. (The Potteries Museum & Art Gallery)

Figure 2.10. Pearlware plate with a blue-painted shell edge from a clearance group excavated at Haregate Hall, Leek, Staffordshire; c.1800–1810. (The Potteries Museum & Art Gallery)

Figure 2.11. Pearlware sauce boat with a mould shell edge, painted blue, from a clearance group excavated at Haregate Hall, Leek, Staffordshire; c.1800–1810. (The Potteries Museum & Art Gallery)

For example, a small clearance group from St Mary's Grove, Stafford, offers a useful insight into the ceramics of a Midlands urban household of a middling sort at this time (Kershaw 1987). Evidence suggests that the group, which comprises 113 individual ceramic vessels, was discarded around 1770. A significant proportion (37%) of the wares are refined table wares, and of these the majority (83%) are of white salt-glazed stoneware which are of quite a poor quality and have been well-used. The forms are primarily plates, soup plates and dishes with all the main moulded edges types being represented, together with small flaring dishes or patties, and two poorly enamel-painted moulded sauce boats. Of the three creamware plates in the group, two – with tortoiseshell decoration – may date to c.1760, while the other, undecorated except for its moulded feather edge (Figure 2.9), was probably produced closer to c.1770. With one exception, the other creamwares, which are few in number and all tea ware forms, also date to the late 1760s or very early 1770s. The contents of the group strongly suggest the discard of old, worn and frequently poor quality ceramics of all types (including seconds and worse) and their replacement with new wares in the latest styles. The creamwares almost certainly represent these new wares and suggest that this household's ceramic table wares were to take on an entirely new appearance during the 1770s.

Another north Staffordshire domestic clearance group, deposited around forty years later in *c*.1805 – 1810, illustrates clearly the development of table ware styles by the early 19th century in a middling social class context. A small pit at Haregate Hall, Leek, contained 178 vessels, of which a significant proportion (30%) were table wares (Barker & Barker 1984). These were split between creamwares (30 pieces), pearlwares (21 pieces), soft-paste porcelain (one piece), and white salt-glazed stoneware (two pieces), but while all but one of the creamwares were undecorated, all the pearlwares (plates, serving plates, dishes and eight sauce boats) had under-glaze painted moulded shell edges (Figures 2.10 and 2.11). By the early 19th century shell-edged pearlwares had become the most widely-used tables wares, but they were also the cheapest decorated table wares available (Miller 1991, 6). Their increased popularity was probably due both to their low price and their simple decoration, for in terms of its ceramics the 19th century was a century of decoration. Painted and slip decoration were in widespread use by *c*.1800, but rarely for table wares. These were most likely to be in undecorated creamware or, increasingly, in decorated pearlware. Printed decoration was initially used for tea wares, but by *c*.1800 it was coming to be more widely used on table wares, as can be seen in the 1796 manufacturers' price list (Appendix 1). By 1820s printed table wares were the dominant types. The Haregate Hall assemblage contains a number of printed vessels, but these are all tea wares. Printed table wares were not yet sufficiently commonplace to be present in a clearance group of this date.

The documentary evidence all reinforces a view of the increased popularity of ceramic table wares during the second half of the 18th century, and presents a picture of an increasingly large number of forms becoming available as the century progresses. This can be seen in both the manufacturers' price lists and in the factory shape books. The price lists represent attempts by manufacturers to counter falling prices for their products by setting prices below which the potter signatories agreed not to sell their wares. These price-fixing agreements are a valuable source of data which George Miller (1980, 1991) has used to create price indices for the types of ware represented in them, but at a most basic level they list the range of wares and vessel forms being produced at a specified date, and with what type of decoration.

What we are seeing with the manufacturers' price lists is not the full the range of forms, but the 'standard' wares which were the mainstays of the trade, and which were aimed at a majority of customers. More elaborate, specialist forms which constituted minority lines and which were aimed at the are not listed, but even so the picture is clear. Over a very short period of time the range of ware of all types of ware increases, with table wares being represented by a greater number of forms. In 1770, there are listed seven (or eight, if a distinction is made between bakers and nappies) table ware forms; in 1783, there are eleven or twelve in what appears to be shell-edged pearlware; the fourteen forms listed in 1795 are in creamware; while the nineteen listed in 1796 occur with (under-glaze) painted or printed decoration, or with no decoration at all (Appendix 1).

For the more specialist forms which were being made by some, if not all factories, we can turn to the factory shape books, although these are few in number. The first of these was produced by Josiah Wedgwood in 1774, to be revised and updated at regular intervals thereafter (Mankowitz 1953, 70–98; Reilly 1989, 329–340). A useful comparison may be made between the 1796 price list (Appendix 1) and the published 1798 Whitehead Catalogue (Whitehead & Whitehead 1798), from the Hanley firm of James and Charles Whitehead. The former has nineteen table ware forms with no decoration, with painted decoration and with printed decoration; the Whitehead Catalogue, by contrast, lists and illustrates fifty different table ware forms (excluding candlesticks) in what seems to be undecorated creamware alone (Figures 2.12 and 2.13).

The Whitehead Catalogue appears to show the complete range of undecorated earthenwares, for which at this time we may read creamwares, made by this one important factory. That other decorated earthenwares and stonewares were being made at the same factory is made clear in the catalogue's title page. Table wares are the dominant item, far exceeding tea wares and toilet wares in both the number and the range of forms, with all of the variations in size and pattern being listed in 119 separate entries. A number of forms clearly have specialist functions at the dinner tables of a limited number of elite customers. Asparagus plates, chestnut baskets, strawberry baskets, herring dishes, fish trowels, and ice cellars, for example, would have served a limited market, and were certainly only a minor part of the factory's output, but they were available.

The Whitehead Catalogue and other late 18th- and early 19th-century shape books illustrate very well the elaborate nature of formal dining in elite, wealthy households, while also including the standard plate, dish, tureen and sauce boats forms that were in more widespread use. Many of the more complex forms will only be seen in museum collections and will be largely absent from domestic archaeological assemblages. However, the archaeology of production sites in north Staffordshire, and elsewhere, is now beginning to reveal evidence for those wares aimed at the more affluent customer. The Greatbatch waster tip, for example, illustrates clearly how a factory was able to adapt its production to

Figure 2.12. Page from the 1798 Whitehead Catalogue (Whitehead & Whitehead 1798) showing tureens, sauce tureens, and sauce boats in both queen's and feather edge patterns, together with a plain covered dish.

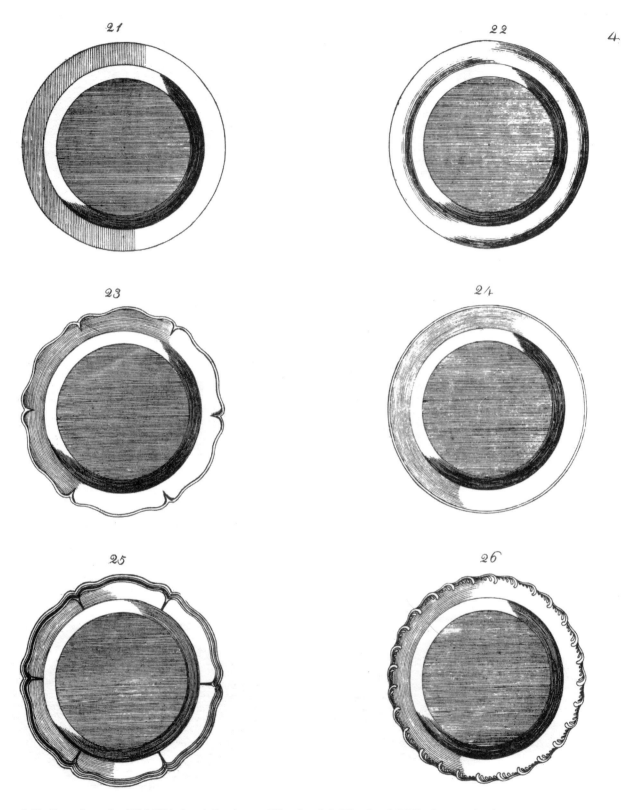

Figure 2.13. Page from the 1798 Whitehead Catalogue (Whitehead & Whitehead 1798) showing the factory's range of standard plate edges – 'T pattern' (No. 21), 'concave' (No. 22), 'royal' (No. 23), 'bath' (No. 24), 'queen's' (No. 25) and 'feather edge' (No. 26) – each of which could be supplied as dinner plates (10 inch diameter), supper plates (9 inches), twifflers, or dessert plates (in diameters from 6 to 9 inches).

meet the needs of requirements of both the elite market and the middle class customer, and is the more important for covering a period during which there were significant developments in dining practices generally and in the more widespread appeal of ceramic table wares specifically. It is important to understand how manufacturers responded to the changing requirements of the consumer, with all the changes in working practices, new processes and more general developments within the factory which might be required for the introduction of new types of ware. In the case of ceramic table wares, the required forms could not have been produced to an adequate standard in the mid 18th century without significant innovation in, and development of the manufacturing processes. Such changes were widespread, affecting every manufacturer and rapidly shaping the whole nature of the ceramics industry and its future direction. General trends will be evident in a range of sources and in extant wares, but for the minutiae of manufacturing production site archaeology has a major contribution to make.

References

Barker, D. (1991) *William Greatbatch – a Staffordshire Potter.* London: Jonathan Horne.

Barker, David (1999) The Ceramic Revolution 1650–1850, in G. Egan and R. L. Michael (eds), *Old and New Worlds*, 226–234. Oxford: Oxbow.

Barker, D. (2004) The Industrialization of the Staffordshire Potteries, in D. Barker and D. Cranstone (eds), *The Archaeology of Industrialization*, Society for Post-Medieval Archaeology Monograph 2, 203–221. Leeds: Maney Publishing.

Barker, D. and Barker, B. (1984) A late 18th century pit group from Haregate Hall, Leek, Staffordshire. *Staffordshire Archaeological Studies* 1, 87–136.

Barker, D. and Klemperer W. D. (1992) An important new discovery of Staffordshire ceramics. *Ars Ceramica* 9, 28–32.

Bemrose, P. (1975) The Pomona Potworks, Newcastle, Staffs., Part II. Samuel Bell: his Red Earthenware Production, 1724–1744. *English Ceramic Circle Transactions* 9:3, 292–303.

Boothroyd, N. (1998) *Archaeological Watching Brief at Fenpark Road, Fenton, Stoke-on-Trent, Staffs., SJ 8977 4450.* Stoke-on-Trent City Museum Field Archaeology Unit Report No. 62.

Elliott, G. (1998) *John Philip and David Elers.* London: Jonathan Horne.

Goodby, M. (2000) Moulds and Modellers in the Early 18th-century Staffordshire Potteries. *English Ceramic Circle Transactions* 17:2, 216–228.

Halfpenny, P. A. (1997) Thomas Whieldon: his life and work. *English Ceramic Circle Transactions* 16:2, 237–254.

Kershaw, M. J. (1987) An 18th Century Pit Group from Stafford. *Staffordshire Archaeological Studies* 4, 60–85.

Mankowitz, W. (1966) *Wedgwood.* London: Spring Books (3rd edition).

McKendrick, N. (1982) Josiah Wedgwood and the Commercialization of the Potteries, in N. McKendrick, J. Brewer and J. H. Plumb (eds), *The Birth of a Consumer Society: The Commercialization of Eighteenth-Century England*, 100–145. London: Europa Books.

Miller, G. L. (1980) Classification and Economic Scaling of 19th Century Ceramics. *Historical Archaeology* 14, 1–40.

Miller, G. L. (1991) A Revised Set of CC Index Values for Classification and Economic Scaling of English Ceramics from 1787 to 1880. *Historical Archaeology* 25:1, 1–25.

Mountford, A. R. (1972). Thomas Whieldon's Manufactory at Fenton Vivian. *English Ceramic Circle Transactions* 8:2, 164–182.

Mountford, A. R. (1975a) A Group of Astbury-Type Pottery Found in Shelton, Stoke-on-Trent. *City of Stoke-on-Trent Museum Archaeological Society Report* 7, 28–38.

Mountford, A. R. (1975b) Documents relating to English ceramics of the 18th & 19th centuries. *Journal of Ceramic History* 8, 3–41.

Reilly, R. (1989) *Josiah Wedgwood.* London: Macmillan.

Richards, S. (1999) *Eighteenth-century ceramics – products for a civilised society.* Manchester: Manchester University Press.

Shaw, S. (1829) *History of the Staffordshire Potteries.* Hanley: Simeon Shaw.

Tyler, K. and Stevenson, R. (2000) *The Limehouse porcelain manufactory: excavations at 108–116 Narrow Street, London, 1990.* Museum of London Monograph Series No. 6. London: Museum of London.

Watney, B. M. (1993) Excavations at the Longton Hall porcelain manufactory. Part 3: the porcelain and other wares. *Post-Medieval Archaeology* 27, 94–108.

Weatherill, L. (1996) *Consumer Behaviour & Material Culture in Britain 1660–1760.* London: Routledge (2nd Edition).

Whitehead, J. and Whitehead, C. (1798) *Designs of Sundry Articles of Earthenware.* Published *c*.1972 as *The Whitehead Catalogue.* Milton Keynes: D. B. Drakard.

Appendix 1. Table ware forms listed in the earliest potters' price lists

1770 Price list (after Mountford 1975b, 3–5)

Dishes (10 to 21 inch)
Nappys [*sic*] & baking dishes (7 to 12 inch)
Tureens (3 sizes)

Twifflers
Butter tubs & stands (3 sizes)
Sauce boats (5 sizes)
Plates

1783 Prices agreed at a general meeting of the manufacturers of Queen's earthenware (after Mountford 1975b, 9)

Plates or Muffins	Edged with Blue	Bakers & Nappies	ditto (8 to 14 inch)
Twifflers	ditto	Tureens with ladles	ditto (4 sizes)
Table plates	ditto	Sauce tureens & stands	ditto (2 sizes)
Table dishes	ditto (10 to 22 inch)	Butter tubs & Stands	ditto (2 sizes)
Covered dishes	ditto (10 to 17 inch)	Sauce boats	ditto (5 sizes)
Salad dishes	blue edges (8 to 14 inch)		

1795 Price list, common cream-coloured ware (after Mountford 1975b, 10)

Table plates
Supper plates
Twifflers
Muffins (6 to 7 inch)
Oval dishes (9 to 21 inch)
Twig baskets & stands (8 to 12 inch)
Sauce boats (4 sizes)

Bakers (7 to 14 inch)
Nappies (7 to 14 inch)
Covered dishes (10 to 17 inch)
Salad dishes (8 to 14 inches)
Large tureens (4 sizes)
Sauce tureens, stands & ladles (3 sizes)
Oval Butter tubs & stands (3 sizes)

1796 Price List (after Mountford 1975b, 11)

Cream Coloured Ware
Dishes (10 to 22 inch)
Covered dishes (10 to 17 inch)
Baking dishes
Nappies
Salad dishes (8 to 14 inch)
Tureens (w/out ladles; 5 sizes)
Sauce tureens (w/out stands & ladles)
Table plates
Supper plates
Twifflers
Muffins (6 & 7 inch)
Twig baskets & Stands (8 to 12 inch)
Sauce boats (5 sizes)
Butter tubs & stands (4 sizes)

Blue and Painted Ware in Colours Under the Glaze
Dishes (10 to 22 inch)
Covered dishes (10 to 14 inch)
Salad dishes (8 to 12 inch)
Tureens (w/out ladles; 5 sizes)
Table plates

Supper Plates
Twifflers
Muffins (6 & 7 inch)
Sauce tureens (2 sizes)
Sauce boats (2 sizes)
Butter tubs & stands

Printed Table Services
Compotiers (8 to 12 inch)
Centrepiece
Shells (2 sizes)
Plates
Twifflers
Muffins (6 to 7 inch)
Dishes (10 to 20 inch)
Tureens (2 sizes)
Baking dishes (8 to 12 inch)
Salads (10 to 12 inch)
Covered dishes (10 to 12 inch)
Root dishes (10 to 11 inch)
Sauce tureens (2 sizes)

Appendix 2. Table ware forms listed in the 1798 *Whitehead Catalogue* (Whitehead & Whitehead 1798))

Oval Tureen (T, Paris, Bath, Feather or Queen's Pattern)
Sauce Boat (T, Bath, Queens or Feather Pattern; w/out stand)
Sauce Tureen (w/out stand & ladle
Cushion Covered Dish Plate (T, Concave, Royal, Bath, Queen's, Feather Edge Pattern)
Supper Plate (9 inch)
Twiffler (6 to 8 inch)
Dessert Plate (6 to 8 inch)
Oval Dish
Round Dish
Soup Dish
Oval Fish Dish
Deep Salad (octagon, round, oval, square scalloped)
Salad Bowl
Compotier (oval or round)
Herring Dish
Fish Drainer for Dishes (10 to 18 inch; oval or round)
Fish Trowel (2 sizes)
Butter Tub & Stands (3 sizes; oval or round)
Oval Canoe
Salt (oval or round)
Round Waiter, complete
Waiter, for Oil & Vinegar (oval)
Single Waiter, for Oil & Vinegar
Sugar, Stand & Ladles (round or melon form)

Cream Bowl, pierced Stand & ladle
Fruit basket (oval or round; 6 to 14 inch)
Sweetmeat Basket & Stands (oval; 3 sizes)
Chestnut Basket & Stand (oval)
Double Chestnut Basket & Stand
Fruit Basket (oval & round)
Strawberry Basket & Stand (pierced; octagon & round)
Fruit Dish (oval & round; 6 to 12 inch)
Lemon Drainer
Double Bucket & Ladle
Double Sauce Boat
Glass Cistern (oval)
Asparagus Plate
Bottle Cooler
Candlestick (low & tall)
Pickle shell
Egg Cup
Pepper Castor
Oil Cruet
Sugar Castor
Mustard Pot (barrel, square, tall)
Table Spoon
Bowl with cover (w/out handles)
Covered Dish
Dessert Plate
Vegetable Dish with Partition & Cover

3

Trade Catalogues: Elaborations and Virtual Collections

Christine Ball

This paper will discuss the catalogues of the cutlery, flatware and hollow-ware trades which were produced from the later 18th century by British manufacturers in, mainly, Sheffield, Birmingham and London for both home and overseas markets. Catalogues are both artefacts in themselves and the illustrations on their pages metaphors for the actual products. Each page is a virtual collection of objects which may, or may not, have ever been manufactured. The requirements for the creation of the catalogues include the recognition that the customer can accept the image as a surrogate for the product. The extent to which the manufacturers helped create their own trade, as the mass markets for railways, hotels, steam ships and institutions developed, will be examined. Finally, there will be a brief look at the catalogue as object, as a prestige production to serve as an image of the firm, but also as a depiction of the work of the many thousands of workers and outworkers employed.

Introduction

'The lavish illustrations in catalogues of every country constitute the main historical source for the development of nineteenth-century ornamental design ... for previous centuries the record of design lies in the sets of prints published in the great artistic centres in order to supply ideas when gentlemen were conferring with local craftsmen' Hyatt Mayor, Curator of Prints at the Metropolitan Museum of Art, New York (1976).

The first part of this statement holds true for the Hawley collection of catalogues of tools, machine tools, cutlery, hollow-ware, agricultural implements, garden tools, surgical and measuring instruments. The collection has some 5000 catalogues, some eight hundred of which are of cutlery and hollow-ware, over 350 firms' histories, ephemera and archives, and an unrivalled collection of tools and cutlery.

The catalogues date from the late 18th century to the present day, tools and cutlery from the medieval period onwards. The Hawley catalogues are still only a fraction of those which once existed, and the examples below are a minute percentage.

How far the second part of Mayor's statement can be applied depends on the interpretation of the *record of design.* The design element in cutlery, hollow-ware and in scientific or measuring instruments can often be a key factor, less so in tools, where evolution from a vernacular original is more usual. Only the larger firms produced catalogues, so any sample is immediately skewed. The intended market must be borne in mind; myriad variations in sizes and qualities promoted reflect the lengths to which firms were prepared to go to accommodate their customers' needs. The requirements of customers are often depicted as being the products of created wants in consumer goods: cutlery, flatware and hollow-ware (Pavitt 2000). The extent to which this is true of edge tools has been explored by Collins (1996), suggesting that even with agricultural tools elaboration was often invented by the manufacturer rather than being solely the manufacturers' response to local needs – a created demand, at least on paper.

Precursors

The antecedents of the illustrated catalogue may be found in the lists, drawings, patterns, sample cards, advertisements, trade cards, shop signs, shop fronts and displays, itinerant salesmen, shopkeepers, market cries, memories, and even illuminated manuscripts, of the medieval and later periods (Amman and Sachs 1973 [1568]; Heine 1996; Willmott 2005). Engravers were employed from the early 17th century in the production of trade cards for the makers of scientific instruments, drawing instruments and precision implements of all kinds (Hambly 1988, 44 and Calvert, 1971).

Figure 3.1. The shop of Thomas Samuel Scudamore, Spiceal Street, Birmingham, late 18th/early 19th century. Note the knives in a fitted box in the left-hand window. Banks and Heal Collection 52.94, courtesy of the Trustees of the British Museum.

Tradesmens' cards, or trade cards were advertisements printed on one side of a card or single sheet of paper (Johnson 2001). The earliest known English card dates from just before 1630, but they did not become relatively common until after about 1720 with the growth of the printing and newspaper trade. The makers, mainly based in London, issued cards which were at first plain printed statements of goods, prices and the location of the shop or warehouse; by the mid18th century these would often contain illustrations and descriptions of the items sold, with the name and address of the supplier.

By the middle of the 18th century cards often had a picture of the shop or sign of the maker's premises (Figure 3.1). Many advertising methods overlapped; trade cards did not cease to be produced simply because a manufacturer issued a printed catalogue. Most frequently, the latter was produced for the wholesaler and was 'trade only' and the card became solely the wholesalers' or retailers' 'give-away' advertising to the public, although frequently offered by the manufacturer to the wholesaler as a additional item; this differentiation persists to the present day. Most comprehensive catalogues of products remain expensive to produce and are generally available only to the retailer; the 'paper' public face of many companies is still the printed flyer, or magazine advertisement; even when the firm has a web site there is often an invitation to request a paper catalogue.

The object of any method of advertising is to sell the product; the illustrated catalogue is a particular form of advertising, whether it is designed for the manufacturer to supply the wholesaler, the wholesaler the retailer, or the retailer the customer. The establishing of the 'brand' name in the 18th century, often the trade or maker's mark, was one of the principal developments in the cutlery trade during the last three hundred years. In the use of such marks the cutlery trades were not unique; in trades such as cloth, and iron, marks had been used to signify quality, individual manufacturers or locations since the middle ages. By the end of the 18th century, an indvidual's mark was being used as an indicator of quality (Higgins and Tweedale 1995).

Form and Significance

Common catalogue elements found at all periods, but not necessarily in every manufacturer's repertoire, include an external view of the premises where a product is made and internal views of the processes of manufacture, the product in use by craftsman, employee, or other satisfied customer, instructions on its correct and safe use, and the artefact itself and its associated 'family' of products. By the early 19th century, the arrangement of the products themselves was often according to agreed 'standard' listings.

Not all elements needed to be present; often a simple, classified listing of products and prices sufficed, the more elaborate productions being either beyond the means or the inclination of the firm. Not all proprietors were convinced of the merits of print as a marketing device. At the other extreme, an elaborate and expensive bound volume of company history, while fulfilling the same purpose at one remove, often dispensed with the listing of actual products, being content to stress the virtues and reliability of the company, and hence of its products. Anniversaries, particularly centenaries, have produced valuable records of company formation, financial operations, factory buildings and layouts, processes, inventions, work forces, and customers, the premise usually being to stress success, triumphs over adversities, longevity, reliability, and overall virtue.

The illustrating and listing of artefacts has been accomplished in diverse media: woodcuts, copper plates, lithographic plates, photography and most recently, computerised catalogues and websites. Developments in 19th-century draughtsmanship, such as in the drawings for machines and civil engineering works, find counterparts in the, albeit often simpler, illustrations of tools and cutlery, works which reached a very high order by 1900 in the work of Pawson and Brailsford of Sheffield, and Billing in Birmingham. The forms of catalogues vary from a single sheet, or even a manuscript list, with or without accompanying prices, to the elaborate numbered, cased and bound volumes of the later 19th and earlier 20th centuries. Histories of printers and printing are numerous (see Steinberg 1996), but most do not consider why certain print items developed except in terms of economics, or technology.

The 18th Century

Why did illustrated catalogues develop at all, and why at the end of the 18th and the beginning of the 19th century when duty on paper was still in place? Changes in markets at home and abroad were leading to initiatives; the colonial markets which had developed strongly in the later 16th and 17th centuries were, in the case of the USA, cut off by revolution and war in the latter part of the 18th, and suppliers in Britain needed to promote themselves in new areas and to an expanding home market (Styles 1993, 2000; Breen 1986, 1993; Weatherill 1988, 1993). By the 1780s Matthew Boulton and John Fothergill of Birmingham were sending out paper designs which could be despatched to wholesaler or retailer 'as a means of inducing orders to mutual satisfaction … a multitude of products might well inspire the customer to substantially increase his order' (Snodin 1987, 28). An illustration can minimise confusion, and it is at this point that the catalogue becomes a recognised and acceptable object for a retailer to have on his counter or shelf. Agreed prices and discounts and adoption of a standard numbering system gave the catalogue a value to, for example, the colonial

retailer. One did not have to have items actually in stock or even available as samples: an illustrated catalogue could be kept as an indication of potential while not having goods sitting idle. The relative merits of actual or metaphorical stock depend to a large degree on the relative certainty of economic conditions and the expectations of the customer; long lead times in production are not seriously compromised by delivery pressures when the transport of goods is by sea and the supplier is relying on his reputation for quality to ensure patience in his customers (Berg 2002, 2004; Breen 1986). Agreed prices and complex systems of discounts were adhered to; whether such agreements stimulated the production of a catalogue, or if the appearance of such catalogues at the same time as agreements were being reached was coincidental, needs further exploration.

There was during the 18th century an increase in the availability of print and of engravers capable of producing acceptable paper metaphors for the sample item. If war disrupted supplies, then paper listings would have to serve. The expansion of demand, as in the 16th and 17th centuries, was chiefly constrained by the cost of paper (Jardine 1996, 162). Acquisition of text was 'comparatively modest'; a price list was cheap in comparison with the cost of preparing an illustration. The installation cost of printing presses was also comparatively low. 'The real expense was the paper … representing two-thirds of the cost of a book's production' (Jardine 1996, 162). A long print run for a book meant a large capital outlay for the stock of paper needed (Steinberg, 1996, 62). The print shops also needed more employment for their skilled workforce. Price lists for trades were only one category among the multitude of single sheet or single-fold items produced to keep the printing shop ticking over between major projects (Jardine 1996, 161); to what extent the craftsman was lobbied by the jobbing printer may be impossible to determine, but the need to advertise may have seemed too obvious to warrant special note in contemporary literature. Many of the 18th- and 19th-century lists would have had their 16th- and 17th-century antecedents. The appearance of the first illustrated printed sheets and catalogues did not immediately supersede price lists, but such ephemera are extremely rare survivals, even from as late as the beginning of the 19th century.

The 19th Century

The earliest illustrated catalogues in Sheffield to include cutlery were produced by Joseph Smith (1816) and Thomas Creswick (1811). Smith's 'Key to the Various Manufactures of Sheffield…designed for the utility of merchants, wholesale ironmongers and travellers' has 169 patterns for handles, 5 types of blade: round (Figure 3.2), dub, scimitar, humped scimitar and pointed; with 11 lengths of blade, this gives 9295 potential variations. If one adds in the different bolsters, there are 743,600, although some bolster shapes are only

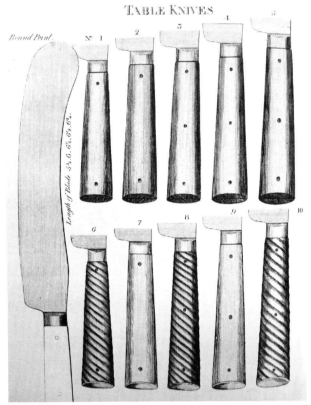

Figure 3.2. Joseph Smith (1816), unpaginated [Table cutlery].

Figure 3.3. Joseph Rodgers advertisement, Gell and Bennett (1821), p. [x].

is no mention of other handle materials such as wood and ivory and for these we have to return to Smith.

These numbers can be compared with the patterns listed in the supplement to the Goldsmith's Journal, the 'Flatware Index' of July 1937; this shows 120 varieties with an index to their makers, although the individual cutlery manufacturers often had their own variations. There is also a note on p. 418 that 'patterns listed as STANDARD are 'parish' patterns, obtainable from any maker, and produced from standard blanks made by specialist manufacturers'. The listing of types is followed by an article by Henry Vander Jr on 'How patterns have evolved' (Vander 1937); he makes the point that spoons and forks, flatware, and knives were not generally found in sets earlier than the end of the 17th century, reflecting the success manufacturers of the late 17th and 18th century had in the marketing of the idea that the host of a meal should provide the cutlery (Vander 1937, 422 and see Leone and Shackel 1987) and thus be presented with the need to make an informed choice which accurately reflected his status and his tastes.

In the early years of the 19th century, several companies began to advertise in the trade directories for Sheffield and Rotherham before going on to produce catalogues in the latter part of the century. There had been two directories produced in the late 18th century which had listed names of manufacturers and their trade marks: Gales and Martin in 1787 and Robinson in 1797, but the first directory to carry advertising was Gell and Bennett in 1821. In this Joseph Rodgers and Sons advertise themselves as 'Manufacturers of all kinds of Cutlery, Wholesale Ironmongers, Hardwaremen and Silversmiths. Orders for Exportation at the shortest Notice', accompanied by an engraving of a coastal scene with three-masted merchantman to reinforce the point (Figure 3.4). Rodgers was prominent in the table, pen and pocket and commercial knife trade to North America. In the next directory, Gell in 1825, they advertise themselves on the page facing their entry as 'Cutlers to his Majesty [George IV]' (Figure 3.4) at 6 Norfolk Street, with an engraving of the 'Manufactory' and coats of arms, one for 'Superior Cutlery' and one for 'Best Sheffield Plate'. Their slogan 'Cutlers to their Majesties' continues throughout their advertising and features on the cover of their company history of 1911 'Under Five Sovereigns' (Figure 3.11); the works was rebuilt and much extended throughout the later 19th century.

In Wm White and Henry and Thomas Rodgers' directories of 1841, James Roberts has an advertisement which is one of many based on the depiction of patent methods for ensuring that the handle of a knife remained firmly attached to the blade (Figure 3.5). The same method is found in a French catalogue of the late 19th century, Rousselon (Figure 3.6): 'Differents types de lame de couteaux de table' are illustrated in Prival's 'Couteaux et Couteliers' (Prival 1990, 93). The idea of selling by advertising durability and 'patent'

associated with certain handle shapes, it is still a substantial number and one has to ask whether all these variations were actually ever produced, or only an indication of what could be made, given an order. Creswick gives us 'Engravings of all the Pressed Horn Handles and Scales Manufactured in Sheffield up to the Fifteenth Day of November 1811', which runs to 132 variations of handle and 35 of scales. In the 'References' he gives the names of all the scales and handles and includes the names of 26 haft pressers with a numerical key to 'every Pattern Manufactured by that House'. There

Figure 3.4. Joseph Rodgers advertisement: 'Cutlers to His Majesty', Gell (1825), facing p. 71.

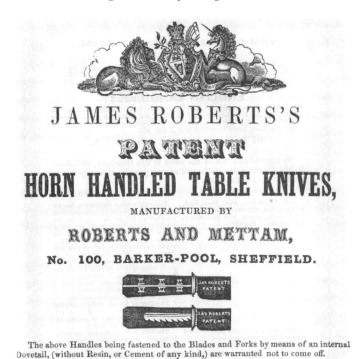

Figure 3.5 (left). James Roberts's patent horn handled table knives, Rodgers (1841).

Figure 3.6 (below). Rousselon catalogue 1908 showing varieties of tang. Courtesy of M Prival (1990, 93).

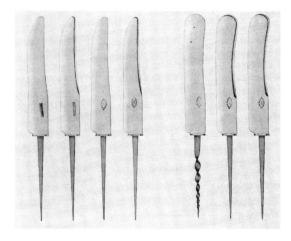

system is a common theme throughout the 19th and early 20th centuries, durability being a particularly desirable property for commercial use.

Testimonials to efficacy and quality from authoritative sources form another important component, ranging from the satisfied customer to the medals awarded at international exhibitions, the latter often accompanied by pictures of the

firm's trade stand as a reinforcement of the prestige of an award. Impetus was given by the Great Exhibition of 1851 (Catalogue 1851), its successor in 1862, and the exhibitions and trade fairs held in other major world cities in the second half of the century (Richards 1990). Firms which had not before produced any kind of catalogue were encouraged by the overwhelming success of such fairs.

The requirements of manufacturers were well catered for by printers and stationers such as R. T. Barras. His advertisement in Melville's Sheffield Directory of 1859 quotes for Engraving and Lithography: 'Plain and Artistic Drawings in Chrome Lithograph, Portraits, Views, Plans, Show Cards, Circulars, Labels, Law-Forms & Abstracts, Briefs &c Lithographed at a moments notice. An Artist will attend to make Drawings at any distance.' The use of 'an Artist' is presumably to make the three-dimensional 'bird's eye' view so frequently reproduced on billheads and in catalogues and firms' histories. In the same directory John Atkinson was promoting his 'Atelier Photographique' at 103 Devonshire Street for the same purposes. The removal of Stamp Duty on advertising in 1853 (Briggs 1948) enabled an enormous increase in the use of illustrated advertisements in directories and newspapers. The abolition of duty on paper in 1861 further increased the potential for advertising and marketing through print.

The Sheffield cutlery trades were also to follow the lead given by the larger steel manufacturers in the second half of the century; the larger steel firms' lavish volumes showed the way, those of Firth, Jessop and Cammell being especially copiously illustrated with photographs.

Cutlery and hollow-ware firms followed from the 1870s, often concentrating on the hotel, transport and restaurant trades. The firm of W. R. Humphreys and Co., Haddon Works, Denby Street, specialised in these trades (Figure 3.7). Their 'New Illustrated Catalogue' of 1913 gives two trade marks, reproductions of the medals won at Cork in 1883, Adelaide in 1887, and Melbourne in 1888–89, as well at home in Sheffield in 1885. A note is also made of their London office and showrooms and the centrepiece is a bird's-eye view of the works. The illustration on p. 20 of the 'Old English' (parish pattern) table knife and fork puts the emphasis on the 'extra strong' and 'heavily sterling silver plated' handles, qualities which would be needed for frequent use in a commercial establishment and would often ensure that the cutlery reached the secondhand market when firms re-equipped or ceased to trade. Page 21 has the 'Rigid Hard Soldered Table Knife' with an exploded view of yet another 'Patent Adjustment of Blade in Handle' and the drawbacks of soldering which caused the knife to fail at the join of bolster and handle (Figure 3.8). The same catalogue has (p. 129) 'The Colonial Cabinet built specially for hot and variable climates'; although the particular countries served are not listed, they would include countries of the then

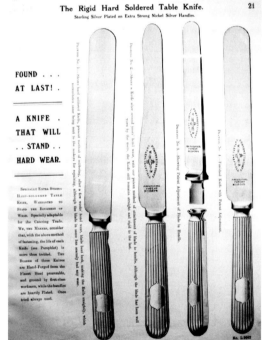

Figure 3.7 (left). Frontispiece, Humphreys (1913) New Illustrated Catalogue, HTC C CUT 314.

Figure 3.8 (above). The rigid hard soldered table knife, Humphreys (1913) New Illustrated Catalogue, HTC C CUT 314.

Figure 3.9. One picture from 'Views of some of our workrooms'. James Deakin and Sons Ltd (1926), HTC C.CUT 338.

VIEW OF CORNISH PLACE IN 1822 *From an old print.*

Figure 3.10. View of Cornish Place 1822 'from an old print'. James Dixon and Sons (1948) HTC C. CUT 058.

British Empire. Customers were also advised that these catalogues were expensive items, often produced in a numbered edition, and manufacturers asked if customers would kindly *not* cut out the illustration from the page to send with an order; the Humphreys catalogue carries such an admonition.

It is ironic that the Haddon Works has been demolished, as its site is adjacent to the now-listed Kenilworth Works and within the Denby Street Conservation Area (SK 350 862). The loss of so many of the larger works is slightly mitigated by the illustrations from their firms' catalogues; but early photographs often only show the exteriors of premises. Pictures of interiors, while showing a carefully-staged and retouched picture of the work force are often the only images we have. Figure 3.9 shows an interior of James Deakin and Sons Ltd, of Sidney Works, Sidney Street from

Figure 3.11. Front cover, Under Five Sovereigns, Joseph Rodgers (1911), HTC FH 233.

Figure 3.12. First showroom, No. 6 Norfolk Street. Joseph Rodgers (1911, 16), HTC FH 233.

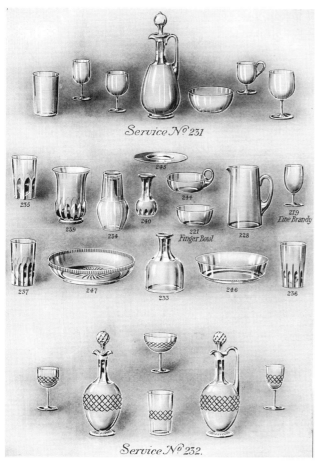

Figure 3.13. Special Nett Price List for Hotels [etc] Mappin and Webb (1922, 60), Glassware, HTC C.HOL 035.

1926: 'Silversmiths at work' and 'One of our hollow-ware buffing rooms', photographs staged to convey the impression of tidiness and order. Excavations and buildings recording in advance of conversion to apartments at the works of James Dixon, Cornish Place by ARCUS are complemented by the illustrations found in Dixon's catalogues. Figure 3.10, from a catalogue of 1948, is a 'View of Cornish Place in 1822' 'from an old print'. Excavations at the works of Thomas Turner and George Wostenholm (Symonds 2007) were informed by the catalogues of the firm, including the views of the works exterior.

The history of the firm of Joseph Rodgers, produced in 1911 (Figure 3.11) illustrates the panoply of the showrooms (Figure 3.12); no workers in evidence here. Mappin and Webb Ltd, of the Royal Works, Norfolk Street, who styled themselves 'Cutlers to also specialised in the trade with: 'Hotels, Steamships, Clubs, Restaurants, Steamships, Clubs, Confectioners and Caterers', with branches in:'Paris, Nice, Monte Carlo, Biarritz, Vichy, Rome, Lausanne, Copenhagen, Johannesburg, Montreal, Buenos Aires, Rio de Janeiro, [and] Sao Paulo' (1922). They aimed to provide a complete range of equipment. Figure 3.13 is a page showing glassware; other pages have china and linen. They also quoted for re-plating hollow-ware and re-blading of table, cheese and carving knives, and the marking of items with the 'crests of establishments' (Figure 3.14).

Catalogue as Artefact and Metaphor

What then of the implications of the catalogue as an artefact in itself? What can be learned from the catalogue-as-object; what from the illustrations of the interiors and exteriors of premises, of past manufacturing processes and the sheer variety of objects enumerated?

Figure 3.14. Special Nett Price List for Hotels [etc] Mappin and Webb (1922, 3), Trade marks, HTC C HOL 035.

'The artifact-document dichotomy is to a great extent artificial; documents are a species of artifact ... they are remnants of the environment of earlier periods, available for direct observation, present new evidence to support historical arguments and suggest new arguments' (Lubar and Kingery, 1993, ix).

In total, the illustrations provide an immense virtual collection of artefacts, far greater than actual items in any of the surviving collections of tools, and excavated assemblages. Collections such as those of Klaus Marquardt (Marquardt 1997) and Bill Brown (Brown 2001) are skewed towards the luxury end of the market. Although the illustrations do have to serve as metaphors for the objects, the firm, the premises, and the docile, efficient (always efficient) workforce, they are of inestimable value, not only for the identification and provenancing of artefacts, but as records of working conditions and material culture in themselves.

Schiffer provides one model for explanations of the cultural meanings of products and how people use and give cultural significance to their artefacts (Preston 2000). His three concepts of technofunction, sociofunction, and ideofunction, with the caveat that a single function is rare and a dynamic multiplicity of acquisition and loss through time more common, can be useful in looking at the 'many-to-many relationship' between form and function. A catalogue has a technofunction in its exposition of the objects it contains, or with instructions it contains. The aim of 19th-century engravers and lithographers was to produce as accurate a representation as possible; the Sheffield firm of Pawson and Brailsford received accolades for the meticulousness of their work (Ferguson 1906; Tweedale 1987). The manufacturer intended the catalogue to serve as the advertisement and reference guide for his representatives who would visit wholesalers and retailers, or for the merchants and agents in Britain or abroad who dealt with overseas orders (Higgins and Tweedale 1995).

In both instances, the catalogue itself becomes the metaphor for the company, one sociofunction. It represents the directors, the workforce, both inside and outside the premises (outworking still played a large part in the activities of the larger firms, particularly in the fulfilling of specialised orders), the premises and the efficiency of the organisation. For the larger companies illustrating the showrooms, the despatch and warehouse areas, whether or not the workforce was present, had an important function in reassuring the anxious customer. This is reinforced by the production of company histories, such as that of Joseph Rodgers (Figures 11, 12), which chronicle, among other topics: success, adversities overcome, the reliability of the workforce and the benevolence of the directors in providing modern and enlightened conditions for them (in their own opinion). These accounts should be used with caution.

In recent investigations into the lives of the inhabitants of the USA, Australia, and Britain by the use of documents such as probate inventories and literary accounts (Bushman 1993; Weatherill 1988, 1993; Young 2003), images (Burke 2001; Chesworth 1984; Parry 1984; Pearce 2000,) and by excavation (Buchli and Lucas 2001; Cantwell and Wall 2001; Karskens 1999; Beaudry *et al.* 1991; Yamin 2001; Yentsch and Beaudry 2001) the place of the objects illustrated can begin to be seen. Young identifies the middle classes through 'unity of aspiration and commonality of expression' (Young 2003, 14) and the cultures of gentility and respectability. Advice literature, etiquette manuals and catalogues demonstrate how to become middle class, and respectable, by exercising self-control and discrimination and by using the correct artefacts. The use of specialised eating utensils and cutlery shows, by the choices made from the profusion of items, how to achieve the desired effects. Karskens and Yamin demonstrate the extent to which these aspirations had moved down the social scale. Studies such as Jameson (1987), Rich (2003) and the many writers on food, dining, manners and consumption in general also set the implements of such activities into context (Day 2000; Ehrman 1999; Glanville and Young 2002; Glennie 1995; Leone and Little 1993; Mennell 1996; Miller 1995, 1998; Pennell 1998, 1999; Visser 1992). The study of the luxury trades and their part in forming the tastes of aspirant middle classes has been a theme for several researchers (Berg 2002, 2004; Berg and Clifford 1999; Berg and Eger 2003; Breen 1986; Brewer and Porter 1993; Clifford 1999, 2004a).

Symonds (2002) and Clifford (2004b) have gone further by investigating the structures where and conditions within which items were produced, by excavation and recording of domestic sites and the study of the records of companies. Examples of finds of cutlery and hollow-ware are few in comparison with pottery. Metal objects can be transported and traded, or a use found for them even if broken – a knife which has lost its handle can still be used as a tool and metal food containers can move down the functional scale – such durable objects can be traded until functionally useless.

Ideofunction may also come into play, with questions of status and acquired meanings, when the catalogue becomes an item which might be worth acquiring, conserving and displaying for its own sake in a museum or art gallery, or reprinted as a scarce collector's piece, as with the Joseph Smith 'Explanation' (1975). The final transformation takes place when artefacts or catalogues themselves become part of works of art (Akin 1996; Cummings and Lewandowska 2000; Hamill 1995; Pearce 2000); the context then becomes that of the collection rather than the real, everyday life of the object.

Acknowledgements

My sincere thanks to the Ken Hawley Collection Trust (HTC), Ken Hawley, the Trustees of the British Museum, and M. Marc Prival for permission to use material from their collections.

References

Directories

Gales and Martin (1787) *A Directory of Sheffield.*

Robinson, J. (1797) *A Directory of Sheffield.*

Gell, R. and Bennett, R. (1821) *Sheffield General and Commercial Directory.*

Gell, R. (1825) *A New General and Commercial Directory of Sheffield and Its Vicinity.*

Blackwell, J. (1828) *Sheffield Directory and Guide.*

White, W. (1833) *History and General Directory of the Borough of Sheffield.*

Rodgers, H. and Rodgers, T. (1841) *The Sheffield and Rotherham Directory.*

White, W. (1841) *General Directory of Sheffield.*

White, W. (1845) *General Directory of Sheffield.*

White, W. (1849) *General Directory of Sheffield.*

White, W. (1852) *Gazetteer and General Directory of Sheffield.*

White, W. (1856) *Gazetteer and General Directory of Sheffield.*

White, W. (1859) *Gazetteer and General Directory of Sheffield.*

White, W. (1862) *Gazetteer and General Directory of Sheffield.*

Melville and Co. (1859) *Commercial Directory of Sheffield and Rotherham and the Neighbourhood.*

Catalogues

[Catalogue, 1851] *Great Exhibition of the Works of Industry of All Nations. Official Descriptive and Illustrated Catalogue, vol. II: section III, Manufactures, Classes 11 to 29; section IV, Fine Arts, Class 30; Colonies.* London, Spicer Brothers.

James Deakin and Sons Ltd (1926) *Silversmiths. Electro-Plate and Cutlery Manufacturers, Sidney Works, Sidney Street, Sheffield, London and Glasgow.*

James Dixon and Sons Ltd (1948) *Manufacturing Silversmiths and Cutlers, Cornish Place, Sheffield, London, Melbourne, and Sydney.*

W. and R. Humphreys and Co. Ltd (1913) *New Illustrated Catalogue. Cutlery and Electro Plate Manufacturers, Haddon Plate and Cutlery Works, Denby Street, Sheffield and London.*

Mappin and Webb Ltd (1922) *Special Nett Price List for Hotels Steamships [etc], Royal Works, Norfolk Street, Sheffield and London.*

Joseph Rodgers and Sons (1911) *Under Five Sovereigns, Norfolk Street, Sheffield.*

Books and Articles

Akin, M. (1996) Passionate possession: the formation of private collections, in Lubar, S. and Kingery, W. D. (eds) *Learning from Things: Method and Theory of Material Culture Studies,* Washington DC, Smithsonian Institution Press, 102-128.

Amman, J. and Sachs, H. (1973 [1568]) *The Book of Trades,* New York, Dover.

Beaudry, M. C., Cook, L. J. and Mrozowski, S. A. (1991) Artifacts and active voices: material culture as social discourse, in McGuire, R. H. and Paynter, R. (eds) *The Archaeology of Inequality,* Oxford, Blackwell, 150–191.

Berg, M. (1999) New commodities, luxuries and their consumers in eighteenth-century England, in Berg, M. and Clifford, H. (eds) *Consumers and Luxury: Consumer Culture in Europe 1650–1850,* Manchester, Manchester University Press, 63–85.

Berg, M. (2002) From imitation to invention: creating commodities in eighteenth-century Britain. *Economic History Review* 54, 1–30.

Berg, M. (2004) Selling consumption in the eighteenth century: advertising and promotional culture. Conference paper at Knowing Consumers: actors, images, identities in modern history, Birkbeck College, London.

Berg, M. and Clifford, H. (eds) (1999) *Consumers and Luxury: Consumer Culture in Europe 1650–1850,* Manchester, Manchester University Press.

Berg, M. and Eger, E. (eds) (2003) *Luxury in the Eighteenth Century: Debates, Desires and Delectable Goods,* London, Palgrave-Macmillan.

Bermingham, A. and Brewer, J. (eds) (1995) *The Consumption of Culture 1600–1800: Image, Object, Text,* London, Routledge.

Breen, T. H. (1986) An empire of goods: the anglicization of colonial America, 1690–1776. *Journal of British Studies* 25, 467–499.

Breen, T. H. (1993) The meanings of things: interpreting the consumer economy in the eighteenth century, in Brewer, J. and Porter, R. (eds) *Consumption and the World of Goods,* London, Routledge, 249–260.

Brewer, J. and Porter, R. (eds) (1993) *Consumption and the World of Goods,* London, Routledge.

Briggs, W. G. (1948) *The Camera in Advertising and Industry,* London, Pitman.

Brown, P. (2001) *British Cutlery: an Illustrated History of Design, Evolution and Use,* York, York Civic Trust.

Buchli, V. and Lucas, G. (eds) (2001) *Archaeologies of the Contemporary Past,* London, Routledge.

Buchli, V. and Lucas, G. (2001) The absent present: archaeologies of the contemporary past, in Buchli, V. and Lucas, G. (eds) *Archaeologies of the Contemporary Past,* London, Routledge, 3–18.

Burke, P. (2001) *Eyewitnessing: the Use of Images as Historical Evidence,* London, Reaktion Books.

Bushman, R. L. (1993) *The Refinement of America: Persons, Houses, Cities,* New York Vintage.

Calvert, H. R. (1971) *Scientific Trade Cards in the Science Museum Collection,* London, HMSO.

Cantwell, A.-M. E. and Wall, D. (2001) *Unearthing Gotham: the Archaeology of New York City,* New Haven, Yale University Press.

Chesworth, M. (1984) *Nineteenth-Century Sheffield through its Billheads and Related Documents,* Sheffield, Sheffield City Libraries.

Clifford, H. (1999) Concepts of invention, identity and imitation in the London and provincial metalworking trades 1750–1800. *Journal of Design History* 12, 241–256.

Clifford, H. (2004a) *Silver in London: the Parker and Wakelin partnership 1760–1776,* New Haven, Yale University Press.

Clifford, H. (2004b) Making luxuries: the image and reality of luxury workshops in eighteenth-century London, in Barnwell, P. S., Palmer, M. and Airs, M. (eds) *The Vernacular Workshop: from Craft to Industry 1400–1900*, York, Council for British Archaeology (Research Report 140), 17–27.

Collins, E. J. T. (1996) Agricultural hand tools and the Industrial Revolution, in Harte, N. and Quinault, R. (eds) *Land and Society in Britain 1700–1914: Essays in Honour of F. M. L. Thompson*, Manchester, Manchester University Press, 57–77.

Cook, I. (1996) The world on a plate: culinary culture, displacement and geographical knowledges. *Journal of Material Culture* 1, 131–153.

Creswick, T. (1811) *Engravings of all the Pressed Horn Handles and Scales Manufactured in Sheffield up to the Fifteenth Day of November 1811*, Sheffield, Wm Todd, Mercury Office.

Cummings, N. and Lewandowska, M. (2000) *The Value of Things*, Basel, Birkhauser.

Day, I. (ed.) (2000) *Eat, Drink and Be Merry: the British at Table 1600–2000*, London, Philip Wilson.

Eatwell, A. (1996) Selling silver, in Glanville, P. (ed.) *Silver*, London, V&A Publications, 102–107.

Ehrman, E. (1999) *London Eats Out: 500 Years of Capital Dining*, London, Museum of London.

Ferguson, G. A. (1906) Sheffield and the graphic arts: a visit to the establishments of Messrs Pawson and Brailsford. *Sheffield Local Pamphlets* 29 (2), Sheffield, Sheffield City Libraries.

Glanville, P. (ed.) (1996) *Silver*, London, V&A Publications.

Glanville, P. and Young, H. (eds) (2002) *Elegant Eating: Four Hundred Years of Dining in Style*, London, V&A Publications.

Glennie, P. (1995) Consumption within historical studies, in Miller, D. (ed.) *Acknowledging Consumption*, London, Routledge, 164–203.

Goldsmith's Journal (1937) Flatware index: first issue. *Goldsmith's Journal*, July 1937, 406–437.

Gordon, R. B. (1993) The interpretation of artifacts in the history of technology, in Lubar, S. and Kingery, W. D. (eds) *History from Things: Essays on Material Culture*, Washington DC, Smithsonian Institution, 74–93.

Graves-Brown, P. M. (ed.) (2000) *Matter, Materiality and Modern Culture*, London, Routledge.

Hambly, M. (1988) *Drawing Instruments 1580–1980*, London, Sotheby's/Philip Wilson.

Hamill, P. (1995) *Tools as Art: the Hechinger Collection*, New York, Abrams.

Harte, N. and Quinault, R. (eds) (1996) *Land and Society in Britain 1700–1914: Essays in Honour of F. M. L. Thompson*, Manchester, Manchester University Press.

Heine, G. (1996) Fact or fancy? The reliability of old pictorial trade representations. *Tools and Trades* 9, 20–27.

Higgins, D. and Tweedale, G. (1995) Asset or liability? Trade marks in the Sheffield cutlery and tool trades. *Business History* 37, 1–27.

Hodder, I. (ed.) (1987) *The Archaeology of Contextual Meanings*, Cambridge, Cambridge University Press.

Hodder, I. (ed.) (2001) *Archaeological Theory Today*, Cambridge, Polity Press.

Ingersoll, D. W. and Bronitsky, G. (eds) (1987) *Mirror and Metaphor: Material and Social Constructions of Reality*, Lanham, University Press of America.

Jameson, R. (1987) Purity and power at the Victorian dinner party, in Hodder, I. (ed.) *The Archaeology of Contextual Meanings*, Cambridge, Cambridge University Press, 55–65.

Jardine, L. (1996) *Wordly Goods*, London, Macmillan.

Johnson, John [collection] (2001) *A Nation of Shopkeepers: Trade Ephemera from 1654 to the 1860s*, Oxford, Bodleian Library.

Karskens, G. (1999) *Inside the Rocks: the Archaeology of a Neighbourhood*, Alexandria, NSW, Hale and Iremonger.

Leone, M. and Shackel, P. A. (1987) Forks, clocks and power, in Ingersoll, D. W. and Bronitsky, G. (eds) *Mirror and Metaphor: Material and Social Constructions of Reality*, Lanham, University Press of America, 45–61.

Leone, M. P. and Little, B. J. (1993) Artifacts as expressions of society and culture: subversive genealogy and the value of history, in Lubar, S. and Kingery, W. D. (eds) *History from Things: Essays on Material Culture*, Washington DC, Smithsonian Institution, 160–181.

Lubar, S. and Kingery, W. D. (eds) (1993) *History from Things: Essays on Material Culture*, Washington DC, Smithsonian Institution.

Lubar, S. and Kingery, W. D. (eds) (1996) *Learning from Things: Method and Theory of Material Culture Studies*, Washington DC, Smithsonian Institution.

Marquardt, K. (1997) *Eight Centuries of European Cutlery: an Art Collection*, Stuttgart, Arnoldsche Verlaganstalt.

McGuire, R. H. and Paynter, R. (eds) (1991) *The Archaeology of Inequality*, Oxford, Blackwell.

Mayne, A. and Murray, T. (eds) (2001) *The Archaeology of Urban landscapes: Explorations in Slumland*, Cambridge, Cambridge University Press.

Mayor, A. H. (1976) [online] *Introduction* www.metmuseum. org/Works_of_Art

Mennell, S. (1996) *All Manners of Food: Eating and Taste in England from the Middle Ages to the Present*, Urbana, University of Illinois Press.

Miller, D. (ed.) (1995) *Acknowledging Consumption*, London, Routledge.

Miller, D. (ed.) (1998) *Material Cultures: Why Some Things Matter*, Berkeley, University of California Press.

Parry, D. (1984) *Victorian Sheffield in Advertisements*, Ridgeway, Sheffield, Private Publication.

Pavitt, J. (2000) In goods we trust, in Pavitt, J. (ed.) (2000) *Brand new*, London, V&A Publications, 18–51.

Pavitt, J. (ed.) (2000) *Brand new*, London, V&A Publications.

Pearce, S. (ed.) (2000) *Researching Material Culture*, Leicester Archaeology Monographs 8/Material Culture Study Group Occasional Paper No 1, Leicester, University of Leicester, School of Archaeological Studies.

Pennell, S. (1999) The material culture of food in Early Modern England c.1650–1750, in Tarlow, S. and West, S. (eds) *The Familiar Past? Archaeologies of Later Historical Britain*, London, Routledge, 35–50.

Pennell, S. (1998) 'Pots and pans history': the material culture of the kitchen in early modern England. *Journal of Design History* 11, 201–216.

Preston, B. (2000) The functions of things: a philosophical perspective in material culture, in Graves-Brown, P. M. (ed.) *Matter, Materiality and Modern Culture*, London, Routledge, 22–49.

Prival, M. (1990) *Couteaux et Couteliers: la coutellerie a Thiers et dans sa region, Metiers, techniques et artisans*, Nonette, Editions Creer.

Rich, R. (2003) Designing the dinner-party: advice on dining and decor in London and Paris, 1860–1914. *Journal of Design History* 16, 49–61.

Richards, T. (1990) *The Commodity Culture of Victorian England: Advertising and Spectacle 1851–1914*, Stanford, Stanford University Press.

Schiffer, M. B. (2000) Indigenous theories, scientific theories and product histories, in Graves-Brown, P. M. (ed) *Matter, Materiality and Modern Culture*, London, Routledge, 72–96.

Smith, J. (1816 [1975]) *Explanation or Key to the Various Manufactories of Sheffield, with Engravings of Each Article*, Burlington, Vermont, Early American Industries Association.

Snodin, M. (1987) Matthew Boulton's Sheffield Plate Catalogues. *Apollo* 126, July, 25–32.

Steinberg, S. H. (1996) *Five Hundred Years of Printing: New Edition Revised by J Trevitt*, London, The British Library.

Styles, J. (1993) Manufacturing, consumption and design in eighteenth-century England, in Brewer, R. and Porter, R. (eds) *Consumption and the World of Goods*, London, Routledge, 527–554.

Styles, J. (2000) Product innovation in early modern London. *Past and Present* 168, 124–169.

Symonds, J. (ed.) (2002) *The Historical Archaeology of the Sheffield Cutlery and Tableware Industry 1750–1900*, Sheffield, ARCUS.

Symonds, J. (2004) Historical archaeology and the recent urban past. *International Journal of Heritage Studies* 10, 33–48.

Tarlow, S. and West, S. (eds) (1999) *The Familiar Past? Archaeologies of Later Historical Britain*, London, Routledge.

Tweedale, G. (1987) 'A day at the works': the nineteenth-century trade and technical press as a source for Sheffield's industrial history. *Hallamshire Historian* 1.2, 25–27.

Vander, H. (1937) How patterns have evolved, in Flatware Index, First issue, *Goldsmith's Journal,* July 1937, 422–423.

Visser, M. (1992) *The Rituals of Dinner*, Toronto, Harper Perennial.

Weatherill, L. (1993) The meaning of consumer behaviour in late seventeenth and early eighteenth century England, in Brewer, R. and Porter, R. (eds) *Consumption and the World of Goods*, London, Routledge, 206–227.

Weatherill, L. (1988) *Consumer Behaviour and Material Culture in Britain 1660–1760*, London, Routledge.

Willmott, H. (2005) *A History of English Glassmaking AD 43–1800*, Stroud, Tempus.

Yamin, R. (2001) Alternative narratives: respectability at New York's Five Points, in Mayne, A. and Murray, T. (eds) *The Archaeology of Urban Landscapes: Explorations in Slumland*, Cambridge, Cambridge University Press, 154–170.

Yentsch, A. and Beaudry, M. C. (2001) American material culture in mind, thought and deed, in Hodder, I. (ed.) *Archaeological Theory Today*, Cambridge, Polity Press, 215–240.

Young, L. (2003) *Middle Class Culture in the Nineteenth Century: America, Australia and Britain*, Basingstoke, Palgrave-Macmillan.

4

Chocolatada! Sensing the Past: Recreating a 17th-Century Chocolate Recipe

Annie Gray

with help from sous-chef, Katharine Boardman

Chocolatada! This Spanish word was in common use in the 17th and 18th centuries, and was used to describe a chocolate party (Morton and Morton 1986, 9). Archaeological recreations – experimental archaeology – can be seen as a bit of fun, an adjunct to the more serious business of excavation and interpretation of surviving material evidence. To view it purely in this light would, however, be a mistake. Investigation of the past through doing can teach us valuable lessons. In the Ironbridge Gorge World Heritage Site in 2001 a group of engineers attempted to build a scale model of the Iron Bridge across the river Severn. They used techniques based upon analysis of a recently discovered painting showing the bridge being built, and what was known of 17th and 18th century bridge construction from other sources (de Haan 2002). Eventually they succeeded in building a half-scale model, and their investigations shed light on the hitherto mysterious construction method, demonstrating that the design and building of the bridge was even more of a remarkable feat of engineering than had previously been thought. The modern version of the bridge can still be seen at the Blists Hill Victorian Town.

Another example of experimental archaeology comes from the Iron Age settlement under excavation in Castell Henlys, Wales. Harold Mytum and students at the yearly training excavation have helped to reconstruct roundhouses, sited on the footprint of the excavated remains (Mytum 1986, 1999). This has not only aided in the archaeological understanding of construction methods, living conditions and daily life, but it is also open to the public. It is a permanent addition to the seasonal archaeological activity at the site, and enables the visiting public to interpret the archaeology more easily than might otherwise be the case.

Through experimental archaeology we can gain an understanding of past behaviour as dictated by physical constraints and technology (Coles 1979). People learn best through personal experience – through doing. In the realm of food and dining practice, for example, the significance of the change from service *à la Française* to service *à la Russe* can best be understood by relating it to our own experience of dining practice: the Christmas spread compared with formal restaurant service. Johnson (1993, 183) argues that historical archaeologists are concerned with the formation of the modern world, and the needs of the future. It is inevitable in this context that contemporary scholars relate their discoveries in the past to their experience of the present (Yamin 2005). Perhaps the discipline should be known as experiential, rather than experimental archaeology, as it impinges upon the senses as much as it is scientific investigation (H. Mytum pers. comm. February 2004; see Mytum 2003 for the impact of Celtic art on the visitor experience of experimental reconstructions). As well as affording us the opportunity for physically experiencing 'the past', it can also act as a salutary reminder that the present is very different to that past, and that we should never forget it.

The following paper, presented in April 2004, took the form of a live demonstration. The methodology and ingredients used were based on several months of experimentation, and the demonstration took the form of a narrated cooking show, as will the rest of this paper. First, I will introduce today's recipe, and then I will discuss each element, be it edible or equipment, as it was used. Naturally the experimental element cannot be recreated within the pages of a book. However, should you wish to try it at home, suggestions are included for easily available alternatives. The result will not be quite the same, but in the spirit of chocolatada, it would still be worthwhile. Good luck if you do!

Why Chocolate?

Why choose chocolate as the subject of experimental archaeology? First of all, because it is a foodstuff which has great appeal in the modern western world. If our primary concern is to look at the development of contemporary society (Johnson 1993, 183), then something with the emotional and market appeal of chocolate is a good subject for an archaeological study. In the 21st century, eating chocolate accounts for around 2.5% of the UK food market (Mintel 2004; this figure is based on the average weekly household spend on food 2000–2001), a significant figure in a sector which includes fruit, bread and meat – all dietary staples. Drinking chocolate, on the other hand, barely registers. Yet it was in the liquid form that chocolate was consumed when it was first introduced to the UK, at the end of the 16th century. It rapidly gained a devoted following, and for a period of around 150 years, chocolate was the drink of choice for many people in coffee houses and drawing rooms across both England and the colonies (Morton and Morton 1986; Dunne 2002, 62–64). It was expensive and, as will be shown, difficult and time consuming to prepare and statistically imports were never very high (Brown 1995, 38). By the 19th century, tea had become the English national drink, and even after technological developments had led to an improved product, chocolate never regained its earlier popularity as a drink (Bailleux *et al*. 1995; Brown 1995, 38). For a brief time though, it was a significant part of the leisure time practices of those wealthy enough to afford it. Group portraits and conversation pieces of the 17th and 18th century abound with chocolate references, the most famous of which is Liotard's *La Belle Chocolatière* (Morton 1986, 30; Brown 1995), later to be reworked as the logo of Baker's chocolate in North America (Williams 1996, 129).

Chocolate therefore has real resonance in both contemporary and past society. It is also a product, which can be used to explore many of the key themes of historical archaeology: consumption, discipline (or a lack thereof) and luxury. Although there were those who came to regard chocolate as a necessity (Camporesi 1994, 115), it fits most definitions of a luxury product. Van der Veen's (2003) consideration of luxury food in a prehistoric context defines a luxury in terms of ease of access (including cost) and desirability. Luxuries are desired by many but obtainable only by a few. Anthropological studies of food have divided the journey from field to table and beyond into stages (Goody 1982). This approach is heavily influenced by the structuralist school, and is open to the same criticisms and provisos. Despite these, the approach is useful to an archaeological analysis of culinary luxury because it can be used as a basic tool for identifying foods, which do not conform to a general pattern. In the historical period structuralist theories fall down, because so many foods do not conform to the culinary triangle of raw-cooked-rotten, but can easily fall in between categories. Chocolate is nevertheless more of an anomaly than other foods. Goody (1982) identifies five stages of consumption: production, distribution, preparation, consumption and disposal. Seventeenth century drinking chocolate had two additional stages of preparation and distribution, to be inserted after the production of the raw ingredients. Like many manufactured foodstuffs, its journey from plant to table was not straightforward. Like other pre-prepared items it was desirable and expensive when first introduced (Brown 1995, 27–38). Indeed, it is the advent of ready-made foodstuffs that poses the biggest challenge to structuralism. It is their introduction from the 17th century on that negates the application of structuralist theories to food in the historic period.

The use of chocolate as a subject for this paper also feeds into a growing awareness of, and interest in, culinary archaeology as a means of understanding the mores and behaviour of past societies (D. Seifert pers.comm. January 2005). Faunal data can inform us, to some degree, as to what was eaten, but is less useful for investigating how. Dining can be defined as the way in which a society consumes food and drink, and as such is a part of every society. An understanding of dining can be a crucial way to study underlying concerns driven by class, culture and education (Gray 2004). Historical archaeologists frequently use dining-related artefacts in their work on individual sites as well as in wider cultural developments. Specific studies of dining using an archaeological methodology are, as yet, relatively rare (some exceptions are Gray 2004; Harbury 2004; Mennell 1996; Samuel 1996), and it remains a small, yet happily interdisciplinary subject.

Cocoa: All About It

Botanically, chocolate originates in Mesoamerica, where people have cultivated it since at least 2000 BC (Coe and Coe 1996). Aztec sources indicate that the beans were used as currency (Coe and Coe 1996, 61). They were also crushed and made into a drink with chilli and water. Chocolate also played a role in human sacrifice, with sacrifices being fed chocolate, the drink of the elites, prior to their death. Pictures show their hearts turning into a cocoa bean (Morton and Morton 1986, 3), but whether this was believed to be the case, or whether it is purely metaphorical is unknown. Sources also indicate that the chocolate was intended to make the sacrifice happy despite his/her imminent death (Coe and Coe 1996). Those who have had the opportunity to sample the product in its recreated form will be able to vouch for this latter effect. In 1521 the Spanish invaded South America and quickly discovered chocolate. At first they hated it (Morton and Morton 1986, 10), but soon developed a taste for it as a hot drink (it was originally consumed cold) and exported it to Spain in large quantities. The spread of chocolate is surrounded by stories – culinary history is especially prone to amusing anecdotes and lengthy digressions which obscure the overall picture – but it is apparent that by the beginning of the 17th century, chocolate was being drunk throughout Europe. The first known import into North America was in 1682 (J. Gay pers.comm. April 2004).

Chocolate was consumed both in the home and in coffee houses, the first of which opened in Oxford around 1650 (Burnett 1991, 36). Pepys and Hooke both drank it with great relish (Dunne 2002, 64), while women also expressed their approval of it. Madame de Sévigné refers to chocolate a number of times in her letters, including this illuminating note on the dangers of over-consumption: 'the Marquise de Coëtlogan took so much chocolate during her pregnancy that she gave birth to a little black boy, who died' (Coe and Coe 1996, 159). Her love-hate relationship with chocolate is indicative of the shaky nature of its beginnings. In the 17th century it was rich, spicy and exotic. It was also strongly associated with sex. Contemporary prints link it with sensuality, and it is frequently present in pictures such as Freudenberger's *Le Bain* (1774), or other examples by Fragonard and Boucher, in which the heroine invariably has one breast prettily exposed. Chocolate is still associated with sex, as well as today's great taboo: calories.

Chocolate was also always regarded as a luxury. In the 17th century it went through a number of preparation stages before consumption. The beans were notoriously difficult to cultivate (Coe and Coe 1996, 21–25; 'Historicus' 1896), and were – and still are largely – harvested by hand. The book from which this section takes its title, *Cocoa: All About It* ('Historicus' 1896) has photographs and illustrations from the end of the 19th century which clearly show the arduous process of cocoa harvesting. Once the beans had been collected they were fermented to bring out the flavour precursors, dried, winnowed and roasted. They were then exported to European or North American ports. Amsterdam, Bristol, Salem, Boston and Newport were all primary centres for chocolate importation (S. Beckett pers.comm. February 2004; J. Gay pers.comm. April 2004; Morton and Morton 1986). They were then sold on to merchants, who ground them. It is very unlikely that the beans themselves were sold to the public (Brown 1995, 29). Cocoa beans have a very high fat content (over 50%), which means that, unlike coffee beans, the grinding process results in a thick paste, known as cocoa liquor, which makes grinding very difficult without specialised equipment (M. Gray pers. comm. March 2004). This paste was then made into a block which resembles a block of modern plain chocolate, but which was extremely brittle and bitter because no sugar had yet been added. In the 17th century it is likely that some manufacturers added spices to the block before allowing it to solidify; this would have then only required the addition of milk or water during heating to produce the final drinkable product.

Just as tea-drinking necessitated a whole range of new equipment, so too did chocolate. The first purpose-designed chocolate drinking vessels were made from the dried-out husk of a cocoa pod, richly ornamented with silver (Figure 4.1, left). These developed into the mancerina, a Spanish-designed cup whose shape derived from that of the cocoa pod, with a saucer, which incorporated a cup holder (Figure 4.1, right). This was probably intended to hold the cup in place at social gatherings, which frequently involved chocolate, but from the experiences of those involved in presenting this paper, it could also have been to stop spillage resulting from a chocolate-influenced euphoria. In French it was known as a *trembleuse*. Chocolate therefore required specialist equipment to prepare it both at the point of grinding the beans and in the home or point of sale. The ingredients required were also, as will be seen, not those commonly found in the 17th century – or the 21st century – kitchen.

Making Chocolate: the Ingredients

'Of cacaos 700, of white sugar 1¼ lbs, cinnamon 2oz, long red pepper 14, cloves ½oz, three cods of the longwood or Campeche tree, or instead of that the weight of 2 Reals or a shilling of Aniseeds. As much of Agiote as will give it colour, which is about the quantity of a hazelnut. Some put in Almonds, kernels of nuts and orange flower water – and I am told it not amiss that sugar be (also) added into it when it is drunk...' (de Ledesma 1644)

This recipe is typical of 17th century recipes. It comes from a Spanish volume, first published in Latin and rapidly translated into English. It uses ingredients, which are, in the main, familiar to us today. We used ready-processed cocoa liquor instead of attempting to grind the beans ourselves. If it is not possible to obtain cocoa liquor, then the purest chocolate available should be used instead (a 99% cocoa product is available), and the amount of sugar changed accordingly. To translate the weights into manageable figures the proportions used in making top-grade dark chocolate today were assumed – roughly 75:25 cocoa liquor to sugar. If using commercially available dark chocolate, therefore,

Figure 4.1. Cocoa pod cup, C17. Courtesy of Mansion House, York (left); Mancerina, Sèvres 1751 (right). Photographed by Annie Gray and reproduced with kind permission of the Earl and Countess of Harewood and the Harewood House Trust.

Figure 4.2 Cocoa liquor and icing sugar. Photographed by Leslie Johansen-Salters.

Figure 4.3. Chocolate spices (clockwise from top right) almonds, aniseed, cloves, chilli and cinnamon. Photographed by Leslie Johansen-Salters.

it should contain no less than 75% cocoa solids (and be aware that every alteration to the recipe will result in a markedly different end product). Figures 4.2 and 4.3 show the various ingredients used in their raw form. The white sheen which can be seen on the liquor (Figure 4.2) is called bloom, and is caused by recrystallisation of unstable cocoa butter crystals to form stable ones. One result of this is the appearance of fat crystals on the surface. (M. Gray pers. comm. March 2004). It can be seen on modern chocolate bars if they are left long enough, or have not been correctly crystallised (tempered) during the production process.

Most 17th and 18th century recipes specify that white sugar should be used to sweeten chocolate. We used icing sugar (Figure 4.2), which gave the end product a smoother texture and was easier to mix into the liquor by hand. The 17th-century version would have been taken from a sugar cone and required crushing prior to being used in this fashion. Sugar was not used in the original Mesoamerican form of chocolate, which instead used honey as a sweetener. The Spanish popularised the use of sugar to such as extent that it was adapted by the native South Americans in what the Coes call the 'creolisation of chocolate' (Coe and Coe 1996, 115). Further sugar could then be added when the drink was served. It should be noted, however, that this brings out the spiciness of the chilli, and is not therefore an action for the faint-hearted!

The spice blend used in the recipe above incorporates both Old and New World ingredients. Aniseed, cinnamon and cloves were all established cooking ingredients, although by the mid 17th century they were no longer as well used as they had been some fifty years previously. Changes in culinary taste and style, primarily influenced by the French, were leading to a less heavily spiced cuisine, which used new world ingredients and better quality meats flavoured with sauces and ragouts (Fernandez-Armesto 2002, 120–123). Chilli was a New World discovery, and a mainstay of South American

chocolate. All of these would have arrived in the home in a dried form, probably whole but occasionally ground. Figure 4.3 shows them after processing in a pestle and mortar – not easy with cinnamon sticks. These spices were all still expensive in the 17th century. They decreased in price as their popularity waned, and their availability grew. By the mid 18th century, chocolate no longer used spices in such variety or quantity. This was partly due to changing tastes. It may also have been an example of the same phenomenon that Muckerji (1983) noted with regard to fabrics: once a product becomes affordable it is open to a wider public, and the elites no longer wish to be associated with it.

The constant drive for differentiation may be one reason why mid to late 18th-century chocolate used vanilla as its main ingredient (Bailleux *et al.* 1995) and had more of a light, flowery flavour. Agiote, which we did not use in this demonstration, is a colourant utilised to give the often pale beans a deeper colour ('Historicus' 1896, 56). In the mid 19th century it was sometimes replaced by brick dust (S. Beckett pers.comm. March 2004; Coe and Coe 1996, 29), which we also opted not to use. Modern beans are of a variety which is naturally darker and do not need colouring in this way (M. Gray pers.comm. March 2004). Our chocolate used ground almonds and we also added orange flower water as suggested, on the grounds that both ingredients appear in other 17th century chocolate recipes and would therefore appear to be representative of the taste that we were trying to recreate.

Making Chocolate Part 2: Equipment and Methodology

'The manner of making chocolate. Set a pot of conduit water over a fire until it boils, then to every person that is drinking put an ounce of choc, with as much sugar into another pot; wherein you must put a pint of the said boiling water and therein

Figure 4.4. (left) Mixing in the milk and aerating the chocolate. Photographed by Leslie Johansen-Salters; (right) Our molinello substitute. Photographed by Annie Gray

Figure 4.5. Molten chocolate goodness. Photographed by Leslie Johansen-Salters.

mingle the choc and the sugar, with the instrument called el molinello, until it be thoroughly incorporated; which done pour in as many pints of the said water as there be ounces of chocolate… the hotter it is drunk, the better it is, being cold it may do harm' (de Ledesma 1644).

De Ledesma's instructions are clear and to the point. They correspond to other recipes, and to what is known about the process from illustrations and descriptions. Figure 4.4 shows the mixing process detailed above in action. That the liquor was first crushed or chopped into small chunks is shown by the existence of specialist chopping basins (Dunne 2002, 62), but it is equally possibly to use a pestle and mortar or chopping board and knife. This crushed liquor is then heated gently to melt it before the addition of the sugar and ground spices. It is not as easy as it sounds. In order to avoid burning the mixture we used a bain-marie. The few illustrations of the chocolate-making process that exist, for example those from Diderot's *Encyclopedie* (Fonteneau 1979), suggest that the liquor was heated over hot coals, in a large version of a chafing dish. This is not something which it is easy to recreate in a lecture theatre. We found it easier to add half the sugar at this stage and half later, after the addition of milk. The spices are also mixed in, and the whole forms a thick, muddy paste, with fats globules glistening in places, and bits of crushed spice clinging to the sides of the bowl. Some of this can be seen in Figure 4.4.

Hot milk is then slowly added to the cocoa mixture, along with the orange flower water. The first part of this can be done using a spatula or spoon, but in order to aerate the product as suggested in our recipe, a molinello substitute had to be found. One method for aerating and frothing the chocolate in the historic period was to pour the chocolate from one vessel to another from a great height. This was used by the Central and South American makers of chocolate, but was rather messy, and in a Western context the hostess

could hardly be called dignified standing on a chair in her drawing room. For our purposes too, this method would not have been practical. The molinello was invented by the Spanish, and although pictures exist of native Central and South Americans using the tool, these are universally westernised, and produced after the mid 16th century (Coe and Coe 1996, 115). Until the mid 17th century chocolate was frothed in the cup, with its distinctive shape as shown above. Later it was used in conjunction with a specially-designed chocolatière, whose central finial would unscrew to allow the insertion of a molinello (Coe and Coe 1996, 160). This could then be vigorously wielded without splattering. The chocolatière declined in popularity from the beginning of the 19th century, after which time a simple coffee pot was used for both beverages. Even the molinello was no longer needed after powdered drinking chocolate became widely available in the 19th century. For the purposes of our chocolate-making experiment, we tried using various types of whisk, small and large, before deciding upon the implement shown in Figure 4.4 (right). This is sold as a honey dipper, but made an adequate molinello.

Mixing and aerating the product is a decidedly manual task. Recipes show the addition of pure milk, half milk/half water, or just water. Whichever combination is used, it needs to be kept very hot in order to keep the chocolate liquor mix fluid. An insulated vessel is therefore a necessity (or for today's version, ready access to a microwave to reheat it as required). Milk was the subject of some worry in the 17th century, when it was not necessarily trusted, but chocolate, along with coffee, was too bitter to drink without it (Brown 1995, 26–27). It therefore gained more widespread acceptance by the end of the century, as evidenced by the introduction of yet another new and specialist piece of equipment: the milk bottle. The bottle, first mentioned in an English context in 1698, rapidly became a jug, but its form remained changeable until the mid-18th century (Brown 1995, 72–74). Figure 4.5 shows the mixing process in action in a modern context.

Once mixed and frothed, the chocolate was served from its chocolatière into suitable drinking vessels. It was drunk straight, or with bread or biscuits. This paper ended with a tasting session to show that all that effort was really worth it. The written word sadly cannot replicate that experience, so it is only by experiment that the reader can enjoy the sensation involved.

Conclusion

Making chocolate according to a recipe which is over 350 years old is a daunting experience. It would be impossible to replicate conditions and equipment exactly (nor would modern health and safety conditions then allow us to serve it to others). Nevertheless, this was an informative exercise. Not only did it inject interest into a fairly standard topic, that of 18th century beverages and the growth of inter-continental trade, but it also raised wider questions about the way in which we view 'the past' and the assumptions, which we habitually make without considering them. Eigteenth-century chocolate was difficult and time-consuming to produce, with many stages of production and preparation. It has a distinctive flavour, which is not to everyone's taste today. It is spicy, strong and very rich. It can also induce euphoria, an interesting side-effect in a small lecture theatre. This paper demonstrates that experimental archaeology has a significant role to play in increasing our understanding of the nature of specific examples of past material culture, and through that the behaviours and attitudes which surrounded such items. We cannot recreate the past – and nor would we necessarily want to – but we can use practical, experiential archaeology as a means of exploring particular aspects of it. Additionally, the chocolate tastes extraordinary and exotic; a salutary reminder of the difference of the past for both researchers and students.

Acknowledgements

Chocolate is not an easy topic to examine from secondary literature, and it has not been the subject of widespread archaeological investigation. This paper therefore drew on the chocolate know-how of a number of individuals. Primary among them are my father, Mike Gray, and a colleague of his, formally at Nestlé UK, Steve Beckett. I am indebted to both of them for knowledge of the technical processes involved in making chocolate and to Steve for the historical background to the development of chocolate. I have been lucky enough to be advised by James Gay at Colonial Williamsburg, and Peter Brown of Fairfax House, on the 18th century aspects of the chocolate trade. Finally, as a live demonstration, this paper would not have been possible without the assistance of the kitchen crew who slaved in the background to make enough chocolate for those present to sample: Rebecca Lane, Katie Webb and Peter Drake. Kitchen equipment was also provided by Harold and Caroline Mytum. Thanks.

References

Bailleux, N., Bizeul, H., Feltwell, J., Kopp, R., Kummer, C., Labanne, P., Pauly, C., Perrard, O. and Schiaffino, M. (1995) *Le Livre du Chocolat*, Paris, Flammarion.

Brown, P. (1995) *In Praise of Hot Liquors*, York, York Civic Trust.

Burnett, J. (1991) 'Coffee in the British diet 1650–1950', in Ball, D. (ed.) *Coffee in the Context of European Drinking Habits*, Zurich, Johann Jacobs Meseum, 35-52.

Camporesi, P. (1994) *Exotic Brew: The Art of Living in the Age of Enlightenment*, Cambridge, Polity Press in association with Blackwells.

Coe, S. and Coe, M. (1996) *The True History of Chocolate*, London, Thames and Hudson.

Coles, J. (1979) *Experimental Archaeology*, London, Academic Press.

Dunne P., in association with *Southern Accents* magazine (2002) *The Epicurean Collector*, Boston, Bullfinch Press (Little, Brown and Co).

Fernandez-Armesto, F. (2002) *Near a Thousand Tables: A History of Food*, New York, Free Press/Simon and Schuster.

Fonteneau, J.-M. (1979) *Les Aventures Merveilleuses du Chocolat et la Petite Histoire des Fines Confiseries Dévoilées aux Gourmandes*, Paris, F Waloszek for Nestlé.

Goody, J. (1982) *Cooking, Cuisine and Class*, Cambridge, Cambridge University Press.

Gray, A. (2004) The Historical Archaeology of Food and Dining, *c*.1750–1850. Unpublished MA thesis, University of York.

de Haan, D. (2002) 'The Iron Bridge – how was it built?' Published at www.bbc.co.uk/history/society_culture/industrialisation/iron_bridge_print.html. Page consulted January 2005.

Harbury, K. (2004) *Colonial Virginia's Cooking Dynasty*, Columbia, University of South Carolina Press.

'Historicus' (1896) *Cocoa: All About It*, 3rd edn, London, Sampson Low, Marston and Co.

Johnson, M. (1993) *Housing Culture: Traditional Archaeology in an English Landscape*, London, UCL Press.

de Ledesma, C. (1644) *Opusculum de Qualitate et Natura Chocolatae*, translated into English by J. Wadsworth (1652). Chocolate recipe can also be found in Brown (1995).

Mennell, S. (1996) *All Manners of Food*, Urbana, University of Illinois Press.

Mintel (2004) *Food Retailing – UK – November 2004*, source: Mintel/National Statistics, available at www.reports.mintel.com. Page consulted April 2004.

Morton, M. and Morton, F. (1986) *Chocolate: An Illustrated History*, New York, Crown.

Mukerji, C. (1983) *From Graven Images: Patterns of Modern Materialism*, New York, Columbia University Press.

Mytum, H. (1986) 'The reconstruction of an Iron Age roundhouse at Castell Henllys, Dyfed'. *Bulletin of the Board of Celtic Studies* 33, 283–290.

Mytum, H. (1999) 'Pembrokeshire's pasts: natives, invaders and Welsh archaeology: the Castell Henllys Experience', in Stone, P. G. and Planel, P. (eds) *The Constructed Past: Experimental Archaeology, Education and the Public*, London, Routledge, 181–193.

Mytum, H. (2003) 'Evoking time and place in reconstruction and display: the case of Celtic identity and Iron Age art', in Jameson Jr., J. H., Ehrenhard, J. E. and Finn, C. A. (eds) *Ancient Muses: Archaeology and the Arts*, Tuscaloosa, University of Alabama Press, 92–108.

Samuel, D. (1996) 'Approaches to the archaeology of food.' *Petits Propos Culinaires* 54, 12–21.

Van der Veen, M. (2003) 'When is food a luxury?' *World Archaeology* 34 (3), 405–427.

Williams, S. (1996) *Savory Suppers and Fashionable Feasts: Dining in Victorian America*, Knoxville: University of Tennessee Press.

Yamin, R. (2005) Discussant at symposium entitled 'Screening the Past: An Archaeological Review of Hollywood Productions, Part II.' SHA Conference, York, 8 January 2005.

5

Conspicuous Consumption: How to Organise a Feast

Joan Unwin

Introduction

In 2005, the Company of Cutlers in Hallamshire hosted its 369th Feast. This internationally famous event has been held almost every year since the Company was incorporated, in 1624. The Company has therefore had a great deal of practice in organising such an occasion and its archives hold a wealth of relevant information. The resources for this description include account books from 1624, minute books from the 1720s, photographs and ephemera, such as newspaper cuttings, programmes and menus from the 19th and 20th centuries. Beginning as a modest dinner at the start of the Master Cutler's year of office, the occasion has developed over the centuries into a major social event – a grand feast, drawing guests from politics, the armed forces and industry. The staging of such a feast requires preparation, food and guests, as well as a reason for going to the trouble and expense, and from the Company archives, it is possible build up a picture of the development of this occasion across the centuries.

Figure 5.1. An outline map of Hallamshire, showing the three parishes of Sheffield, Handsworth and Ecclesfield. (Leader 1905, 3).

Sheffield is known internationally as a manufacturing centre for cutlery and steel, benefiting from a strong base of craft skills and local technological developments. From the medieval period, the town was one of several places in England making common knives in a market dominated by the London trade. Although Sheffield was geographically remote, it had physical advantages in the form of ironstone, which had once provided metal for the local craftsmen, sandstone for grinding the blades, and rivers providing waterpower.

In the 16th century, the regulation of the cutlery trades in Sheffield – taking apprentices, registering craftsmen's identifying marks and imposing fines – was in the hands of the Lords of the Manor of Hallamshire, though their manorial courts. The last resident Lord, the 9th Earl of Shrewsbury, died in 1616, and Sheffield cutlers looked to Parliament for a framework for their trade organisation. The Act of Incorporation in 1624 established the Company of Cutlers in Hallamshire, with the right to continue many of the procedures established under the manorial court. The role played by the Lord of the Manor was now invested in the Cutlers' Company of 33 men, elected annually.

The original craftsmen covered by the 1624 Act were those who made knives, scissors, shears, and sickles, and who lived in an area called Hallamshire, comprising the medieval parishes of Sheffield, Ecclesfield and Handsworth (Figure 5.1). Although Hallamshire covered 72,000 acres, the Act gave the Company further jurisdiction over craftsmen living within six miles of the Hallamshire boundary, potentially giving it an enormous area of control. However, the Company effectively controlled only men in Hallamshire, plus the men in Norton and Eckington parishes adjacent to the southern borders of Hallamshire. The Company's rules dictated that masters could only train one apprentice at a time, except their own sons, and by carefully registering the identifying marks of the trained craftsmen, the Company could maintain a measure of quality control. By-laws stated that the cutting edges of all blades had to be of steel and the Company had the right to search out and destroy 'deceitful wares', that is, without steel edges or those that were stamped with another man's mark.

In the later 17th century, the Company made great efforts to support the craftsmen, taking on the government in its opposition to the payment of the Hearth Tax on cutlers' smithies. The relative success encouraged other metalworking craft groups in Hallamshire to submit to the control of the Company. In the 1670s and 1680s, the awlbladesmiths, filesmiths, and scythesmiths joined, resulting in a large proportion of the local working population being linked to the Company, either as craftsmen or suppliers of raw materials and subsidiary services.

Figure 5.2. The Badge of Office of the Master Cutler, showing the Company's Coat of Arms.

The Occasion

The Cutlers' Company is headed by the Master Cutler, who is elected for a year from the rest of the 'Company', which consists of two wardens, six searchers and 24 assistants. The rest of the craftsmen and manufacturers are known as the Commonalty and have always had little say in the running of the Company. The Company employed a Beadle to act as a caretaker/handyman, with ceremonial duties at the installation and the Feast. There was also the company Clerk, often with legal training, who maintained the records. The Master's year originally ran from August to August (now from October to October). Once a year, the Company settled the accounts of the outgoing Master Cutler, elected a new Master, installed him in his office, which involved a church service, and had a celebratory dinner. Originally, all this took place on the same day! The first account book (D1/1) shows that the dinner was a modest affair, probably in a room in a local tavern, which in 1625 cost the Company six shillings (30p). The Company bought its own Hall in 1638, and by the 1650s, the dinner was held there with costs having risen to 30 shillings.

During the 1670s and 1680s, this occasion took on features that would be recognisable today. In its fight against the imposition of the Hearth Tax, the Company realised it could lobby for support in parliament by inviting local landowners and nobility to its annual dinner, first referred to as a 'Feast' in 1682. Throughout the 18th century, the Feast continued to be held in August on the same day as the installation of the new Master (the election was moved to a few weeks earlier). It was an event for the whole town of Sheffield, which saw it as a holiday, with stalls and entertainment outside the Hall, opposite the parish church. In the latter half of the 19th century, the installation and Feast became two separate events. The newspaper cuttings

Figure 5.3. An unknown artist's impression of the first Cutlers' Hall.

Figure 5.4. The second Cutlers' Hall, built in 1725 and demolished in 1832.

Figure 5.5. A drawing of the third Cutlers' Hall, 1906 (Leader 1905, frontispiece).

from the 19th and 20th centuries show the Feast as a high social event when the Master Cutler could invite people from the London livery companies, the government, industry, and the Church, when he could repay the hospitality he had received in his year of office, and of course, provide an opportunity for guests to 'network'.

The Venue – the Halls

In the first few years of its existence, the Company met in a room in one of the inns or taverns in Sheffield town centre. In 1638, the Company purchased property on Church Street, opposite Sheffield parish church, now the cathedral. There is some confusion about the appearance and function of the first Hall, but it is clear from the accounts that only one room was used by the Company for its meetings. There are no details of the building though there is a drawing, of unknown provenance (Figure 5.3), which suggests an imposing property, possibly an inn (Harper 1997, 115). However, the Company thought it had a room sufficiently large to hold all 33 members and an increasing number of influential guests.

In the 1720s, the Company demolished the first Hall and built a second bigger and better Hall, on the same site (Figure 5.4). Details from Company records indicate that the building did not have a large 'hall' in which to hold its Feast, but had several rooms, rather sparsely furnished, in

which to entertain guests. From this time, the accounts show increasing expenditure on furniture, fittings and tableware.

At the end of the 18th century, the fortunes of the Company were at a low ebb and it was at odds with most of the cutlers in the town, eventually resulting in the loss of most of its guild powers in 1814. The Feast had lost its appeal, with tickets being offered for sale, but as the 19th century advanced, the Company regained its status and confidence, resulting in the demolition of the second Hall and the building of its third and present Hall in 1832. The second Hall had been increasingly criticised as providing poor accommodation for the Feast and in 1833, the Company could finally sit down together with its 200 guests in its brand new first floor dining hall, which is now called the Old Banqueting Hall. Extensions to the third Hall in 1866 provided a grand and even larger banqueting hall (Figure 5.5).

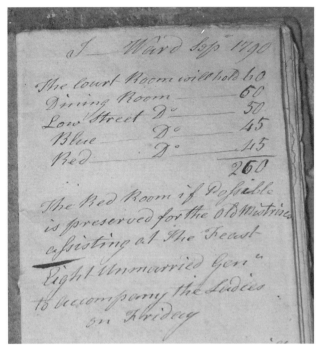

Figure 5.6. The allocation of guests in the rooms in the second Hall, details from the papers of Joseph Ward, Master Cutler, 1790/91 (P8/1).

The Venue – the Rooms

One can only speculate on the appearance of the rooms in the first and second Halls. The first account book lists annual work such as whitewashing the Hall and repairing benches and the cushions on them. The 1682 account shows that two men were paid ten shillings (50p) to prepare the Hall Chamber in which 'to entertain the noble persons att the Feast' with 'Coales to dry the Roome with'. In the Hearth Tax return of 1672 (E179/262/15), the Cutler's Hall was listed as having only one hearth and one might therefore suppose it was the Hall Chamber which had the fire, lit on this occasion, for drying out the room after cleaning. Either that, or the building was terribly damp!

The second Hall is better documented, showing that increasing amounts were spent to improve the facilities and comforts for the Feast. The Company was prompted to purchase new furniture, such as an oval table, deal tables and three dozen chairs in 1726 and 42 leather-bottomed chairs in 1739, with more being bought in 1767. From the accounts, it seems that the benches had cushions, which required regular recovering and re-stuffing and the leather seats on chairs had to be replaced. There were brass hat pegs, dressers, mirrors, and a marvellous Coat of Arms, painted in 1727. The account books summarise expenditure, but surviving dockets and receipts from the year of Joseph Ward, Master Cutler in 1790, show more details relating to the organisation of his Feast (P8/1). His papers show that the second Hall had at least five rooms, each large enough

to seat 45–60 people on chairs and benches (Figure 5.6).

An inventory of 1807 (D10/1) suggests that the Court Room was the main room and had a fireplace, a painting (possibly the Coat of Arms), and a hat rail with 70 brass hat pegs. The dining arrangements consisted of six oak dining tables, two tables – one was 14 foot long and one was five foot long – but only 17 chairs and three benches. In this room, Joseph Ward hoped to entertain 60 guests. The Red Room had 112 feet of deal table, 68 feet of deal forms, twelve chairs and a side table. The deal tables were probably trestle tables, since men were paid to set up 'the deals' prior to the Feast. Joseph Ward wanted 45 guests to be seated here, including the Past Mistress Cutlers.

It is clear that the accommodation could be cramped. Thomas Asline Ward, who was Master in 1816, kept a diary which was edited and published in 1909 by Alexander Bell. During the early years of the 19th century, the Cutlers' Company was facing financial hardships and loss of prestige following the turmoil which resulted in the slackening of its hold over the local cutlery trades. In 1812, after three years when there was no Feast, Asline Ward commented that, 'Instead of the hundreds who were formerly invited, only a few noblemen or gentlemen who were accustomed to present us with venison were this year sent to, and instead of the squeezing which in older times incommoded the company, we had on this occasion plenty of elbow room.' He also goes on to say that in better times, the ladies had had a feast on the second day 'and it was their custom, as well as that of the gentlemen, to be ready seated at the table an hour or two before dinner was served up, for fear they should not get a good seat in the principal room, or at the first table'(Bell 1909, 190).

In 1832, the Company began the building of its third and present Hall. The Feast was cancelled that year and it cost 10/6d to send messages to the 'nobility' telling them it was off, and the money allowed for the Feast, a total of £73, was given to the poor. The accounts for 1832 list the expenses involved, not only in the building of the new Hall, but in the furnishings required. In 1831, the Company had sold off its old furniture for £55, indicating its intention to have a completely new set of dining furniture. Unlike the second Hall, which seems to have had more benches for seating, an unknown number of chairs were purchased from Nathan Glossop, who was paid around £40 a month for five months in 1833. One chair, which survives from this time, is the magnificent mahogany chair made for the Master Cutler by George Eadon. The building of the third Hall, with its spacious dining hall meant that for the first time, the Company could sit down together with its guests. In 1833, 233 people accepted the invitation from the Master Cutler, Thomas Ellin, to the first Feast in the new Hall. The dining hall was the largest room in the town and was seen as an appropriate space for displaying full-sized portraits of 'the great and the good', the first in 1838, being that of the

Figure 5.7. The dining room in the third Hall, now called the Old Banqueting Hall. This illustration shows the 1853 Feast of William Matthews, who was both Mayor of Sheffield and Master Cutler in that year (London Illustrated News, 10 September, 1853).

Figure 5.8. The Cutlers' Feast of Mark Firth, Master Cutler in 1867, in the new Great Banqueting Hall (London Illustrated News, 9 September, 1867).

Reverend Thomas Sutton, who was Vicar of Sheffield from 1805 to 1851.

Grand though this dining hall was, by the mid 19th century the Company felt the need to extend its Hall and built the impressive Great Banqueting Hall. For decades, there had been a gradual shift in manufacturing emphasis in Sheffield, which the Company could no longer ignore. Although the traditional cutlers still numbered in tens of thousands, they were being eclipsed in power by the steel and edge-tool manufacturers who had never been under the jurisdiction of the Company. In 1860, an Act of Parliament allowed those who were in these metal-working industries to be admitted as Freemen and so into the Company. In 1867, Master Cutler Mark Firth, a steel manufacturer, moved the date of his Feast to October, in order to celebrate the opening of the Great Banqueting Hall. This grand affair was covered by the *Illustrated London News*, which had been reporting the Cutlers' Feasts for several years (Figs 7 and 8).

The Great Banqueting Hall continues to be an incomparable venue for the Cutlers' Feast (Harper 1997, 135). Above a dado of marble, the walls are now hung with twelve full-size portraits of local and national figures, including Reverend Sutton, who has been moved from the Old Banqueting Hall. The hall was originally lit by two gas chandeliers, but is now lit with three chandeliers and at the Feast, these lights reflect off the silver and glass on the long tables, which can accommodate almost 400 people. At one end of the hall is the ladies' gallery, used by the guests of the Mistress Cutler on the day of Feast, to listen to the after-dinner speeches.

The provision for ladies can be traced through the records. The wife of the Beadle is mentioned during the preparations for the Feast and the wife of the Master, as Mistress Cutler, gradually moved out of the kitchen into having a social role. The papers of Joseph Ward indicate that the Mistress, and the Past Mistresses, had their own festivities in one of the rooms in the second Hall. When the third Hall had space for all the Master's guests in the banqueting hall, the guests of the Mistress met on a different day, but during the 20th century, traditions were established whereby the ladies either met in a nearby hotel or in the Hadfield Hall (directly below the Great Banqueting Hall) on Feast night.

Preparations for the Feast

Throughout the 18th century, the accounts show that the Beadle had a new set of clothes at the beginning of the Cutlers' Company year, presumably to be smart for the installation and Feast. The accounts also show that the Feasts involved the Beadle and his wife in work, for which they were paid extra. For instance, in the late 1750s, the new Beadle, Thomas Ragg, had the usual new set of clothes and his wife, Betty, was paid twelve shillings 'for her Care and Trouble at the Feast'.

Some of the most illuminating references to the Feasts relate to the preparations made by the Company to ensure the success of the occasion. Before 1682, when the Company invited the local nobility, the accounts simply mention the small amounts allowed to the Master for the dinner. From 1682, however, preparations became increasingly elaborate, costing more money and time, but greater involvement with the local gentry brought benefits with gifts of food being sent from the nearby country estates.

Preparations for the Feasts began with the cleaning of the Hall, the pewter (later the silver plate), knives and linen, refurbishing the furniture and repairing the cooking equipment. The preparations in the first Hall are not specified, apart from such references in 1682 as 'Payd William Bulles for work in the Hall Chamber in prepareing it to entertain the noble persons att the Feast 4/6d'. More details are given for the second Hall where the recurring expenses indicate that not only was there the annual cleaning and refurbishment, but that many items had to be specifically bought or hired for the Feast.

The building of the second Hall seems to have stimulated the Company to purchase more cutlery and tableware, and sometimes the accounts list purchases under the heading 'Bought for the Company use'. From the beginning of the 18th century, the Company began to identify its purchases of knives and forks, as in 1716, it bought six dozen knives and forks from Robert Bridges for £1/16/0 (£1.80p) and three years later, another six dozen were bought for a slightly cheaper price of £1/4/0. Between 1724 and 1729, the Company bought 348 knives, but interestingly, only 156 forks and no spoons. It is likely that spoons and forks were among the unspecified items hired in for the Feast. In 1739, the Company had to re-imburse Mr Marriott 2/6d. (12.5p) for the loss of a silver teaspoon.

The Company continued to purchase knives, and some forks, throughout the 18th century, potentially amassing an enormous number. In 1739, they bought 144 stag handled knives and forks and 84 ivory-handled knives and forks. In 1740, John Green was paid 3/8d for cleaning 250 knives. The continual purchase of knives makes one wonder what happened to them all – were they lost, stolen, or did they break? From the details in Joseph Ward's papers, it would seem that 250 was the maximum number of people who could be entertained at one time, so why was there the need to buy more? Did it indicate that guests' place-settings included more than one knife and fork for the different dishes or was there a natural desire to replace old knives with the newer designs?

It is clear from the earlier accounts, and it continues today, that the Company could not own enough tableware, furniture and staff to mount its annual Feast. Although it continued to purchase cutlery, linen, glasses and cooking equipment, the accounts show that the Beadle was responsible for listing the items borrowed. Mr Horsfield of the Rose and Crown in the Market Place was an important supplier and the Company often had to repay him for losses; as in 1733 when a plate was lost; in 1734 three shillings were paid for lost pewter and again in 1737, another plate was lost. The loan of items thought necessary for the Feast continued into the 19th century, but whereas the loans in the 18th century came from local inns, the Company borrowed increasingly from the town centre shops and from the major manufacturers, especially for the silver to decorate the tables.

In the last years of the 18th century, the internal troubles of the Company had led to the easing of the requirements necessary to become a Freeman. For several years, the Company seems to have lost it way and the Feast reflected this. The Company's fortunes and influence declined, culminating in 1814, with an Act of Parliament, which removed many of its functions, such as the enrolling of apprentices. There was no Feast 1809–1811 because of the poor state of its finances and the Company seems only to have had a 'dinner' at the installation until 1816, when Thomas Asline Ward was allowed 40 guineas for his Feast, about half the amount provided for Joseph Ward's Feast in 1790. Gradually however, the Company regained its confidence and in 1825, £75 was allowed, but no details were given. In 1834, in the new Hall, the Master was allowed £100 for the Feast, but there were extra costs such as £4 for hiring waiters. In September 1840, the details once again indicate the preparations and costs.

Ringers	£3/3/0
Revd James Knight	£1/1/0
Gratuities to gamekeepers and carriage of game	£6/6/9
Cook's wages and men for cleaning plate etc	£9/9/6
Beadle's bill for waiters & his expenses for taking invitations to the Feast	£10/10/11
Beadle for horse hire	£2/5/0
Cleaning the Hall before and after the Feast	£13/10/1
Norton for washing	15/3
Foster for music	£3/6/0
Chapman for cleaning knives	£2/10/0
Renwick for spoons	1/4
Dixon for the Beadle's top coat, etc	£4/11/6

The 'Ringers' were paid to ring the bells of the parish church across the road from the Cutlers' Hall. The ringers had probably been ringing the church bells for the installation of the Master from the Company's inception and later for the Feasts. In 1688, the Company paid £48/15/0 to Houmfrey Wilkinson of Lincoln, Bellfounder, 'for the new Bell called Cutlers Bell', and in the 18th century, it seems to have been used to call Company meetings. The minister had always been paid a guinea for his sermon at the Installation, plus a bottle of wine.

The Food and the Table

It has been shown that each Cutlers' Company used the start of its year to establish the tradition of an increasingly important and opulent Feast, involving it in a great deal of expense and preparations. Evidence for the food served throughout the 18th century comes indirectly from the purchases made following the rebuilding of the Hall in the 1720s. The new Hall had a kitchen, a cellar and a new 'furnace', while the 1736 accounts show the Company bought a pair of stand racks, six stewpots, two larger stewpots, two large pancheons and two sieves. The following year, they bought another stand rack, two more pancheons, two stewpots, two hair sieves, two squirts (whatever they may be), a bowl and two new pasty pans. These items seem to form the core of the kitchen equipment; more were bought and many were repaired each year. The cooking and preparation for the Feast fell to the wife of the Beadle and no doubt, other helpers were taken on and in the 19th century, cooks, chefs and waiters were hired, costing an increasing amount in wages.

Purchases of food are not listed specifically in the accounts. Indications of what was served come from the details of the gifts, existing menus and the few surviving dockets and receipts. The account books record contributions in kind from the local landowners, the first indication being in 1688, when Lord Castleton of Sandbeck started to send venison. However, the delivery of game meant that carriage had to be paid and the Company had the expense of 'treating' the gamekeepers and even providing them with gifts. For instance, in 1705, the keeper from Hardwick Hall was given a shoulder knife costing 2/6d, and in 1818, the keepers were treated to beef and ale costing 14 shillings. In 1790, Joseph Ward had a scale for presents to the gamekeepers (P8/1/1). For 'Every Buck or Doe 10/6 a Knife and a Razor All other Smaller Presents as Game Fruite etc According to Vallue or as you Please'. Such expenses cease in the 1890s.

In 1854, the Master Cutler, Thomas Moulson, listed the cost of the game sent in (P1/1). Venison came from the Earls of Scarbrough, and Fitzwilliam, from the Duke of Devonshire, and from Lord Wharncliffe, amounting to £3/9/8d in carriage. A total of 17 brace of grouse, five couple of rabbits and two hares were given by the Dukes of Norfolk, and Rutland; from Mr Ellison, the Duke of Norfolk's agent, and from Willis Dixon, silver manufacturer. The total cost for carriage was £1. Obviously, game and meat provided the main courses of the Feast and in the later 19th century and early 20th century, meat courses were extensive as can be seen in the menu for the 1906 Feast of William Fawcett Osborn. The entrée course included quails; the removes included saddle of mutton, sirloin of beef, haunch of venison, boiled turkey and roast chicken. The game course consisted of grouse, pheasant and partridge.

One other animal which often featured on the Feast menu was the turtle. The first was sent by Mr John Kaye from Liverpool in 1774, and the Company seems to have enjoyed the experience of eating it at Mr Glanville's (which cost them eleven guineas). Samuel Glanville was the innkeeper of the Angel Inn in the Market Place, a short walk from the Cutlers' Hall and one of the main inns in the town centre. From then on, these creatures were on the menu and were sent live to the Hall; the spectacle of the animals walking down the corridor to the kitchens is described by many people. Turned into soup, which was served in the shell, the turtles are remembered as several of their shells and heads decorate the Hall. Needless to say, this no longer happens.

Apart from the cost of carriage for game, the 18th century accounts do not give details of the Feast menus. The papers of Joseph Ward in 1790 list some of the other ingredients for his Feast, as in September 1790, the following vegetables were purchased – peas, turnips, carrots, onions, celery, horseradish, 'Hartychoaks' and potatoes. Ann Pearson received 13 shillings for oat bread, and Pearson and Brown provided confectionary such as, preserved apricots, eight 'raised figures', six 'flat figures', two currant cakes, two raspberry cakes and five pound of Savoy biscuits. Compare these desserts with those listed in the 1906 menu, when guests were served Datzic jelly, Curaçao soufflé and fruit cream; cheese straws and savouries; strawberry, melon and pineapple ices and petits fours.

In the days before the Feast, the Company would draw up its guest lists and deliver its invitations, additional staff were employed to cook and serve the food and entertainers were brought in. On the day, though, the guests would see only the tables, the food and the drink. The appearance of the table would change over the decades as more, and different, food was deemed necessary. Changes in style occurred as more dishes were placed on the table all together, and then as food was served in separate courses. These changes involved the Company in expenses such as the purchases of serving dishes, and in hiring the wide range of plates, glasses and spoons, plus waiters.

The details in the accounts for the second Hall suggest that rooms were set out with trestle tables, round tables, and at least one oval table. These were covered with tablecloths. In 1727, the Company bought diaper (a cloth with a woven diamond pattern) and huckaback (a strong, coarse linen) which were made into tablecloths and napkins, and cost over £11. More linen was bought in 1729 and in 1733 a tablecloth for the oval table was purchased, with six diaper napkins and a small tablecloth. In 1744, it cost 14/6d to have the Company's linen washed, which is a continuing cost to the present day. Guests would have eaten off pewter plates (later delft plates were bought) and using Sheffield-made knives, forks and spoons. In 1708, six dozen pewter plates, twelve dozen trenchers and four dozen knives and forks were bought specifically for the Feast. The cutlery had

stag-horn handles, some had ivory and some even had silver, especially towards the end of the 18th century, when the Sheffield silver industry was getting into its stride and manufacturers and innkeepers were able to lend the Company more top quality cutlery. Although the Company bought in substantial amount of tableware, the wish to present a good table meant they had to hire silver spoons and glasses.

The purchases detailed in the account books may well indicate increasing refinement in the meals throughout the 18th century, as well as the changes in the manner of dining. Purchases show that the Company increasingly provided a wider range of knives and forks, together with an array of glasses for syllabub and jelly. Drinking vessels in the 1730s were mugs and gills, with ale served from pitchers, drawn from barrels in the cellars. It may be that more glasses were hired from local taverns. In 1732, the Company purchased six syllabub glasses; in the mid-1760s, a punch bowl and ladle were bought, and in 1774, they bought a large teapot. By the end of the 18th century, the Company had an assortment of wine glasses and decanters. Although purchases of tableware continue to be itemised until the 1770s, an inventory of 1807 (D10/1) shows what all these purchases amounted to, and what the Company could put on its tables. This inventory, together with the Company's purchases, indicates the variety of the food and drink being served. The glass collection is impressive, jelly being a favourite food, and there was obviously a hierarchy implied in the quality of the glasses.

> 99 cut glass wine glasses at 1/2d each
> 120 wine glasses at 6/- each
> 89 ale glasses at 1/- each
> 4 orange glasses at 1/- each
> 66 quart decanters at 2/6 each
> 28 pint decanters at 1/3 each
> 4 pair cut quart decanters 15/- each
> 60 tart glasses at 1d. each
> 45 cut sweetmeat glasses at 3d each
> 5 small glass dishes at 5d each
> 168 jelly glasses at 3/- each
> 156 jelly glasses at 2/6d each
> 82 jelly glasses at 2½d each
> 38 large jelly glasses at 6d each
> 16 glass salts at 6d each
> 9 cut glass salts at 1/- each

All the purchases of cutlery resulted in the Company, in 1807, having 492 sets of knives and forks with a variety of handles including ivory, horn and silver. There were also 84 pairs of 'old' knives and forks. There were 25 pairs of carvers matching these knives and forks, indicating that carving the meat was a 'public' affair, unlike today when meat is served ready sliced. To make the occasion of the Feast more splendid, the Company owned some silver and silver-plated items. It had 68 silver teaspoons and twelve tablespoons, plus 168

Figure 5.9. A survivor from a set of dinner plates and serving plates purchased by Thomas R. Ellin for use at his Feast in 1841. The set was loaned to subsequent Masters for their Feasts. The flower and foliage pattern is predominantly blue and red with a gold rim.

plated teaspoons and 76 plated tablespoons. It had 24 plated decanter labels (which still survive) plus nine plated fruit baskets and nine sets of casters. The tables could be lit with candlesticks and candelabra, nine of which are described as being plated with three light branches.

The desire to make display of fine cutlery, glass and linen is understandable, and as the 18th-century accounts show, the Company had to hire many items and this continued into the 19th century, though with the building of the third Hall and its more impressive dining space, the Company naturally wanted more display (Figure 5.9). Two newspaper illustrations of Feasts in the Hall in 1853 and in 1867, show the tables groaning under the weight of silver, fruit and flowers, with candlesticks and epergnes down the centres of the tables.

In the third Hall, the illustration for the 1853 Feast (Figure 5.7) shows the Old Banqueting Hall with guests sitting at three long tables down the length of the room, and a top table across the end. In the new Great Banqueting Hall, the 1867 Feast is shown with the top table on the left along the length of hall (Figure 5.8). This position is dictated by the location of the serving doors in the right-hand wall, when facing the ladies' gallery, as in the illustration. The other long tables are set at right angles to it and this layout continues, except that the top table is raised on a dais. These illustrations of the two Halls in the third Hall clearly show the guests sitting on chairs and it seems the Company had enough chairs not to have to hire any.

Figure 5.10. The Cutlers' Feast, 2005. Photograph Seamans.

Compared to the tables shown in the 19th-century illustrations, the tables and the menu today are much more restrained. Each place is set for four courses, with glasses for red and white wine, port and water; the food being served from dishes carried by waiters and waitresses, who are hired for the evening. One notable difference from the 19th century Feasts is the impressive display of the Company's silver. Prior to the middle of the 20th century, the Company owned very little plate with which to decorate the tables and the hall, and had to borrow from silver manufacturers such as

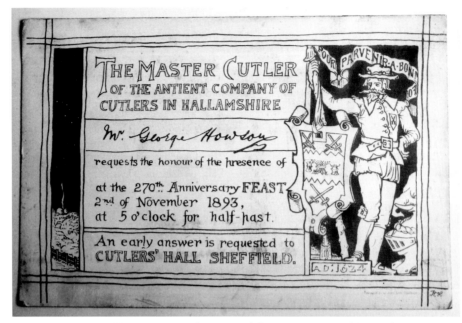

Figure 5.11. Invitation to the Feast of George Howson, 1893 (P2/1).

Bradbury's and from local department stores like John Walsh. Today, however, the Company has enough silver candlesticks and candelabra for all the tables and is able to set out an array of stunning silver behind the top table (Figure 5.10).

The Guests

In 1682, the first effect of inviting the gentry and nobility was the business of delivering invitations. Not only did members of the Company jostle for the right to ride round with the invitations, which was costing five pounds in the mid 18th century, but there were also costs involved simply in the *meeting* held to decide who would get to go. Drawing up a list of guests, preparing invitations, delivering or sending them seems to have required many meetings. Precise details survive in the papers of Joseph Ward, Master Cutler in 1790. He has left a small booklet with the names of his guests, ticked off or crossed out. He was very particular in his instructions for the invitations, referred to as 'tickets'. An engraved copper plate was required for printing the invitations and Ward specified that letters were 'to bee written on gilt paper, and the ladies' and gentlemen's tickets to be folded in gilt paper'. The Company and their wives' tickets were folded in paper. The same was for the burgesses and town and country friends. The surviving invitations from the 19th and 20th centuries show the changes in stylistic details and in printing techniques (Figure 5.11).

In 1906, a local antiquarian, Robert Eadon Leader produced an impressive two volume history of the Cutlers' Company. Volume I describes the fortunes of the Company as it strove to regulate the trade of making cutlery. Not

surprisingly, a chapter deals with the Feast and guests in which Leader traces the involvement of the local gentry and nobility and includes several 18th-century newspaper reports. In Volume II, he includes lists of people invited to several of the Feasts. From the papers of Joseph Ward, Leader transcribed and printed all who were invited, though not necessarily those who accepted (Leader 1906, 59). Although Ward could only accommodate 250 guests in five rooms, he sent invitations to 340 woman and 370 men to be spread over two days. His list of guests was divided in to groups. Seventy 'Nobility and Gentry' included the Dukes of Devonshire, Leeds, and Norfolk; the Earls of Bute, Effingham, Fitzwilliam, Scarbrough, and Strafford; four other lords; two knights or baronets, and three Members of Parliament, including William Wilberforce. The twelve Sheffield Church Burgesses were invited, together with thirteen Town Trustees, the 32 members of the Company and 17 clergymen. The general guests amounted to more than 240. In addition there were the ladies who were the wives and daughters of these guests. Although this is an impressive list, it is not clear who came. The hall could accommodate around 500 guests over two nights, so there would be a fair number who declined his invitation. The assumption is that the main evening was Thursday, with the Past Masters Cutler, and the 19 Past Mistresses and widows of Past Masters were invited for Friday. Twenty-four couples were invited 'For the Dance'. One wonders in which room this was held.

For the Feast of 1833, the first in the third Hall, Thomas Ellin invited 321 people and 232 accepted, all being able to sit down together. The top table included Lords Morpeth and Wharncliffe; Earl Manvers; seven Justices of the Peace; nine clergymen; the two county Members of Parliament and the two newly elected Sheffield MPs. However, there were notable absences, such as the Dukes of Devonshire, Norfolk, Portland, and Rutland; Earls Fitzwilliam and Surrey; Lord Howard of Effingham, and Francis Chantrey, the local sculptor.

Invitations continue to be sent to the nobility, members of the government, the clergy and captains of industry. During the 20th century, the list of guests who have attended is impressive. It includes three members of the Royal family: HRH Prince Philip, The Duke of Edinburgh, HRH The Princess Royal, and HRH The Duke of Kent, plus 49 titled guests. The political scene has been represented by 52 MPs, including five Prime Ministers, ten High Commissioners, two foreign Prime Ministers, and six foreign Ambassadors, including those from America, Japan, and China. There have also been ten members of the clergy including the Archbishops of York and Canterbury, 61 members of the armed forces, and nine captains of industry. It is interesting to see how the invitations reflect the fortunes of Sheffield's industry – its desire to sell to the armaments trade or to highlight foreign trade issues and obstructive regulations. An important occasion in the history of the Feast occurred in 1934, when, continuing the practice of inviting the Lord Mayor of Sheffield, the first lady to be invited was Mrs Longden, Sheffield's first female Lord Mayor.

Conclusion

The Cutlers' Feast represents an amazing example of the development and survival of a tradition, which over the centuries, changed from being a simple dinner in a tavern to a spectacular and costly display of corporate dining. In 1624, Sheffield was a small town with a metal-working industry, which involved a large proportion of its inhabitants, which had some physical advantages, but which was geographically remote from London and the ports. Within 60 years, the Company had established a 'Feast' to which it felt comfortable in being able to invite a mix of nobility, landed gentry, merchants, clergy, and working cutlers. It may seem surprising that there was a desire on the part of the gentry etc. to attend and even in today's sophisticated age, an invitation to the Feast is still coveted. The Company has been able to mount its Feast successfully in each of its three Halls, each of which had different rooms and features. There can be no doubt that the desire to entertain more lavishly determined the layout, decoration and refurbishment of the third Hall, culminating in its most impressive Great Banqueting Hall.

Over the centuries, the Company has responded to circumstances and has cancelled the Feast, so it has not had the 381 Feasts since its foundation. In 1798, there was no Feast because of internal problems and the £200 earmarked was given to the Government. In 1809–1811, no Feasts were held because of depression in local trade and in 1832 and 1866, the building of the third Hall and extension prevented the celebrations. In the 20th century, the Feast was cancelled during the First World War and again in 1921, because of the depression in the country.

The records of the Company holds details of all the hard work which went into the preparations – the cleaning of the Hall, linen and tableware and the assembling of the food. The cost of the occasion has increased enormously from the modest amount spent in 1625, not just on the day, but in the purchases of cooking equipment, furniture and tableware. The meetings required to draw up the guest lists show how important this was and is, in the minds of the Company and while the preparations today do not involve making seat reservations, with breakfast, on the London trains, the Company still plans for the reception of its main guests. The Feast, its preparations, and the occasion itself, can be seen as a fascinating reflection of the fortunes, not just of the Company, but of the Sheffield metal-working trades.

References

Cutlers' Company archives

Accounts of the Master Cutlers, 1811–1889, D1/3.
Company Guard Book, P2/1
Company Minute Book, 1727–1785, C9/1.
Company Minute Book, 1785–1803 C9/2.
Company Minute Book, 1803–1830, C9/3.
Company Minute Book, 1830–1860, C9/4.
Company Minute Book, 1860–1880, C9/5.
First account book, 1625–1790, D1/1.
An inventory of the Cutlers' Hall, 1807, D10/1.
Papers of Joseph Ward, Master Cutler, 1790/91, P8/1.

Sheffield Archives

Hearth Tax, 24 Chas II, Strafforth and Tickhill Wapentakes, E179/262/15.

Books and Articles

Bell, A. B. (ed.) (1909) *Peeps into the Past, being passages from the diary of Thomas Asline Ward*, Sir W. C. Leng and Co, Ltd., Sheffield.
Harper, R. (1997) A history of the Cutlers' Hall, in Binfield, C. and Hey, D. (ed.) *Mesters to Masters*, Oxford, Oxford University Press, 115–161.
Leader, R. E. (1905–1906) *A History of the Company of Cutlers in Hallamshire Vols I and II*, The Company of Cutlers in Hallamshire, Sheffield.
MacDonald, J. (1997) The Cutlers' Feast, in Binfield, C. and Hey, D. (ed.) *Mesters to Masters*, Oxford, Oxford University Press, 225–240.

6

Dining at Endcliffe Hall

Julie Banham

This chapter examines the building and furnishing of Endcliffe Hall in the 1860s by Sir John Brown one of Sheffield's leading Victorian industrialists. It considers some of the issues facing men whose business activities demanded homes which reflected not just their success but their tastes, sophistication and allegiances. By the mid-19th century it was possible for the keen observer to deduce from the style and furnishing of a home whether they shared similar outlooks and aspirations or whether substantial philosophical differences existed between them. Then, as now, much business was secured through networks supported by home entertaining and so presenting the right image was an important and potentially fraught issue.

By the mid-19th century, the ability to present oneself as a gentleman simply by subscribing to the polite forms and fashions of the day had became seriously compromised. Whilst personal comportments were increasingly regimented by etiquettes and conventions the range of styles available with which to build and furnish a home was increasing quite dramatically. The third edition of Robert Kerr's (1871) *The Gentleman's House* offered ten styles ranging from Elizabethan, Palladian and Rural Italian to Scottish Baronial. By the end of the century trade journals such as *The Furnisher* and *The Furniture Record* regularly featured a dozen different styles whilst more ambitious publications could offer 30 or more modes including Chinese, Japanese, Roman, Byzantine, Pompeiian, Moorish, Adam, Italian Gothic, Spanish, Dutch and New British with which to adorn the discerning gentleman's home (Binstead 1904).

This plethora of styles plus the inexperience of many into whose hands the baton of fashion now passed generated an abundance of anxious commentaries and guide books eager to assist the *nouveaux riches* in making the same discerning and tasteful judgements as their 18th-century aristocratic predecessors. Smith (1808), Loudon (1833), Arrowsmith (1840), Eastlake (1864), Mrs Beeton (1861), and Mrs Haweis (1876), the 'arbiter of elegance', all offered advice to ensure that new wealth followed old taste.

Classicism was no longer the mainstay of a gentleman's home and whilst variety was actively pursued, the popularity of these works with many middle-class readers suggests an underlying terror that choosing the wrong style would not just expose a lack of sophistication, but could result in a loss of face amongst their peers, superiors and clients.

This chapter takes as its theme John Brown's journey from his early beginnings in Sheffield to his dining table at Endcliffe Hall. It considers whether such fears were justified or whether the energy, innovation and acumen that such men applied to their businesses enabled them to blend tradition with technology and modernity to create homes which reflected both an ease with success and their role in society.

As with many Sheffield industrialists, John Brown was a self-made man and the first of his family to enjoy considerable wealth. Born in 1816, the son of a local builder and slater, he was apprenticed to Earl Horton and Co., file and cutlery manufacturers, where he soon became a partner. In 1844 he started his own steel manufacturing business achieving considerable success with his invention of coiled spring buffers for railway carriages. In 1856 he opened the Atlas Works and employed 200 men to make armour plate from Bessemer steel. By 1863 he employed 2,500, and 5,000 by 1872. His works soon covered some 21 acres and by 1867 was generating an annual turnover of around £1,000,000 (Tweedale 1986).

Brown held many local posts including Mayor of Sheffield, Master Cutler, Deputy Lieutenant of the West Riding of Yorkshire, Justice of the Peace, Council Member of the Sheffield School of Art, Chairman of the Sheffield School Board and he was also a Town Trustee. A generous benefactor, he gave money to religious, welfare and educational causes. Remaining childless, he and his wife directed much of their attention to putting on recitals, parties and concerts in order to foster his business, charitable and social aims (*The Sheffield and Rotherham Independent*, 28 December 1896).

In 1862, Brown's firm won a gold medal at the International Exhibition, where he escorted Queen Victoria round the Sheffield stand. In the same year Lord Palmerston spent a week at Brown's home Shirle Hill when he visited the Atlas Works (*Sheffield Daily Telegraph*, 11 August 1862). In the following year a reception was held there for the Lords of the Admiralty and 'all the neighbouring nobility' after they had inspected the rolling of armour plate at his works – an event fully covered by the *Illustrated London News* (21 Nov 1863). In 1867 he was the first Sheffield industrialist to be knighted.

Following the practice of local manufacturers, Brown had first lived alongside his works in the town centre in order to be on hand at all times. With success and a growing management structure, Brown began the arriviste's trek westwards away from factory noise and pollution to the affluent suburbs of Sheffield amongst the Pennine foothills. During the second half of the 19th century successful Sheffield industrialists were producing goods of international repute earning them considerable wealth and status. Instead of forsaking the town for areas such as York, London or Cheltenham as their 18th-century counterparts had done, once their wealth had been made, (Reid 1973), they began to build large, architect-designed, expensively furnished residences in secluded parklands in which to raise families, receive guests, and pursue their ambitions. They acquired moorland shoots, farmed estates and collected art, shaking off the provincialism that had dogged the town for much of its history (Walton 1948).

Whilst land was readily available for development and house-furnishers, cabinetmakers and architects were quick to supply their needs, Sheffield's *nouveaux riches* nevertheless lacked an articulate and varied building tradition. A poor civic and domestic heritage plus a focus on business affairs meant many rising industrialists lacked the visual vocabulary shared by the gentry, professionals, aristocrats, and merchants of other towns.

Sheffield's demographic landscape was unusual as the development of vast iron and steel works demanded considerable areas of flat space which were found to the east of the town alongside the few roads and waterways linking the area to neighbouring communities. Their growth forced many gentry families out of the area or caused them to relocate to the relatively narrow segment in the foothills west of the town safe from factory development (Hunt 1956). Such a concentration of middle-class dwellings, away from all but the most determined visitor, may have helped form a local code of attitudes and aspirations which were expressed through the design and furnishing of middle-class homes. Many aspiring *nouveaux riches* saw what I describe as 'the Sheffield code' as a more successful entrée into society than subscription to fashions which had not yet secured the benefits of local endorsement (Linton 1956).

When success and a developing business structure enabled Sir John to move the family home away from his factory, he first chose a house set on a fashionable road leading towards the Pennine foothills, followed by a move to Shirle Hill, a substantial Georgian property set within its own grounds to the south-west of the town. Surrounded by the homes of fellow industrialists and merchants it was '...fitted up with every convenience and decorated at great cost for the owner's occupation and comfort'. It had dining, drawing and breakfast rooms, a butler's pantry, seven bedrooms, one dressing room and one bathroom. Outside there were pleasure grounds a conservatory, stabling, a vinery, peach house, pine pits, potting house and a large amount of land (*Sheffield Daily Telegraph* 6 May 1865).

However, across the valley from Shirle Hill in the comparatively remote district of Ranmoor, Brown could see his commercial rival Mark Firth building a home in the new Italian style. The Duke of Norfolk was also refurbishing his Sheffield home in the gothic style whilst further afield manufacturers such as Crossley, Salt and Lister were building homes incorporating the latest fashions and technology (Sheeran 1993). Brown therefore decided to leave '...the comfortable gentility of Shirle Hill at Sharrow for the magnificent empty spaces of Endcliffe Hall' (Walton 1948, 225).

Throughout the 19th century Sheffield was constantly criticised for its lack of good buildings and the dire condition of its streets. As late as 1900 *The Court Guide to the West Riding of Yorkshire* acknowledged Sheffield's rank as the second largest city in Yorkshire but dismissed it as 'the blackest, dirtiest and most smokey town in Yorkshire ... The public buildings in the town are comparatively few, and of little interest'.

Comments were also made on the unusual nature of Sheffield society. It was observed that 'there is not that marked line of difference between the rich man and the poor man which is becoming annually more observable in other places' (Parker 1830). And again in 1860:

> the line of demarcation separating the two classes from each other is easily overstepped and indeed can scarcely be accurately drawn... Master and men, in consequence, do not hold aloof from one another to the same extent as is the case in most places (Hill 1860).

The integration and easy transposition between master and men was in part responsible for the higher standard of living enjoyed by many of Sheffield's workers when compared to other industrial communities. However, it also fuelled the homogeneous and tightly-knit structure of the cutlery industry which failed to see need or value in acquiring any 'outward trappings of civic dignity' (Pollard 1959, 3). George III's condemnation of Sheffield as a 'damned bad place' was not just a consequence of its sympathies towards

French Revolutionaries and republicanism but that from the outside it was seen as a rough and impolite town.

Sheffield presented a paradox whereby its fame as a producer of polite goods for the table was rarely reflected in fine architecture or high culture. It was essentially a plebeian society content to pursue practices and forms which had long sustained the cutlers' culture.

Against this background, Sir John determined that Endcliffe Hall should be a showhouse not just for himself, but also for the town and its skills. Using local craftsmen whenever possible, Endcliffe's function was to combine technology, sophistication and fashion to enhance the standing of a technocrat at ease with industrialists, politicians and aristocrats and to advertise a town which was home to some of the nation's largest and most important companies. Whilst ambitious, this was neither simple naivety nor vanity on Sir John's part, but the recognition that modern business life required far more than just good products. In a volatile economy success demanded confirmation through the outward trappings and assurances which most effectively demonstrated technical expertise and efficiency with the values of stability, efficiency and longevity. Choosing a style which accurately reflected these values and caught the mood of the market was essential.

Thus, whilst locally admired, Shirle Hill failed to reflect either Sir John's national standing and ambitions or his company's modernity and innovation. In addition, by the early 1860s it was clear that the status of the area was rapidly losing ground to the more cosmopolitan suburbs of Ranmoor to the west of the town.

Sir John therefore acquired a 40 acre site overlooking Oakbrook, the home of his business rival Mark Firth. Before building could commence, a much earlier hall, dating in part from the 13th century, was demolished and all traces removed except for a beam which was incorporated into the ktichen of the new hall. Sir John was not nostalgic. Designed by the Sheffield architects Flockton and Abbot the 36-room hall was completed in less than two years (Figures 6.1 and 6.2). Italianate in the French manner was the style chosen which had the effect of rendering Firth's mere Italianate style as *passé*. The use of the latest classical interpretation was calculated to emphasise Sir John's status as a sophisticated gentleman acknowledging his technologically innovative business whilst aligning him with a classical tradition endorsed by the establishment for over 200 years.

Endcliffe was a modern building. A long driveway lit by ornamental gaslights took visitors from the main road to a covered plate glass carriage porch flanked by sculptures (Figure 6.1). The entrance hall led directly from an inner porch to the grand staircase passing all the major rooms – fulfilling Kerr's requirement that classical entrance halls must be symmetrical and that their route should be both direct and central. Iron joists and concrete floors made it virtually fireproof and a large cistern provided power for a 32-stop organ in the saloon as well water for fire hydrants and domestic use. All the principle bedrooms were equipped with bathrooms. Oakbrook had to wait until the impending stay of the Prince and Princess of Wales in 1875 prompted extensive alterations and the provision of modern facilities. The ground-floor windows were protected against burglary and sunlight by retractable Belgian-made louvered iron shutters. At night, large mirrors stored in the wall cavities were drawn across the windows to mask the louvers and throw light back into the rooms (The Public Advantages of Personal Munificence, *Sheffield Daily Telegraph* 24th May, 1865).

Gas and candlelight were available throughout the house. It is possible that Sir John – or his wife – were aware that even though Prince Albert had installed gas at Windsor, many considered its light vulgar and lacking intimacy so, torn between modernity and taste, both systems were in use. Two large conservatories adjoining the Hall were inspired perhaps by Paxton's Crystal Palace or his work at nearby Chatsworth and used the same technology of plate glass inserted into cast iron ribs extending from a masonry base. Service areas were grouped together on the north side of the building whilst a network of corridors enabled all major rooms to be quickly serviced with the minimum disruption. The cooking ranges could use gas or coal whilst all rooms were linked by an electric bell system to the kitchen and benefited from central heating (Hindmarch and Podmore 1990).

Amongst other local manufacturers and suppliers the two well-established Sheffield firms of John Manuel and Son and George Eadon and Son were commissioned to produce the furniture (Figures 6.4, 6.5 and 6.7) (Ball 1978; Banham 1999). Both supplied detailed drawings and room plans for approval prior to any work being undertaken. A third firm, William Johnson and Son, was equally well-established but the few surviving drawings provided by them are of poor quality and little appears to have been commissioned from them. All schemes were presented to Sir John for his approval meriting ticks, crossings out or comments on the plans (SA AP 38. 1–62). His wife, Lady Mary, appears to have had little direct input although it is assumed her views were accommodated. As the designer of his own works and used to being involved in all stages of development, it is evident that Sir John continued this practice at home.

Contemporary etiquette pervaded the schemes with each room using the appropriately designated woods to reflect their masculine or feminine status (Banham *et al.* 1991, 27–43). In particular, great attention was lavished by Manuels on the furnishing of the State Bedroom Suite comprising bedroom, dressing room, bathroom and boudoir. All the furniture was made from: 'Italian walnut woods with carved work and ornamentations of light and dark woods, inlaid with marquetry, ebony and tulip woods with ebonised mouldings' (Maple and Co. 1893, 45).

Figure 6.1. View of Endcliffe Hall from the front, showing long driveway and entrance porch. (Endcliffe Hall, Sheffield, Yorkshire, Sale Particulars. Maple & Co., Ltd, London & Eastbourne, 1893)

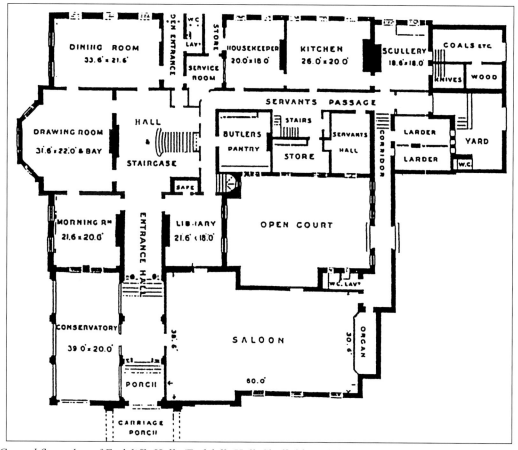

Figure 6.2. Ground floor plan of Endcliffe Hall. (Endcliffe Hall, Sheffield, Yorkshire, Sale Particulars. Maple & Co., Ltd, London & Eastbourne, 1893)

This is where the discerning visitor would have realised the full extent of Sir John's ambitions. In contemporary etiquette walnut was deemed a feminine wood: its Latin name was *juglans regia* meaning 'fit for a queen'. The seal of a royal visit would be the ultimate social accolade he could achieve and Endcliffe was to be the vehicle of that ambition.

Inspiration for the furniture designs reflect a mixture of high fashion and flamboyance tempered by the familiar and comfortable. References can be seen to designs presented at the Great Exhibition of 1851, and the International Exhibition of 1862 when Sir John escorted Queen Victoria around the Sheffield stand and his company's gold medal display of armour plating. The drawing room mantelpiece and stove described as 'very chaste pieces of art work of great merit' by the London auctioneers Maple and Co. in 1893 were bought directly from the 1862 Exhibition (Maple and Co. 1893, 10). Whilst exhibition designs could ultimately reflect and merge with popular styles, Symonds and Whineray noted that:

> it is important to remember that it [exhibition furniture] was not entirely typical of the furniture trade as a whole…. These pieces were designed to attract as purchasers, kings, noblemen, governments, museums and immensely wealthy people and it was not intended that the ordinary middle class householder should do anything but observe and wonder (Symonds and Whineray 1987, 59).

Sir John was keen to be recognised by the fashionable title of the time as a merchant prince. The spatial and material provisions for dining at Endcliffe can be judged against a contemporary backcloth of practices to assess the degree of Sir John's conformity to cosmopolitan ideals and also as unwitting evidence of the way fashions and practices were tempered by regional communities to conform to local judgements of good taste. As indicated by Sarah Paston-Williams (1995, 321) in *The Art of Dining*, 'Giving dinner parties was a direct route to obtaining a "footing in society" and there was no surer or better passport than having a reputation for giving "good dinners"'. Dining was of such importance to Sir John's social, business and political ambitions that two rooms were created to accommodate every form of occasion.

To the right of the entrance hall was the long and impressive saloon some 60 ft long and almost 40 ft wide (Figure 6.3). Containing a 32-stop organ, the saloon could be used as a reception area, concert hall, ballroom, art gallery or dining room for grand and formal occasions (*Sheffield Daily Telegraph* 9 May, 1865). Its location on the north-east corner of the hall conformed again with Kerr who claimed a dining room used in the evening needed to catch the rays of the setting sun and look well in candlelight (Kerr 1871, 91). Natural light entered through a row of long windows and a series of skylights featuring three large graduated domed rotundas. The ceiling was heavily embellished with painted

Figure 6.3. Photograph of the Grand Saloon taken in 1893. (Endcliffe Hall, Sheffield, Yorkshire, Sale Particulars. Maple & Co., Ltd, London & Eastbourne, 1893)

Figure 6.4. Spanish mahogany dining table with three extra leaves extending to 16 ft with shaped ends and quadruple centre legs. George Eadon and Sons for the saloon. (Drawings for the Furniture at Endcliffe Hall, Sheffield City Archives Library AP 38–39)

Figure 6.5. Spanish mahogany and green velvet saloon chairs, made by George Eadon and Sons. (Drawings for the Furniture at Endcliffe Hall, Sheffield City Archives Library AP 38–39)

decorative plasterwork based upon a baroque grid iron beam design.

Two ormolu, china and steel stoves with carved figures, ornaments and painted plaques provided additional heat and focal points on the long internal wall. The woodwork and furniture were made from Spanish mahogany with green velvet upholstery and best quality horse-hair stuffing as required (Figure 6.5). Matching green velvet curtains contrasted with a patterned crimson, black, blue and green Brussels carpet whilst the walls were filled with paintings hung in layers from a rail running just below the coving. The suite of furniture made by Eadons comprised 38 chairs, six sofas and couches ranging from 5–12 ft in length, a 7ft 6 inch wide china cabinet with plate glass doors, an 11ft 6inch wide mirror back sideboard and two dining tables each of which could extend from 5–16 ft in length (Figure 6.4). It is tempting to speculate that local tastes which held durability, practicality and comfort in high esteem may have dissuaded Sir John and Lady Brown from completing the effect of the saloon by choosing light, gilt furniture with pale upholstery rather than the heavier and more reliable forms offered by Eadons.

Decorative items and tableware were in the French manner. They included Louis XVI ormolu candelabras supported by cupids, Sèvres vases with painted panels in the style of Watteau, a Louis XVI table dessert in dead and bright gold, and French china jardinières with painted flower panels (Maple and Co. 1893). The tables had shaped ends and a massive frame supported by four corner and four central legs that would take the additional weight of the leaves as the table was extended. Unlike Georgian tables which were made in sections displayed separately around the edge of the dining room until required, Victorian tables remained *in situ* and were extended according to the number of diners. This was achieved by the use of one or two large steel corkscrews connected to the underframe which were wound out to the required length by strenuously turning a handle placed in a socket at each end. The tables in the Endcliffe saloon would be seen from a considerable distance down the length of the room adding to the need for them to appear substantial and aesthetically pleasing from any angle and this helps to explain the intricate acanthus carving and capitals which form the legs and the gadrooning around the usually unseen lower moulding of the table frame.

To the rear of the room a water closet was sited thoughtfully behind a recessed annexe whilst a service corridor led directly to the kitchen enabling hot food to be served speedily and discreetly. Much of the cooking at Endcliffe was prepared by staff in the kitchen but documents indicate that for large events food was bought in – the newly opened Victoria Hotel in the centre of the town being a frequent supplier as were the two leading inns, The Angel, and The Tontine (*Newspaper Cuttings Relating to Sheffield*, Vol.10, 81).

For more intimate and less formal occasions a smaller rectangular dining room 33 ft long and 22 ft wide was provided at the far south-west of the Hall overlooking the gardens and park and, both conventionally and conveniently, next to the drawing room effecting ease of entrance from one to the other. Whilst drawing rooms were designated female spaces and furnished appropriately in light, curvaceous forms using walnut or rosewood, Loudon (1833) echoed the popular view that the characteristic colouring of a dining room should be warm, rich and substantial. Kerr added that the dining room should also possess an overall appearance of 'masculine importance' (Banham *et al.* 1991, 35). This meant the timbers should be thought of as masculine which popular convention deemed oak or mahogany. Eadon's scheme for the dining room involved furniture in oak with green morocco upholstery, blue and crimson table cloths and crimson curtains (Figure 6.6). The floor was covered with a large Turkey carpet to which a plain border, some 3ft wide, gave the appearance of a fitted carpet. Turkey carpets, not Axminster or Brussels, were considered appropriate for the dining room and, like the dining table they had to be the same shape as the room they occupied (Arrowsmith 1840).

The importance and solemnity attributed to dining was acknowledged by the Art Journal Illustrated Catalogue of the 1867 Paris Exhibition:

> The dining room furniture of England, as distinguished from the furniture suited to a drawing room, should be substantial, massive, handsome, and in colour somewhat sombre rather than gay. The sideboard is the *pièce de résistance* in which these characteristics usually reach a climax…

Kerr endorsed the contemporary view that for ease of serving, food should be delivered via a service door located next to the sideboard and behind the master's chair at the head of the table. Furthermore, the sideboard should be against the north wall – ideally in a recess – so that the mirror would reflect light back into the room from the southerly or westerly facing windows. Endcliffe did not have a recess but as the service door flanked one side of the sideboard a false door was placed on the opposite side to add balance and symmetry to the room. Kerr advised that a corridor should separate the service room from the dining room to reduce odours and smells and this plan was duly incorporated into Endcliffe's design.

The sideboard was described as beautifully made in oak, carved and panelled with bold pedestals, spiral columns, having three drawers in the frieze, massive back with reflecting plate, shaped sliding trays and revolving decanter holder (Figure 6.7) (Maple and Co. 1893). By the mid-19th century sideboards had become more substantial than their Georgian counterparts and whilst they still possessed a recess which would have held a matching wine cooler the storage of drink for the table was now incorporated into the body of the sideboard.

Figure 6.6. View of the dining room taken in 1893. (Endcliffe Hall, Sheffield, Yorkshire, Sale Particulars. Maple & Co., Ltd, London & Eastbourne, 1893)

Figure 6.7. Dining room sideboard in polished oak by George Eadon and Sons. (Drawings for the Furniture at Endcliffe Hall, Sheffield City Archives Library AP 38–56)

The table could accommodate up to ten extra leaves – the case for which was stored out of view in the service room. Large ceramic castors supported the six substantial legs allowing the table to be wound out to its required length. Fourteen gentlemen's chairs, 15 ladies' chairs and one carver could be called upon for seating – each having Sir John's coat of arms gilded upon the back. Motifs from Sir John's coat of arms such as a bee and coil spring were incorporated into many of the furnishings and fabric of the building. The Hall and its furnishings were made between 1863– 1865 and yet Sir John did not receive his knighthood until 1867 (Death of Sir John Brown, *Sheffield and Rotherham Independent,* 28th December, 1896).

The scheme was completed by an elaborately moulded, gilt and painted ceiling, with gilt mirrors, pier and console tables placed between heavy sweeping silk curtains held back by gold tassels and supported by large carved gilt pelmets. The curtains draped along the floor – a fashion vilified by Eastlake (1864) but one which remained highly popular in Sheffield and which was still being offered by local firms in 1900. Conversely, Eadon's design for Endcliffe's dining room sofa, made between 1863 and 1865, pre-empts the style produced by Richard Charles of Warrington in 1867 (Thornton 1984, 218). This evident mixture of old and new styles suggests a far more complex attitude towards design in the provinces than simple provincialism or time-lag would explain.

Endcliffe Hall was the largest and most ambitious housing project Sheffield had seen and as such has remained unparalleled. It was claimed that the building cost some £100,000 with an additional £60,000 spent on furnishings and decoration. Upon completion in 1865, such was the interest that for three days prior to occupancy the public were allowed to process through the Hall and wonder at its marvels and the prestige of its owner as a true 'merchant prince' (The Public Advantages of Personal Munificence, *Sheffield Daily Telegraph* 24th May, 1865).

Although Endcliffe Hall was large and imposing by Sheffield standards, on a national level it never fully abandoned the familiarity, practicality and comfort of local middle-class life for the higher reaches of contemporary avant-garde fashion. At the same time as Endcliffe was being built, less than 30 miles away Brodsworth Hall was redesigned in the Italianate style for the wealthy Thelluson family of financiers. Italian architects were employed to create an exuberant and flamboyant style, whilst furnishings were purchased from London and the continent. The drawing room conformed to the required feminine style but whereas Endcliffe's was furnished with practical amber curtains and brown ribbed upholstery, Brodsworth confidently embraced the more ambitious and complimentary decorating schemes of pastels, white and gilding. Although geographically only 30 miles apart and sharing similar architectural schemes, the two houses reflect very different attitudes to cosmopolitan

ideals and fashions. Endcliffe willingly embraced technology but moderated fashions through the conservative filter of local tastes. Brodsworth's wealth and urbanity were demonstrated by a confident use of marble, scagliola, and damask wall coverings to create rich decorative schemes which incorporated both fashion and individuality.

Sheffield was home to some of the nation's largest companies but its dependence upon a relatively narrow range of industries meant it was vulnerable to the volatile economic climate of the day. Whilst capable of producing innovative and groundbreaking solutions for heavy engineering and the metal industries, it was less confident in employing design to reflect status, achievement or prestige.

> Sheffield's response to polite tastes in architecture and town planning were both tardy and modest. Though … the wealthiest inhabitants erected houses with classical facades, the scale of individual buildings was modest and the sole classical square was not completed until the 1770s. Sheffield did not have a group of wealthy merchants … comparable with those in Leeds or Nottingham, nor did it have the unitary government institutions to provide the fine public buildings…The meeting houses were no more than brick boxes… (Hey 1991, 280–281).

In the building of Endcliffe Hall, Sir John was determined to reverse this perception but still he remained bound by the Sheffield code. Limited links with other communities had created a parochial society which further lacked a dynamic architectural heritage or the stimulus of a cosmopolitan society. To be acceptable to local society, new styles had to conform to an established code of meanings and values. It is unreasonable to argue that this created a series of regional styles each of which nuanced aspects of local cultures, rather than such codes reflecting the time it took metropolitan styles and fashions to be accepted and integrated into the local vocabulary. Delay had the virtue of transient and costly styles being avoided whilst the popularity of some forms long after they had become outmoded in more metropolitan areas suggests a useful mechanism for avoiding costly purchases in times of economic uncertainty. The argument put forward by Cain and Hopkins (1993). that industrialists were more hostile to and found greater difficulty integrating with court and county life than their professional or service counterparts does not appear to be fully supported in Sheffield. Sir John embraced these institutions and advertised his affinity with them through the architecture and furnishing of his home. Whilst the description of Ranmoor as 'a centre of local fashion, but not of taste' (Walton 1948, 225) may accurately describe the attempts of many in their desire to acquire the trappings of sophistication and respectability, the furnishing of Sir John Brown's dining rooms reflect integration with, not opposition to, the social mores of the day.

Alas, Endcliffe Hall never received its royal visitor – that honour was won by Mark Firth in 1875, who welcomed the

Prince and Princess of Wales to his newly extended house, Oakbrook, decorated in the Aesthetic style (The Royal Visit, The Royal Apartments at Oakbrook, *Sheffield Daily Telegraph* 14th August, 1875). After several poor business ventures and increasing ill health, after the death of his wife Sir John retired to friends in the south of England. Apart from a skeleton staff, Endcliffe remained empty until the entire contents and premises were auctioned in 1893 – fetching, on the estimate of the local press, a sixth of their original cost.

References

Archives

Drawings for the Furniture at Endcliffe Hall. Sheffield City Archives Library *AP,* 1–62.

Soirée and Ball of the Mayor and Mayoress. *Newspaper Cuttings Relating to Sheffield* Vol. 10, 5 November 1863.

Books and articles

Arrowsmith, Henry and Aaron (1840) *The House Decorator and Painter's Guide*, London, John Murray.

Ball, J. (1978) John Manuel and Son of Sheffield. *Furniture History* XIV, 62–65.

Banham, J. (1999) Furnishing a City: the Design and Production of Furniture in Nineteenth-Century Sheffield. MPhil thesis, Sheffield Hallam University.

Joanna Banham, Sally MacDonald, Julia Porter. (1991) *Victorian Interior Design*, London, Cassell.

Beeton, M. I. (1861) *The Book of Household Management*, London, S.O. Beeton.

Binstead, H. E. (1904) *The Furniture Styles*, London, Alfred H. Botwright.

Cain and Hopkins (1993) *British Imperialism: Innovation and Expansion 1688–1914.* London, Longman.

Eastlake, C. E. (1864) The fashion of furniture. *Cornhill Magazine* IX, 337–349.

Graves, J. J. (1900) Successor to the Manuel Galleries of High Class Furniture. Catalogue of Goods, Sheffield.

Haweis, M. M. E. (1876) *Art of Decoration*, London.

Hey. D. (1991) *The Fiery Blades of Hallamshire: Sheffield and its Neighbourhood 1660–1740*, Leicester, Leicester University Press.

Hill, F. H. (1860) *An Account of Some Trade Combinations in Sheffield*, Special Volume: Trade Societies and Strikes. National Association for the Promotion of Social Sciences.

Hindmarch, D. and Podmore, M. A. J. (1990) *Endcliffe Hall in the Manor of Hallamshire*, Sheffield, The Officers' Mess 4th Battalion Yorkshire Volunteers.

Hunt, A. J. (1956) The morphology and growth of Sheffield, in Linton, D. L. (ed.) *Sheffield and its Region: A Scientific and Historical Survey*, Sheffield, Local Executive Committee, 228–242.

Kerr, R. (1871) *The Gentleman's House; or How to Plan English Residences, from the Parsonage to the Palace*, London, John Murray.

Linton, W. (ed.) (1956) *Sheffield and its Region: A Scientific and Historical Survey*, Sheffield, Local Executive Committee.

Loudon, J. C. (1833) *Encyclopedia of Cottage, Farm and Villa Architecture and Furniture*, London, Longman, Rees, Orme, Brown, Green and Longman.

Maple and Co. Ltd (1893) *Endcliffe Hall Sheffield. A Catalogue of the Costly and Very Valuable Furniture, Statuary, Bronzes, Oil Paintings... and Other Effects*, London, Brighton and Eastbourne, Maple & Co Ltd.

Parker, J. (1830) *A Statement of the Population etc. of the Town of Sheffield*, Sheffield.

Paston-Williams, S. (1995) *The Art of Dining: A History of Cooking and Eating*, London, National Trust Enterprises Ltd.

Pollard, S. (1959) *A History of Labour in Sheffield*, Liverpool, Liverpool University Press.

Reid, C. (1973) *Middle Class Values and Working Class Culture in Nineteenth-Century Sheffield*, Unpublished Ph.D., University of Sheffield.

Sheeran, G. (1993) Brass Castles. *West Yorkshire New Rich and their Houses 1800–1914*, Ryburn Ilkely.

Smith, G. (1808) *A Collection of Designs for Household Furniture and Interior Decoration*, London.

Symonds, R. W. and Whineray, B. B. (1987) *Victorian Furniture*, London, Studio Editions.

The Court Guide and County Blue Book of the West Riding of Yorkshire (1900) London, Charles William Deacon & Co.

Thornton, P. (1984) *Authentic Décor: the Domestic Interior 1620–1920*, London, Weidenfeld and Nicolson.

Tweedale, G. (1986) *Giants of Sheffield Steel: the Men Who Made Sheffield the Steel Capital of the World*, Sheffield, Sheffield City Libraries.

Walton, M. (1948) *Sheffield: its Story and its Achievements*, Sheffield, the Sheffield Telegraph and Star Ltd.

7

Privy to the Feast: 'Eighty to Supper Tonight'

Mary C. Beaudry

Introduction

Elites constitute an important element of social systems characterized by inequality in access to rewards, resources, and services. Anthropologists have been interested in examining 'the principles and expectations that regulated distribution of social, economic and political advantage' (Villamarin and Villamarin 1982, 125) and the special roles played by elites in colonial and post-colonial society. Membership in the colonial and post-colonial Anglo-American elite was not wholly ascriptive; elite status could be achieved through acquisition of wealth and scrupulous conformity to the principles of behavior subscribed to by the established elite. Elites share cross-cultural characteristics, one of which revolves around food and social display through hospitality extended in the form of tea and supper parties as well as, on special occasions, large banquets.

Colonial elites tended to perceive of themselves as distinct from the rest of society on the basis of having a good reputation, being honorable, virtuous, trustworthy, and courageous, by possessing clear consciences, living orderly and moderate lives, through demonstrating generosity and by doing good deeds, though without doubt 'a series of double standards in sexual mores and business affairs existed' (*ibid*. 130, 127). The fundamental requirement was to demonstrate lineage by having a well known ancestral mansion and estate; service to the crown or government was also important both in maintaining reputation and as a way of obtaining elite status and associated rewards.

Maintenance and transmission of elite status was closely linked to lineage; alliances through proper marriages were critical: 'Marriage into a traditionally recognized elite family was important not only for establishing oneself . . ., but also for the dowry involved'(*ibid*. 133). Women brought money, lands, and other goods – including slaves and servants – that could be used by their husbands, with their consent, and married women could make claims against their dowries. Elite women were vested with power, real (through their

own lineage and reproductive fertility; *cf.* Hall 1995) and financial, always within the context of family relations.

Wealth, of course, was critical: 'Poverty was incongruous with nobility; instead wealth increased the luster and importance of the noble [or elite] family...It was expected that those who were noble [or elite] would have enough money or goods to support themselves without having to engage in lowly occupations or trades . . .' (*ibid*. 129). Elites were obliged to manifest their wealth in a manner that reinforced status, through ownership of land, houses, furnishings, clothing, servants and slaves, food, manners, and the trappings of everyday life.

However rigidly delineated and carefully maintained, the stratified social system of which elites formed the apex was far from static. Families experienced shifting fortunes as a result of changing political and economic circumstances; those for whom the dynamics of the system spelt decline found that sustaining good standing required balancing economic, social, and political resources. Useful here is Wolf's concept of *funds* (1966, 7–10), one for wealth accumulation; a social fund; a religious fund; and a political fund. As interpreted by Villamarin and Villamarin (1982, 144), the concept constitutes 'the purposeful setting aside or apart of personnel and quantities of material or other resources for their accumulation, from which present and future generations might draw rewards to maintain or increase their wealth and highly valued, culturally sanctioned style of life'.

De Cunzo employs this concept in her study of Delaware merchants as culture brokers, whose success, she notes, 'depended on their accumulation, management, and deployment of resources, knowledge, and relationships'. Economic and social funds comprised an inextricable amalgam. Like elites elsewhere, Delaware merchants 'communicated powerful messages' through architecture and 'other components of their material life' (De Cunzo 1995, 196). Social funds were endowed through marital alliances, inheritance, and other family strategies, and social,

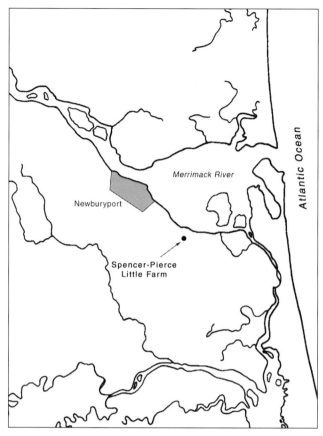

Figure 7.1. Location of the Spencer-Peirce-Little Farm in Newbury, Massachusetts. (Drawing by Stefan H. Claesson)

multifarious transformations of the early republic had a direct and dramatic impact upon the social position and daily lives of almost everyone – especially upon people of means, established elites and aspirants alike. Of interest here is the roles of material culture pertaining to hospitality and entertaining in the discourses surrounding the construction of post-colonial cultural identities.

Spencer-Peirce-Little Farm and its Late 18th-Century Owners

Newburyport was never a serious rival to the larger ports of the Atlantic seaboard, but in its 18th-century heyday it was nevertheless a bustling *entrepôt* and home base for some of Massachusetts' wealthiest and most powerful merchant families. Newbury has a history tied intimately to adjacent, urban Newburyport, which broke off from its parent town in 1764 after decades of rivalry between competing interests of merchants who controlled the port, or 'waterside', and farmers tilling 'land side' – rural backcountry – of the community (Labaree 1962, 2–3; Benes 1986).

The land that became the Spencer-Peirce-Little Farm was granted to John Spencer, one of the founders of the town of Newbury, in 1635 (Figure 7.1); it was conveyed to Daniel Peirce, Sr in the 1660s; it is possible that his son, Daniel Peirce, Jr built the surviving house following his father's death in 1677 (Figure 7.2; Beaudry 1993). The house is cruciform in plan, constructed of stone; the porch is brick, and brick trim surrounded the original window openings. For its time, it was an imposing dwelling. This far-from-humble farmhouse was from its earliest days emblematic of the coexistence of traditional agrarian values alongside what was perceived as the profit-oriented arena of mercantile capitalism. By the 19th century, it was labeled on local maps as 'Mansion House'.

The Peirces established a pattern of discontinuous residence at the farm; through several generations the family had at least one residence at the waterside and used the farmhouse as a part-time home. By the late 18th century, the house had acquired a patina of age that made it an appropriate country seat for urban merchants who amassed great fortunes through shipping and privateering and formerly had lived in grand houses in town.

Nathaniel and Mary Lee Tracy

One such individual was Nathaniel Tracy. Nathaniel 'prepared' at Boston Latin, attended Harvard College (class of 1769), Yale College (1772), and received an honorary A. M. from the College of New Jersey (Princeton, 1773), making many friendships and forging alliances that served him well throughout his business career (Lee 1916; Shipton 1975). Nathaniel married Mary Lee, daughter of a leading merchant family of Marblehead (Lee 1906, 63; Shipton 1975, 248). Mary Lee Tracy's sisters married into other

political, and religious funds through church membership, military service, voluntary associations, and political office-holding (*ibid.* 199–200). What becomes clear in anthropological and archaeological studies such as these is that elite status involved and was imbedded in a complex of behaviors that were reinforced and communicated in material form; in order to consolidate and sustain elite status, families had to mobilize all their 'funds' in an ongoing process of 'prestige negotiation' and reiteration, never slipping in the appropriate observances in any aspect of their public and private lives.

The conditions in post-revolutionary America produced a set of behaviors that highlight issues surrounding the operation of power and agency; the decades when the new nation was forming comprised a period of flux during which former colonials were forced to construct new identities. Elite status was being renegotiated. The intersection of social, political, and economic forces put in motion by the separation from England resulting from the Revolution with the changes wrought by the consumer revolution produced, if not a 'flashpoint' in history, an unsettled era in which fashionable consumerism played such an important role that the period has an especially pronounced material – and hence archaeological – signature. The complex and

Figure 7.2. The Spencer-Peirce-Little House in the 1880s. Photograph by Wilfred A. French. (Courtesy of Historic New England)

merchant families, forming a tight network of kin-based alliances within the mercantile elite (Lee 1917; Porter 1937). In 1778 Nathaniel Tracy purchased the Peirce farm from two Peirce heirs.

Tracy entered international trade as a sedentary merchant after a short apprenticeship in his father's countinghouse, forming a partnership (Jackson, Tracy and Tracy) with his younger brother John and college friend Jonathan Jackson. The firm shifted to coastal trade as tension between Britain and the colonies heightened prior to the Revolution (Porter 1937, 7, 16). Tracy, Jackson, and Tracy received a commission from the government to act as privateers in 1776 (Allen 1927, 48). Privateering in the Revolutionary period was a high-risk venture – a form of entrepreneurial patriotism – that could produce vast fortunes or financial ruin (Porter 1937, 20). Tracy fitted out the first American privateer to sail in the Revolution, eventually owning or having interest in 110 merchant vessels and 24 cruising ships (Allen 1927; Eastman 1928). Tracy had a hand in the capture of 120 vessels that were sold for $3,950,000. He made a large loan ($167,000.00) to the new government of the United States that was never repaid, and, despite having had millions during the revolutionary years, suffered financial setbacks that reduced his fortune. After 1785 he was forced to mortgage or sell much of his property, which included many houses, and,

briefly, title to the Farm. Tracy and his household 'retired' to the Peirce Farm in Newbury, and, after a series of complex transactions (Grady 1992), he regained title to the property.

Nathaniel's decision to resolve the dilemma of his business failure through dignified retirement was one of the acceptable courses of action a merchant in his position might take. That he elected to do so at the Peirce Farm is not without import. The property, the house, and its associations served as an instrument in the long-term social and economic strategies of the Tracys. The prestige of the 'house' (in the sense of family continuity) and the power relations signified in the interplay between kinship, property, and moveable wealth could be preserved in this context.

In the late 1780s and early 1790s, travelers and diarists, including Thomas Jefferson and John Quincy Adams, recorded their visits to Tracy and his wife living in relative seclusion at the Farm (Grady 1992, 30–35). Adams spoke of him with regard: 'This gentleman was in the course of the war peculiarly fortunate and accumulated an immense fortune; but he has since been equally unlucky and is now very much reduced. The generosity of his heart is equal to any estate whatever' (1902, 397).

At the height of his mercantile success, Tracy and his family lived in a luxurious manner and underscored their position and wealth through overt display. The reverse in Tracy's fortunes meant that, after 1786, he could no longer indulge in elaborate entertainments and public display for which he had once been celebrated.

Lavishing hospitality upon guests in one's home provided the choicest opportunity for enhancing prestige, for in such contexts the wealth, taste, and social genius of host and hostess could be displayed in a multiplicity of ways. A banquet hosted by Tracy is described by Winsor in his *Memorial History of Boston* (Winsor 1881, 166–167). Tracy wished to regale members of the French squadron that arrived in Boston in 1778 with a delicacy of their own country.

> Mr. Nathaniel Tracy, who lived in a beautiful villa at Cambridge, made a great feast for the admiral, Count D'Estaing, and his officers. Everything was furnished that could be had in the country to ornament and give variety to the entertainment…two large tureens of soup were placed at the ends of the table… Tracy filled a plate with soup which went to the admiral, and the next was handed to the consul. As soon as L'Etombe put his spoon into his plate he fished up a large frog, just as green and perfect as if he had hopped from the pond into the tureen. Not knowing at first what it was, he seized it by one of its hind legs, and, holding it up in view of the whole company, discovered that it was a full-grown frog…The company, convulsed with laughter, examined the soup plates as the servants brought them, and in each was to be found a frog. The uproar was universal. Meantime Tracy kept his ladle going, wondering what his outlandish guests meant by such extravagant merriment. 'What is the matter?' asked he, and raising his head, surveyed the frogs dangling by a leg in all directions. 'Why don't they eat them?' he exclaimed. 'If they knew the confounded trouble I had to catch them, in order to treat them to a dish of their own country, they would find that, with me at least, it was no joking matter.'

Unless this was his little joke on the French, Tracy's attempt at 'refined hospitality' (Winsor 1881, 167) by raiding the swamps of Cambridge to provide his distinguished guests with what he believed to be a national dish of France turned into an episode recounted to ridicule the ignorance of Americans. Not all of Tracy's entertainments had so droll an outcome, however, as the archaeological record at the Spencer-Peirce-Little Farm reveals.

Feasting Fashionably or Living on the Land? The Tracy / Kitchen Stairwell Deposit

Excavations beneath the floor of the kitchen resulted in the discovery of a filled-in stairwell along the north edge of the central chimney stack (Figure 7.3; Beaudry 1992). The north leg of the brick arch of the chimney base formed one cheek of the stairwell; the other was faced with stone. A short flight of wooden steps had been seated into a ramp sealed over with clay.

Soon after he acquired it, Tracy undertook a modified 'Georgianization' of the house, giving symmetry to the

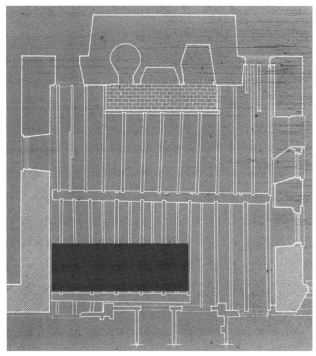

Figure 7.3. Floor framing diagram of the Spencer-Peirce-Little kitchen, with location of filled-in stairwell indicated. (Drawing by Bruce Blanchard, courtesy Historic New England)

fenestration, reworking the fireplaces and center chimney stack. The chimney was dismantled down to its support arch in the cellar, and a double stack of two flues meeting at a second arch in the attic was built. A new entry from the kitchen to the cellar was created between the two flues, and the old cellar stairwell opening was filled with a combination of demolition debris, kitchen waste, and soil mined from outside the house. Artifacts from the fill provide a TPQ of *c.*1780 (Scarlett 1992, np), suggesting that it was deposited early in Tracy's ownership, while he was one of the wealthiest men in the new republic, flush with the riches of his privateering ventures.

The stairwell cavity had been used as a receptacle for kitchen waste, including numerous animal bones that seemed fresh and perfect, having suffered not at all from exposure or weathering (Landon 1991a, b; 1992). Cooking activities went on even in the midst of the disruption and inconvenience of the renovations. Artifacts within the stairwell fill included ceramics, half of a small grindstone, cutlery, and wine bottle glass (Scarlett 1992); charred seeds were abundant (Pendleton 1990). Many of the artifacts and seeds found their way into the deposit in soil from outside the house, however, as pollen and seed analysis reveals (Kelso 1992; Pendleton 1990).

Eighteen genera of plants were identified from the lower levels of the stairwell deposit: '3 are domesticated plants, 6 are exploited for their edible fruits, 2 are inedible grasses, 1 is an inedible herb,' and the remaining six were wild plants

Table 7.1. Taxonomic representation of faunal remains recovered from the kitchen stairwell.

Taxonomic identification	TNF	%TNF	WT	%WT	MNI	%MNI
Bos taurus (cow)	82	2.5	2226.7	40.2	2	2.7
Ovis aries/Capra hircus (sheep/goat)	34	1.0	193.3	3.5	2	2.7
Ovis aries (sheep)	[6]	0.2	[50.9]	0.9		
Ovis/Capra/Odocoileus (sheep/goat/deer)	3	0.1	10.2	0.2		
Sus scrofa (pig)	168	5.1	803.9	14.5	6	8.1
Felix domesticus (cat)	1	*	1.2	*	1	1.4
Mephitis mephitis (striped skunk)	1	*	1.5	*	1	1.4
Procyon lotor (raccoon)	1	*	9.4	0.2	1	1.4
Mus musculus (house mouse)	9	0.3	0.9		2	2.7
Rattus sp. (rat)	66	2.0	14.9	0.3	11	14.9
Rattus norvegicus (Norway rat)	[20]	0.6	[7.0]	0.1		
Sciurus carolinensis (eastern gray squirrel)	7	0.2	3.8	0.1	1	1.4
Marmota monax (woodchuck)	5	0.2	3.9	0.1	1	1.4
Rodentia (rodent)	6	0.2	0.9			
Small mammal	35	1.1	3.9	0.1		
Small-medium mammal	10	0.3	3.8	0.1		
Medium mammal	239	7.2	395.9	7.1		
Medium-large mammal	33	1.0	116.5	2.1		
Large mammal	59	1.8	696.9	12.6		
Unidentified mammal	**301**	**9.2**	**279.4**	**5.0**		
Cyanocitta cristata (bluejay)	4	0.1	0.5	*	1	1.4
cf. *Turdus migratorius* (probable robin)	1	*	0.1	*	1	1.4
Passeriformes (perching birds)	5	0.2	0.5	*	1	1.4
Columbidae (passenger pigeon/rock dove)	96	2.9	17.6	0.3	8	10.8
cf. *Sterna* sp. (probable tern)	2	0.1	0.3	*	1	1.4
Charadriidae (plovers)	3	0.2	0.3	*	2	2.7
Meleagris gallopavo (turkey)	35	1.1	53.2	1.0	5	6.8
Gallus gallus (chicken)	45	1.4	53.9	1.0	6	8.1
Phasianidae	2	0.1	0.9	*		
Galliformes	1	*	0.1	*		
Aix sponsa (wood duck)	2	0.1	0.8	*	1	1.4
Anas crecca/discors (teal)	3	0.2	1.4	*	1	1.4
Anas sp. (duck)	15	0.4	17.9	0.3	2	2.7
Branta canadensis (Canada goose)	28	0.8	62.8	1.1	5	6.8
Anatidae (swans, geese, and ducks)	3	0.1	4.2	0.1		
cf. *Phalacrocorax* sp. (probably cormorant)	1	*	1.2	*	1	1.4
Unidentified bird	**553**	**16.8**	**116.2**	**2.1**		
Taxonomic identification	**TNF**	**%TNF**	**WT**	**%WT**	**MNI**	**%MNI**
Rana sp. (frog)	3	0.1	0.3	*	1	1.4
Salienta (small frog or toad)	**4**	**0.1**	**0.4**	*	**1**	**1.4**
cf. Mugilidae (probable mullet)	2	0.1	0.2	*	1	1.4
cf. *Micropterus* sp. (prob. freshwater bass)	2	0.1	0.2	*	1	1.4
Roccus saxatilis (striped bass)	1	*	0.2	*	1	1.4
Percoidea (small perch, sunfish, or bass)	1	*	0.2	*	1	1.4

Table 7.1. Continued.

Taxonomic identification	TNF	%TNF	WT	%WT	MNI	%MNI
Gadus morhua (cod)	10	0.3	20.2	0.4	2	2.7
Melanogrammus aeglefinus (haddock)	2	0.1	7.9	0.1	1	1.4
Gadidae (cods, hakes, and haddocks)	14	0.4	5.7	0.1		
Acipenser sp. (sturgeon)	9	0.3	15.2	0.2	1	1.4
Unidentified fish	639	19.5	109.4	2.0		
Homarus americanus (lobster)	**1**	*	**0.6**	*	**1**	
Crassostrea virginica (eastern oyster)	32	1.0	26.3	0.5		
Spisula sp. (surf clam)	9	0.3	63.6	1.1		
Mya arenaria (soft shell clam)	15	0.4	32.9	0.6		
Geukensia demissa (Atlantic ribbed mussel)	1	*	0.1	*		
Mytilus edulis (blue mussel)	19	0.6	2.0	*		
Mytilidae (mussels)	2	0.1	0.2	*		
Mercenaria mercenaria (northern quahog)	9	0.3	25.2	0.4		
Bivalvia (bivalves)	110	3.3	36.3	0.7		
Gastropoda (gastropods)	1	*	0.1	*		
Mollusca (mollusks)	16	0.5	6.0	0.1		
Unidentified bone	523	16.0	81.1	1.5		
Total	**3284**	**100.0**	**5533.1**	**99.7**	**74**	**99.7**

TNF = total number of fragments; WT = weight in grams; MNI = minimum number of individuals
* <0.1
Numbers in brackets [£] are subsets of a preceding category.
Source: Landon 1992.

that 'could have been harvested for their edible leaves, seeds, or flowers' (Pendleton 1990, 40). Kernels of New England eight-rowed flint corn were the most common among the botanical remains. It is possible that the botanical remains, especially the charred corn, represent food-processing and preparation by the Tracy household.

The faunal remains in the lower fill were contemporary with the remodeling episode, and several lines of evidence point to a rapid filling. The seeds, pollen, and faunal remains indicate that the feature was filled over the course of a few days or up to a week in spring (Pendleton 1992; Kelso 1992; Landon 1992). The faunal assemblage (Table 7.1) is exceedingly varied and contains butchered elements of both domesticated and wild animals (Landon 1996, 40–41).

Both saltwater and freshwater fish are represented, as are a wide variety of edible shellfish, including lobster, oyster, soft-shell clam, and blue mussel...Pigeons are the single best represented bird, followed closely by chickens, turkeys, and geese...there are smaller numbers of ducks (including some that were clearly wild), plovers, tern, bluejay, robin, and an unidentified perching bird. These wild birds...played an important role in the spring diet. The small wild mammals represented were probably not all eaten, but the squirrel and woodchuck were; bones of both these animals had distinct butchery marks... (Landon 1992, np).

The butchered squirrel and woodchuck are complemented by poor-quality cuts represented by the cattle bones and by the large number of pig foot bones with butchery marks that testify to the consumption of pigs' feet. In contrast to this seemingly humble fare, the assemblage also contained the remains of three suckling pigs with cut marks on the jaw bone likely made by cutting open the mouth to stuff it – perhaps with an apple. The diversity of wild species, each represented by one or a few individuals, is highly suggestive of the waste generated by preparation of a hearty, gumbo-like stew combining shellfish with meats from miscellaneous beasts and fowl (incorporating, perhaps, some of the herbs and plants represented in the floral remains – especially, perhaps, corn); the songbirds, seabirds, and pigeons may have been included in such a stew, or served individually as part of a multi-course meal, or included in a popular dish like pigeon pie. The remains of suckling pigs with the butchery and preparation marks observed by Landon suggest not pie or stew, however, but a formal presentation of roast suckling pig for a banquet or very special meal. Is it possible that Tracy celebrated his newest acquisition of property with a splendid banquet – even though this would have forced his servants to struggle with the hindrances and disarray of a renovation in progress? The written record is silent in the matter, but the archaeological record hints as much.

An explanation for the composition of the faunal assemblage from the stairwell is that it represents two ends of the social scale: on the one hand, victuals – grub – caught, collected, scavenged any way possible, by servants or by the workmen engaged in the renovations; and, on the other, fine and elegant meals, prepared by a cook and helpers for Tracy and guests, blending delicacies of barnyard, field, woods, river, and ocean. Wild species often appear on the tables of the elite as part of status display (Goody 1982), and it is no surprise to find large numbers of bird bones, especially pigeon bones, among the food remains at the site. However many wild species in whatever exotic preparations were presented to guests at Tracy's country home in Newbury, they were, no doubt, received with far more gustatory enthusiasm than the unfortunate amphibians served up at Tracy's earlier 'frog frolic' in Cambridge.

Offin and Sarah Tappan Boardman

Mary Lee Tracy sold the Farm to Offin Boardman in 1797. Boardman had become one of Newburyport's leading merchants after serving as a ship captain. Unlike Tracy, whose route to the mercantile life had been via the countinghouse, Boardman seems to have established his career by way of the quarterdeck. Indeed, Boardman commanded Tracy privateers during the Revolution (Allen 1927, 202, 321).

Captured at sea in 1776, Boardman was taken to Mill Prison in Plymouth, England, from which he escaped twice, eventually making his way to France. There he recorded in his diary how impressed he was by the grandeur of country estates of the nobility. He met outside Paris with American Commissioners Franklin and Adams, and became involved with John Paul Jones's plans to outfit a fleet of privateers, sailing home on one of the ships in the resulting convoy (Boardman 1779–1780). Back in Newburyport he built wealth through straightforward business dealings and inheritances from his own and his first wife's family. He attempted to defraud his siblings out of their inheritance, however, by tricking his father on his deathbed into signing a will handing Boardman's entire estate over to son Offin. The other heirs successfully brought suit against Offin, but the rift was so deep that the rest of the Boardman family refused to have anything further to do with him. Hence during his years at what he called the Tracy Farm, where he took up residence with his second wife Sarah Tappan Boardman in 1799, his social connections were largely through his wife's family (Dempsey 1993b).

Boardman made the most extensive changes to the external appearance of the house of all its owners, including constructing a wood addition to the west wing of the stone house with an up-to-date federal-period parlor and a sleeping chamber for his wife. The additions to the stone house left it intact, though of course the extensions modified its external appearance and increased interior living and sleeping spaces.

The rift with his consanguinial family did not dampen his energies or ambitions. The diary he kept of his time at the farm 'reflects a variety of interests and activities…He describes farm activities as well as town interests…He gives equal time to…work and his leisure, making particular note of comings and goings of members of his family and his household, and of parties and visits he hosts and attends' (Dempsey 1993b, 9). The diary entries reveal 'how kinship reinforced friendships and business relationships…[through a] web extending and thickening through the years' (Dempsey 1993b, 10).

After Boardman's death in 1811, Sarah sold the property, reserving her dower rights. Boardman's assets did not cover his debts. His will gives no indication that he was aware of potential difficulties, but it was written in 1808, three years before his death (Boardman 1811). He suffered losses during the Jeffersonian Embargo that paralyzed Newburyport shipping (Labaree 1975, 151–152) and could scarcely have recovered after the Embargo was lifted when his wharf, shop, and other property were destroyed in the fire that swept through the waterfront in May, 1811 (Faulkner *et al.* 1978, 128; Gilman and Gilman 1811). Boardman's estate was auctioned in 1813 and the proceeds divided among his heirs and creditors (Salem Registry of Probate 1813, 29).

A map of the property generated by the estate settlement shows the farm, its outbuildings, and fences (Figures 7.4, 7.5), representing Boardman's vision for the farm. He must have taken great satisfaction succeeding his one-time employer as owner of the Tracy Farm. Boardman made many improvements and changes to the landscape and farmyard that, apparently, went well beyond what Tracy had been capable of during his retirement.

The Boardman Privy at the Spencer-Peirce-Little Farm

The plan reproduced as Figure 7.4 depicts a small structure just to the east of the house; it is the only unlabeled structure on the map. In 1990 a crew of volunteers completed excavation of the unlabeled structure (Beaudry 1987), a stone-lined privy vault, *c.*3.03 m square (Figure 7.6). Beneath a clay cap or seal lay *c.*1.212 m of clean sand, deposited in the late 1860s. The sand overlay a rich organic layer with artifacts from the late 1830s. Several inches of organically enriched matter separated this layer from an artifact-abundant layer containing hundreds of fragments of ceramics and glass as well as other items such as a coin, buttons, fragments of a writing slate, and a few pieces of animal bone – including several vertebrae from a mature, ocean-going shark, unlikely to have been part of a meal. The intervening layer seems to have been formed through steady use between *c.*1810–*c.*1840 and consisted of nightsoil with relatively few artifacts

Much of the ceramic and glass in the lowest level of the privy was manufactured between 1800–1810 (*cf.* Miller

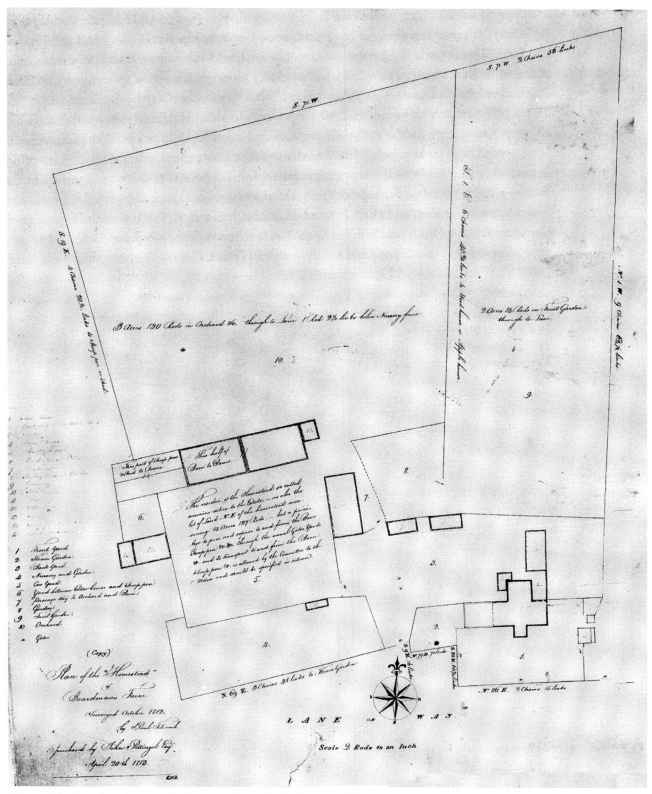

Figure 7.4. Plot plan showing the Spencer-Peirce-Little Farm c.1812. (Drawn by P. Titcomb, surveyor, courtesy Historic New England)

1 Stone House
2 Wood part of Dwelling House
3 Scullery
4 Farm House
5 Poultry House
6 Wood House Old
7 Hoghouse
8 Poultry House in Garden
9 Granery
10 Stable
11 Barn
12 Cider House
13 Shed
14 Sheep Pen and Shed
15 Linter and Shed

A Front Yard
B Flower Garden
C Back Yard
D Nursery and Garden
E Cow Yard
F Yard between Cider House and Sheep Pen
G Passageway to Orchard and Barn
H Garden
I Fruit Garden
J Orchard

Conjectural Drawing by Bruce Blanchard, 1993

1812

Based on the survey
"Plan of the Homestead of Bournbanks's Farm"
by Paul Titcomb, 1812

Spencer-Peirce-Little Farm - Newbury, Massachusetts

Figure 7.5. Artist's interpretation of the structures and fencing shown on the 1812 Titcomb plan of the Spencer-Peirce-Little Farm. The privy is the small square structure east of the main house. (Drawing by Bruce Blanchard, courtesy Historic New England.)

Figure 7.6. Excavation of the Boardman-era privy in progress during the summer of 1990. (Photograph by Mary C. Beaudry.)

2000), although numerous items pre-date this period, and the plates bear evidence of heavy use, in the form of scratches and cut marks. Local redwares, English refined earthenwares, and English wine and case bottles predominate, but local stonewares, Chinese export porcelain, Silesian wine glasses, and blue French condiment bottles are also present in the assemblage, giving it an unmistakably international character.

Several lines of evidence indicate that the privy was constructed several years after the Boardmans moved to the farm in 1799, but before Boardman's death in 1811. Among the hundreds of vessels recovered from the lowest stratum were items of glassware bearing the initial B – the Boardmans were the only family whose name began with B who ever lived at the site.

The vault was lined with fieldstones with remains of wooden planks at its base, *c.*4.78 m below grade. The majority of artifacts at the base of the privy were deposited intentionally to provide drainage (cf. Roberts and Barrett 1984). Several nearly intact vessels lay *underneath* the stones making up the north wall of the privy. The depiction of the privy on the 1811 survey (Figure 7.4) provides a *terminus ante quem* of 1811 for the basal deposit: it is highly unlikely that artifacts, especially nearly intact vessels, could have gotten *below* the stones of the privy vault *after* it was constructed. It seems clear that Boardman was responsible for the privy construction and used an accumulation of household debris for a drainage layer in the bottom.

Plant remains from the privy are varied (Table 7.2; Smyth 1994), with a minimum of 22 species present, almost all of which could be used for food or medicine. Cultivated species, such as table grapes, may have been brought to the

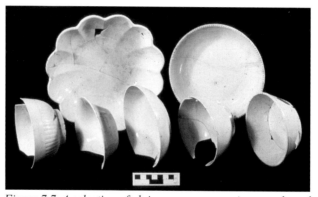

Figure 7.7. A selection of plain creamware serving vessels and punch bowls from the Boardman privy. (Photograph by Michael Hamilton)

site, but white clover was probably grown there. Blueberries, elderberries, and blackberries or raspberries may have been cultivated, though they grow wild in brushy areas at the farm today. Bulrushes and sedges are likewise found in the nearby marshes. Most of the macrofossils fall into the category of herbs and could have been gathered from the wild or cultivated. Boardman alludes to herbal preparations in his diary several times in recounting his own ailments. Once he mentions drinking herbal tea for medicinal purposes. He frequently took doses of salts to relieve pain in his joints; on one occasion he administered an emetic to himself, perhaps a home remedy (Dempsey 1993c).

The ceramic vessels (Table 7.3) deposited in the Boardman-era stratum of the privy (minimum number of vessels=272) include utilitarian items related to hygiene – chamber pots of debased scratch blue stoneware and plain creamware. Vessels for dairying, although extremely bulky,

Table 7.2. Identified plant remains from Feature 6, stone-lined privy, at the Spencer-Pierce-Little Farm, and their possible uses.

Latin Name	Common Name	# Seeds	# Frags.	Food	Medicine	Nonfood	Other Uses
Amaranthus sp.	Pigweed	2		x	x		ornamental
Brassica nigra	Black Mustard	298	19	x	x		improves soil
Chenopodium album	Lambsquarter	186	57	x	x		
Cuscuta pentagona	Field Dodder	6	1		x		
Cyperus sp.	Flatsedge	1		x			
Hypericum perforatum	St. Johnswort	4			x		
Lepidium virginicum	Pepperweed	4		x	x		
Mollugo verticillata	Carpetweed	5				x	
Morus sp.	Mulberry		1	x	x		wood; dye; silk industry
Oxalis sp.	Wood Sorrel	1		x	x		
Plantago spp.	Plantain	62	7	x	x		
Polygonum sp.	Smartweed	9		x	x		insect repellent
Portulaca oleracea	Purslane	54		x	x		
Ranunculus sp.	Buttercup	14			x		
Rhus glabra	Smooth Sumac	24		x	x		dye; tannin
Rubus spp.	Raspberry/Blackberry	10,342	329	x	x		
Sambucus canadensis	Elderberry	2,508	63	x	x		wood; dye; hedgerow shrub
Scirpus/Carex	Bulrush/Sedge	1		x			
Tradescantia ohiensis	Spiderwort	2	2			x	ornamental
Trifolium repens	White Clover	24	5	x			smoking mixture; animal fodder & forage; sachet; beekeeping
Vaccinium sp.	Blueberry	1	x	x			dye
Vitis sp.	Grape	1,941	453	x			livestock food; tannin

Table 7.3. Ceramic vessels from the Boardman-era stratum of Feature 6, stone-lined privy.

Vessel form	Ware type/decoration	MNV	% by category
Food Preparation and Storage – Dairy			
milk pan	lead-glazed redware	3	
butter pot	lead-glazed redware	9	
Total food preparation and storage – dairy		12	4.41
Food Preparation and Storage – Kitchen			
dish	black-glazed redware	1	
bowl	black-glazed redware	1	
batter bowl	lead-glazed redware	1	
bottle (large)	brown stoneware	1	
bottle (small)	black-glazed redware	1	
Total food preparation and storage - kitchen		5	1.84
Food Consumption			
dinner plate	creamware, plain	46	
dinner plate	Chinese porcelain, Imari type	1	
dinner plate	pearlware, blue shell-edged	6	

Table 7.3 Continued.

Vessel form	Ware type/decoration	MNV	% by category
dinner plate	pearlware, green shell-edged	1	
small plate	creamware, plain	47	
small plate	pearlware, blue shell-edged	4	
Vessel form	**Ware type/decoration**	**MNV**	**% by category**
small plate	pearlware, green shell-edged	7	
small plate	pearlware, blue transfer-print	6	
small plate	pearlware, hand-painted polychrome [?]	1	
soup plate	creamware, plain	2	
small bowl	creamware, plain	18	
small bowl	pearlware, hand-painted polychrome	1	
small bowl	pearlware, hand-painted, brown stars	1	
small bowl	pearlware, green transfer-print	1	
Total food consumption		142	52.21
Food Distribution			
platter	creamware, plain	1	
platter	pearlware	4	
serving bowl	creamware, plain	11	
serving bowl	pearlware	4	
tureen	creamware, plain	1	
tureen cover	creamware, plain	1	
tureen + cover	pearlware, green shell-edged	1	
sauce boat	creamware, plain	1	
sauce boat	pearlware, blue shell-edged	1	
sauce boat	pearlware, green shell-edged	1	
sauce dish	creamware, plain	6	
Total food distribution		32	11.76
Beverage Distribution			
cream/milk pot	pearlware, hand-painted polychrome	2	
pitcher	creamware, plain	4	
pitcher	creamware, brown transfer-print	1	
pitcher	pearlware, hand-painted polychrome	2	
teapot	creamware, plain	1	
teapot	pearlware, hand-painted blue Chinoiserie	1	
teapot lid	pearlware, hand-painted polychrome	1	
teapot lid	black-glazed redware	1	
sugar dish	pearlware	1	
sugar dish lid	pearlware	2	
Total beverage distribution		16	5.88
Beverage Consumption			
can	creamware, plain	2	
mug	creamware, plain	3	

Table 7.3 continued.

Vessel form	Ware type/decoration	MNV	% by category
punch bowl	creamware, plain	20	
punch bowl	pearlware, hand-painted blue Chinoiserie	7	
punch bowl	pearlware, hand-painted polychrome	1	
punch bowl	Chinese porcelain	1	
tea bowl	creamware, plain	2	
tea bowl	pearlware, hand-painted polychrome	2	
tea bowl + saucer	pearlware, hand-painted polychrome	1	
saucer	pearlware, hand-painted polychrome	1	
Vessel Form	**Ware type/decoration**	**MNV**	**% by category**
tea bowl	pearlware, hand-painted blue Chinoiserie	1	
tea bowl	pearlware, blue transfer-print	1	
tea bowl + saucer	pearlware, blue transfer-print	1	
tea bowl + saucer	Chinese porcelain	4	
tea bowl	Chinese porcelain, Batavia type	1	
tea bowl	Chinese porcelain	2	
chocolate cup	black-glazed redware	2	
Total beverage consumption		52	19.12
Toilet/Hygiene			
chamber pot	debased scratch blue stoneware	2	
chamber pot	plain creamware	7	
chamber pot	lead-glazed redware	1	
Total hygiene &c.		10	3.68
Non-Food/Ornamental			
spill vase	pearlware, hand-painted polychrome	2	
figurine/"toy"	pearlware, hand-painted polychrome	1	
Total non-food/ornamental		**3**	**1.10**
Total ceramic vessels		**272**	**100.00**

MNV = minimum number of vessels.

comprised only 4.41% of the ceramic assemblage; food preparation and food storage vessels for kitchen use of local redware and stoneware constituted only a tiny 1.84% of the total. The preponderance of the assemblage was for entertaining, or at least feeding and refreshing, large numbers of people (Figure 7.7). Vessels for food consumption dominated the assemblage (52.59%, n=142), followed by beverage consumption (19.26%, n=52). Forms include serving and punch bowls, tureens, platters, sauce boats, pitchers and jugs, and multiple sets of dinner plates and twifflers. The latter included large numbers of plain creamware plates with differing rim patterns as well as a small set of blue shell-edged pearlware. Green shell-edged

vessels were present in the assemblage in small numbers, chiefly in forms for food distribution.

Tea wares comprised a large proportion of the beverage consumption vessels, but punch bowls dominate that category, indicating a household in which formal entertainments included tea parties as well as evenings 'passed rapidly with the aid of agreeable conversation and a few glasses of punch' (de Chastellux 1963 [1780–1782]). This notwithstanding, it is clear that tea could be served fashionably and from sets of differing quality, ranging from hand-painted and transfer-printed pearlwares to Chinese porcelain.

The glass vessels (n=102; Table 7.4) round out the

Table 7.4. Glass vessels from the Boardman-era stratum of Feature 6, stone-lined privy.

Vessel form	Type	MNV	% by functional Category
Food Preparation and Storage – Kitchen			
condiment bottle	blue metal (French), wide mouth	8	
sauce bottle	blue metal (French)	1	
Total food preparation & storage – kitchen		9	8.82
Food Distribution			
salt cellar	molded, clear metal	1	
Total food distribution		1	0.98
Beverage Distribution			
decanter	clear metal	6	
cellaret bottle	acid-etched, Stiegel type	1	
wine bottle	olive green	19	
wine bottle	blue metal (French)	5	
aquavit bottle	blue metal (French)	1	
case bottle	olive green	2	
case bottle, large	pale green	1	
beer bottle	olive green	2	
Total beverage distribution		37	36.28
Beverage Consumption			
tumbler	spiral	7	
tumbler	fluted	16	
tumber	acid-etched (1 w/initial "B")	2	
tumbler	plain	19	
stemware (wine/cordial)	acid-etched	7	
Total beverage consumption		51	50.00
Toilet/Hygiene/Medicinal			
pharmaceutical bottle	aqua metal	1	
pharmaceutical bottle	clear metal	2	
perfume bottle		1	
Total hygiene &c.		**4**	**3.92**
Total glass vessels		**102**	**100.00**

MNV = minimum number of vessels.

beverage distribution and consumption categories in the form of wine glasses, tumblers, and decanters. Glass bottles of both English and French origin are present; while only 8.82% of the assemblage, the food containers of blue-green French glass testify to the use of commercially distributed exotic foodstuffs such as olives and capers (Jones 1993, 33; Jones and Smith 1985; Harris 1978).

The range of spirits represented by the bottles in the privy assemblage is impressive, for it includes not just wine and beer but aquavit and gin bottles. These, the nearly 30 punch bowls, and Boardman's diary entries revealing he brewed his own beer and regularly put up hundreds of gallons of cider (Dempsey 1993c) leads to the conclusion he was well prepared to extend hearty hospitality to his guests.

The assemblage resembles other, similar deposits (e.g. Edwards *et al.* 1988) but does not include the quantities and qualities of, for instance, Chinese porcelain that appear in

Table 7.5. Selected excerpts from Offin Boardman's farm diary that mention entertaining.

22 October 1799	Sally & Famely hear This Night A Compney of 30 . . . had . . . Mutton Rosted & Pudins
28 November 1799	had the Honnor of My Father & Mother Sister Pike Richd Pike Amos & Wife Rhoada Mr Mareses & Wife Offin Tm. Bm. to Dinner
10 September 1800	Mrs Hichcock & Wife Person & Wife & other Gm. & L to taik Tea
21 January 1801	A Larg partey to Dinner this Day in Compney with Brother & Sister Dunlop A Very Agreabel Day 22 in Compney
12 February 1802	Fryday Revd bodley & Lady with Sister Dunlop & partey of 30 to dinner this Day
20 December 1802	Hannah Clarke Amos Sisters Pike & Obrian Polley Obrian Macey greenleaf R Dunlop & R OB to taik Tea & Miss G & B O Brian Lodgd hear
15 February 1803	This Day taiken Up In maiken Readey for Compney Revn J Giles & A partey of 45 to Dinner & Tea Spend the Day & Eving
16 February 1803	A partey of 16 to Diner & 13 to Tea
1 December 1803	20 In Number to petaik of Dinner
27 October 1806	A partey of 14 to taik Tea
2 February 1807	A Larg partey To Tea 30 Gentm & lades
25 March 1807	Amos t & famely for the Day Sister P & R to taik Tea
30 May 1807	A Larg partey to Tea
12 June 1807	Amos t & Hannah & Children Sister Boardm to Dinner on pig
26 November 1807	Amos Hannah Sally & Clakson to Dinner Ver igrebl Day
2 February 1808	Brother & Sister Dunlop hear for the Day A Dinner Rost pig & veail Brother & Sister Dunlop Mr Duning Wife & Children to Taik Tea Sister OBrian & Pike
6 July 1808	6 in Compney to Tea
20 September 1808	A Larg partey to Tea 14 . . . for the Most part the Embager the Cheaf News of the Day when It will Rise I Cannot Say Ships Still Laying their stumps
23 September 1808	6 to Breckfarst
14 October 1808	A partey of 80 to Supper
27 October 1808	A partey to Tea Miss Boardman & Sam 8 Lades Am & Hannah
10 January 1809	A partey to Dinner 12 in Compney A very Agreebel Day allth Cold
8 February 1809	A partey to taik Brackfrst Revr John Chaplin & Wife Child Miss Dunin & Jeremiah OB
23 February 1809	Sister Pike & 9 other Ladeys to taik Tea & 3 Gentm
24 February 1809	Offin & Judey Amos & Clakson hear to Tea the Gals took Slay Ride
9 June 1809	Brother J Tappan Am Tappen & Hannah to Diner on A fine Turkey
2 August 1809	A partey to Dine on Pig & Leg Veal Mrss Jn. Boardman I OBrian & Brother OB & Bm John Giles H Topan Agreeabel Day
25 August 1809	A partey to Breckf of 9
7 September 1809	A partey of 16 to Tea & plesunt day
15 September 1809	Genral Farnum & Ladey took A Repast with us at the Farm at 9 am . . . A Compney of 10 Gm & Ladeys from Newton took Dinner & Tea hear
12 October 1809	Miss Boardman & son Mis Tucker Am & Hannah & 3 Gentm to Tea
14 October 1809	Judey with 4 Children Am & Hannah heer to Din & Spent the Day Mis Greenleaf & Marcy heer the Night
15 October 1809	Miss Greenleaf Marcy & S Sims with our One Famely Clakson & Tm Tappen heer to Dinner at 6 pm Wm Boardman & Wife & Sam with Sarvent Arivd Suppd & Lodgd
5 May 1810	A partey hear to Tea of our frinds

| *Source*: | Extracts from the diary of Capt. Offin Boardman, from "A Journal on the Farm," 1799. |
| *Note*: | The original of the diary has not survived and what is available for researchers was transcribed by a descendant in the early 20th century; here the spelling given in the transcription has been retained, although it is far from certain that Boardman's words were transcribed exactly as he wrote them. Dempsey 1993c is an annotated version, with spelling regularized and modernized. Hence the entries that appear here are excerpts from what already were extracts from, presumably, a more detailed and comprehensive journal. |

urban deposits associated not just with wealthy merchants but with widows of middling status. There are, however, enough plates, bowls, saucers, and dishes to serve large dinner and tea parties. Boardman's diary reveals that he and his wife entertained lavishly (Table 7.5), once serving 80 guests at supper. The diary entries reveal a seasonal pattern to entertaining and visiting, most social visits and house parties occurring during the coldest winter months when travel was easier (Nylander 1993, 237–238; Carson 1990:75). The Boardmans hosted husking parties in the fall, offering a feast to guests who assisted in shucking the newly harvested corn; on October 22, 1799, a 'company of 30' stayed on after husking. They were fed '5 mutton roasted & pudding' (Dempsey 1993c).

The excavated material culture provides an entry point for interpreting rituals for establishing and maintaining elite status. Artifacts can be interpreted in terms of the roles they play in the discourse of prestige negotiation – rituals of exchanging visits, dining, taking tea, attending church services as well as meetings of voluntary associations. In order to participate in these rituals, Boardman and others of his milieu constructed for themselves a material life 'above vulgar economy', as Jane Austen put it: 'In the meantime for Elegance & Ease & Luxury…I shall eat Ice & drink French wine, & be above vulgar economy' (quoted in Ellis 1982, 2).

An explicit code of behavior dictated that elite families should live in luxury and ostentation; inability to display wealth would be humiliating in the extreme. 'Their display of wealth served to mark them off from the rest of society. A considerable amount of money and energy was spent in competition among families of high position, and was expressed in terms of large expenditures on houses, clothes, dowries and festivities' (Villamarin and Villamarin 1982, 135). Boardman's deliberate pursuit of 'bourgeois personhood' (*cf.* Barker 1984; Bourdieu 1987; Comaroff and Comaroff 1992), indeed, the very fact that, like most members of his class, he recorded his actions in a diary, reflect a self-conscious construction of identity incorporating the outward projection of an image of gentility and control over personal destiny.

Conclusion

Thinking again of Wolf's notion of funds, it appears that, finding their economic fund diminished beyond recourse, the Tracys husbanded their social fund carefully through scrupulous maintenance of dignity and respectability that underscored their gentility. Mary Lee Tracy, from her tea or dinner table, was the ultimate broker of this fund as she steered the course of conversation and oversaw social interaction in her role as hostess.

For the late 18th-century owners of the Spencer-Peirce-Little Farm, the house's age and association with an agrarian life and its virtues vitiated the negative connotations of urban commerce upon which their fortunes had been based and overrode its lack of stylishness and failure to meet the standards of taste for the time. McCracken refers to this phenomenon as the 'patina' system of consumption: 'Patina, as both a physical and a symbolic property of consumer goods, was one of the most important ways that high-standing individuals distinguished themselves from low-standing ones, and social mobility was policed and maintained' (McCracken 1990, 31). Although largely supplanted by the 'fashion' system of consumption by the late 18th century (the latter system exemplified by the once-fashionable goods thrown into the privy), it remained a status strategy among the very rich. Among the items in the Boardman privy assemblage dated to *c*.1800 were two mid-18th-century vessels of Chinese porcelain – a Batavia tea bowl and an Imari dinner plate. Whether these had once been owned by the Tracy or Boardman household is less significant than the fact that they were at least half a century old before they were discarded. The symbolism of the age of objects, houses, and perhaps even landscapes served not just to represent high standing, wealth, and taste, but also to legitimate status claims through implications of longevity and generational continuity (McCracken 1990, 32). More than anything else, it was the house's association with the town's founding families that provided its near-mythical patina; the aura of antiquity was associational and largely overrode the reality of renovations and remodelings that successive owners undertook to assure their own comfort or to provide themselves with a fashionable parlor.

The house served as frame and setting for elite behavior, as it had since the 17th century, and, through its patina of antiquity, imbued its current owners, regardless of how reduced their circumstances, with an image of gentility, dignity, and long-standing 'roots' in the land. The house's quality as a 'genealogical mnemonic' carried with it not just the implications of antiquity and rootedness; it was a medium that carried and conveyed in some measure the status of former owners – four generations of descendants of a town founder – upon new ones. It was also a medium that helped to maintain the prestige of owners like the Tracys whose reversal of fortune rendered them unable to participate fully in the rituals of prestige negotiation, or Boardman who lived grandly until his death but whose administrators were forced to sell his estate at auction to settle egregious debts. In the socially fluid and economically challenging decades after the Revolution, both the Tracys and the Boardmans participated in dual systems of consumption, engaging in fashionable consumerism while at the same time they relied upon the strategy of employing patina to bolster their attempts to consolidate their identity and power as part of the elite.

For elites negotiating their social position in the early republic, to economize was vulgar. Yet extravagance in service of social display and competition could lead to debt and social decline – as it did in the cases of Tracy and Boardman. Families like the Derbys of Salem (Thornton 1989) ascended to the upper echelon as members North Shore's consolidated elite; descendants of Nathaniel Tracy and Offin Boardman did not. Tracy's dignified retirement preserved the family's social fund, assuring that the family name continued to be respected. Boardman had both economic and social funds when he moved to the Farm, though he jeopardized his social fund through his sleight-of-hand with his father's will. He nevertheless kept strong ties with his affinal relations and his own children and grandchildren, was active in local affairs, and took great interest and pride in erecting new buildings and renovating others at the Farm while maintaining his shipping business. The 1807 Embargo and the Great Fire in Newburyport in 1811 both made serious inroads into Boardman's fortune and hence there was no economic fund to pass down to his family. Boardman's time at the Farm was anything but a retirement; his household's impact on the archaeological record is a pronounced one that reflects perhaps unwise outlay on the trappings of elite life. The archaeological record reveals that both Tracy and Boardman engaged in prestige negotiation as their means allowed through hosting teas, suppers, and grand feasts. This underscores the great importance such hospitality played in the renegotiation of elite status in the new American republic – yet with no guarantee of success. But the stories of the losers can be as informative as those of the winners.

References

Adams, J. Q. (1902) The Diary of John Quincy Adams [1788], *Massachusetts Historical Society Collections* (2nd Series) 16.

Allen, G. W. (1927) *Massachusetts Privateers of the Revolution*, Massachusetts Historical Society. Cambridge, Massachusetts, Harvard University Press.

Barker, F. (1984) *The Tremulous Private Body: Essays on Subjection*, London, Methuen.

Beaudry, M. C. (1987) Limited Archaeological Reconnaissance of the Spencer-Peirce-Little Property, Newbury, Massachusetts. Unpublished report on file, Boston, Massachusetts, Department of Archaeology, Boston University.

Beaudry, M. C. (ed.) (1992) *Beneath the Kitchen Floor*, Archaeology of the Spencer-Peirce-Little Farm, Interim Report No. 3. Unpublished report on file, Boston, Massachusetts, Department of Archaeology, Boston University.

Beaudry, M. C. (1993) Puzzling over the pieces: the 1992 field season at Spencer-Peirce-Little Farm. *Context* (the newsletter of the Center for Archaeological Studies at Boston University, Boston, Massachusetts) 11:1–2, 5–7, 24.

Benes, P. (1986) *Old-Town and the Waterside: Two Hundred Years of Tradition and Change in Newbury, Newburyport, and West Newbury, 1635–1835*, Newburyport, Massachusetts, Historical Society of Old Newbury.

Boardman, O. (1779–1780) Diary of Offin Boardman, January 4, 1779 to March 18, 1780, transcript prepared by Mrs. John

Bradbury, typescript on file, Newburyport, Massachusetts, Historical Society of Old Newbury.

Boardman, O. (1811) Will of Offin Boardman, March 1, 1808; proved September 5, 1811, Essex County Registry of Probate, Boston, Massachusetts State Archives.

Bourdieu, P. (1987) *The Biographical Illusion*, Working Papers and Proceedings of the Center for Psychosocial Studies 14, Chicago, Center for Psychosocial Studies.

Carson, B. (1990) *Ambitious Appetites: Dining, Behavior, and Patterns of Consumption in Federal Washington,* Octagon Research Series, New York, American Institute of Architects Press.

Comaroff, J. and Comaroff, J. (1992) *Ethnography and the Historical Imagination*, Boulder, Colorado, Westview Press.

De Chastellux, F. J., Marquis (1963) *Travels in North America*, 2 vols. [1780–1782], Chapel Hill, University of North Carolina Press.

De Cunzo, L. A. (1995) The culture broker revisited: historical archaeological perspectives on merchants in Delaware, 1760–1815. *North American Archaeologist* 16:3, 181–222.

Dempsey, C. W. (1993a) Nathaniel Tracy and Mary Lee Tracy, research essay on file, Boston, Massachusetts, Society for the Preservation of New England Antiquities.

Dempsey, C. W. (1993b) Offin Boardman and Sarah Tappan Boardman, research essay on file, Boston, Massachusetts, Society for the Preservation of New England Antiquities.

Dempsey, C. W. (1993c) Extracts from Offin Boardman's Farm Diary, transcribed and annotated, draft version, research manuscript on file, Boston, Massachusetts, Society for the Preservation of New England Antiquities.

Eastman, R. M. (1928) *Some Famous Privateers of New England*, Massachusetts, privately printed by the State Street Trust Company.

Edwards, D., Pendery, S. R. and Agnew, A. B. (1988) Generations of trash: ceramics from the Hart-Shortridge House, 1760–1860, Portsmouth, New Hampshire. *American Ceramic Circle Journal* 6, 29.

Ellis, M. (1982) *Ice and Icehouses through the Ages, with a Gazetteer for Hampshire*, Southampton, Southampton University Industrial Archaeology Group.

Faulkner, A., Peters, K. M., Sell, D. P. and Dethlefsen, E. S. (1978) *Port and Market: Archaeology of the Central Waterfront, Newburyport, Massachusetts*, prepared for the National Park Service, Interagency Archeological Services, Atlanta, Georgia. Newburyport, Massachusetts, The Newburyport Press.

Gilman, W. and Gilman, J. (1811) *Account of the Great Fire in Newburyport*, Newburyport, Massachusetts, W. and J. Gilman.

Goody, J. (1982) *Cooking, Cuisine, and Class*, Cambridge, Cambridge University Press.

Grady, A. A. (1992) *Spencer-Peirce-Little House Historic Structures Report*, Boston, Massachusetts, Society for the Preservation of New England Antiquities.

Hall, M. (1995) The architecture of patriarchy: houses, women, and slaves in the eighteenth-century South African countryside, in D'Agostino, M. E., Prine, E., Casella, E. and Winer, M. (eds) *The Written and the Wrought: Complementary Sources in Historical Archaeology*, Kroeber Anthropological Society Papers No. 79, Berkeley, Department of Anthropology, University of California, 61–73.

Harris, J. E. (1978) Eighteenth-century French blue-green bottles from the fortress of Louisbourg, Nova Scotia. *History and Archaeology* 29, 83–149.

Jones, O. R. (1993) Commercial foods, 1740–1820. *Historical Archaeology* 27:2, 25–41.

Jones, O. R. and Smith, E. A. (1985) *Glass of the British Military ca. 1755–1820*, Studies in Archaeology, Architecture, and History, Ottawa, Ontario, Environment Canada-Parks.

Kelso, G. K. (1992) Pollen analysis of stairwell fill under the kitchen, in Beaudry, M. C. (ed.) *Beneath the Kitchen Floor*, Archaeology of the Spencer-Peirce-Little Farm, Interim Report No. 3. draft, not paginated, Boston, Massachusetts, Department of Archaeology, Boston University.

Labaree, B. W. (1975) *Patriots and Partisans: The Merchants of Newburyport 1764–1815*, New York, Norton and Company.

Landon, D. B. (1991a) *Zooarchaeology and Urban Foodways: A Case Study from Eastern Massachusetts*, PhD thesis, Boston University, Ann Arbor, Michigan, University Microfilms International.

Landon, D. B. (1991b) The potential applications of tooth cement increment analysis in historical archaeology. *Northeast Historical Archaeology* 17, 85–99.

Landon, D. B. (1992) Pigs' feet and pigeon pie: faunal remains from the Spencer-Peirce-Little Farm Kitchen, in Beaudry, M. C. (ed.) *Beneath the Kitchen Floor*, Archaeology of the Spencer-Peirce-Little Farm, Interim Report No. 3. draft, not paginated, Boston, Massachusetts, Department of Archaeology, Boston University.

Landon, D. B. (1996) Feeding colonial Boston: a zooarchaeological study. *Historical Archaeology* 30:1.

Lee, T. A. (1906) The Tracy family of Newburyport. *Essex Institute Historical Collections* 52 (April, 1906).

Lee, T. A. (1916) Nathaniel Tracy, Harvard, 1769. *Harvard Graduates Magazine* 25 (December, 1916), 193–197.

Lee, T. A. (1917) *The Lee Family of Marblehead*, reprinted from the Essex Institute Historical Collections. Salem, Massachusetts, Essex Institute.

McCracken, G. (1990) *Culture and Consumption: New Approaches to the Symbolic Character of Consumer Goods and Activities*, Bloomington, Indiana University Press.

Miller, G. L. (2000) Telling time for archaeologists. *Northeast Historical Archaeology* 29, 1–22.

Nylander, J. (1993) *Our Own Snug Fireside: Images of the New England Home, 1750–1860*, New York, Charles Scribner's Sons.

Pendleton, S. (1990) The Plant Remains from the Spencer-Peirce-Little Kitchen: An Historical Ethnobotanical Analysis. Unpublished MA thesis, Boston University.

Pendleton, S. (1992) Plant remains from the kitchen crawlspace, in Beaudry, M. C. (ed.) *Beneath the Kitchen Floor*, Archaeology of the Spencer-Peirce-Little Farm, Interim Report No. 3. draft, not paginated, Boston, Massachusetts, Department of Archaeology, Boston University.

Porter, K. W. (1937) *The Jacksons and the Lees: Two Generations of Massachusetts Merchants 1765–1844*, Volume I, Cambridge, Massachusetts, Harvard University Press.

Roberts, D. G. and Barrett, D. (1984) Nightsoil disposal practices of the 19th century and the origin of artifacts in plowzone proveniences. *Historical Archaeology* 18:1, 108–115.

Salem Registry of Probate (1813) Account Sales of Real and Personal Estate on Account of the Estate of Offin Boardman by John Porter Auctioneer on the 20th 22 and 23 April 1813 at Public Auction. Newburyport, Massachusetts, Folios 27–29 of unnumbered bound volume in the collections of the Historical Society of Old Newbury.

Scarlett, T. J. (1992) Through the cracks: artifacts from three and one-half centuries under a kitchen floor, in Beaudry, M. C. (ed.) *Beneath the Kitchen Floor*, Archaeology of the Spencer-Peirce-Little Farm, Interim Report No. 3. draft, not paginated, Boston, Massachusetts, Department of Archaeology, Boston University.

Shipton, C. K. (1975) Nathaniel Tracy. *Sibley's Harvard Graduates Volume XVII: 1768–1771*, Boston, Massachusetts Historical Commission, 247–251.

Smyth, M. M. (1994) The Plant Remains from the Spencer-Peirce-Little Privy: A Historical Archaeobotanical Analysis. Unpublished MA thesis, Boston University.

Thornton, T. P. (1989) *Cultivating Gentlemen: The Meaning of Country Life among the Boston Elite, 1785–1860*, New Haven, Connecticut, Yale University Press.

Villamarin, J. A. and Villamarin, J. E. (1982) The concept of nobility in colonial Santa Fe de Bogotá, in Ackerman, K. (ed.) *Essays in the Political, Economic and Social History of Colonial Latin America*, Occasional Papers and Monographs 3, Newark, Latin American Studies Program, University of Delaware, 125–153.

Winsor, J. (ed.) (1881) *The Memorial History of Boston, Volume III, 1630–1880*, Boston, Massachusetts, Tichnor and Co.

Wolf, E. (1966) *Peasants*, Englewood Cliffs, New Jersey, Prentice Hall.

8

Separating the Spheres in Early 19th Century New York City: Redefining Gender among the Middle Class

Diana diZerega Wall

Prologue

In 1979, I was fortunate to be able to work on the first large-scale archaeological project in New York City. The Landmarks Preservation Commission was interested in incorporating archaeological assessments into the city's environmental review process. They had identified the Stadt Huys Block, where the city's first city hall had been built in the 1640s, as a test case to show that important archaeological resources could be preserved beneath the Wall Street district in lower Manhattan, a heavily urbanized area in the heart of Dutch New Amsterdam and English colonial New York. Together with Nan Rothschild, I co-directed the excavations there. Before we began to dig, we were afraid that we would find nothing. But of course our fears were completely unfounded; instead of finding too little, we found too much: literally tons and tons of artifacts.

The excavations at the Stadt Huys Block were the beginning of my on-going passion for the archaeology of New York City. One of the leitmotifs of that passion has been the study of women's roles in New York during the late 18th and 19th centuries, a study that was inspired over a quarter of a century ago by a discovery that we first made in the archaeological trenches of the Stadt Huys Block. What caught my attention as we were trying to roughly date the strata in the field was the fact that there were plenty of ceramics that we could use to date the early layers, but there were very few ceramics in the more recent layers, those that dated to the mid- and later 19th century. Of course I soon learned that what I was observing in the ground was the fact that there had been an enormous cultural transformation in New York during the early 19th century, and as part of this shift, wealthy and middle-class New Yorkers had moved their homes (and their dishes) away from lower Manhattan. This part of the city, which since the time of the Dutch settlement of New Amsterdam almost two centuries earlier had been subjected to mixed residential and commercial

use, had become a business district where very few people lived. I was fascinated by this transformation and have devoted much of my career to exploring its ramifications. Of course it is related to the global process of the development of the capitalist world system (Wallerstein 1980) as well as to local changes in the cultural constructions of gender, race, and class. One of the ways that I have explored this transformation among the middle class has been by looking at the changes in the composition of the household and by examining the dishes that middle-class women used to set their tables in late 18th and 19th century New York. This is one of those studies. It is derived from my dissertation (1987; 1994) and is included here in the hope that it will provide a helpful example for a new audience of the power of using a combination of the material culture from archaeological excavations along with historical sources to address a research question about the relatively recent past.

Introduction

During the half century that followed the American Revolutionary War, New York changed from a provincial colonial city to the economic hub of a new nation. One of the ramifications of that transformation was the development of what Americans today look on as the 'traditional' definition of gender, with men going out to work and women staying at home and devoting themselves to domestic life. In this study, I explore the extent to which middle-class women contributed to this redefinition of gender by examining innovations in the composition of the people who were living in these middle-class homes and the dishes that middle-class women used to set their tables.

The Revolution, in effecting the transformation of the colonies to independent status, removed all of Britain's mercantile restrictions and opened up innumerable possibilities for the economic expansion of trade and manufacture. At the beginning of the Revolution, American

80

seaboard cities like New York 'stood poised between tradition and modernity; and the Revolution...greatly accelerate[d] the transition between older and more modern forms of economic and political life' (Foner 1976, 68). After the war, the city, which had been fourth in terms of port activity among the British American colonial cities in 1770, soon jumped to first place. By the mid 19th century, it had also become the manufacturing center of the nation, and its population swelled from 33,000 in 1790 to 312,000 in 1840, an almost ten-fold increase (Rosenwaike 1972). New York, with its access to a vast hinterland, had developed into a core economic area within the capitalist world system, with a new *laissez-faire* ideology that promulgated the view that the self-interested pursuit of gain, free of regulations for the common good and the tenets of the 'moral economy', provided the greatest benefits for society (Gilje 1987; Thompson 1971). Its social relations of production as well as of gender and domestic life were transformed.

In 18th century New York, before this transformation, domestic and work life for the developing middle class – its craftsmen and shopkeepers – were much more integrated than they were a century later. The middling household was a tightly-knit, corporate unit, with most of its members working and living together. Men ran their businesses from their homes, with their shops in the front rooms of their houses; men, women, and children spent much of the day working together side-by-side. Men were responsible for the moral and physical well-being of household members, who in addition to family included workers like journeymen, apprentices, clerks, and enslaved Africans, who all lived with the family. Although their wives had primary responsibility for running the household and caring for infants, they also helped their husbands in the business. Children learned their adult roles at home, with older children working alongside their parents. Daughters helped their mothers with household tasks while sons helped their fathers in the family trade. Some sons apprenticed in other trades; they tended to board with the families where they worked.

By the middle of the 19th century, the structure of the middle-class household had changed completely. Homes and workplaces were no longer combined in the same buildings and in fact were often located in different neighborhoods. Furthermore, there was a strict division of labor governing the roles of family members. The primary responsibility for men was for the economic well-being of the household, which they now fulfilled *outside* the home and often in the business district, whereas their families now lived in middle-class residential neighborhoods. Older children no longer learned their adult roles at home, but instead went off to school. Workers no longer boarded with their employers. The enslaved were finally emancipated in 1827, and they along with other members of the working class, which came to be made up more and more of foreign immigrants as the century progressed, now lived in separate working-class neighborhoods.

Middle-class women, along with their small children, were the only ones at home during the day. They ran the house, raised the children, and became the caretakers of the moral, physical, and emotional well-being of household members. Part of their responsibility included enhancing home life so as to create an appropriate environment for raising children and a haven for other family members. The importance of their new role was directly related to the importance of raising the sons who would serve as the future citizens of the new republic. Historians refer to this new importance that was bestowed on motherhood and the new domestic emphasis in the roles of American middle-class women and the associated enhancement of home life as the 'cult of domesticity', which was marked by the redefinition of domestic life as 'woman's sphere' (Ryan 1981). The private arena of the home, instead of being a 'little commonwealth' or a 'microcosm of society' as it had been in the colonial period, had become a 'haven in [the] heartless world' of the marketplace (Demos 1970; Ryan 1981; Lasch 1977).

Framing the Question

The question addressed here is how this transformation of domestic life took place. Theoretical approaches used to explain it fall roughly into two groups: those that view women as relatively passive victims who were thrust into 'woman's sphere' (as described by Scott 1986), and those that look on women as active agents in redefining the spheres (e.g. Cott 1977; Sklar 1973; Ryan 1981). One way to explore this question is to see when women began to enhance the quality of their homes. If, on the one hand, they began to enhance it *before* the separation of the home and workplace, it implies that women (as well as men) contributed through their actions to the development of woman's sphere and the transformation of family life itself. If, on the other hand, they began enhancing home life only *after* the separation of the home and workplace occurred, it suggests that they merely reacted, or adapted, to economic changes that were initiated in the larger society. So the physical separation of the home and workplace can be used as a watershed in looking at this question.

The period that is relevant for this study is the half-century after the American Revolutionary War, from the 1780s to the 1830s. We know that the transformation accelerated after the war, which marked the end of the US's status as a colony (Foner 1976; Bender 1978), and we know that this new way of life was the ideal in the 1830s, when a whole new literature prescribing the new definition of women's roles began to appear (Cott 1977).

But before looking inside their homes, we need to find out when the middle class separated their homes from their

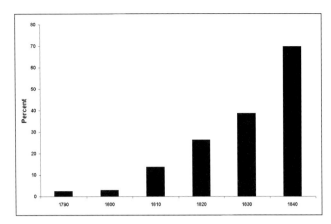

Figure 8.1. The percentage of middle-class households that were separated from the workplace, 1790–1840.

workplaces. To answer this question, I looked at 2% samples of the people who were listed in the city's directories at ten year intervals over a 50 year period, from 1790 to 1840 (see Wall 1994, Appendix A for a full description and discussion of this methodology). These directories are similar to telephone books today in that they list the names of the heads of the city's businesses and households and either a single address (for those who lived in combined homes and workplaces) or separate work and home addresses (for those who had already separated their homes and workplaces). I then cross-checked those listed in the directory samples with their listings in the New York City tax assessment records, so that information about assets could be used to make inferences about class. The data show that the separation of the home and workplace among the middle class was a gradual, slow process until the 1830s, when the proportion of middle-class families who maintained separate homes and workplaces almost doubled (Figure 8.1).

Addressing the Question: Household Composition

With that information in hand, the next (and most important) question to be addressed is whether the enhancement of domestic life and the beginnings of woman's sphere began inside the city's combined homes and workplaces, before the spatial separation occurred, or whether it began only afterward, in homes that had already been separated. One way to explore this question involves looking inside some of these combined homes and workplaces at the people who were actually living there. There were several changes in the composition of the household, which were closely related to the enhancement of home life and the development of 'woman's sphere'. One was the decline in the number of children in the middle-class family. With the re-definition of domestic life, children were no longer looked on as

'helpful little hands' but instead came to be regarded as responsibilities who had to be educated for their future role of citizen. Another change was in the increase in the number of women working as servants in each household because the enhancement of domestic life entailed a great deal more housework than had been considered necessary in the 18th century. Finally, there was a decline in the number of male employees living in these households, because as the home became a 'private haven', employers no longer provided room and board for their employees.

The best way to examine this shift in household composition is to look at the census records. I took the middle-class families that I had identified in the samples from the directories and the tax assessment records and looked them up for the appropriate year in the United States Federal decennial census returns for the years 1810 through 1840 (see Wall 1994, Appendix D). The data show that the number of children in each of these households began to fall beginning in the second decade of the 19th century (Figure 8.2). In addition, there was a sharp increase in the number of women, many of whom were presumably domestics, living in these households between 1810 and 1830; a plateau was reached around 1830 and the numbers stayed relatively high between 1830 and 1840. But the data for the adult men were quite different: first, the numbers of men living in the middle-class households rose consistently from 1810 until 1830, but then in the 1830s, there was a drop-off in their numbers. What the data suggest, then, is that although middle-class families began to change their concept of family life by having fewer children and hiring more domestic servants *before* the 1830s, when most of them were still living in combined homes and workplaces, they only began to stop providing accommodation for their employees *during* the 1830s, at the same time that many families were separating their homes and workplaces.

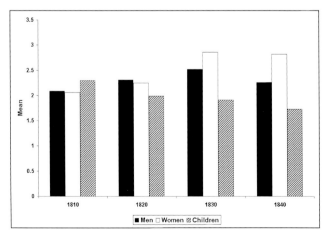

Figure 8.2. The mean numbers of children, adult women, and adult men in the middle-class households, 1810–1840.

Addressing the Question: the Dishes

Another way to examine this same question is by looking at changes in the dishes that middle-class women were using to set their tables during the period when they and their families were still living in combined homes and workplaces. The best way to do this is to look at the sherds from those dishes that became part of the archaeological record. We can use both the styles of these dishes and the amounts of money that women were willing to spend for them as barometers of the changes that were taking place in domestic life. But before we do this, we have to set the stage by providing, first, the cultural context for some of the meals that women served in these homes – family dinners and social teas – and, second, identifying who actually shopped for the dishes that were used in these homes, to be sure that it was women who were making these consumer decisions.

The Cultural Context

Travelers who visited the city in the late 18th and early 19th centuries provide the basis for developing a cultural context for these meals. Their accounts show that among the middle class in New York City, dinner was apparently a private, family meal throughout this whole period, with dinner parties becoming common for the middle class only much later in the 19th century (Clark 1986). However, there were some changes in the meaning of family dinner during this period (adapted from Wall 1994). In the 18th and very early 19th centuries, family dinner both expressed and reinforced the tightly knit, corporate nature of the household. The meal was consumed in the middle of the day, and often consisted of a single, one-pot dish, such as a soup or stew, which was served with bread. Each household member was served from the communal serving dish and ate from an individual bowl or plate. More elaborate dinners could consist of a number of dishes served as a single course or as a series of courses. During this period, the table was set in the Old English or covered-table plan (Carter 1802; Figure 8.3). The shared serving dishes covered the table in a balanced and symmetrical table setting, with none of these dishes serving as the visual focal point of the table.

By the mid 19th century, with most men commuting downtown to work, dinner was no longer held in the afternoon but in the evening, and it had also become much more important than it had been before. In the 18th century, with most family members working together, family dinner had relatively little social significance in daily life. In the 19th century, with men and older children away from home all day, family dinner took on new meaning as a secular ritual – it became a 'constant and familiar reunion', as Calvert Vaux put it (quoted in Clark 1986, 42), because it was the only occasion in the day when all family members were gathered together. As such, it reinforced the family ties and the moral values of home life.

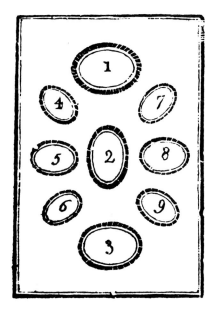

ARRANGEMENT OF A DINNER OR SUPPER TABLE, CONSISTING OF NINE DISHES.

Figure 8.3. Setting the table at the turn of the nineteenth century (Carter 1802).

Family dinner's new importance as a secular ritual can be seen in several innovations that were introduced into the meal. First of all, it had become more elaborate for most of the members of the middle class. The one-course, one-dish meals popular in the 18th century were much less common a century later. Now, the meal was composed of several courses which were specialized in their content. Meats and vegetables made up a first main course, pies and puddings a second one, with dessert forming the last course of the meal (Belden 1983; Pope-Hennessy 1931; Hooker 1981).

A second change was in the table setting. Although women continued to set their tables according to the old English plan, a new and important change was introduced. In the 18th century, the food had been the visual focus of the table, with no particular dish serving as a single focus of attention (Belden 1983; Williams 1985). But by the middle of the 19th century, the focus of the table was no longer on the food, but rather on a centerpiece which might be a castor (or condiment stand), a celery glass, or even a vase of flowers (Beecher 1846; Belden 1983; Figure 8.4). It seems the material culture of domesticity had replaced the food as the focus of the meal.

Throughout the same period, 'tea' was also an important meal but one that had a very different cultural meaning than family dinner: tea was a social event, the meal to which

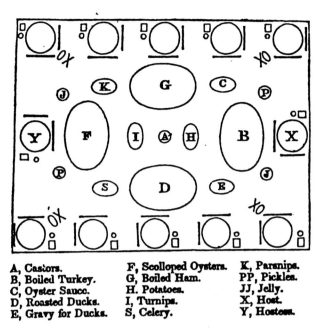

A, Castors.
B, Boiled Turkey.
C, Oyster Sauce.
D, Roasted Ducks.
E, Gravy for Ducks.

F, Scolloped Oysters.
G, Boiled Ham.
H, Potatoes.
I, Turnips.
S, Celery.

K, Parsnips.
PP, Pickles.
JJ, Jelly.
X, Host.
Y, Hostess.

Figure 8.4. Setting the table in the mid-nineteenth century (Beecher 1846).

guests were invited into the home (Smith 1972; Perkins 1960; Scott 1952). It provided an arena for the negotiation of household status with outsiders. The tea ceremony was held either in the late afternoon (during the period when dinner took place at noon) or in the evening, when it became the focus of evening parties and might be accompanied by supper or desserts. When family dinner shifted to the evening, these parties took place after dinner, later in the evening, while afternoon tea became a feminine social ritual, to be indulged in by middle-class and elite women alike (Belden 1983; Williams 1985).

The Shoppers

A final issue to consider before examining the dishes themselves is whether women (as opposed to men) went shopping for the dishes and if so, whether they seem to have put thought into their purchases. The diary of Elizabeth Bleecker, a New York broker's daughter, suggests that yes is the answer to both these questions. After her marriage in 1800, Bleecker and her husband lived with her parents while they set up their new home. Bleecker records shopping on several occasions over a period of months for the dishes she needed. She first mentions going shopping for dishes in early July, when her mother bought her some 'Cups and Saucers'. Throughout the summer and into the fall, even after she and her husband moved into their own house in August, she mentions shopping for tea pots and plates and serving dishes several times. Occasionally, she shopped alone, but she usually went shopping with another woman, sometimes a relative and sometimes a friend (Bleecker 1800, *passim*). So Bleecker's diary entries suggest that women

not only made consumer choices when it came to dishes, but also that they put a lot of thought into choosing them.

The Dishes

Having established the changing cultural context of these meals and the fact that women seem to have been the primary shoppers for ceramics, the next step involves looking at the actual dishes that they bought in order to see when the changes in the meanings of these meals took place. The dishes examined here come from the archaeological assemblages from 11 middle-class households in New York City (see Wall 1994, Appendix E, for a discussion of the assemblages and their analysis). The dishes were used in family dinners and social teas in combined homes and workplaces dating from the 1780s to the 1820s. Based on the mean dates of manufacture for the dishes that make up the assemblages, the households fall into three chronological groups: the 1780s, around 1805, and the 1820s (see Wall 1994, Appendix E). I looked at changes in two different aspects of the dishes from these households – the kinds of motifs that were used to decorate them and their relative value or cost – to see what the dishes could show about the enhancement of home life inside these combined homes and workplaces.

The Styles of the Dishes

Many archaeologists study style as an aid in exploring the definition and maintenance of social boundaries, particularly the social boundaries between groups (Wobst 1977; Hodder 1979). But the analysis of style can also provide information on the definition and maintenance of boundaries between social arenas, where different messages are being conveyed, within the same social group. In addition, changes in style through time can also express changes in the social meaning of the context in which artifacts were used – as the social meaning of the context in which an object is used changes, the object's style usually changes as well. Conversely, if we can see changes in the style of an object, we might also say that the social meaning of that object is changing too.

Therefore in looking at the dishes from New York City, I expected the styles used for tea dishes and dinner dishes to be quite different from each other throughout the whole period examined here, because the social meanings of the contexts where these dishes were used were very different from each other throughout the period of study. In addition, if the social meanings of these meals were changing, with tea becoming feminized and dinner becoming more important as a family ritual, we would expect to see changes through time in the styles of the vessels that were used in these meals.

The styles of the motifs used to decorate most of the tewares and the tablewares from the 11 New York City households fall into four broad groups: neo-classical molded white vessels, shell-edged vessels, romantic vessels decorated

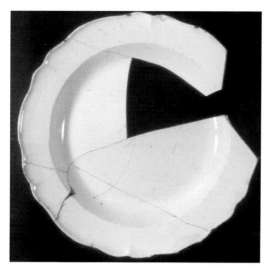

Figure 8.5. An earthenware plate in the royal pattern.

Figure 8.6. An earthenware plate in the shell-edged pattern.

Figure 8.7. A porcelain plate in the Canton pattern.

Figure 8.8. An earthenware plate in the willow pattern.

with Chinese landscapes, and vessels with floral motifs. As expected, the motifs on both the teawares and the tablewares are consistently different from each other within each of the different periods, and the kinds of motifs popular for both of them change through time. For the early group, dating to the 1780s, most of the plates are plain white neo-classical vessels in the royal pattern (Figure 8.5). The teawares, on the other hand, are evenly represented by those decorated with Chinese landscape and floral patterns. For the middle group, dating to *c.*1805, most of the plates in all four households are decorated with blue or green shell-edged motifs (Figure 8.6), although cream-colored plates with plain rims were popular too. Teawares with floral motifs had also become more common. Finally, for the later group, dating to the 1820s, there is a marked and clear-cut change between the motifs preferred for both the tablewares and the teawares: whether made of costly porcelain or cheaper earthenware

(Figures 8.7 and 8.8), most of the tablewares in all the assemblages are decorated with romantic Chinese landscapes, while most of the teacups continue to be embellished with floral motifs.

So, the dishes show that middle-class women in New York used different kinds of motifs to mark the tea ceremony and family meals as different social arenas with different social meanings. Furthermore, the fact that there were changes in the kinds of motifs on the tablewares and teawares, respectively, used from the 1780s to the 1820s supports the interpretation that the social meanings of these meals were changing inside the combined homes and workplaces of the city's middle class.

The Cost of the Dishes
The next question involves looking at how much money the women in these households were willing to spend on the

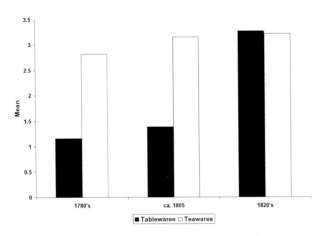

Figure 8.9. The relative costs of the teawares and tablewares for each of the three periods.

dishes that they used to present these meals. George Miller has shown how to assign relative values to both earthenware and porcelain dishes by using information from the price lists of the English potters who made the earthenware dishes that were popular in the United States at this time and from the records of local merchants who imported Chinese porcelain from Canton (Miller 1991, pers. comm.). The relative costs of the tablewares and the teawares for the three chronological groups are quite different from each other (Figure 8.9). Those for the teawares start relatively high in the 1780s and stay relatively high with only a slight increase through time, suggesting that the goal of the mistress of the house was always to have a showy teaset for entertaining her friends, and that she continued to be able to achieve this goal throughout the period. This is what we might expect for dishes used in a social ceremony like tea, which was continuously and consistently used to display a household's status to outsiders.

The tableware dishes used at family meals, on the other hand, show a marked increase in value in the same period (Figure 8.9). During the first three decades of the century, middle-class women in New York were willing to spend ever-increasing amounts of money on the dishes that they used for family meals. By the 1820s, the mistresses of these households were willing to spend as much for their tableware dishes, which were usually seen and used only by household members, as for their teaware dishes, which were used to entertain outsiders. This consumer decision suggests that family meals and domestic life were becoming more and more important inside the combined homes and workplaces of the city's middle class.

But another striking thing about the dishes is how standardized the patterns were that women used to serve family meals. All of the households in the early group had more plates decorated in the royal pattern than in any other style; all the households in the middle group had more plates

decorated with shell-edged motifs than in any other style; and all the households in the later group had more porcelain plates decorated in the Canton pattern than in any other style (Wall 1994, Appendix E). The standardization among the tablewares from all of the households for the later 1820s period is particularly striking when we take into account the efforts of the English potters to compete for the American market after the War of 1812. The potters began to produce vessels decorated with American motifs (including those of American institutions such as prisons and mental hospitals) and national heroes. As you might imagine, most of these were never popular for family meals in American homes – it is hard to imagine mothers urging their children to 'eat your peas, dear, so we can see the picture of the lovely prison on the plate' – and they almost never turn up in American archaeological assemblages dating from this period (see also Ewins 1997, 38–43). The standardization in tableware patterns from the New York City households from all three periods indicates that, like Elizabeth Bleecker, most women had very precise ideas about what was 'suitable' when they went shopping for dishes.

The matched teaware cups and saucers are quite different in this regard and are not standardized at all. The most popular pattern in teawares from each of the households was depicted on an average of only about a third of the tea vessels in each assemblage, and very few of these patterns turn up in the assemblages from more than one household.

The lady of the house may well have used sets of tablewares in each period to emphasize to the members of her household the importance of the communal values of family life. As the social meaning of home life and family dinner was rapidly changing, the standardization of these sets may have been important so that their message came through loud and clear. This standardization is particularly striking when we remember that these objects were regularly seen primarily only by household and family members.

The mistress used the teawares, on the other hand, for entertaining friends of the same class at tea parties. The diversity of the patterns on the teacups may have expressed the different messages different households were sending out about their position in this highly diversified society. Perhaps the hostess did not use matched sets of teawares because she did not care to stress the communal values shared by household members and their guests.

This study of the dishes shows that the mistresses of these middle-class families were well on their way to elaborating dinner and other family meals into the secular rituals of the woman's sphere by the end of the 1820s. Furthermore, it suggests that they began this ritualization process even earlier, in the first decade of the 19th century, in the integrated homes and workplaces of the city's middle class, before the separation of the home and workplace took place.

Conclusion

All in all, this study of changes in household composition and in the kinds of dishes that women used to set their tables suggests that women were active agents in developing a woman's sphere inside the combined homes and workplaces of the city's middle class. The interpretation that women, as well as men, may have actively contributed through their social actions to the separation of the spheres has ironic implications. If we look on this structural transformation as a consequence – albeit unintended – of changing social practice on the part of both men *and women*, it implies that women were at least in part responsible for their own ultimate seclusion in the home – a seclusion that many middle-class western women have been struggling against for the last few decades (Ryan 1981). But of course, as Foucault put it over two decades ago, '[p]eople know what they do; they often know why they do what they do; but what they don't know is what what they do does' (personal communication in Dreyfus and Rabinow 1982, 187).

Finally, I should note that this particular redefinition of gender roles was apparently unique to the United States. The observations of two European travelers who visited New York in the early 19th century support this inference. When Englishman Basil Hall arrived with his wife, Margaret, in the late 1820s, he was 'struck...with this strong line of demarcation between the sexes' (1964, 152). The men 'are almost exclusively engaged abroad by occupations which the women cannot possibly comprehend; while the women, for their part, are quite as exclusively engaged at home, with business equally essential and engrossing, but with which the men do not meddle in any way' (1964, 156). He went on to compare the situation in America with that of England, where, he said, '[t]he virtual control which women in England exercise over the conduct of the men, extends to every thing public as well as domestic' (1964, 159). The Frenchman Alexis de Tocqueville made similar observations when he visited the United States a few years later (Tocqueville 2003). What we seem to be seeing here is the beginning of a peculiarly American definition of gender, as distinct from a British or European one.

This new definition of gender was probably part of the beginnings of an American, as distinct from a British, cultural tradition, which included its own construction of domestic life. We know that a separate domestic tradition becomes visible in the material culture of meals later, at mid-century, when white granite molded dishes in the gothic pattern become popular among American middle-class women (Figure 8.10). In fact, the British potters manufactured these wares exclusively for the American market (Sussman 1985; Ewins 1997) at the same time that their British customers preferred dishes in a multitude of transfer-printed

Figure 8.10. An ironstone plate in the gothic pattern.

patterns both at home in Britain and abroad in the British colonies (Brooks 2003; Lawrence 2003; Malan and Klose 2003). These gothic dishes were used in dining rooms filled with gothic-style furniture and were in the same style that characterized the churches that were being built in New York City at the time. Elsewhere, I have suggested that the use of gothic dishes in gothic dining rooms, with their ecclesiastical associations in mid 19th century New York, helped middle-class women in constructing their role as the moral guardians of society (1991). We do not know how this separate American domestic tradition began or when it first appeared. I suspect that the American Revolutionary War, which marked the independence of the United States from Britain and its entrance as a separate entity into the capitalist world system, provided the catalyst for the negotiation of a new cultural tradition in post-colonial New York which in turn resulted in these changes in gender relations and domestic life. But this is a question that we should be able to address by comparing the material culture associated with domestic life, including the dishes that women actually used to set their tables, in British and American homes in the late 18th and early 19th centuries.

Acknowledgments

I thank James Symonds for inviting me to participate in his symposium on 'The Table: The material culture and social context of dining in the historical periods' at the University of Sheffield in 2004. It was he who requested that I present this particular study, because as he noted although it was originally written up over a decade ago, it had yet to be disseminated in Britain. I am also grateful to Arnold Pickman for his help with the graphs.

References

Beecher, C. (1846) *Miss Beecher's Domestic Receipt-Book, Designed as a Supplement to Her Treatise on Domestic Economy*, New York, Harper.

Belden, L. C. (1983) *The Festive Tradition: Table Decoration and Desserts in America, 1650–1900*, New York, W. W. Norton.

Bender, T. (1978) *Community and Social Change in America*, New Brunswick, Rutgers University Press.

Bleecker, E. (1799–1806) Diary Kept in New York City, Rare Books and Manuscripts Division, New York Public Library.

Brooks, A. (2003) Crossing Offa's Dyke: British ideologies and late eighteenth- and nineteenth-century ceramics in Wales, in Lawrence, S. (ed.) *Archaeologies of the British: Explorations of Identity in Great Britain and Its Colonies 1600–1945*, London, Routledge, 119–137.

Carter, S. (1802) *The Frugal Housewife*, Philadelphia, Matthew Carey.

Clark, C. E., Jr. (1986) *The American Family Home, 1800–1960*, Chapel Hill, University of North Carolina Press.

Cott, N. F. (1977) *The Bonds of Womanhood: A Woman's Sphere in New England*, New Haven, Yale University Press.

Demos, J. (1970) *A Little Commonwealth: Family Life in Plymouth Colony*, New York, Oxford University Press.

Dreyfus, H. L. and Rabinow, P. (1982) *Michel Foucault: Beyond Structuralism and Hermeneutics*, Chicago, University of Chicago Press.

Ewins, N. (1997) 'Supplying the present wants of our Yankee cousins...': Staffordshire ceramics and the American market 1775–1880. *Journal of Ceramic History* 15.

Foner, E. (1976) *Tom Paine and Revolutionary America*, New York, Oxford University Press.

Gilje, P. A. (1987) *The Road to Mobocracy: Popular Disorder in New York City, 1763–1834*, Chapel Hill, University of North Carolina Press.

Hall, B. (1964) *Travels in North America*, 3 vols, Graz, Austria, Akademische Durck-U.

Hodder, I. (1979) Economic and social stress and material culture patterning. *American Antiquity* 44, 446–454.

Hooker, R. J. (1981) *Food and Drink in America: A History*, Indianapolis, Bobbs-Merrill.

Lasch, C. (1977) *Haven in a Heartless World: The Family Besieged*, New York, Basic Books.

Lawrence, S. (2003) Archaeology and the nineteenth-century British Empire. *Historical Archaeology* 37:1, 20–33.

Leslie, E. (1844) *The House Book, or, a Manual of Domestic Economy for Town and Country*, Philadelphia, Carey and Hart.

Malan, A. and Klose, J. (2003) Nineteenth-century ceramics in Cape Town, South Africa, in Lawrence, S. (ed.) *Archaeologies of the British: Explorations of Identity in Great Britain and Its Colonies 1600–1945*, London, Routledge, 191–209.

Miller, G. L. (1991) A revised set of cc index values for classification and economic scaling of English ceramics from 1787 to 1880. *Historical Archaeology* 14, 1–40.

Perkins, B. (ed.) (1960) *Henry Unwin Addington's Residence in the United States of America, 1822–1825*, University of California, Publications in History, 65, Berkeley, University of California Press.

Pope-Hennessy, U. (ed.) (1931) *The Aristocratic Journey, Being the Outspoken Letters of Mrs. Basil Hall, Written During a Fourteen Month Sojourn in America, 1827–1828*, New York, G. P. Putnam's Sons.

Rosenwaike, I. (1972) *Population History of New York City*, Syracuse, New York, Syracuse University Press.

Ryan, M. P. (1981) *Cradle of the Middle Class: The Family in Oneida County, New York, 1790–1865*, New York, Cambridge University Press.

Scott, F. D. (trans. and ed.) (1952) *Baron Klinkowstroem's America, 1818–1820*, Evanston, Northwestern University Press.

Scott, J. W. (1986) Gender: A useful category of historical analysis. *The American Historical Review* 91:5, 1053–1075.

Sklar, K. K. (1973) *Catharine Beecher: A Study in American Domesticity*, New Haven, Yale University Press.

Smith, T. E. V. (1972) *The City of New York in the Year of Washington's Inauguration, 1789*, Riverside, Chatham Press.

Sussman, L. (1985) *The Wheat Pattern: An Illustrated Survey*, Ottawa, National Historic Parks and Sites Branch, Parks Canada.

Thompson, E. P. (1971) The moral economy of the English crowd in the eighteenth century. *Past and Present* 50, 76–136.

Tocqueville, A. de (2003 [1835,1840]) *Democracy in America*, translated by G. E. Bevan, Penguin Books, London.

Wall, D. diZ. (1987) At Home in New York: The Redefinition of Gender among the Middle Class and Elite, 1783–1840. PhD Thesis, New York University.

Wall, D. diZ. (1991) Sacred dinners and secular teas: constructing domesticity in mid-19th century New York. *Historical Archaeology* 25(4), 69–81.

Wall, D. diZ. (1994) *The Archaeology of Gender: Separating the Spheres in Urban America*, New York, Plenum.

Wallerstein, I. (1980) *The Modern World System*: Vol. 2. *Mercantilism and the Consolidation of the European World Economy*, New York, Academic Press.

Williams, S. (1985) *Savory Suppers and Fashionable Feasts: Dining in Victorian America*, New York, Pantheon.

Wobst, H. M. (1977) Stylistic behavior and information exchange, in Cleland, C. E. (ed.) *For the Director: Research Essays in Honor of James B. Griffin, Michigan Anthropological Papers* 61, 317–342.

9

Domesticity and the Dresser: An Archaeological Perspective from Rural 19th Century Pembrokeshire

Harold Mytum

Introduction

Historical archaeologists have recently begun to examine the role of domesticity as a concept held in 19th century households (Praetzellis and Praetzellis 1992; Wall 1991, 1994). Domesticity was linked to the increasing dichotomy of home and the workplace, with 'separate spheres' of male workplace and female dwelling. The woman undertook the roles of homemaker and childcarer, and retreated from a more public role. She could have some power and significance within the household, though in an unequal relationship with her husband. This was most manifested in the middle classes, and indeed was seen as a consequence and essential part of the identity that the middle-class created (Vickery 1993, 384). Part of the woman's role within the framework of domesticity was the construction of menus, and the associated sequence of activities from the purchase of raw materials through preparation and cooking to the setting in which consumption took place. In middle-class households, servants could be responsible to the woman of the house, but in working-class contexts the roles were not delegated, or only to other family members, such as daughters.

The 'separate spheres' framework was the dominant North American model in women's history until the late 1980s (Kerber 1988; Ryan 1981), and this is reflected in the archaeological literature (Wall 1991, 1994). In Britain and Europe, a similar emphasis developed, and again concentrated on the middle-classes (Davidoff and Hall 1987; Simonton 1998, 89). More recently, however, the 'separate spheres' model has come under some criticism. The extent to which the strictures of moralists were heeded by middle-class women has been questioned (Vickery 1993, 385). Moreover, the model was seen as overly simplistic and did not recognise the agency of individuals, both male and female, in the construction and negotiation of relations within the home and beyond. This less distinct binary opposition is also emphasised when working-class gender relations have been examined, and archaeologists have noted that variability in

behaviour and attitudes was greater than that implied by the moralising tracts (Spencer-Wood 1994, 1996). Not only did many women work in factories or the fields, but middle-class values may not have been held as an ideal by the working-classes in the early 19th century (Simonton 1998, 131). Many historians have assumed that emulation of the middle classes would have been the aim of those less well off, and that only their material conditions prevented this. Thus Rendall (1991, 83) argued whilst the more affluent could embrace domesticity:

> This was not the case for the working-class wife and mother. For her, notions of domesticity, privacy and respectability were far removed from her environment. Neither the rural cottage nor the housing of the early industrial revolution offered such possibilities.

It would seem that from the middle of the 19th century, however, there was a shift to more differentiation based on gender and associated with domesticity in all social groups. Married working class women began to withdraw from the world of work and concentrate on the domestic realm (Bourke 1994; Rose 1992). This was in part their choice, though it was also caused by male attitudes to women in the workplace where they could be a threat to their jobs or wage levels (Clark 1992; Simonton 1998, 172). This affected rural areas as well as cities (Simonton 1998, 122–125) and created the dynamics in gender relations that were clearly in force in the 20th century. The models of gender differentiation outlined in the 20th-century ethnographic studies used here can be seen to carry back to the late 19th-century through direct experiences of informants, and even further with indirect experience and family memories. Thus, the rise of gender differentiation linked to domesticity can be seen to be relevant in 19th century rural Wales. From an archaeological perspective it is therefore necessary to consider the material evidence that can inform such social relations and cultural aspirations.

Material Culture of Domesticity

The locales of particular relevance to the study of domesticity lie within the homes of the population under study, whether working-class labourers or middle-class tenant farmers. Material culture relevant to such a study is domestic architecture, furniture (largely now removed from its original context), and ceramics (in museum collections but also recovered from excavation).

A long-term research project in north Pembrokeshire, south-west Wales, has been investigating the ways of life and death of rural communities, with some comparative work in the small town of Newport. This has involved the survey and limited excavation of a range of settlements (Mytum 1988), which has run alongside recording of the graveyard memorials of the region (Mytum 1994, 1999a, 1999b, 2002). In addition, the small community museum at Penrhos near Maenclochog is a valuable survivor illustrating the architecture of a low status dwelling, combined with a collection of furniture and other artefacts originally used in this house, augmented by others donated by local families (Figure 9.1). Collections such as those in the Carmarthenshire County Museum, and the Museum of Welsh Life, St Fagans, also provide important comparanda for the study.

The information from material culture can be combined with historical sources and ethnographic studies in west Wales (mainly the adjacent region of southern Cardiganshire) to allow some understanding of the domestic lives of inhabitants across a range of classes. In this context the role of eating in the home and workplace can be seen as one of the major structuring principles of the daily round, and as such important for the creation, negotiation and recreation of social relations (Bourdieu 1977). Meal preparation was a female activity, but aspects of consumption were also gendered. By the late 19th-century concepts of domesticity can be seen to be applicable in the tenant farms, and it can be argued was also present in some form in the lower status households.

The physical arrangement of relatively fixed built space and attitudes to gender and class created structure within which actors operated. Nevertheless, there was flexibility in terms of the social composition of dining groups, the arrangement of movable furniture and even more so with portable artefacts such as ceramics and textiles. Of particular cultural importance was the dresser, a functional item of furniture under female control that also allowed for display, and can be seen as a symbol of domesticity in the later 19th century. Only some of these elements may be recovered through archaeological excavation and survey, but it is possible to combine these with other sources to understand aspects of material existence in rural 19th century Pembrokeshire.

Domesticity in Wales

Given the debates over the relevance of the 'separate spheres' model of domesticity, it is necessary to consider how relevant this was to the circumstances of 19th century rural Pembrokeshire. Evidence from Wales comes from a variety of sources: contemporary magazine articles, including many written by women (Jones 2000, 206); interviews conducted during various government enquiries; and travellers' accounts. These all suggest that gender differentiation was important, and that increasingly during the 19th century the concept of domesticity not only took hold but was indeed positively acted upon. The concept of the 'separate spheres' gained particular prominence in Wales during the second half of the 19th century and applied to all social classes, including labourers (Jones 2000, 180). How these 'separate spheres' were manifested, however, clearly depended on many factors, including class and the range of options regarding income sources and levels, work patterns, and type of housing. Clearly gender roles and domesticity would be manifested differently in a mariner's household where the man was absent for long periods of time compared with that of a farm labourer, or a tenant farmer.

The contrast between middle-class descriptions of working-class homes and the photographic, oral history and archaeological evidence suggests that the differences between reality and perception were no less in Wales than in Five Points, New York (Fitts 2001), or in The Rocks in Sydney (Karskens 1999). This can be seen from this description of a visit to Merionethshire:

> The house accommodation is wretched ... They comprise but one room, in which all the family sleep. This is in some cases separated from the rest of the hut by whisps of straw, forming an imperfect screen. These squalid huts appear to be the choice of the people, who are not more poor than the peasantry in England. They are well supplied with food, clothing and fuel ... But they have never seen a higher order of civilization, and though they have the means to live respectably, they prefer from ignorance the degraded social condition above described. Nor is this confined to the labouring population. The farmers, who might raise the standard of domestic comfort and civilization, although they live well and dress in super-fine cloth, are happy to inhabit huts scarcely less dark, dirty and comfortless (Report of the Commission of Inquiry into the State of Education in Wales, 1847, 3, Appendix 136, quoted in Owen 1991, 32; these volumes are also widely known as the Blue Books and caused considerable protest at their bias even at the time).

Here, as elsewhere, class and racial assumptions coloured the description. This can be contrasted with the image in Figure 9.2, dated about 1910, and with comments of more sympathetic observers such as George Borrow who observed in 1854, that: 'We sat down on stools by a clean white table in a little apartment with a clay floor' (quoted in Lowe 1985,

Figure 9.1. Penrhos cottage, near Maenclochog, now a community museum. Top; exterior view, showing two-ended house plan with narrow room added later. Bottom, interior view of central room; note timber panel room partition and the dresser in a prominent location.

Figure 9.2 Interior of cottage, Bardsey Island (sketch derived from photograph in Lowe 1993, 4). D = dresser with crockery; F = fire; M = shelf over fire with crockery; S = settle; ST = stool; T = table; V = large ceramic vessels.

5). These suggest that, whilst the poorest and most inadequate members of Welsh rural society lived in abject physical conditions, many were able to make through their efforts a home of some dignity, and in a style of their own choosing. That included creating a home where the values of domesticity could be championed, even within the rural poor where women also had to contribute to manual work on smallholdings and through small-scale home production such as knitting.

Magazines were published during the 19th century that concentrated on a female readership, and extolled the virtues of domesticity (Jones 2000). Some such publications were in Welsh, first *Y Gymraes* from 1850, and the more popular *Y Frythones* issued from 1879 until 1889 (Howarth 2000, 168). Welsh women were encouraged to be the wives, mothers and domestic servants, emphasising the concept of the 'separate spheres'. Whilst this rhetoric could have been largely unheeded, it provided a source of aspiration that was also reinforced by Nonconformist culture that was prevalent in Wales and so was emphasised in local active contexts, not just in print. The untidy homes described by some observers were criticised by women anxious that appropriate domestic ideals should be upheld. Poor behaviour and inattention to housework was often linked to gossiping, and is recorded from a range of sources (Jones 2000, 192–193).

It would seem that the widespread desire to have a clean and tidy home, well brought up children, and a loyally supported husband was therefore positively desired and not merely enforced in the second half of the 19th century. Such attitudes created arenas where female responsibilities were paramount, and this can be read within the ethnographic evidence (Jenkins 1971; Rees 1975). Nowhere could this cleanliness and quality, often linked to concepts of Welsh culture and identity, be more clearly seen than with the dresser. Though widespread in Britain, this item of furniture became closely associated with Wales (Twiston-Davies and Lloyd-Johnes 1950), and so became an active part of Welsh identity as viewed from outside, but also accepted and developed by the Welsh themselves. Moreover, strong regional traditions of dressers developed (Davis 1991) which further emphasised identity and place.

The dresser (Figure 9.3) had developed out of an elite furniture item for storing food in closed cupboards and with space for display of vessels above, though by the 19th century it was found across all social classes (Davis 1991). Thus, in Carmarthenshire, for example, the dresser could be used to subdivide the single room house into two, given its bulk (Report of the Commission of Inquiry into the State of Education in Wales, 1847, 2, 56, quoted in William 1995). Peate (1946, 90) notes that evidence from various parts of Wales indicates that box beds could be placed back to back to split a single room into two sections. In some cases these beds were fitted with shelves on which the crockery could be placed, in effect creating a form of dresser. Even poor families thus had some power in the segregation and

Figure 9.3. Oak dresser from Cil-y-cwm, Carmarthenshire, with its 19th-century ceramic assemblage. It has an open potboard and three drawers in the base and three shelves above. Photograph: Carmarthenshire County Museum.

organisation of their domestic space, and in which display of household objects could be given some prominence.

The dresser could display not only the everyday items used on the table, but also ceramics used on special occasions, and indeed ornaments and display china never to be placed on the table (Vincentelli 1994). Archaeologically, most artefacts of the dresser are under-represented in assemblages as they would rarely suffer breakage. Moreover, most museum displays of dressers are recreations, rather than actual collections from households. This is even the case at the local Penrhos museum; the main items reclaimed by the descendants of the ladies who had lived in the cottage had been the ceramics from the dresser, though most other items were left to form the core of the collection. Nevertheless, the combination of oral history (Vincentelli 1994), occasional survivals with original assemblages such

as those donated to Carmarthenshire County Museum (e.g. http://www.gtj.org.uk/en/item1/17734), and the range of artefacts from excavations, suggest that a colourful array was possible given the material recovered. All these sources underline that the role of the dresser in 19th century rural Pembrokeshire should not be underestimated.

Vincentelli (2004, 234) notes how blue and white plates, copper lustre ware, and Staffordshire dogs were particularly popular on Welsh 19th century dressers. Depositional factors explain the lack of dogs in the excavated assemblages, but lustreware (Figure 9.4) and blue transfer-prints are present in sufficient quantities in the archaeological record to support this. Bebb (1997, 38) comments that 'Asiatic Pheasant' was popular on North Welsh dressers, which often had an emphasis on a blue and white colour scheme. Given that this is a common design from the Pembrokeshire excavations its success may have been more widespread. Dressers in South Wales could be more colourful in their ceramic assemblage (Bebb 1997, 38), and an array of individual lustre ware jugs and hand-painted gaudy wares augment the blue and white transfer-printed set present on the Carmarthenshire County Museum dresser. A colourful display can be suggested for the excavated sites by the presence within the transfer-printed material of red, green, and black designs. Moreover, the sponge-decorated cawl bowls Bebb (1997, 38) describes are frequent site finds (Figure 9.4).

It may be that, in the poorer households of the two-ended cottages discussed below, much of the everyday china was displayed between meals on the dresser. In such contexts the archaeologically recovered material may more accurately indicate the aesthetics of the home than the middle-class dresser with its display china, and the everyday tableware stored out of sight. Certainly the range of colours and designs present on the painted and transfer-printed ceramics from such dwellings suggests that the dressers could have given a bright and colourful appearance to the main living room. Moreover, the choice of ceramics and their arrangement on the dresser was a form of statement of control by the woman of the house who could employ her own agency to emphasise aspects of individual style and taste on the one hand, and national or religious identity on the other, through purchase and display of ceramics on the dresser.

The role of transfer-printed ceramics in the creation and reinforcement of national identities has begun to be appreciated (Brooks 1997, 1999). The national costume of Wales was deliberately designed in the 1830s, mainly through the efforts of Augusta Waddington, Lady Llanover, from the red tweed cloaks and black hats that had been until recently worn in rural areas even though harking back to a fashion of the early 17th century (Morgan 1983, 79–81). It rapidly became popular, and its acceptance as a national icon in rural Pembrokeshire can be seen in the transfer-printed cup with 'traditional' Welsh scenes on it from Parcau

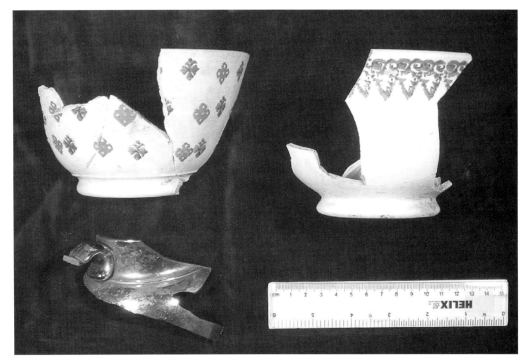

Figure 9.4. Sponge-decorated cawl bowls and lustreware jug fragment, excavated from Fron Haul two-ended house.

Figure 9.5. Transfer-printed cup with 'traditional' Welsh scenes, excavated from Parcau single house.

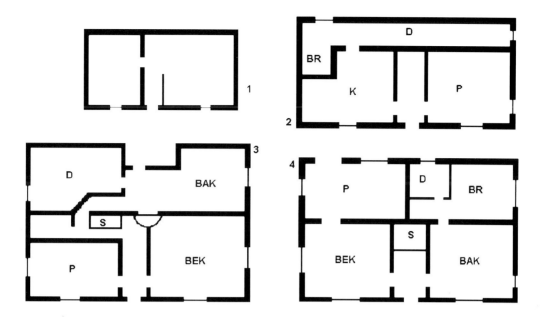

Figure 9.6. Schematic plans (not to scale) of the main house types in rural Pembrokeshire (after Jenkins 1971). 1 Two-ended house; 2 Single house; 3 Double house; 4 Double house. Room key: BAK = Back kitchen; BEK = Best kitchen; BR = Board room; D = Dairy; K = Kitchen; P = Parlour; S = Stairs.

(Figure 9.5). Other transfer-printed ceramic designs could be associated with cultural and religious figures, places or events. Rich and complex messages could thus be provided by the dresser and its display collection.

Linked to aspects of identity, the items on the dresser had become important possessions partly because of their heirloom qualities. The objects on the dresser all had a history and personal associations that were known and could be recalled (Rees 1975, 44). The female acquisition of items, and the control over memories so evoked, gave the woman of the household considerable social power through the knowledge of family and community history, triggered by the items on the dresser. These were not the only material culture items linked with memories, but in the Welsh household they were amongst the most visible and culturally valued. This tradition of stories linked to particular items has been maintained up to the present, sometimes still linked to family, in other cases associated with the acquisition and appreciation from a collector's viewpoint (Vincentelli 1994, 238–240); this, too, may have been present earlier. The power of the woman of the house in teaching children and maintaining family history through stories has not been greatly appreciated (Langellier and Peterson 1993). In a Welsh context those memories illustrated or triggered by heirlooms from the dresser, or indeed constructed via the individual items and the whole assemblage on display, is an avenue of research currently being explored.

The role of domesticity was given special prominence by Nonconformist values (Jones 2000, 195). The majority of labourers and farmers were of this persuasion in the region, and chapels were numerous and well-attended (Mytum 2002). The need to assert national identity was recognised at the time (the publication *Y Gymraes* translates as *The Welshwoman*). Education of children in the home was essential to preserve many aspects of Welsh culture including language, and the mother was responsible for this (Jones 2000). The morality of the Welsh, and particularly their womenfolk, had been challenged by the 1847 Commission of Enquiry, and this further increased the need to emphasise domesticity. The dresser was the most obvious and important feature in the house by which such domestic standards could be demonstrated. It had a functional role that did not challenge Nonconformist concerns about frippery and ostentatious display (Vincentelli 1994, 234), yet allowed demonstration of cleanliness, order and taste.

The Houses

Welsh vernacular architecture is extremely regional, just as were the dressers, but the western areas of Gwynedd in the north-west and Dyfed (Pembrokeshire, Cardiganshire and Carmarthenshire) in the south-west share many architectural features. Today, most of the rural working housing has been either abandoned or has been heavily modernised, often for holiday homes, whilst the larger farmhouses have been continuously occupied and greatly changed internally in the face of 20th century needs.

Many standing buildings have been recorded, sometimes prior to conversion or abandonment, beginning with the early efforts of Peate (1946) and subsequent work of other folk life researchers and staff from the Royal Commission for Ancient and Historic Monuments for Wales (Lowe 1985). Relatively few of the buildings in north Pembrokeshire have been so fortunate, but a small number of farmhouses have been recorded though not published by the Royal Commission for Ancient and Historic Monuments for Wales. In addition, one cottage has been rescued by the local community at Penrhos near Maenclochog, and is now a small museum (Figure 9.1). The survey and partial excavation at ruined sites, often now overgrown by trees, has provided a unique range of material that can augment the ethnographic and wider architectural studies. Their fragmentary state can allow study of the building fabric, and excavation allows the recovery of associated material culture rarely possible at still-occupied sites with extensive concrete and paved yards.

The homes that form the core of the study are the two-ended house or cottage, the single house, and the double house (Figure 9.6). These three types were inhabited by all but the few gentry families, or those tenant farmers who were living in over-large and decrepit gentry houses that had been abandoned by landowners as estates were consolidated during the 18th and 19th centuries. One such residence, Henllys Farm, has been extensively excavated and was in many respects used as a version of the double house (Mytum 2010). Nevertheless, most houses in the region fall into clear typological categories that allow generalisations to be made.

The two-ended cottage consisted of two rooms, and could have a half-loft above, lit by a window in the gable end (Jenkins 1971). The people who lived in these houses were landless workers, largely agricultural labourers, but also mariners. They were often associated with very small holdings of land, but the occupants relied on wage labour to augment their limited agricultural production from their rented home.

The single houses were farmhouses, and were used on tenant farms greatly varying in size. Two or three rooms were arranged on the ground floor, accessed from a hallway that also contained the stairs, and rooms in the loft generally matched those below. There was often a lean-to at the rear that served as the dairy. The main rooms were the parlour, best kitchen, dairy and often a board room. The use of these rooms will be discussed later.

The larger farmhouses were termed double houses and had the same types of ground floor rooms as the single houses but crucially had two kitchens, the best kitchen and the back kitchen, and generally the rooms were larger. There were more upstairs rooms, making sleeping arrangements far more segregated. These tenant farms employed more servants and labourers, but the pattern of segregation was as with the single houses.

Two-Ended Cottages

Fieldwork has been conducted on several two-ended cottages, and here Fron Haul in Newport parish will be used as an example of such a structure. Fron Haul may have begun as a single-roomed dwelling, later extended to the south with the addition of a second room. Entrance was gained through a single door roughly mid-way along the long eastern side, and the fireplace and larder occupied the northern gable end. The western wall was set against the steep valley side, a trench being dug at its base to encourage rainwater to flow around the building. The additional room, butt-jointed onto the first, was approached through a door against the west wall of the dwelling. A small fireplace at the gable end of the additional room was fitted with a small cast iron grate.

Several little fields for the small holding lay to the east, with a pig sty to the south and a boiler for clothes washing built into the steep bank to the north. Most social activity would have been concentrated in the one room, with the large stone-hooded fireplace forming the centre of attention.

The census returns indicate that a widow and four children between the ages of 7 and 15 lived in the house in 1841, a labourer, his wife and 21-year-old daughter in 1851, and a mariner and his wife in 1871 (Mytum 1988, 35). Fron Haul was not a home occupied by anyone for a long period, the shifting population reflecting the uncertainties of employment in rural west Wales.

How was life conducted in this small dwelling, and how was food produced and consumed? A rare interior photograph of a two-roomed cottage is known from Bardsey Island, Gwynedd (Lowe 1985, 4), and this perhaps provides a guide, though the shifting occupants may have had even fewer possessions than this image indicates. The Bardsey Island cottage has a central fireplace with a mantelpiece, a safe shelf for foodstuffs and a washing bowl (Figure 9.2). The asymmetrical Pembrokeshire cottage fireplace may have had such a shelf, though no evidence survives on the lintels in the surveyed cottages. It is likely, though, that the Pembrokeshire fireplace contained a large cooking pot, around which could be placed small three-legged stools, a settle and table, and significantly a dresser on which china would be placed. Other utensils would be kept in the drawers, and large cooking vessels stored on the base.

Ethnographic evidence from the early 20th century in south Cardiganshire (Figure 9.7) gives details of the furniture found in the two-roomed cottage in south-west Wales (Jenkins 1971, 95), and this supports the relevance of the Bardsey Island photograph. Moreover, 19th century documentary sources list the same items of furniture, though do not give details as to their location (William 1995). A bed would occupy a considerable amount of space in the main room, together with several items of furniture for storage.

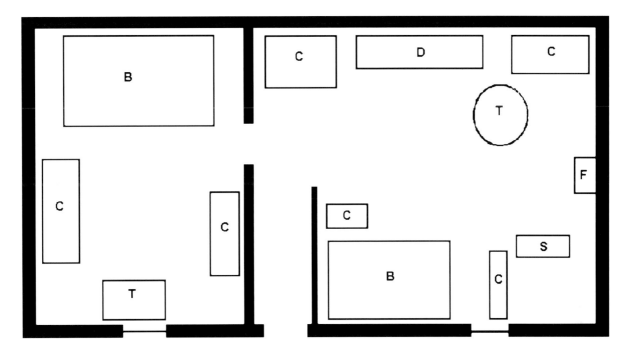

Figure 9.7. Schematic plan of furniture in a two-ended house (after Jenkins 1971). B = Bed; C = Coffers and chests; D = Dresser; F = Fire; S = Settle; ST = Stairs; T = Table.

The dresser would dominate one wall, and so could provide a prominent arena for display associated with but not always directly linked to dining. If there were room there would be a rectangular table, but sometimes only a smaller circular table was placed near the fire. The second room, accessed off the first, was as little-used as possible, though if there were boys and girls in the family the latter slept in there and the boys on the half loft if there was one. Important family items such as photographs, the family Bible and other books including hymn books, were kept here, and there could be a cupboard for other more valuable china not placed on the dresser. This may have housed the tea ware used for visitors, though the excavation evidence suggests that this was not a matched set. The room may also have been used to tend the sick and lay out the dying, but was not a room normally given much use (Rees 1975, 46).

The Penrhos cottage has a bed which folds away in the kitchen, and a parlour, though an addition to the building, probably in the 20th century, created a separate bedroom and the original large fireplace was removed at this time. The features and furnishings are largely complete and original, apart from the contents of the dresser which were retained by descendants of the two sisters who had lived there till the mid 20th century. These suggest that the pattern of arrangements in north Pembrokeshire, and so Fron Haul and the other investigated two-room houses, were much as described for south Cardiganshire.

Sleeping, cooking and eating therefore all largely took place in the one space, with the fire the centre of heat and light. The Fron Haul cottage, as with the other Pembrokeshire two-roomed dwellings surveyed, had a bread oven built into the wall by the fireplace, heated with coals from the fire. Otherwise all cooking was done over the fire, and mainly within the one large pot. The diet of the poor is not well-known, but it is thought that most survived on the produce of the smallholding, with limited additional purchased supplies. Breads were augmented by a range of sloppy foods, including *sopas* (oatmeal and buttermilk), *potsh* (mashed potatoes and buttermilk), *uwd a laeth* (gruel and milk) and various forms of *cawl* (broth or stew) (Lewis 1972, 192). Wooden or ceramic bowls were used with wooden spoons.

The finds from all the sites have been examined by a number of people. Peter Drake catalogued the glass and has noted here, and at the other sites, a reasonable number of beer bottles. The ceramics were initially examined by Helen Grundy, and latterly by Alasdair Brooks (2000).

Fron Haul finds were largely recovered from a deposit against the field wall running next to the path leading north from the dwelling, and belong largely to the late 19th and very early 20th centuries. A significant number of bowls suitable for cawl were recovered, but there was also a wide range of other ceramics including decorative items, simple earthenware tea pots and tea wares. In contrast, it should be noted, clay pipes are rare. It is likely that the ceramic assemblage reflects vessels for everyday use, and some decorative items from the dresser or parlour cupboard which were discarded either when broken or when the family moved on. We should also remember that the poorer sections of the population also used wooden bowls and spoons, now archaeologically invisible. It is not known how many meals the cottage-dwellers had a day, and at what times, though the structure experienced by the farm labourers when working at the farms, described later, may have been followed as far as could be allowed given the limited and no doubt varying supplies.

The Single House

Parcau house represents the single house form, with a central door leading into a hall with stairs leading to the first floor and a small underground store below, with the parlour on the right and the kitchen on the left. To the rear was a lean-to room only behind the kitchen, added at a later date and largely robbed away by the time of the excavations. This may have been a dairy or the board room where any additional labourers were fed whilst working the farm. Here the same limited use for the parlour would have applied, and most activity must have taken place in the kitchen, though the upstairs bedrooms provided more and separate sleeping space than in the two-room houses. Parcau is the smallest form of single house, and is relatively late in its present form, with bricks used in the lintel of one upstairs window and in the bread oven built into the fireplace in the kitchen.

The artefacts from the midden against a field bank defining the yard opposite the house reveal an assemblage not dissimilar to that at Fron Haul, but it is larger and contains a very high percentage of bowls. This may be because fewer were of wood than at the Fron Haul cottage.

Double House

No double house has been excavated, though recent excavations at Henllys Farm have uncovered a house that in the 19th century housed a prosperous tenant farmer who would have had more subdivided space than in the houses described so far, and his neighbours would have been living in double houses (Mytum 2010).

The standard double house has four main rooms downstairs and four bedrooms upstairs, and with a dairy the length of the building built at the back. In the double house there was sufficient space for a more segregated and socially structured form of dining. The master and mistress ate in the best kitchen, with the rest of the family (apart from children too small to feed themselves), house servants and farm workers eating together in the board room if there was one, or otherwise the back kitchen (Jenkins 1971). Even the eldest son ate there, though if he visited another family in a double

house, he was invited to join the master and mistress in the best kitchen as an honoured guest.

Many of the larger farms employed a number of labourers, though these could be laid off without pay at slack times of the year. Previously housed in lofts above outbuildings, they normally now lived in rented two-ended cottages, but had their meals provided for at the farm whilst working on its land. Jenkins (1971, 98–100) has recorded the pattern and typical menu of such meals in the late 19th and early 20th century. We can thus see how all social levels on the farm had their waking hours structured by eating times which were varied in character and with different types of social interaction.

After dealing with the livestock, a breakfast at seven o'clock was tea, bread and butter, and cheese. The master ate alone in the back kitchen, the mistress ate there later after all had been fed, and if the family and servants were too many to eat at once, the men ate first followed by the women. Breakfast was often followed by a short Bible reading and prayer, led by the master or some elderly and respected servant known for his religious faith, and in which women said little. At mid-morning 'ten o'clock food' was taken to wherever people were working, again tea, bread and butter and cheese, though some broth was served at the 'good places' where the food was seen as best, and which tended to have a stability in their labour force for that reason.

At noon or half past the next meal was indicated, and the arrangements were as at breakfast. This was the largest meal of the day, with broth in bowls followed by the salt bacon or beef and vegetables that had been cooked in the broth, followed by dumplings or rice pudding. At harvest time the main meal was eaten in the fields, and was adapted accordingly. Afternoon tea was the same as 'ten o'clock food', and consumed at work, and the final meal was around seven o'clock in the evening and consisted of leftovers of all the previous meals. Again the master and mistress were separated in their dining, whilst everyone else was together in the board room or back kitchen.

The double house arrangement largely followed the communal cross-class mealtimes, and all consumed the same food. Here, though, the most important couple were separated physically and socially. The food was undoubtedly better than that enjoyed by the poor back in their two-roomed cottages, but was not greatly superior. It was probably more plentiful and could be relied upon, and may have been of better quality, but was different more by degree than kind. Only the master and mistress in the double house, and their visitors, experienced a different physical context for dining, and even they had shared the communal lifestyle until they took over the farm. Visitors who did not do agricultural manual labour, such as the minister or an auctioneer, would be invited into the best kitchen, but other craftsmen, even respected ones such as the blacksmith, ate in the board room.

Conclusion

Most 19th-century rural dwellings have been greatly altered or survive only in ruins, and the furniture they contained has largely been destroyed or is now treated as a separate decontextualised commodity and bought and sold as antiques. The item most likely to have been retained within a household is the dresser, which may have limited information regarding date and context. Now dressers either present developing private collections, or display static but recreated assemblages, even if in original buildings, as at the St Fagan's National Folk Museum (Davis 1991). Authentic contextualised collections have rarely survived for the social classes discussed here, though Carmarthenshire Museum does have some important exceptions.

The archaeological assemblages from the north Pembrokeshire sites contain a variety of material, some of which was in midden deposits, but some seems to have been deposited at times of house clearance when even some normally curated items from the dresser may have been deposited as no longer wanted. The ceramics on the dresser were sometimes intrinsically valuable, but many were mementos of events and gifts from friends and relations that gave them great value within a living family, but not necessarily any value to others. Material may therefore have been deposited at any of the many changes in tenancy of the two-roomed houses, or after some accident within the house.

Although the cramped living and eating arrangements of the two-roomed cottage and the single house, and the segregated dining of the double house, have all now gone the use of the dresser for a repository of memories enshrined in china continues to this day (Vincentelli 1994). The archaeological assemblages give us contexts for the past, and the dresser can give us a link to the present. China previously used in dining may now act as an antique commodity for display, and such changes in use lives should be recognised within the 19th century. This may lead to a wide range of ceramic manufacture dates in the assemblages, even if deposited at one time.

Folk life, architectural history and archaeological fieldwork on buildings, deposits and artefacts can together provide a feast of information on Welsh lifeways and foodways. The structuring of the day around mealtimes provided points of social contact for workers who could spend much of their time isolated or in small working parties. Meals provided an important and visible aspect to women's work, and the authority of the woman of the house was acknowledged and reinforced in these routines. Moreover, the domestic roles involving the teaching of language and culture could be elaborated in part at least through the preparation and serving of meals, and through maintenance and display of the dresser, able to symbolise through its ceramics the aesthetic and cultural values of Wales.

Acknowledgements

Excavation and survey of the settlements described here took place with volunteers from Earthwatch, Center for Field Research, and students from the University of York, under the supervision of Julian Ayre. I would like to thank Chris Delaney and Ann Dorsett of Carmarthenshire County Museum for information on the dressers in their collections, and for permission to reproduce Figure 3. Kate Chapman annotated Figures 2, 6 and 7.

References

Bebb, L. (1997) *Welsh Pottery*, Princes Risborough, Shire Publications.

Bourke, J. (1994) Housewifery in working-class England 1860–1914. *Past and Present* 143, 167–197.

Bourdieu, P. (1977) *Outline of a Theory of Practice*, translated by R. Nice, Cambridge, Cambridge University Press.

Brooks, A. M. (1997) Beyond the fringe: nineteenth-century transfer prints and the internationalisation of Celtic myth. *International Journal of Historical Archaeology* 1 (1), 39–55.

Brooks, A. M. (1999) Building Jersualem. Transfer-printed wares and the creation of British identity, in Tarlow, S. and West, S. (eds) *The Familiar Past? Archaeologies of Britain 1550–1950*, London, Routledge, 51–65.

Brooks, A. M. (2000) The Comparative Analysis of Late 18th and 19th Century Ceramics: A Trans-Atlantic Perspective. Unpublished DPhil, University of York.

Clark, A. (1992) The rhetoric of Chartist domesticity: gender, language and class in the 1830s and 1840s. *Journal of British Studies* 31 (1), 62–88.

Davidoff, L. and Hall, C. (1987) *Family Fortunes: Men and Women of the English Middle Class, 1780–1850*, London, Hutchinson.

Davis, A. T. (1991) *The Welsh Dresser and Associated Cupboards*, Cardiff, University of Wales Press and the National Museum of Wales.

Fitts, R. (2001) The rhetoric of reform: the Five Points missions and the cult of domesticity. *Historical Archaeology* 35 (3), 115–132.

Howarth, J. (2000) Gender, domesticity and sexual politics, in Matthew, C. (ed.) *The Nineteenth Century*, Oxford, Oxford University Press, 163–193.

Jenkins, D. (1971) *The Agricultural Community in South-West Wales at the Turn of the Twentieth Century*, Cardiff, University of Wales Press.

Jones, R. (2000) 'Separate spheres'? Women, language and respectability in Victorian Wales, in Jenkins, G. H. (ed.) *The Welsh Language and its Social Domains 1801–1911*, Cardiff, University of Wales Press, 177–213.

Karskens, G. (1999) *Inside The Rocks: The Archaeology of a Neighbourhood*, Sydney, Hale and Iremonger.

Kerber, L. (1988) Separate sphere, female worlds, women's place: the rhetoric of women's history. *Journal of American History* 75, 9–39.

Langellier, K. L. and Peterson, E. E. (1993) Family storytelling as a strategy of social control, in Mumby, D. K. (ed.) *Narrative and Social Control: Critical Perspectives*, Newbury Park, Sage, 29–76.

Lewis, E. T. (1972) *North of the Hills – a History of the Parishes of Eglwyswen, Eglwyswrw, Llanfair Nantgwyn, Meline, Nevern*, Clunderwen, E. T. Lewis.

Lowe, J. (1985) *Welsh Country Workers Housing 1775–1875*, Cardiff, National Museum of Wales.

Morgan, P. (1983) From death to a view: the hunt for the Welsh past in the Romantic Period, in Hobsbawm, E. and Ranger, T. (eds) *The Invention of Tradition*, Cambridge, Cambridge University Press, 43–100.

Mytum, H. (1988) The Clydach Valley: a nineteenth-century landscape. *Popular Archaeology* March, 33–37.

Mytum, H. (1994) Language as symbol in churchyard monuments: the use of Welsh in nineteenth- and twentieth-century Pembrokeshire. *World Archaeology* 26 (2), 252–267.

Mytum, H. (1999a) Welsh cultural identity in nineteenth-century Pembrokeshire: the pedimented headstone as a graveyard monument, in Tarlow, S. and West, S. (eds) *The Familiar Past? Archaeologies of Britain 1550–1950*, London, Routledge, 215–230.

Mytum, H. (1999b) The language of death in a bilingual community: nineteenth-century memorials in Newport, Pembrokeshire, in Blench, R. and Spriggs, M. (eds) *Archaeology and Language III: Artefacts, Languages and Texts*, One World Archaeology 34, London, Routledge, 211–230.

Mytum, H. (2002) A comparison of nineteenth- and twentieth-century Anglican and Nonconformist memorials in North Pembrokeshire. *Archaeological Journal* 159, 194–241.

Mytum, H. (2010) Biographies of projects, people and places: archaeologists and William and Martha Harries at Henllys Farm, Pembrokeshire. *Post-Medieval Archaeology* 44(2).

Owen, T. M. (1991) *The Customs and Traditions of Wales*, Cardiff, University of Wales Press.

Peate, I. (1946) *The Welsh House: a Study in Folk Culture*, Cardiff, University of Wales Press.

Praetzellis, A. and Praetzellis, M. (1992) Faces and facades: Victorian ideology in early Sacramento, in Yentsch, A. and Beaudry, M. (eds) *The Art and Mystery of Historical Archaeology: Essays in Honor of James Deetz*, Boca Raton, CRC Press, 75–100.

Rees, A. D. (1975) *Life in a Welsh Countryside*, Cardiff, University of Wales Press.

Rendall, J. (1991) *Women in an Industrializing Society: England 1750–1880*, Oxford, Blackwell.

Rose, S. O. (1992) *Limited Livelihoods: Gender and Class in Nineteenth-Century England*, Berkeley, University of California Press.

Ryan, M. (1981) *Cradle of the Middle Class: the Family in Orieda County, New York, 1790–1865*, Cambridge, Cambridge University Press.

Simonton, D. (1998) *A History of European Women's Work: 1700 to the Present*, London, Routledge.

Spencer-Wood, S. M. (1994) Diversity and nineteenth-century reform: relationships among classes and ethnic groups, in Scott, E. (ed.) *Those of Little Note: Gender, Race, and Class in Historical Archaeology*, Tucson, University of Arizona Press, 175–208.

Spencer-Wood, S. M. (1996) Feminist historical archaeology and the transformation of American culture by domestic reform movements, 1840–1925, in De Cunzo, L. A. and Herman, B. L. (eds) *Historical Archaeology and the Study of American Culture*, Winterthur, Henry Francis duPont Winterthur Museum, 397–446.

Twiston-Davies, L. and Lloyd-Johnes, H. J. (1950) *Welsh Furniture*, Cardiff, University of Wales Press.

Vickery, A. (1993) Golden age to separate spheres? A review of the categories and chronology of English women's history. *Historical Journal* 36, 383–414.

Vincentelli, M. (1994) Artefact and identity: the Welsh dresser as domestic display and cultural symbol, in Aaron, J., Rees, T., Betts, S. and Vincentelli, M. (eds) *Our Sisters' Land: The Changing Identities of Women in Wales*, Cardiff, University of Wales Press, 228–241.

Wall, D. D. (1991) Sacred dinner and secular teas: constructing domesticity in mid-19th-century New York. *Historical Archaeology* 25 (4), 69–89.

Wall, D. D. (1994) *The Archaeology of Gender: Separating the Spheres in Urban America*, New York, Plenum Press.

William, E. (1995) 'Home-made homes': dwellings of the rural poor in Cardiganshire. *Ceredigion* 12 (3), 23–40.

10

'We Lived Well at the Hagg': Foodways and Social Belonging in Working-Class Rural Cheshire

Darren Griffin and Eleanor Conlin Casella

Introduction

In his classic study of *The Making of the English Working-Class*, the Marxist historian E. P. Thompson noted, 'The rich lose sight of the poor, or only recognise them when attention is forced to their existence by their appearance as vagrants or delinquents' (Thompson 1966, 322). The primary significance of historical archaeology lies in its ability to subvert such negative depictions by challenging the dominant historical transcripts that serve to reinforce the brutal inequalities of our modern era. The Alderley Sandhills Project was designed to illuminate the transformative roles of industrialisation and de-industrialisation on working-class rural England. By focusing on a domestic site, the project was able to examine how the men, women and children of ordinary rural working households struggled to maintain and improve their conditions of everyday life in the face of the rapid socio-economic revolutions of the 18th to 20th centuries. One of the main aims of the ASP research design was to explore the nature and operation of class mobility within the social world of Alderley Edge, Cheshire.

Background: Historical Archaeology in a European context

The sub-field of historical archaeology developed during the 1960s and 1970s in the former Western European colonies such as the US, Canada, South Africa, Australia and New Zealand. In the beginning it was driven by historians interested in examining the origins and evolution of their respective nations. As a consequence, historical archaeologists focused on specific sites related to important historical events or people.

In the 1970s, the type of sites studied by historical archaeologists around the world began to diversify. The emphasis shifted to mining sites, boom towns, missions, and frontier sites. In these places historical archaeologists not only studied the material remains of European colonialists but also the material remains of indigenous peoples who were in contact with them (Lightfoot 1995). The result of this increased academic interaction with indigenous peoples and issues was that historical archaeology increasingly incorporated post-colonial paradigms into their research directions, and adopted anthropological frameworks in order to present their interpretations of the colonial past. Researchers began to listen to other voices from the past which until then had been silent. Historical archaeology was seen as a way of democratising the past: of highlighting and researching the role of the people who were not well represented in the historical documents; the people who were written about, but who never did the writing; people from different genders, races, religions, ages, ethnicities and socio-economic backgrounds to the wealthy, white men who created the western European written histories (Delle 1998, 1).

While this was happening in the post-colonial world outside of Europe, back in the Old World, there was no such self reflection of the western European nations' role in the creation of new settler societies across the globe. Historical archaeology in England emerged from a completely different theoretical background. The majority of the researchers were industrial archaeologists who were, as a general rule, more interested in the history of machines than the people who worked them (Symonds 2005). As a consequence post-colonial perspectives and self-reflexivity have begun to emerge with British studies of the 'post-medieval' period only within the last 10 years. This limited engagement with critical approaches has maintained the attitude that there is no multi-ethnic, race, gender or class conflict visible in the archaeology of modern Britain (Horton 2003).

Part of the problem is that historical archaeologists in England are still arguing about the definition of historical archaeology. If it refers to the archaeology of 'literate societies', then should it go back to the Romans (Moreland 2001)? Should it include the medieval or post-medieval world or should it just be about the Victorians (Clark 1999)? In the former colonies it is easier to put a start date to historical archaeology because it necessarily links to the arrival of western Europeans. But how does that disciplinary definition fit in with the long established archaeological periods of Europe?

Perhaps an answer can be reached through a focus on the archaeology of capitalism, as argued by many American influenced scholars (Orser 1996; Paynter 2001; Delle 1998; McGuire 1991; Shackel 1996; Johnson 1996; Leone 1999). The colonial expansion across the rest of the globe from the late 15th century onwards was fuelled by the development of capitalism. All historical archaeological sites are in some way related to western European attempts at placing the other peoples they encountered within this socio-economic system. At no other time in human history has one socio-economic system been so globally dominant. The study of how this system developed and spread and how people related, reacted and resisted this system provides a unique insight in to how our modern world emerged. Therefore, as James Delle explains, either the explicit or implicit goal of most historical archaeologists with international projects is the analysis and understanding of the historical processes of European capitalist expansion across the world (Delle 1998, 2).

Of equal significance were the profound socio-economic processes that nurtured and consolidated the brutal inequalities of capitalist systems within the British landscape (Johnson 1996). Across the island, revolutionary changes transformed local communities as long-stable populations uprooted and relocated, abandoned craft traditions and joined the expanding industrial wage economy. The Alderley Sandhills Project was developed to focus explicitly on the material conditions of these wider socio-economic transformations. By exploring the everyday material worlds of these rural households, we were able to consider the operation of class hierarchies as this local community moved from an agrarian to industrial and eventually post-industrial landscape order.

The Hagg Cottages

Located approximately 25 km south of Manchester, Alderley Edge is a natural rocky outcrop with views across both Greater Manchester and the Cheshire plain. Archaeological evidence demonstrates the region was mined for copper deposits during both the Bronze Age and Romano-British periods. During the 1850s, a series of Italianate 'villas' were constructed at Alderley Edge, and sold to the newly wealthy mill barons or 'cottontots', desperate to escape the dank urban grime of industrial Manchester. At the same time, an early rail line was established to link central Manchester to the growing service town, thereby making Alderley Edge the first commuter suburb of Great Britain. From the 1780s through the 1890s, the Edge was extensively mined for copper, lead and cobalt deposits. Thus, from the 18th

century, the region supported a complex mix of agricultural, industrial and service-based economic activities.

The Sandhills site is presently located on private land adjacent to the forested nature reserve now owned and managed by the National Trust. The Sandhills area was notified as a Site of Special Scientific Interest by English Nature in 1993. It was granted Scheduled Ancient Monument status by English Heritage in 2001 due to its proximity to the subterranean Romano-British mineshafts.

The study area became locally known as the Sandhills because of the large quantities of acidic sand dumped outside West Mine as a by-product of the 19th-century copper mining activities. During this period the Alderley Edge Mining Company developed an acid-leeching process in order to extract copper from the sandstone matrix. As a result, the waste sand was steeped in hydrochloric acid, with the pH of the remaining sandhills discouraging regrowth of plant species, and helping preserve the unique landscape features.

The Sandhills site itself comprises of the remains of two cottages, used by the Alderley Edge Mining Company for the accommodation of the families of men who worked at the local mines (Figure 10.1). They were both two-storey structures that were internally divided to accommodate four separate households. The site also contains their associated outbuildings, privies, middens, domestic gardens, and a well. Parish records indicate that the eastern cottage was built during 1747 on Lord Stanley's Estate in a local architectural style known as the Stanley type cottage. The Stanley-type cottage was a two storey brick Georgian structure. The main distinguishing characteristic of this type of cottage was the chimneys on each end and the entrance gable in the middle of the house. The Stanley-type cottage at the Alderley Sandhills site was originally built for agricultural tenant farmers. The date of construction and original function of the southern building was unknown, although excavated architectural features and a pipe-stem date suggested a possible late 17th-century origin (Casella *et al.* 2004). Both structures appear on the 1787 Lord Stanley Estate plan. Since both structures were built on Hagg Lane they became locally known as the Hagg Cottages.

By the turn of the 20th century, mining activity in the area had completely ceased, and the occupants of the cottages all worked in the service economy of Alderley Edge village. Residents of the four households consisted of the Barrow, Ellam, Perrin, and Barber families. Members of these families – Mrs Edna Younger (née Barrow), Mr Roy Barber and Mrs Molly Pitcher (née Barber) – visited the site during the excavations (Figure 10.2). Their recollections of living in the cottages form the bulk of the oral history relating to the site.

The cottages were occupied until immediately after the Second World War but were demolished in the early 1950s by the Nield family. Having privately purchased the

Figure 10.1. Hagg Cottages, facing east, c.1930. Photo taken by George Barber, father of former residents Roy Barber and Molly Pitcher (née Barber). Photo courtesy of R. Barber.

Figure 10.2. Roy Barber, Edna Younger (née Barrow), and Molly Pitcher (née Barber), site visit September 2003. Inset: Edna Barrow, Roy Barber and Molly Barber at the Hagg, c.1930. Photo courtesy of E. Younger.

surrounding land following the Stanley estate sale of 1938, the Nields removed the majority of the sandhills intermittently from the 1930s to the 1960s, and sold the acidic sands to the local council as an aggregate road base. In addition, the Nields used the abandoned mine shafts and immediate region for extensive landfill operations, on contract with the local council.

Foodways and the Production of Community

Through the material culture and oral histories collected during the excavation of the Hagg cottages in the summer of 2003, a detailed analysis of the socio-economic identity of the residents of these cottages was developed. From this identity we were able to place domesticity at the Hagg Cottages into a wider social context.

Given our central focus on the material culture of everyday life that expressed socio-economic identity, our research started with a basic underlying question: what constituted a working-class household? British social historians have generally dismissed the 'nuclear family' as a meaningful unit of social organisation because of increased overcrowding in the rural population from 1800 (Rule 1986). The first two decades of the 19th century witnessed an average increase of 37% in the labouring population of rural English counties. In a subsequent 1864 Parliamentary survey of 821 rural English parishes, a total of 69,225 cottages were recorded, housing 305,567 persons. This produced an average of 4.4 occupants per one-room household cottage. The Alderley Sandhills site reflected this wider demographic pattern. Parish census data on the Hagg Cottages, collected from 1841 through to 1901, demonstrated the prevalence of extended and multi-generational households, with the core families most frequently augmented by renting lodgers, fostered nieces and elderly relatives (Casella *et al.* 2004).

Further, complex neighbourly and kinship affiliations linked households into the wider rural community. Workers maintained and elaborated these enduring networks of social belonging to ensure survival for those vulnerable members of their households. Distinguishing the English working-class by an 'ethos of mutuality', E. P. Thompson argued:

Every kind of witness in the first half of the 19th century – clergymen, factory inspectors, Radical publicists – remarked upon the extent of mutual aid in the poorest districts. In times of emergency, unemployment, strikes, sickness, childbirth, then it was the poor who 'helped every one his neighbour' (Thompson, 1966, 423).

While such a concentration on 'mutuality' has been disparaged as an overly romanticised perspective, these historical studies have emphasised the community as a dominant social unit in the formation of English working-class culture – a change in scale that holds direct implications for the intertwined foodways of rural working-class communities. Drawing from Ferguson (1992), we define

foodways as the food itself, the material culture used to make and present the food, and the cultural practices of food consumption. By way of example, during oral history interviews, one of the Hagg Cottage's former residents Mrs Edna Younger repeatedly recalled her shared breakfasts with Mr Ellam, the elderly father of her neighbours in the adjoining cottage:

And their father, of course, was a very old Cheshire man. He used to say 'Oo wants a strawberry, doesn't Oo.' [Laughs]. You know, the old fashioned way of talking. … And I used to share his porridge in the morning. Father would bring the paper up from the night before, and the following morning, I used to deliver it. Before I went to school, this was. When I was very young. I'd go round with the paper to Mr. Ellam, and he'd be sat, having his porridge. And he'd say, 'Oo wants a bit of porridge, doesn't Oo. Sit 'r' on me knee.' And I'd sit on his knee, and he'd give me another spoon, and we'd both have it out of the same dish [Laughs] (Mrs Edna Younger interview with ASP, August 2003).

Thus, for the residents of the Hagg Cottages, the consumption of food served as a performance of hospitality and social belonging, as much as a performance of prestige or bourgeois aspiration.

Characterising small agricultural settlements as 'complete and integrated' communities, the British social historian John Rule has described the 'intermingling of neighbourhood, friendship and kin links developed over time' as a product of the reciprocal relationships that structured their world (Rule 1986, 157). Importantly, this sense of community emerged from the ability of inhabitants to 'know' each other both *socially* in the present, and *temporally* through the dimension of previous generations. You knew who each other's people were, and you knew where you belonged. Later in interviews, Mrs Edna Younger explained to us:

You felt part of a very big family. That's gone now hasn't it? I mean, if you live in a town, you don't belong to anyone but your own few people, do you? Whereas, you felt belonging to everybody in the parish. You felt safe with everybody (Mrs Edna Younger interview with ASP, July 2003).

However, a sense of community and of social belonging did not create egalitarian social structures. Life within a 'complete and integrated' community meant a life of rigid social hierarchies – a life where everyone else knew your ancestors, and everyone else knew where you belonged.

Consumer Choice in a Working Community

Assemblages traditionally interpreted as archaeological evidence of class aspiration were recovered from the Hagg Cottages. The excavation of the 1747 Georgian-style 'Stanley Cottage', revealed numerous examples of ceramics that appeared to suggest a concern with domestic gentility and bourgeois sensibilities. These artefacts were specifically concentrated in the north-western half of the Area A trench. As part of our post-excavation analysis strategy, we decided to focus more closely on this question of class aspiration. Funding parameters necessitated a sampling strategy for specialist analysis of the cultural materials recovered from stratigraphic deposits within Area A. The northern-most unit of Area A (Unit 1) was selected as a representative sample because this specific trench had exposed the greatest extent of the cottage interior. Additionally, during preliminary processing of the collection, the project ceramic specialist had earmarked this unit as worthy of further detailed identification and analysis (Casella *et al.* 2004).

Table 10.1 demonstrates the results from that secondary analysis of Trench A, Unit 1. Tablewares constituted the largest single identifiable category of ceramics within this representative sample of the ASP Collection. While local coarse earthenwares do appear in small quantities, the sample was characterised by its relative lack of locally produced coarse earthenwares, when compared to other regional sites (Cumberpatch 2004). The two types that formed the bulk of the Area A/Unit 1 ceramic sample were transfer-printed whitewares and porcelain/whitewares. Analysis of ceramic forms indicated an emphasis on cups, saucers, plates and mugs. There were a small number of bowls present, although these items represented tablewares (as opposed to food preparation or kitchenwares). The tablewares recovered from Area A/Unit 1 were further distinguished by a (perhaps unsurprising) absence of high-quality wares, and a concentration of cheap mass-produced items (like whitewares) with a limited range of standard decorative motifs that represented a lower end of wares available to consumers from the mid-19th through early 20th centuries. For example, 'Asiatic Pheasant' and 'Willow Pattern' designs were produced in vast quantities, and were the most common transfer-printed designs that survived the imposition of British copyright laws in 1842. These designs are well represented within the ASP ceramic assemblage. The general trend in ceramic fashion from 1860 to 1880 produced a shift from white dinner services to plates with decorative printed boarders and plain white centres (Coysh and Henrywood 1989, 11). The more traditional designs, including 'Asiatic Pheasant' and 'Willow Pattern', were relegated to the inexpensive end of the market.

In the early 20th century, fashion again shifted to plain white dinner services with silver or gold lustre lines around the rims and bodies (Figure 10.3). Evidence of this stylistic change was apparent within the ASP assemblage from Area A. While similar to the hand-painted decorations on the under-glaze painted creamwares and pearlwares of a previous generation, these wares still represented the lower end of the available ceramic market.

Nonetheless, the relative absence of high-end ceramic wares did not indicate that inhabitants of the Hagg Cottages

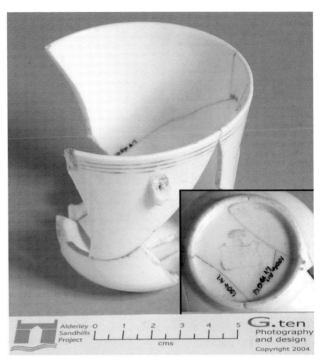

Figure 10.3. ASP Collection, whiteware cup, c.1911–1940. Artefact commissioned by the Co-operative Wholesale Society through the Windsor Pottery, Longton, UK.

were in any sense destitute. They appeared to prioritise alternative modes of consumer activity. Figure 10.3 represents a 'porcelain-type' whiteware cup, marked on the underside of the base with a wheatsheaf symbol and the words 'CWS WINDSOR CHINA' (Cumberpatch 2004). The Co-operative Wholesale Society (established in Greater Manchester in 1863) employed the Windsor Pottery, Longton as a supplier from 1911 (Godden 1991, 170) in order to produce decent quality tablewares for working-class households. The presence of this artefact suggests the residents of Area A either directly participated in, or indirectly purchased from, the Co-operative Wholesale Society movement. While in middle-class households dining had become an increasingly formalised ritual, a performance of 'gentility' that served as a distinctive class marker (Fitts 1999, 49), workers' households apparently communicated their class conscious-ness through the purchase of commodities affiliated with the wider English labour movement. Such an open association with an explicitly working-class political movement would hardly reflect a primary concern with aspirations towards socio-economic mobility.

Like thousands of working people in Northern England, Hagg residents enjoyed day trips and longer breaks at seaside resorts (Benson 1994, 102–103). Examples of these workers' holidays appeared within the ceramic collection as decorative souvenir plates, with one example recovered from each Hagg Cottage. While a small porcelain saucer-sized plate

Table 10.1 Tablewares from Area A, Alderley Sandhills Project.

	Bottle	Bowl	Cup	Cup/bowl	Dish	Dish/saucer	Eggcup	Flat ware	Flowerpot	Hollow ware	Jam jar	Jar	Jug	Large bowl	Lid	Mug	Mug/Jug	Plate	Saucer	Serving dish	Stopper	Teapot	Tureen lid	U/ID	Grand Total
Blue Banded ware										13															13
Brown Bodied ware																						1		2	3
Brown Glazed Coarseware																								11	11
Cane Coloured ware												1												7	8
Colour Glazed ware																						9		36	45
Creamware				2	3												1	1						17	24
Edged ware					1													4							5
Horticultural Vessel									14																14
Late Blackware																								16	10
Lustre Ware																						1			1
Marbled slipware																						1			1
Mocha ware																								3	3
Mottled ware								1				1												1	3
Pearlware																								8	8
Porcelain			17		2	1	1	1		5					2	5		12	8					89	143
Redware type																								2	2
Slip Banded ware																								8	8
Slipware																								2	2
Sponged ware		1																							1
Stoneware	1	1									1	2							1					21	28
Transfer Printed Pearlware																				1					1
Transfer Printed Porcelain								1					1					1						12	15
Transfer Printed Whiteware	1		12					10					1				1	22	1	3				82	133
Unidentified																								3	3
Whiteware		37	9		2			17		11			4	1		14		27	15		1		1	316	455
Whiteware/Porcelain																		1	1						2
Grand Total	2	39	38	2	8	1	1	30	14	29	1	4	6	1	2	19	2	68	26	4	1	12	1	636	947

depicting the Blackpool Tower in polychrome overglaze and black transfer-print was recovered from within the Area B cottage, sherds from two small, matching porcelain vessels depicting an association with the Isle of Man were recovered from Area A trenches (Cumberpatch 2004). Studies of English working-class consumer patterns have noted that the tradition of extending the day trip to a week-long holiday was established in the north-west region a generation before it became commonplace elsewhere in the country (Benson 1994, 84–85).

Class Aspirations or Destined to be the Underclass?

Additionally, a surprising quantity of highly decorative items were recovered, including fragments of three Black Basalt teapots, two royal commemorative vessels, a Wedgewood Jasperware lidded jar, an opaque light-blue glass ornamental 'lustre', and polychrome figurines with both historic and pastoral themes (Table 10.2). The Jasperware jar (missing lid) was the only vessel from the ASP Collection to have been produced by the Wedgewood Factory of neighbouring Stoke-on-Trent, Staffordshire. A matte blue body with moulded white classical designs applied externally, the jar depicts tableaux consisting of groups of two, and three, female figures with small winged cherubs at their feet (Figure 10.4). Although this decorative type of ceramic ware originated in the 18th century, it has been continuously produced to the present day. The ASP specimen was dated to the early 20th century through the addition of a 'MADE IN ENGLAND' stamp in the maker's mark on the underside of the vessel.

Within the English ceramic industry, the best known type of decorative figurines were probably 'Pratt wares', dated to between 1780 and 1840 (Cumberpatch 2004). The figurines recovered from the Hagg Cottages were stylistically linked to this manufacture tradition, particularly in their depiction of archetypical human figures in vaguely 18th or early 19th century pastoral dress. The first example from Area A/Unit 1 consists of three female figures supporting a shallow receptacle with an orange interior. The glazed white earthenware body was moulded in two halves (back and front), and reinforced internally with strips and rods of clay prior to the joining of the two halves. The details of the faces, hair and dress of the figures is emphasised in underglaze paint. This ornament is moulded in a form known as 'flatback', a type of manufacture technique common throughout the 19th century. This popular form allowed the figurine to either be displayed on a shelf or mantelpiece (Hughes 1981), or alternatively attached to a hook on the wall through a small hole in the back of the piece. Such figurines were produced widely by numerous English potteries, thereby preventing attribution to a particular manufacturer.

The example from Area A/Unit 1 depicts two children and the trunk of a tree with the upper part elaborated to form a small dish-like receptacle. It too was produced in a two-piece mould (front and back) in white earthenware. Inexpensive and mass-produced forms, both examples were originally designed as matching pairs, although only one of each was archaeologically recovered.

A third figurine recovered from the assemblage sample represented a creature first identified as a horse (Figure 10.5). However, following closer examination, Chris Cumberpatch,

Figure 10.4. ASP Collection, Jasperware jar, Wedgewood Potteries, Stoke-on-Trent, UK. Scale 1:1.

Table 10.2 Decorative Ceramics from Area A, Alderley Sandhills Project.

Context	Quad	Type	Material	No	Wt	ENV	Form	Decoration
1001	A/1	Figurine	Whiteware	1	61	1	Figurine	Part of a moulded tree, matches the more complete example from 1004 A/1 (Figure 75)
1001	A/2	Figurine	Porcelain	2	8	1	Figurine	Androgynous figure with long hair wearing a bicorn hat
1001	A/3	Figurine	Whiteware	1	9	0	Figurine	Part of the body of the zebra figurine
1004	A/1	Encrusted ware	Whiteware	24	123	2	Vase	Beige body encrusted with fine clay chips and applied flowers
1004	A/1	Figurine (?)	Porcelain	2	2	1	Figurine (?)	Moulded design, not large enough to determine the design
1004	A/1	Highly Decorated ware	Earthenware	47	377	1	U/ID	A coarse white fabric with brightly coloured applied slip relief designs externally
1004	A/1	Porcelain	Porcelain	3	41	1	Ornament	Moulded base with single over-glaze transfers externally
1004	A/1	Red Stoneware	Stoneware	27	219	19	U/ID	Relief moulded classical design and Egyptian style heads
1004	A/1	Whiteware	Whiteware	4	108	1	Figurine	Head of a horse or zebra; black mane and a black striped body
1004	A/1	Whiteware	Whiteware	24	471	1	Figurine	Two figures; girl and a boy with stylised tree stump on oval base
1004	A/1	Whiteware	Whiteware	50	1064	1	Figurine	Figurine; three women in C18th style dress supporting small dish-like receptacle
1004	A/1	Whiteware	Whiteware	7	26	1	Figurine	Parts of a figurine, similar to Ill. 75
1004	A/1	Whiteware type	Whiteware	3	120	1	Vase	Moulded base with gold line on foot
1004	A/1	Whiteware type	Whiteware	8	214	1	Vase	Floral design, overglaze transfer with applied gold lines outlining flowers on pale cane coloured bk'ground
1004	A/1	Whiteware type	Whiteware	22	490	1	Vase	Overglaze painted flowers outlined with raised gold lines and gold lustre handles
1004	A/1	Whiteware type	Whiteware	6	27	4	Vase	Overglaze painted flowers outlined with raised gold lines
1004	A/1	Whiteware type	Whiteware	13	49	9	Vase	Over glaze painted flowers outlined with raised gold lines
1004	A/1	Whiteware type	Whiteware	4	45	1	Vase	Over glaze painted flowers outlined with raised gold lines
1004	A/1	Whiteware type	Whiteware	8	3	8	Vase	Over glaze painted flowers outlined with raised gold lines
1004	A/1	Whiteware type	Whiteware	4	24	1	Vase	Over glaze painted flowers outlined with raised gold lines and moulded flared rim
1004	A/1	Whiteware type	Whiteware	7	42	7	Vase	Moulded gold handle sherds
1004	A/1	Whiteware type	Whiteware	42	322	39	Vase	Overglaze transfer floral design externally
1004	A/1	Whiteware type	Whiteware	2	22	2	Vase	Pinkish finish with gold lines on moulded rim
1004	A/2	Encrusted ware	Porcelain	7	172	1	Figurine	A hand holding an encrusted egg-like object decorated with flowers; wrist also encrusted & has floral wreath
1005	A/1	Figurine	Whiteware	6	20	0	Figurine	Parts of the body and legs of the zebra
1005	A/1	Figurine	Whiteware	1	5	1	Figurine	Part of the body of an unidentified figurine
1035	A/2	Encrusted ware	Porcelain	1	1	1	U/ID	Small fragment of an encrusted ware ornament or vessel
1035	A/2	Figurine	Whiteware	4	16	4	Figurine	Moulded white figurine
1001	A/1	Lidded jar	Jasper Ware	1	13	1	BS	Matte blue body with applied white classical designs externally
1004	A/1	Lidded jar	Jasper Ware	22	145	0	Base	Matte blue body with applied white classical designs externally
1004	A/1	Lidded jar	Jasper Ware	12	117	0	BS	Matte blue body with applied white classical designs externally
1004	A/1	Lidded jar	Jasper Ware	2	60	0	BS	Matte blue body with applied white classical designs externally
		Total		367	4416	112		

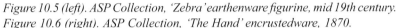

Figure 10.5 (left). ASP Collection, 'Zebra' earthenware figurine, mid 19th century.
Figure 10.6 (right). ASP Collection, 'The Hand' encrustedware, 1870.

project ceramic specialist from ARCUS (University of Sheffield), determined that the black horizontal stripes visible on neck and body fragments identified the animal as a *zebra* – although one portrayed with the mane of a horse (Cumberpatch 2004). His further research suggested this specimen dated to the early to mid-19th century, with depictions of exotic animals gaining wide popularity over those decades as a result of touring fairs, circuses and wild beast shows.

A dramatic example of an 'encrusted-ware' sculpture was recovered additionally from the Area A sample (Figure 10.6). This last type of 19th-century ornamental ceramic was identified by the application of crumbs of dried clay to the slipped surface of the vessel prior to firing, yielding a distinctive 'pebble-dashed' exterior appearance (Cumberpatch 2004). On its base, a diamond registration stamp, was recorded. Reflecting a ceramic registration system used in England between 1842 and 1883, the series of letters and numbers used on the ASP specimen indicated a manufacture date of 1870.

Specialist analysis of glass produced similar results, with the assemblage distinguished by a remarkable number and variety of non-functional display items. Examples included two 20th-century press-moulded vases, three opaque white vases, and a particularly decorative pedestal bowled 'lustre'. A popular Victorian era mantelpiece ornament, the 'lustre' vessel was moulded of opaque blue glass, decorated with a worn band of gilding, and retained seven of eight original cut and faceted glass drops which hung from small holes drilled through the body. Dated to 1860 through 1880 by Hugh Willmott, project glass specialist from ARCUS, the artefact appeared to have undergone careful curation until discard during abandonment of the Cottages after World War II (Willmott 2004).

Decorative household ornaments, and figurines in particular, have been linked to the expression of 'good taste', with their presence in domestic assemblages serving 'to extend gentility from the table to other aspects of the public arena' (Brighton 2001, 24). Extending this theoretical approach, the highly decorative items recovered from the Area A household would be typically read as material examples of class aspiration – with their garish or flashy appearance revealing an 'unsophisticated', or somehow failed, attempt at bourgeois sensibilities. In other words, they would be interpreted as a gallery of simple 'poor' taste. However, evidence from oral history sources, collected during the 2003 field season, indicated a far more complicated socio-economic dynamic operated within the hierarchical world of Alderley Edge.

When these curious decorative artefacts were shown to our oral history participants, they invariably linked the items to a specific resident of the Hagg Cottages – Mrs Lena Perrin, the final occupant of the northern half of the 1747 Stanley Cottage. Through the oral history stories, Mrs Perrin emerged as a formidable character within the community. A member of the local Cheshire clan of Barbers, she was the great-aunt of former residents Molly and Roy Barber. Mrs Perrin lived in the northern half of their internally subdivided Stanley Cottage, first with her husband Mr Perrin (who delivered papers, and sold half-candles for a penny to tourists exploring the disused Alderley mines) and later alone as a childless widow (Mrs Molly Pitcher interview with ASP, August 2003).

Our oral history participants generally remembered her as 'a bit frightening'. Mrs Edna Younger and Mrs Molly Pitcher both described her 'big flashing eyes' and her dramatic emotional outbursts (Figure 10.7). All the former

Figure 10.7 Residents on the Sandhills, c.1930. From right: Mrs Lena Perrin, Mr Perrin, visiting Barber cousins. Hagg Cottages visible in background. Photo courtesy of E. Younger.

residents also commented on Mrs Perrin's love of the costume jewellery she wore to accompany her Edwardian era dress. While this might appear a direct example of bourgeois aspirations, a further ethnographic interview revealed the hierarchical relations of class that rigidly structured the social landscape of Alderley Edge.

During excavations the archaeological team was visited by the Parkinson sisters, who agreed to be interviewed and filmed during their site tour. Pamela and Mary Parkinson explained that they had lived down Whitebarn Road during the 1930s, and had played with Molly, Roy and Edna as children. When we showed them examples of the decorative ceramics from Area A, they also immediately linked the objects to Mrs Lena Perrin. Pamela repeatedly used the word 'tranklements' to refer to Mrs Perrin's ceramic ornaments, which we misunderstood as 'tranquil-ments' – objects that helped her feel tranquil (Misses P. and M. Parkinson interview with ASP, August 2003).

The reference was passed on to Tony Willmott, the English Heritage Project Officer for the Alderley Sandhills Project, who discovered the true etymology of Pamela Parkinson's term the following week. While he was eating a pub lunch he suddenly realised the chutney accompaniment was embossed with the word 'tranklement'. We realised that Miss Pamela Parkinson had not been conjuring a nostalgic memory of Mrs Perrin's gentile tranquillity. She had referred to Mrs Perrin's ornaments as a food condiment – with subtle overtones of 'mutton dressed as lamb'. In essence, she had subtly identified Mrs Perrin as 'poor white aspirational trash'. It was only then that we realised the implications of what

had been casually described as 'living down Whitebarn Road'. The Parkinson Sisters were daughters of the wealthy families who lived in the villas. They had gone up to the Sandhills to play with their servants' children who lived at the Hagg.

Conclusions

We offer three reflections on this ethno-archaeological data to summarise the central points of this chapter. Firstly, a community scale of social life was centrally important to the working-class residents of the Alderley Sandhills site. A sense of 'social belonging' operated on a much wider scale than that of the 'nuclear family'. As a result, domestic practices – including food production, distribution and consumption – served as performances of community solidarity as much as performances of prestige or gentility (Beaudry *et al.* 1991). Secondly, such expressions of community life did not negate the existence of individual expressions of class aspiration, as was manifest in the fine and decorative ceramics recovered during excavations. A yearning for elevated social standing and improved living conditions infused the everyday lives of working people who occupied the Hagg Cottages. However, as a final point, rather than a straightforward adoption of the 'etiquette and equipage of upward socio-economic standing' (Paynter 2001), residents of the Hagg understood that mobility would prove ultimately elusive. As recent studies have suggested, working-class households may have held no desire to emulate middle-class forms of dining and decorative etiquette (Fitts 1999, 49). In other words, as the British sociologist Annette Kuhn recently noted, class inequalities reside deep within people's fundamental subjectivities:

Class is not just about the way you talk, or dress, or furnish your home; it is not just about the job you do or how much money you make doing it; nor is it merely about whether or not you went to university, nor which university you went to. Class is something beneath your clothes, under your skin, in your psyche, at the very core of your being (Kuhn, 1995, 98).

All residents of this 'complete and integrated' community knew their relative status, and could (and did) perform that hierarchy to the archaeologists who were initially misreading these signs. As Roy Barber patiently explained during the last interview, 'it was always, *always*, them and us. You always knew where you stood' (Mr Roy Barber, interview with ASP, September 2003).

Acknowledgements

This project was sponsored by English Heritage through the Aggregates Levy Sustainability Fund, and directed in partnership with Professor John Prag, Keeper of Archaeology at the Manchester Museum. We enjoyed the generous support of Paul and Jutta Sorensen, landowners of the Sandhills site. Analysis of the ASP Collection was undertaken by ARCUS at the University of Sheffield, UK. Thanks are due to Jim Symonds, Chris Cumberpatch, Hugh Willmott, and Joan Unwin for this valuable work. We would like to thank all participants in the 2003 field season. Meg and Wendy of the Wizard Tea Rooms provided wizard teacakes to a hungry crew. Photographs of the ASP Collection were done by Derek Truillo, G.10 Photography and Design Unit, Manchester University. Sarah Croucher, Sarah Whitehead, Laura Brenton, Zoe Sutherland, Sophie Pullar, and Sam Bolton assisted with processing the collection during field and laboratory stages of research. Special thanks are due to Mrs Edna Younger, Mrs Molly Pitcher, and Mr Roy Barber for sharing their memories and photos of life at The Hagg.

References

Beaudry, M. C., Cook, L. J. and Mrozowski, S. A. (1991) Artifacts and active voices: material culture as social discourse, in McGuire, R. and Paynter, R. (eds) *The Archaeology of Inequality*, Oxford, Blackwell, 150–191.

Benson, J. (1994) *The Rise of Consumer Society in Britain 1880–1980*, Longman.

Brighton, S. (2001) Prices that suit the times: shopping for ceramics at the Five Points. *Historical Archaeology* 35:3, 16–30.

Casella, E. C., Griffin, D. and Prag, A. N. J. W. (eds) (2004) The Alderley Sandhills Project: A Final Report, unpublished report for English Heritage and the National Trust, London.

Clark, K. (1999) The workshop of the world: the Industrial Revolution, in Hunter, J. and Ralston, I. (eds) *The Archaeology of Britain*, London, Routledge, 280–296.

Coysh and Henrywood (1989) *The Dictionary of Blue and White Printed Pottery 1780–1880*, Volume 2, Antique Collectors Club.

Cumberpatch, C. (2004) Pottery report, in Casella, E. C., Griffin, D. and Prag, A. N. J. W. (eds) The Alderley Sandhills Project: A Final Report, unpublished report for English Heritage and the National Trust, London.

Delle, J. (1998) *An Archaeology of Social Space*, Plenum, New York.

Ferguson, L. (1992) *Uncommon Ground: Archaeology and Colonial African-America*, Washington, DC, Smithsonian Institution Press.

Fitts, R. (1999) The archaeology of middle-class domesticity and gentility in Victorian Brooklyn. *Historical Archaeology* 33:1, 39–62.

Godden, G. (1991) *Encyclopaedia of British Pottery and Porcelain Marks*, Barrie and Jenkins.

Horton, M. (2003) Commentary. Presentation within the symposium 'What is all the CHAT about?' TAG, Lampeter, UK, December 2003.

Hughes, T. (1981) *Pottery and Porcelain Figures*, Country Life Books.

Johnson, M. (1996) *An Archaeology of Capitalism*, Oxford, Blackwell.

Kuhn, A. (1995) *Family Secrets: Acts of Memory and Imagination*, London, Verso.

Leone, M. (1999), Setting some terms for historical archaeologies of capitalism, in Leone, M. and Potter, Jr., P. (eds) *Historical Archaeologies of Capitalism*, New York, Kluwer Academic/Plenum, 3–20.

Lightfoot, K. (1995) Culture contact studies: redefining the relationship between prehistoric and historical archaeology. *American Antiquity* 60, 199–217.

McGuire, R. (1991) Building power in the cultural landscape of Broome County, New York 1880–1940, in McGuire, R. and Paynter, R. (eds) *The Archaeology of Inequality*, Oxford, Blackwell, 102–124.

Moreland, J. (2001) *Archaeology and Text*, London, Duckworth.

Orser, Jr., C. E. (1996) *A Historical Archaeology of the Modern World*, New York, Plenum.

Paynter, R. (2001) The cult of whiteness in western New England, in Orser, Jr., C. E. (ed.) *Race and the Archaeology of Identity*, Salt Lake City, University of Utah Press, 125–42.

Rule, J. (1986) *The Labouring Classes in Early Industrial England 1750–1850*, Harlow, Longman.

Shackel, P. A. (1996) *Culture Change and the New Technology: An Archaeology of the Early American Industrial Era*, New York, Plenum Press.

Symonds, J. (2005) Experiencing industry: beyond machines and the history of technology, in Casella, E. C. and Symonds, J. (eds) *Industrial Archaeology: Future Directions*, New York, Springer.

Thompson, E. P. (1966) *The Making of the English Working Class*, Vintage Books, New York.

Willmott, H. (2004) Glass report, in Casella, E. C., Griffin, D. and Prag, A. N. J. W. (eds) The Alderley Sandhills Project: A Final Report, unpublished report for English Heritage and the National Trust, London.

11

The Material Manifestations of 19th Century Irish America

Stephen A. Brighton

Introduction

The research question driving this study involves how material evidence documents the socio-cultural transition from mistrusted immigrant group to Irish-Americans. Timothy Meagher (1986, 2001), an historian of late 19th century Irish-America, argues that by the 1880s an Irish-American identity emerged across America. This subtle shift in identities was not an act of assimilation, as such a term cannot adequately account for the experiences of the Irish in America. Like other diasporic groups who have maintained many traditional cultural attributes, the Irish have always retained some of their social behaviors and institutions. They did not arrive as blank slates quickly adopting new social values and material culture; rather they came to this country with entrenched social dispositions communicated through material signs (Brighton 2005). Understanding the types of material culture used in Ireland to express the identities of the rural poor classes (e.g. those making up Famine-period emigration) provides a basic comparable foundation to identifying the diachronic material transformations in America.

The author recognizes that there are many factions within any ethnic or class group. This multiplicity creates tensions, as they negotiate conflicting ideologies. It is not the intention here to represent the Irish immigrant and Irish-American communities as 'whole cultures' static and unchanging through time and space, but rather to study two localized contexts in order to identify and give meaning to changes in the material culture over time. Archaeology can be at times a limited discipline in that conclusions can only be made from existing evidence. At this moment there are only a handful of sites in America relating to Irish immigrants and Irish-Americans. The sites used in this chapter were chosen because of their close proximity to each other, and the fact that each assemblage covers very important periods in Irish and Irish-American history. Therefore, the inter-pretations and conclusion offered here do not represent the

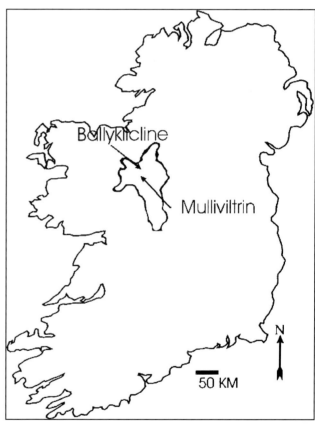

Figure 11.1. Map of Ireland showing the location of County Roscommon (highlighted) and the two excavation sites.

end of the material study of Irish and Irish-American identities but rather the beginning, as it is arguably one of the first attempts to bring a transnational or transatlantic approach to the material and historical evidence of 19th century Irish and Irish-American identity.

The importance of this study is the transnational approach. I detail material continuities and change over time and space through examination of tea- and tableware ceramic vessels

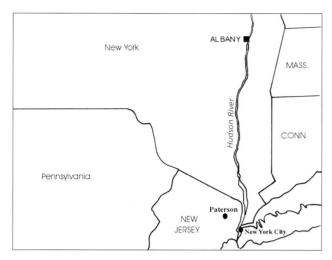

Figure 11.2. Map of New York and New Jersey showing the locations of Paterson and New York City.

recovered from archaeological sites in Ireland and America in order to interpret cultural and behavioral shifts from Irish to Irish-American identities. To further support and emphasize interpretations glass tableware vessels, as well as faunal remains are used. A detailed inventory of the data is not presented here as it has been discussed at length in each of the site-specific technical reports. For the purposes of this chapter, the Irish data is from the excavation of two stone cabins in County Roscommon, Ireland (Figure 11.1). The cabins were occupied by the Nary family in the townland of Ballykilcline (1820–1848). In America the sites include two privy deposits associated with Irish immigrant tenements at the Five Points, Manhattan (*c*.1850–1870), and privy deposits from two single-family houses owned by Irish and Irish-American families in the Dublin section of Paterson, New Jersey (*c*.1880–1910) (Figure 11.2).

Rural Ireland, Eviction and Emigration: Ballykilcline, County Roscommon

The project area within the townland of Ballykilcline is located in the north-east corner of County Roscommon. The county itself is the most eastern border of the province of Connacht. Traditional Irish land divisions consisted of four types, the first and largest being the *baile* (Scally 1995, 3). The remaining and lesser divisions include a quarter, a cartron, and a gnive. The townland was located in the parish of Kilglass in the barony of Ballintober North consisting of 620 statute acres or in Irish measurement 371 acres, 2 roods, and 30 perches. The exact population total varied over the decades prior to the Famine, but its maximum was 526 individuals; prior to the clearances the lowest was 470. On average Ballykilcline included 500 individuals forming 100 families (Orser 1998, 1–2; Scally 1995, 4).

The townland's landscape was filled with third and fourth-tier housing that greatly outnumbered the larger and more durable dwellings. The numbered tiers refer to the categories created in 1841. The four tiers were based on quality and durability, such as building materials (e.g. stone vs. mud), the number of rooms, and other architectural elements including roofing material, windows, and gable-end hearths, which in turn affected the values (social and economic) placed on dwellings (Aalen *et al.* 1997; Donnelly 2001; Gailey 1984; Mokyr and Ó Gráda 1984).

Based on the information drawn from 1836 Ordnance map of the townland of Ballykilcline, the property and the two cabins located on the land that are the focus of this study belonged to the Nary family. The map shows that the neighboring cabins belonged to Mark Nary and his sons, James, Luke, and Edward. The early history of the Narys is unknown except that they settled at Ballykilcline by 1820 (Scally 1995, 80). The Brassington and Gale map shows the location of the Nary property. The two cabins in the quarters of Kiltullyvary and Bungariff are listed as belonging to Mark Nary and his sons, James, Luke, and Edward (Hull and Brighton 2002,1). The Nary family lived in Ballykilcline until they were forcibly evicted sometime between September of 1847 and April of 1848. The rents of all tenants had been in arrears since 1834 (Scally 1995, 105–129).

In total, the Nary family unit had a holding size approximately 44 acres. It was divided over six fields and six Nary members. Individually, each family member's holdings averaged seven acres. It is unclear at this time whether the Nary family represents a group of middling or small farmers. Taken as a whole the land rented by the Nary family would place them in the social class of middling farmer. They are documented as paying rent directly to the crown and not to a strong farmer or grazier. This is problematic because even middling farmers were thought to pay rent to a landowner. Furthermore, there are no known records stating that the Nary family members hired laborers. It is possible that the work was done through the large family network, and they had no apparent need for outside employment. The question that needs to be asked is 'does it matter?' Based on the historical evidence of economic downturns experienced by the middling farmer after 1815, this class did not fare much better than small farmers, therefore it is really of no consequence here which label is put to them since it is evident that the Nary family, represented by the two cabin sites, was a family living just above the subsistence level. Based on individual holdings, the Narys are presented here as small farmers.

Land is central to any study of pre-Famine rural Ireland. It dictated social position based on a complex web of socio-economic relations with a stratified social structure centered on access to and control of land (Beames 1978; Guinnane 1997; Quinlan 1998). Members of the landowning class were at the top of the socio-economic structure and

Figure 11.3. Brassington and Gale 1836 Survey Map of the holdings at Ballykilcline. The Nary holdings are in the lower left corner.

controlled most of the rural Irish landscape. Their large estates were subdivided and leased to the farming class, who consisted of commercial farmers and graziers earning a profit from their produce. In turn, members of this class subdivided sections of their holdings and leased them to the majority of the population known as the rural poor (Fitzpatrick 1980, 68). The large numbers of people making up the rural poor classes held the least amount of land.

Small farmers were part of the rural poor (Clark 1982; Johnson 1990, 264; Langan-Egan 1999, 53; Marx and Engels 1972, 62; Quinlan 1998, 253; Shanin 1987). This class practiced full-time subsistence-based agriculture. Farming typically consisted of two crops. The first was the potato, the staple of the family's diet. The second crop was corn, which was sold at market. The proceeds would be used to meet the annual rent. Although small farmers were part of the rural poor, they differed from cottiers and landless laborers in two distinctive ways. First is the amount of land leased. On average, small farmer holdings ranged from 5 to 20 acres, and as a direct result they were able to subsist without needing to sell their labor to the farming classes (Miller 1985, 50–51).

The total amount of land leased by the Nary family represents the third largest tenant holdings in Ballykilcline. The largest belonged to the McDermott family, who held 49.75 acres (four holders), and the Donnellan family, with 48.30 (two holders) (Orser 2004, 219). This is in direct contrast to the cottiers and laborers in the townland like the Coyle family with 4.89 acres (two holders), the Toolan family with 1.22 acres (one holder), the Pellegren and Ginty families each with 0.50 acres (one holder), and the smallest was the Mahon family with only 0.41 acres (one holder) (Orser 2004, 219).

Ballykilcline ceased to exist after the mass clearances sometime between 1847 and 1848. Precipitating the large-scale evictions was a decade-long rent strike and subsequent assassination of the then landowner Denis Mahon (Coleman 1999, 46). Mahon was shot and killed in November of 1847 by a group of tenants from his estate. His murder was a direct result of the eviction scheme and 'assisted emigration'. The process of ridding his land of what he considered the redundant population consisted of removing the tenants in 'batches' beginning in the spring of 1847. The eviction was recorded as swift and violent. Cabins were demolished and completely leveled under the armed protection of the British cavalry and infantry and a large contingent of police. In Kilglass parish alone, 150 families comprising approximately 800 to 900 people were cleared from the land (Coleman 1999, 51–52). The Nary family, like many other Ballykilcline families, emigrated to America.

From 1998 to 2002 archaeological surveys located and excavated these cabins and recovered 9,000 artifacts relating to the daily lives of this farming family. The conditions were ideal for archaeological investigations because the site had been undisturbed since the evictions of the 19th century (Orser 1998, 2). The field investigations were conducted as part of Orser's annual field school. The excavations exposed architectural debris and other structural remains such as interior and exterior drains, pathways, cobble and hard-packed floor surfaces. The cabins were third-tier housing.

The fact that the Brassington and Gale map includes them reflects the structures' durable nature, and the archaeological remains confirm it (Figure 11.3). Subsurface wall remnants of both cabins consisted of mortared fieldstones. The eviction process of burning the roof and toppling the walls is clearly visible at Ballykilcline. A stone scatter three courses deep just north of the north cabin's packed stone foundation reflects the wall collapse from the outside (Hull and Brighton 2002, 11; Orser and Hull 2001, 12).

Coming to America: Irish and Irish-American Communities, 1850–1910

Five Points, Manhattan, 1850–c.1870

The Five Points emerged as a distinct neighborhood within New York City's Sixth Ward during the first decade of the 19th century (Figure 11.4). It earned its name from the intersection of Cross (later Park), Orange (later Baxter), and Anthony (later Worth) Streets. As a neighborhood it offered crowded living conditions to the city's poorest, immigrant population. From 1840 to 1880 newly or recently arrived Irish made up most of that population. In 1991, 22 features associated with 14 lots were investigated as part of a larger federally mandated project conducted by John Milner Associates (for a full account of the excavation and artifact database see Yamin 2000). The excavations focused on shaft features, such as privies, cesspools, wells, and cisterns, located in the rear lots of the tenement buildings. The data recovered from two privies (designated Features O and J), dating from 1850 to 1870, belonging to tenements housing all Irish-born families at 472 and 474 Pearl Street, are used for this study.

The tenement at 472 Pearl Street was a large five-storey brick tenement constructed in 1850 by then Irish-American landlord Peter McLoughlin (Yamin 2000, 98). In 1864 he sold the property to William Clinton. Sometime after Clinton's purchase (c.1870s), he built a second tenement building in the rear lot. The new building reduced the open space in the courtyard to a mere 20 by 50 feet (Yamin 2000, 98).

The number of tenants ranged from 58 to 107 people between 1850 and 1870 (NYC State Census 1855, 1865; US Bureau of the Census 1850–1870). At this time all of the tenement dwellers were Irish with the exception of German families; first the Finck family, a German-born husband and wife, and the Lutz family replacing them in the 1860s. The first tenants were recently arrived immigrants. Families like the Currys, Callahans, Cronins, and McLoughlins had been in America for no more than five years. Many, for example, the Sears, Barry, Papard, Killoran families, had been in American less than three years. On average the Irish tenants at 472 Pearl Street had three children.

Living with most of the families were at least two boarders, making seven people the average number who lived in the small apartments. The Garvey family was the exception. They had five boarders totaling ten people. In the Garvey case, it seems that the boarders were relations. Since the census does not provide any information regarding to the date of entry into the country, the estimated time of residence for each family is determined by each child's age and place of birth. By 1870 the number of households increased to 18 and totaled 96 individuals. Fifteen households represented families new to the tenement, although they were not new to America. According to the census those families had been in the country more than ten years.

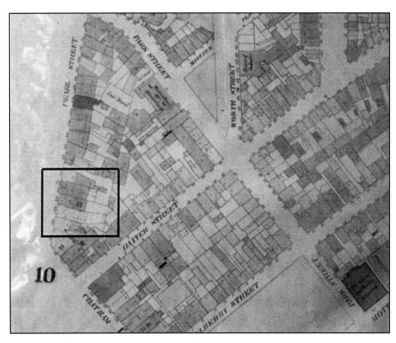

Figure 11.4. Perris Insurance Map of the Five Points in 1857. The tenements along Park Street (top) and Pearl Street (left) were inhabited mostly by Irish families and boarders. The two tenements in the center of the box are used for this study.

At 474 Pearl Street was a two-story wood-framed structure as old as the Five Points itself, having been constructed as early as 1790. A store was always present on the first floor. Two grocers rented the front of the building between 1814 and 1840. After 1840, the store was converted into a porterhouse and oyster saloon (Yamin 2000, 109, 114). Ownership of the saloon changed hands between 1850 until its closure in 1866. Owners included Irishmen James Doyle (1850–1857), John Sullivan (1865–1866), and John Lysaight (1866–1873). Sometime after 1870 a brick tenement was constructed in the rear of the lot. James Doyle was listed as a liquor dealer and ran a saloon on the first floor (Yamin 2000, 114). In comparison to the large tenement next door there were far fewer families living at this address. The tenement houses on average about 23 people (NYC State Census 1855, 1865; US Bureau of the Census 1850–1870). In 1850 none of the tenants had been living in America for more than five years. All of the household members were Irish-born and had at least two boarders.

Dublin Section, Paterson, New Jersey, c.1888–1910

The industrial city of Paterson, New Jersey, is located 19 miles (30.4 km) west of New York City in the northeastern corner of New Jersey (Figure 11.5). The original street grid of Dublin was planned around the existing raceways and mill sites in the 1820s. The area became known as Dublin after the influx of Irish laborers, who, upon completion of the Morris Canal in 1830, settled here to work in the surrounding mills and factories (Yamin 1999, 10). Dublin's Irish population grew with the arrival of individuals and

families forced to leave Ireland during the Famine. By the end of the 1850s, Dublin expanded southward. While the northern section developed into a multi-ethnic area that included Irish, first-generation Irish-American, English, and Scots, the southern section remained predominantly Irish or first-generation Irish-American until 1910 (De Cunzo 1983, 83).

Housing in Paterson was much different than in Five Points. The Dublin section was not home to large brick tenements. Although there were a few five-story brick tenements constructed to meet the housing need in 1860, for the most part housing consisted of wood-framed row houses in the style of Greek Revival and averaging two and one-half stories (Cotz *et al*. 1980). Towards the end of the 19th century many of these wood-framed buildings were refitted to accommodate the increasing population. The rear courtyards consisted of open space, gardens, and of course privy vaults.

The first excavations in Paterson began in 1973. The initial work focused on the industrial development of Paterson (Cotz *et al*. 1980). The excavations included the study of the raceways constructed to harness the waterpower of the Great Falls, various industrial buildings and complexes, and factory and mill workers' housing. The second excavations were conducted in 1978 and 1979. Archaeological testing included various important industries in Paterson and mill operatives' houses (Ingle 1982, 239). Finally, in 1989, John Milner Associates investigated 14 house lots comprising two blocks along Oliver Street in the southern section of Dublin. Twenty-two privies were excavated in the back lots associated with

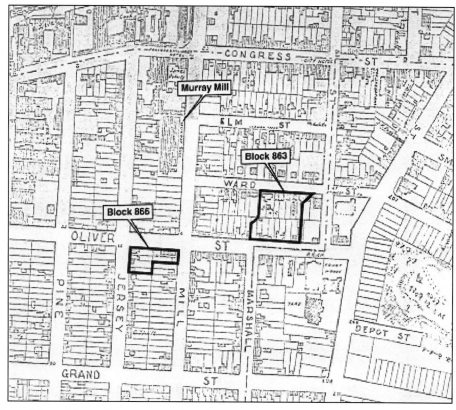

Figure 11.5. Beran Map of the southern section of Dublin, 1860. Marked in the figure are the project areas under study.

Irish and Irish-American workers' housing (Yamin 1999, 99). Artifacts recovered from two privies (designated Feature 10 at 46 Oliver Street and Feature 63 at 32 Ward Street) during the 1989 excavations are used here. The privies are associated with the Irish-born Mackel family and the first-generation Irish-American McGill family.

In 1895, Thomas and Ann McGill purchased the lot and house at 46 Oliver Street. Thomas McGill, American-born, was the son of Daniel McGill, Irish-born, who owned 84[92] and 86[94] Mill Street. He operated a porterhouse there beginning in 1861. Both Thomas and Mary Ann's parents were born in Ireland. Like the Mackel family, their children remained in school well past the working age. The house was a two-story, wood-framed rowhouse, with a raised basement. The structure was converted from a multiple family dwelling into a single-family residence by the 20th century. The time coincides with the census data as the McGills ceased to have tenants at this address by 1900. The McGill family continued to live at this address until it was sold to an Italian family in 1911.

The house at 32 Ward Street was a wood-framed two-and-a-half story structure. In 1866 James Mackel purchased the property. Prior to moving his family to this address he refitted it to allow for more occupancy space. James Mackel, his wife Sarah, two daughters, and son were born in Ireland. According to the 1870 Federal Census, the Mackels had been in America

for less than a year when he purchased the property. James Mackel was a semi-skilled machinist in one of the nearby mills. Although James Mackel was listed in the 1880 Federal Census, he died sometime between then and 1888. According to the 1888–1889 city directories, Sarah Mackel was listed as widow. By 1895, Sarah moved away, but remained the owner of the property until it was sold in 1909.

The Materialization of Social Identities: Negotiating Continuities and Change

Material culture reflects broader social behaviors and value judgments. Comparing the patterns of continuities and changes in decorative types and complexities in the ceramics and glass assemblages with the Irish data marks the starting point towards illustrating the physical manifestation of an Irish-American identity and consumer culture. Continuities in the data show that newly arrived Irish obtained familiar forms similar to those owned by the rural poor classes in Ireland, but more importantly differences over time reveal new behaviors and desires resembling an American, non-Irish, consumer culture (Brighton 2005).

Ireland

In Ireland, there is a distinct pattern between ceramic functional categories and decorative types. With the exception of the transfer-printed 'Willow' pattern tableware and the *Lucano* serving piece, in the Nary assemblages all of the transfer-printed vessels are teacups. At this time in 19th-century Ireland transfer printing would have been the most costly decoration on refined earthenware (Brighton and Levon-White 2006).

Based on the archaeological assemblages in Ireland it is evident that tea was consumed by the rural poor classes beginning as early as the first decade of the 19th century. Economic historians, however, consider tea to be a luxury item with limited consumption at that time, if it at all (Mokyr and Ó Gráda 1988, 217). Nevertheless, the teacups and saucers in each assemblage indicate that the rural classes were drinking tea. Its importance is reflected by the emphasis on the vessels' contemporary decorative styles. Jane Gray (1993, 251) argues that all classes of the rural poor were drinking tea by the first decade of the 19th century. Drinking tea was recognized by the tenant farmers and laborers as a luxury and leisure activity, and because of its social context became a cultural symbol of a collective consciousness (Gray 1993; Harlow 1997; McGowan 2001). The importance of tea-drinking remains an important part of social activities in many areas of rural Ireland and has been noted by folklorists and anthropologists (Arensberg 1988; Arensberg and Kimball 1940).

The cabin assemblages range in date between 1820 to the end of the 1830s. It can be said with some degree of certainty that both Nary families did have two sets of dishes, one for everyday use and a smaller one for display on shelves or atop a chest of drawers (Brighton and Levon-White 2006). The pattern contradicts the historical context of Ireland at the time consisting of rent strikes, violent evictions, poverty, and famine. Nevertheless, research on 19th century rural communities reveals that refined earthenware was a feature in most tenant farming cabins, not only in Ireland, but on the far-off islands in Scotland (Grant 1961; Thorton 1978).

James Symonds (2000) has identified 19th-century refined earthenware (both Scottish and Staffordshire) from poor tenant sites on the marginal island of South Uist in the Outer Hebrides (a chain of islands northwest of Highland Scotland). Conditions of poverty, famine, and ultimately eviction on South Uist are similar to the conditions in rural Ireland during the first half of the 19th century, and it was not uncommon, in fact it was a point of pride, for poor tenants living in small thatched cabins similar to those in Ireland, to own dressers with three or four shelves for displaying plates, bowls, and teacups.

The Nary's ownership of refined earthenware illuminates and to an extent challenges the validity of non-Irish travelers forming much of the descriptive record of the living conditions for much of Ireland's rural poor. For example, Arthur Young (1780) in his travels wrote

the cottages of the Irish, which are called cabins, are the most miserable looking hovels that can well be conceived. The furniture of the cabins is as bad as the architecture; in very many, consisting only of a spot for boiling their potatoes, earthenware, a bit of a table, and 1 or 2 broken stools; beds are not found universally, the family lying on straw, equally partook of by the cows, calves, and pigs. I very generally found that these acquisitions were all made within the last 10 years...I think the bad cabins and furniture are the greatest instances of Irish poverty.

Young's remarks are revealing. First, he somewhat begrudgingly acknowledges the presence of material culture in many of the cabins visited, even though the condition of the items are not to his level of satisfaction and comfort. Second, Young's dating of the material culture is close to accurate. The ceramic vessels in both cabin assemblages were at least ten years old at the time of the Narys' eviction in 1847 – with some exceptions, most of the vessels date to the 1820s. Young viewed the lack of contemporary material culture as a sign of Irish poverty, which is indicated and reflected by the piecemeal purchasing patterns of each of the three assemblages. Furthermore, the fact that the most recent ceramic vessels are from the 1830s is also indicative of the turbulent early years of the 1840s and ultimately the clearances and forced emigration to American between 1847 and 1848.

Comparing the Material Culture from Ballykilcline and the Five Points

Scholars have argued that the driving force of consumer patterns in America was the middle classes (Praetzellis *et al.* 1988, 192–193). Therefore any interpretation of the archaeological manifestations of identity and consumption, Irish immigrants and Irish-Americans must be compared with the larger structure of American consumer culture. In the 19th century, American consumerism was believed to communicate distinctive positions in society. This notion was drawn from the emerging consumer habits of the middle-classes. The new consumer culture of the middle-classes was the result of changing attitudes in American Protestantism after the Second Great Awakening (1800–1830). Religious ideology changed from the predetermined salvation to the belief that morality and piety was the responsibility of each individual. The outward expression of this was through the necessary material culture (Green 1983; Kasson 1990; McLoughlin 1978; Rosenberg 1971). In contrast, those not who did not possess the outward material signs of Christian piety were judged immoral, thus un-American (Bushman 1993; Clark 1988; Grier 1988; Ryan 1981). Those considered on the lowest rung of American society established a consumer culture in reaction to the appropriate middle-class Protestant privileges in order to gain a certain level of respectability (Mullins 1999, 3, 26).

Archaeological evidence of the middle-classes dating throughout the last half of the 19th century demonstrates the meaning and importance of material culture symbolizing the ideologies of respectability and morality. Matching ceramic tea, tableware, and serving forms in the prescribed numbers, as well as the incorporation of religious piety and naturalism galvanized a consumer demand in forms such as Christian-inspired pattern names and forms (Fitts 1999, 2000; Fitts and Yamin 1996; Praetzellis and Praetzellis 1992; Praetzellis *et al.* 1988; Wall 1994, 2001). The patterns of change in the assemblages are assessed by comparing the data to contemporary American-born, non-Irish households in Manhattan and Paterson. In order to identify cultural change, it is important to understand and interpret the basis of continuities in the Irish immigrant community. From here it is possible to reveal the expression of new behaviors, consumer culture, and desires of respectability and civic citizenship and the transformation of Irish identity in America (Brighton 2001, 2005).

Continuities exist between Irish immigrant data in Manhattan and the assemblages in Ireland. Figure 6 shows similarities in the ratio of teaware to tableware; teaware is consistently higher than the proportion of tableware vessels. Furthermore, continuities occur in transfer-printed scenic patterns, or less expensive polychrome floral patterns, on teaware, and inexpensive tableware either in blue shell-edged or 'Willow' pattern. In the Irish and Irish-American communities the level of vessel complexity increased as the 19th century progressed (Brighton 2005). In comparison to the traditional assemblage from Ireland, it appears that serving pieces were a part of the Nary household (Brighton and Levon-White 2006, 126, 132–134). In America, serving pieces do not factor to a large degree in the material culture of recently arrived Irish immigrants, most of whom would have been landless tenants in Ireland.

The continuities with Ireland become more prevalent when the Irish immigrant data are compared to a contemporary American-born working-class assemblage from the Greenwich Mews in Manhattan (Geismar 1989) (Figure 11.7). The Greenwich Mews site housed two families each owning at least three serving vessels. In comparison, the percentage of serving pieces at the Five Points is low considering the number of households living in the tenement. The serving platters and various sized dishes in the data average roughly one vessel per household at 472 Pearl Street between 1850 and 1860, and approximately one serving vessel for every other household between 1860 and 1870, and one serving vessel per family at 474 Pearl Street.

This pattern can be explained in two ways. In one instance serving vessels cost much more than other vessel types, and owning such vessels might have been cost-prohibitive to the recently arrived Irish households (Brighton 2001). Families at the Five Points were either semi-skilled or unskilled, and in the case of 472 Pearl Street all of the households by the 1860s consisted of unskilled laborers. Along with cost, the low percentage of vessel complexity

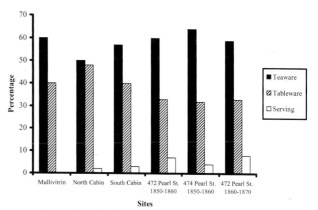

Figure 11.6. The distribution of ceramic functional categories between the sites in Ireland and the Five Points.

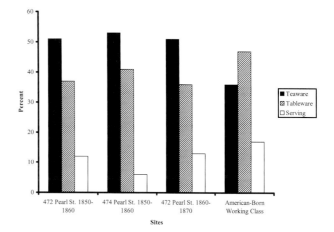

Figure 11.7. The distribution of ceramic functional categories between the Five Points assemblages and a contemporary American-born working class household from the Greenwich Mews, Manhattan.

at the Five Points might reflect a lack of experience owning and using serving pieces as each Nary assemblage had only a platter and tureen. Referring back to the daily diet of the rural poor in Ireland it is not surprising that there was no great demand to acquire these forms, but with the availability of different foods, especially meat, in Manhattan, there was a developing need to acquire these new ceramic forms.

The increase in vessel complexity over time is directly correlated with the length of time in America. An emergence of social dining activities instead of social tea-drinking in the 1860s upper deposit at 472 Pearl Street represents the emergence of a new pattern of learned behaviors and practices of a larger group transformation (Brighton 2005). Unlike the ceramics and glass from the privy's lower deposit associated with families such as the Kellys, Callaghans, Loftuses, Barrys, Morrises, and Flynns, who had been recent arrivals to America, the tableware and serving forms from the upper deposit belonged to Irish families that had lived in the country for well over ten years. The overall length of residence suggests that change in vessel complexity was a transgenerational process as a result of negotiation with external social pressures of assimilation (Mintz 1996, 112). In order to gain social and economic opportunities after being considered the 'foreign other' for nearly 30 years, the Irish were forced to reshape behaviors and world view to acceptance and citizenship in the eyes of American society.

The Five Points and Dublin section, Paterson, New Jersey

Vessel complexity increases further by the 1890s, and continuities in ceramic form and function between Ireland and the Irish in America cease to exist. At first glance, Figure 11.8 seems somewhat deceptive because the serving category in Paterson is only slightly higher than at the Five Points. Again, as with the comparison with the American-born assemblage, each Paterson assemblage represents a single family and contains at least three serving vessels per household. This similarity is seen in the American household in New York, also a contemporary non-Irish American-born working class household from the north end of the Dublin Section (Figure 11.9). The increase in serving pieces represents a change in the consumer culture and dining

habits – reflecting what was considered a respectable American form/way of eating (Brighton 2005).

Gradual increases in glass tableware over time provide further evidence of continuity and change. When ceramic functional categories are evaluated with the addition of glass vessels a new pattern emerges (Figure 11.10). The data from Irish immigrant households at both Five Points tenements remains relatively the same; there was an emphasis on owning more decorative teaware in comparison to tableware and serving vessels. This pattern strongly resembles that of the pre-Famine Irish data. However, a shift occurs by the end of the 1860s. The data from the upper privy deposit at 472 Pearl Street is more reflective of a pattern similar to the non-Irish American-born assemblages. This material change is further buttressed by the pattern of both Paterson assemblages, where tableware vessels with the inclusion of glass vessels outnumber teaware. Therefore with the introduction of glass vessels into the data set, in addition to an increase in vessel complexity, the emergence of an Irish-American material assemblage begins as early as 1870 and develops by the 1890s (Brighton 2001, 2005) (Figure 11.11).

While changes in vessel complexity and the increase in glass tableware occurred between 1870 and 1900, a pattern

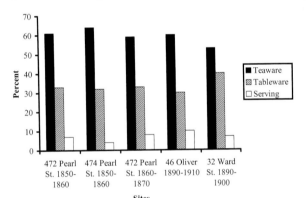

Figure 11.8. The distribution of ceramic functional categories between the Irish immigrant tenements at the Five Points, Manhattan and the Irish and Irish-American households at the Dublin section, Paterson, New Jersey.

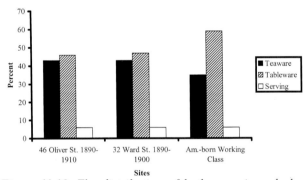

Figure 11.10. The distribution of both ceramic and glass functional categories between the Irish immigrant tenement assemblages at the Five Points and the Irish and Irish-American assemblages at the Dublin section, Paterson, New Jersey.

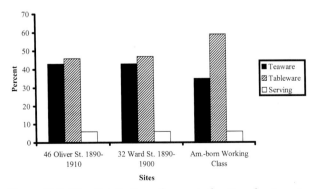

Figure 11.9. The distribution of ceramic functional categories between the Irish and Irish-American households and an American-born, non-Irish household in Paterson, New Jersey.

Figure 11.11. The distribution of ceramic and glass functional categories of Irish and Irish-American and a contemporary American-born, non-Irish, working class household at the Dublin section, Paterson, New Jersey.

emerges in the numbers of plain and molded white granite vessels. At the time the lower deposit in Feature J at 472 Pearl Street and the deposit in Feature O at 474 Pearl Street were created, sometime after 1860, the Five Points assemblages had a low percentage of white granite vessels, mostly teacups and saucers. The total number of white granite pieces from all functional categories increased in the upper deposit of Feature J, created after 1870. By the end of the 19th century, it replaced all ceramic types in the Dublin assemblages. The presence of white granite and its eventual predominance in the Paterson data marks the subtle and gradual social process of incorporation into American consumer culture.

White granite is valued as a ceramic type because the demand for the austere white and thickly potted ceramic type overrode the popularity of all other decorative ceramic types by the 1840s. White granite vessels first appeared on the American market as early as 1840 and quickly became the most popular and sought-after ware type in tea and tableware. Its arrival marked a dramatic shift in ceramic form and decoration, and differed greatly from the colorful transfer-printed vessels it replaced (Miller 1991). The values are compared with the archaeologically recovered ceramic vessels within the established date range for that particular archaeological context. Higher priced ceramics in a particular functional category, for example teaware, over another indicates a greater social and cultural emphasis on tea drinking. In this study, the changes in decorative types in conjunction with the increase in the amount and different types of white granite and glass tableware and serving pieces reflect new consumption patterns.

Diana Wall (1994, 153–154) argues that white granite marked a new American consumer pattern reflecting an ideology that formed the American middle class. She links the revival of Gothic style architecture in churches to the acquisition of the sterile white granite plates and teacups molded in the Gothic pattern. Because of its symbolic association with the sanctity and morality of the church, Wall (1994, 158) suggests that white granite became highly sought after by Victorian Americans. The social meaning of white granite became infused with the ideal of 'the home's role as sanctuary from the heartless world of business' and therefore outwardly demonstrated the household's social position, citizenship, and thus respectability (Wall 1994, 6).

It is not clear whether white granite and glass tableware and serving pieces held the same meaning for Irish-born and Irish-American families as they did for non-Irish, American households. White granite vessels are present in very small numbers in the mid-century data. Like the increase in glass and ceramic complexity, the percentage of white granite vessels increases by the 1860s. Three decades later it is the only ware type in the Paterson assemblages. The question then becomes why the change in the material culture between 1860 and 1890?

There are two possible and interdependent reasons why late 19th century Irish households would have goods associated with American ideologies. The first explanation is cost. By the end of the 1860s various patterns of white granite tea and tableware flooded the marketplace causing a considerable drop in cost, perhaps even for the Irish-born laborer class (Miller 1991). By 1890, the Mackel and McGill families, homeowners rather than tenants, were acquiring white granite; by this time, America's ceramic industry stabilized and became a competitive industry. American potteries were mass-producing large quantities of white granite at cheaper prices than their English-made counterparts (Gates and Ormerod 1982; Potteries of Trenton Society 2001). Trenton and East Liverpool, both manufacturers with products present in the Paterson data, were producers of inexpensive white granite products that thrived commercially throughout the last decades of the 19th century (Gates and Ormerod 1982, 128; Potteries of Trenton Society 2001, 10).

While affordability is one facet, the other is demographics and the symbolism of respectability and civic citizenship associated with owning these objects. The McGill family was American-born. It is quite possible that neither Daniel nor his wife were exposed to patterns of traditional Irish material culture. The same could be said for the Mackel family. Although both Sarah and James Mackel were born in Ireland, they had lived in Paterson for over 30 years at the time of the deposit. The white granite vessels may reflect their conscious efforts to acquire objects similar to those owned by their Irish-American neighbors. It is most likely that the McGill family, and perhaps the Mackel family, viewed themselves as American citizens first and foremost. Therefore acquiring the objects associated with the American consumer culture would be an expression of their desire for inclusion which separated them from the stigmas and stereotypes of the Irish as the foreign other.

The physical evidence of gradual incorporation between the Five Points and Dublin section is further supported through faunal remains. The changes in the percentages in the variety of animal remains, especially when compared to the non-Irish American-born households, reflect the same pattern of incorporation as the ceramics and glass (for complete faunal analysis see Davis 1989; Milne and Crabtree 2000; O'Steen 1999).

Nineteenth-century American eating habits were stratified and the meaning of food was a cultural product of the social structure. Choices in diet and how meals were presented and eaten held enormous significance; in one form or another such choices were a declaration of social position (Mintz 1996, 4–6, 13). Throughout the 19th century Americans' consumption of beef, and then chicken, ranked the highest in relation to other meats such as lamb and salted pork (Davis 1989, 202; Rothchild and Balkwill 1993, 74). Salted pork was preferred over fresh pork when used for meals.

Eschewing fresh pork stemmed from its association with food-born illness and the animals' tendency to live in filth and eat garbage (Davis 1989, 202).

The consumption of new types of foods in upper privy deposit at 472 Pearl Street and deposits from the Irish and Irish-American households in Paterson indicate learned behaviors and new meanings of food presentation and consumption. Similar to the changes in tableware and serving forms, change takes place in the faunal assemblage once it becomes part of the daily lives of the Irish and Irish-American community, and when this happens many of the older patterns seen at the Five Points are replaced by the new ones that resemble non-Irish, American assemblages.

The lower privy deposits for both tenements at the Five Points (*c.*1850–1860s) represent recently arrived Irish immigrants. The percentage of meat in their daily diet presents a new pattern of a consumer culture. Meat did not form the foundation of the diet for the Irish rural poor. The availability of meat had an enormous impact on the immigrant group after the experience of the Famine, and therefore meals and the daily serving of meat had an additional social importance (Mintz 1996, 4). Unlike the American meat consumption of beef and chicken, the newly arrived Irish consumed predominantly pork in the form of ham hocks and pigs feet (Milne and Crabtree 2000, 181, 188). Beef and sheep are present in the assemblages but in small numbers and represent the cheapest cuts. The sheep remains, for example, are mostly from the shank end of older animals or mutton. There is little difference in the faunal assemblage between the earlier deposits from both tenements and the later dating upper deposit at 472 Pearl Street, with the exception of a slight rise in cuts of beef (Milne and Crabtree 2000, 181).

A change in the dietary patterns of Irish and Irish-American families occurs by the last decade of the 19th century when there is a shift in the types of meat consumed. This pattern begins to resemble the dietary pattern of non-Irish Americans, specifically in the consumption of beef and chicken. Based on the recovered faunal remains, the Mackel family consumed more beef and lamb, rather than pork and mutton. Pork represents less than 7 per cent of the entire faunal assemblage (O'Steen 1999, 9). Slightly different, but remaining in the context of American food consumption pattern, is the McGill family. This family had a higher percentage of poultry, predominantly chicken, with lesser amounts of beef and lamb (O'Steen 1999, 9).

The gradual acceptance of new consumer patterns and incorporation is indicative of practice into action. The developing complexity of ceramic and glass forms in conjunction with the introduction of new and different foods is the evidence of learning and accepting of new cultural patterns that replaced many of the traditional patterns (Mintz 1996).

Conclusion

Material culture forms an important part of social relations in the construction of the everyday world. Continuities may evoke a shared heritage reinforcing traditional social behaviors and values, while change reflects the introduction and acceptance of new socio-cultural identities. The ceramic vessels used in this chapter, as well as supporting glass and faunal evidence, are the physical evidence of the daily experiences of desire, and the gradual process of adopting new social behaviors.

The manifestation of an Irish-American identity is found in both continuity and change. There is an overall pattern between the data from Ireland and that belonging to the recently arrived in Manhattan. For example, there is an emphasis on the importance of tea drinking in both Ireland and America; this is manifested in the large numbers of tea-related vessels. The forms are decorated in transfer-printed patterns considered a more expensive form of decoration. Furthermore, the level of vessel complexity is low in the Five Points assemblages. As with the traditional assemblage from Ireland, serving pieces do not factor to a large degree in the material culture. This is reinforced when the Irish immigrant data are compared to a contemporary American-born working-class assemblage.

Material commonalities between Ireland and the Irish in America declined as the last half of the 19th century progressed. The overall length of residence suggests that change in vessel complexity was a transgenerational process. The gradual acceptance of new consumer patterns and incorporation is indicative of practice into action. The developing complexity of ceramic and glass forms in conjunction with the introduction of new and different foods is evidence of Irish immigrants and first generation Irish-Americans learning new cultural patterns. The McGill family was American born and the Mackel family had lived in Paterson for over 30 years at the time of the deposit. The white granite and glass tableware and serving pieces owned by each household reflect their conscious efforts to acquire objects that expressed their own view of themselves as American citizens.

The physical evidence of gradual incorporation between the Five Points and Dublin section is further supported through faunal remains. A change in the dietary patterns of Irish and Irish-American families occurs by the last decade of the 19th century. At that time there is a shift in the types of meat consumed which begins to resemble the dietary pattern of non-Irish Americans. The Mackel family consumed more beef and lamb, rather than pork and mutton, and the McGill family consumed a higher percentage of poultry. Changes in diet are indicative of new and learned behaviors.

Meagher has argued that the historical record indicates a period of transition and change in the social behaviors of the Irish in America. The archaeological data provides firm evidence of that transition in practice. The ceramic data suggests that by the turn of the 19th century the Irish have incorporated an American-like pattern of tableware and serving forms, and such shifts represent adoption of new socio-cultural behaviors and outlook establishing the formation of a new Irish-American identity and consumer culture.

References

Aalen, F. H. A., Whelan, K. and Stout, M. (eds) (1997) *Atlas of the Rural Irish Landscape*, Toronto, University of Toronto Press.

Arensberg, C. M. (1988) *The Irish Countryman: An Anthropological Study*, Prospect Heights, IL, Waveland Press.

Arensberg, C. M. and Kimball, S. T. (1940) *Family and Community in Ireland*, Cambridge, MA, Harvard University Press.

Beames, M. R. (1978) Rural conflict in pre-Famine Ireland: peasant assassinations in Tipperary, 1837–1847. *Past and Present* 81, 75–91.

Brighton, S. A. (2001) Prices that suit the times: shopping for ceramics at the Five Points. *Historical Archaeology* 35:3, 16–30.

Brighton, S. A. (2005) An Historical Archaeology of the Irish Proletarian Diaspora: The Material Manifestations of Irish Identity in America, 1850–1910, Ann Arbor, MI, UMI Dissertation Service/ProQuest.

Brighton, S. A. and Levon-White, J. (2006) English Ceramic Exports to Ballykilcline, in Orser, Jr., C. E. (ed) *Unearthing Hidden Ireland: Historical Archaeology in County Roscommon*, Bray, Wordwell Press, 109–139.

Bushman, R. L. (1993) *The Refinement of America: Persons, Houses, Cities*, New York, Vintage Books.

Clark, C. E., Jr. (1988) Domestic architecture as an index to social history: the romantic revival and the cult of domesticity in America, 1840–1870, in St. George, R. B. (ed.) *Material Life in America, 1600–1860*, Boston, Northeastern University Press, 535–549.

Clark, S. (1982) The importance of agrarian classes: class-structure and collective action in nineteenth-century Ireland, in Drudy, P. J. (ed.) *Ireland: Land, Politics, and People*, Cambridge, Cambridge University Press, 11–36.

Coleman, A. (1999) *Riotous Roscommon: Social Unrest in the 1840s*, Dublin, Irish Academic Press.

Cotz, J. A., Rutsch, M. J. and Wilson, C. (1980) Salvage Archaeology Project, Paterson, New Jersey, 1973–1976, Volume II: Paterson's Dublin: An Interdisciplinary Study of Social Structure, ms. prepared for Great Falls Development, Inc. and the New Jersey Department of Transportation.

Davis, B. (1989) Faunal analysis, in Geismar, J. H. (ed.) History and Archaeology of the Greenwich Mews Site, Greenwich Village, New York, Unpublished report submitted to the Greenwich Mews Associates, New York, 190–214.

De Cunzo, L. A. (1983) Economics and Ethnicity: An Archaeological Perspective on Nineteenth-Century Paterson, New Jersey, unpublished dissertation, University of Pennsylvania, Philadelphia.

Donnelly, J. S. Jr (2001) *The Great Irish Potato Famine*, Gloucestershire, Sutton.

Fitts, R. K. (1999) The archaeology of middle-class domesticity and gentility in Victorian Brooklyn. *Historical Archaeology* 33:1, 39–62.

Fitts, Robert K. (2000) *The Five Points reformed, 1865–1900. In Tales of the Five Points: Working-Class Life in Nineteenth-Century New York, Volume 1, A Narrative History and Archaeology*, ed. by Rebecca Yamin, pp. 67–89. Philadelphia, John Milner Associates.

Fitts, R. K. and Yamin, R. (1996) *The Archaeology of Domesticity in Victorian Brooklyn*, Philadelphia, John Milner Associates.

Fitzpatrick, D. (1980) The disappearance of the Irish agricultural laborer, 1841–1912. *Irish Economic and Social History* 7, 66–92.

Gailey, A. (1984) *Rural Houses of the North of Ireland*, Belfast, H.M.S.O.

Gates, W. C. Jr. and Ormerod, D. E. (1982) The East Liverpool, Ohio, Pottery District: Identification of Manufacturers and Marks. *Historical Archaeology* 16:1–2, 1–358

Geismar, J. H. (1989) *History and Archaeology of the Greenwich Mews Site, Greenwich Village, New York*, New York, J. H. Geismar.

Grant, I. F. (1961) *Highland Folkways*, London, Routledge and Kegan Paul.

Gray, J. (1993) Gender and plebian culture in Ulster. *Journal of Interdisciplinary History* 24:2, 251–270.

Green, H. (1983) *The Light of Home: An Intimate View of the Lives of Women in Victoria America*, New York, Pantheon Books.

Grier, K. C. (1988) *Culture and Comfort: Parlor Making and Middle-Class Identity, 1850–1930*, Washington, DC, Smithsonian Institution Press.

Guinnane, T. W. (1997) *The Vanishing Irish: Households, Migration, and the Rural Economy in Ireland, 1850–1914*, Princeton, NJ, Princeton University Press.

Harlow, I. (1997) Creating situations: practical jokes and the revival of the dead in Irish tradition. *Journal of American Folklore* 110(436), 140–168.

Hull, K. L. and Brighton, S. A. (2002) A Report of Investigations for the Fifth Season of Archaeological Research at Ballykilcline Townland, Kilglass Parish, County Roscommon, Ireland. Unpublished report submitted to Dúchas the Heritage Service and the National Museum of Ireland.

Ingle, M. (1982) Industrial site-building: implications from the 1978–1979 investigations at the Rogers Locomotive Works, Paterson, New Jersey, in Dickens, R. S. (ed.) *Archaeology of Urban America: The Search for Pattern and Process*, New York, Academic Press, 237–256.

Johnson, J. H. (1990) The context of migration: the example of Ireland in the nineteenth century. *Transactions of the Institute of British Geographers* 15:3, 259–276.

Kasson, J. (1990) *Rudeness and Civility: Manners in Nineteenth-Century Urban America*, New York, Hill and Wang.

Langan-Egan, M. (1999) *Galway Women in the Nineteenth Century*, Dublin, Open Air.

Marx, K. and Engels, F. (1972) *Ireland and the Irish Question*, New York, International Publishers.

McGowan, J. (2001) *Echoes of a Savage Land*, Cork, Mercier Press.

McLoughlin, W. (1978) *Revivals, Awakenings, and Reform*, Chicago, University of Chicago Press.

Meagher, T. J. (1986) Introduction, in Meagher, T. J., *From Paddy to Studs: Irish-American Communities in the Turn of the Century Era, 1880 to 1920*, New York, Greenwood Press, 1–25.

Meagher, T. J. (2001)*Inventing Irish America: Generation, Class, and Ethnic Identity in a New England City, 1880–1928*, South Bend, University of Notre Dame Press.

Miller, G. L. (1991) A revised set of CC index values for classification and economic scaling of English ceramics from 1787 to 1880. *Historical Archaeology* 25:1, 1–25.

Miller, K. A. (1985) *Emigrants and Exiles: Ireland and the Irish Exodus to North America*, New York, Oxford University Press.

Milne, C. and Crabtree, P. (2000) Revealing meals: ethnicity, economic status, and diet at the Five Points, 1800–1860, in Yamin, R. (ed.) *Tales of Five Points: Working-Class Life in 19th-Century New York: Volume II. An Interpretive Approach to Understanding Working-Class Life*, West Chester, PA, John Milner Associates, 130–196.

Mintz, S. (1996) *Tasting Food, Tasting Freedom: Excursions into Eating, Culture, and the Past*, Boston, Beacon Press.

Mokyr, J. and Ó Gráda, C. (1984) New developments in Irish population history, 1700–1850. *The Economic History Review* 37:4, 473–488.

Mokyr, J. and Ó Gráda, C. (1988) Poor and getting poorer? Living standards in Ireland before the Famine. *The Economic History Review* 41:2, 209–235.

Mullins, P. R. (1999) *Race and Affluence: An Archaeology of African-America and Consumer Culture*, Kluwer Academic/ Plenum Press, New York.

New York State Census (1855–1865) Census Returns for the Sixth Ward of the City of New York in the County of New York. Manuscript returns on file, Department of Records and Information, Municipal Archives of the City of New York, 31 Chambers Street, New York.

Orser, Jr, C. E. (1998) *A Report of Investigations for the First Season of Archaeological Research at Ballykilcline Townland, Kilglass Parish, County Roscommon, Ireland.* Unpublished report submitted to Dúchas the Heritage Service and the National Museum of Ireland.

Orser, Jr, C. E. (2004) *Race and Practice in Archaeological Interpretation*, Philadelphia, University of Pennsylvania Press.

Orser, Jr, C. E. and Hull, K. L. (2001) *A Report of Investigations for the Third Season of Archaeological Research at Ballykilcline Townland, Kilglass Parish, County Roscommon, Ireland.* Unpublished report submitted to Dúchas the Heritage Service and the National Museum of Ireland.

O'Steen, L. (1999) Zooarchaeological remains from site 28PA151, Block 866 and Site 28PA152, Block 863: 19th – early 20th-century Irish, English, and Italian immigrant diet in Paterson, New Jersey, in Yamin R. (ed.) *With Hope and Labor: Everyday Life in Paterson's Dublin Neighborhood,* Volume II, West Chester, PA, John Milner Associates, 1–34.

Potteries of Trenton Society (2001) *From Teacups to Toilets*, Trenton, NJ, Potteries of Trenton Society.

Praetzellis, A. and Praetzellis, M. (1992) Faces and facades: Victorian ideology in early Sacramento, in Yentsch, A. E. and Beaudry, M. C. (ed.) *The Art and Mystery of Historical Archaeology: Essays in Honor of James Deetz*, Boca Raton, FL, CRC Press, 75–99.

Praetzellis, M., Praetzellis, A. and Brown, M. (1988) What happened to the silent majority? Research strategies for studying dominant group material culture in the late 19th century, in Beaudry, M. C. (ed.) *New Directions in Archaeology: Documentary Archaeology in the New World*, Cambridge, Cambridge University Press, 192–202.

Quinlan, T. B. (1998) Big Whigs in the mobilization of Irish peasants: a historical sociology of hegemony in pre-Famine Ireland (1750s–1840s). *Sociological Forum* 13:2, 247–264.

Rosenberg, C. S. (1971) *Religion and the Rise of the American City: The New York Mission Movement, 1812–1830*, Ithaca, NY, Cornell University Press.

Rothchild, N. A. and Balkwill, D. (1993) The meaning of change in urban faunal deposits. *Historical Archaeology* 27:2, 71–89.

Ryan, M. P. (1981) *Cradle of Middle Class: The Family in Oneida County, New York, 1790–1865*, Cambridge, Cambridge University Press.

Scally, R. J. (1995) *The End of Hidden Ireland: Rebellion, Famine, and Emigration*, New York, Oxford University Press.

Shanin, T. (1987) *Peasants and Peasant Societies*, Oxford, Blackwell.

Symonds, J. (2000) The Dark Island revisited: an approach to the historical archaeology of Milton, South Uist, in Atkinson, J. A., Banks, I. and MacGregor, G. (eds) *Townships to Farmsteads: Rural Settlement in Scotland, England, and Wales*, Oxford, British Archaeological Reports Series 293, 196–209.

Thorton, P. (1978) *Seventeenth-Century Interior Decoration in England*, New Haven, CT, Yale University Press.

US Bureau of the Census (1850–1870) Population and Manufacturing for the Sixth Ward, US Bureau of the Census. New York, New York Public Library.

Wall, D. D. (1994) *The Archaeology of Gender: Separating the Spheres in Urban America*, New York, Plenum Press.

Wall, D. D. (2001) Family meals and evening parties: constructing domesticity in nineteenth-century middle-class New York, in Delle, J. A., Mrozowski, S. A. and Paynter, R. (eds) *Lines That Divide: Historical Archaeologies of Race, Class, and Gender*, Knoxville, University of Tennessee Press, 109–141.

Yamin, R. (1999) *With Hope and Labor: Everyday Life in Paterson's Dublin Neighborhood* Volume 1: *Data Recovery on Blocks 863 and 866 within the Route 19 Connector Corridor in Paterson, New* Jersey, West Chester, PA, John Milner Associates.

Yamin, R. (2000) People and their Possessions, in *Tales of the Five Points: Working-Class Life in Nineteenth-Century New York,* Volume 1, *A Narrative History and Archaeology*, West Chester, PA, John Milner Associates.

Young, A. (1780) *A Tour of Ireland with General Observations on the Present State of that Kingdom made in the Years 1776, 1777, and 1778*, London, T. Cadell and J. Dodsley.

12

The Ceramic Revolution in Iceland 1850–1950

Gavin Lucas

Introduction

Until the mid 19th century, the majority of the population in Iceland were effectively aceramic; at least from the 18th century food preparation was largely through wooden or metal vessels, and eating and drinking was performed using personalized wooden vessels held in the lap. Over the later 19th and early 20th century, such a pattern was transformed by the mass importation of English and Scottish industrial whitewares, leading to more cosmopolitan styles of consumption at the table. This paper explores how this transition occurred, in particular looking at how the highly personalized nature of traditional vessels negotiated this transition from wood to ceramic, and how the different material properties of these objects, acted back upon and altered the patterns of consumption and people's relationships to vessels used for eating and drinking.

Ceramic studies in Iceland are relatively undeveloped – indeed there have effectively been only two projects specifically dedicated to the topic, one of them an unpublished Master's thesis. The first analysis of any kind was by Guðrun Sveinbjarnardóttir published in 1993 on medieval pottery (Sveinbjarnardóttir 1993), which was later expanded into a monograph on all pottery up to c.1800, published in 1996 in both Icelandic and English (Sveinbjarnardóttir 1996). Sveinbjarnardóttir's research mainly involved constructing a typology and drawing general conclusions on trade links. The second work is by Natascha Mehler, who wrote her Master's thesis on medieval pottery from Iceland in 2000 (Mehler 2000). Apart from some minor differences of identification, the main difference in Mehler's work was that she was able to study a much larger assemblage of medieval pottery than Sveinbjarnardóttir, and thus able to produce statistical data on the sources of pottery imported into Iceland. Mehler's thesis and an updated summary (Mehler 2004) showed the dominance of Rhenish ceramics in medieval Iceland, except for a short peak in English wares in the 14th century.

It might seem odd that there have only been two studies of ceramics in Iceland, and these only in the past decade, but this needs to be put in context. First, pottery in Iceland is fairly rare until the 14th century; although settled in the late 9th century, Iceland was essentially aceramic until the later medieval period. Only two vessels are known from settlement and immediate post-settlement period sites (AD 850–1150), and only 28 in the early medieval period (AD 1150–1350). It is not until the later 14th century that ceramic imports dramatically rise (65 vessels for the period 1350–1600) and are likely to be found on a normal settlement, but even then, only in small amounts except for the higher status (i.e. ecclesiastical) settlements. Numbers steadily rise in the post-medieval period (post-1600), though here exact figures are lacking, but it is not until after the revolution in industrial ceramics in 19th century that they occur in anything like substantial proportions on most sites. There is no evidence that pottery was ever made in Iceland and all of it is imported, even today – except for some studio pottery. A number of small trading sites occur around the island, and Iceland was until the mid 19th century almost exclusively linked to Baltic trade networks, and usually under restricted conditions because of its colonial status. Although settled as an independent island, it became a colony, first of Norway from the early 13th century, and then of Denmark from the late 14th century; it only gained full political independence in 1944. It was not until 1855 that free trade was allowed, which also coincides with the increase in imported material culture, especially ceramics, found on most sites throughout the country.

Documentary data on ceramic imports are rare, and mainly come from the 19th and 20th centuries. The earliest Danish records of pottery imports are from 1844, but it is not until 1870 that they are at all regular (Halldór Bjarnason, pers. comm.). The early Danish records primarily distinguish between earthenwares and porcelain and give figures in kilograms (Figure 12.1). Imports rise over the course of the

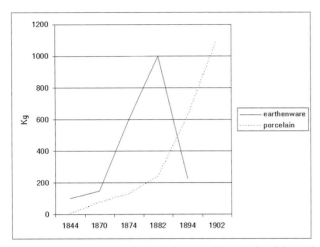

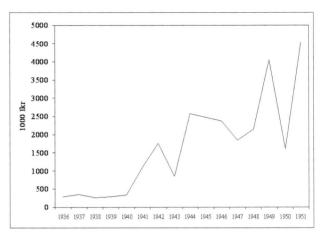

Figure 12.1. Quantities of pottery imported into Iceland through Danish merchants, 1844–1902 (Source: Halldór Bjarnason).

Figure 12.2. Quantities of pottery imported into Iceland, 1936–1951 (Source: Jónsson and Magnússon 1997).

latter half of the 19th century, especially earthenwares, but absolute numbers are not high: in 1870 only 150kg was imported into the whole country – that could be estimated at *c.*500 vessels for a population of *c.*70,000! Furthermore, earthenwares show a marked decline after the 1880s, while porcelain starts to rise dramatically. However, the decline in earthenwares only reflects the decline of *Danish* trade in earthenwares; what is probably happening is that with the establishment of free trade in 1855, the Danish merchants gradually cede the earthenware market (but probably not porcelain) to English and Scottish merchants. Documentary research is clearly needed on British exports to Iceland to substantiate this, but based on archaeological finds, it seems probable. Records for the early 20th century are amalgamated for all sources, and shows that pottery imports may have reached a plateau in the early 20th century until the Second World War, when they start to rise dramatically again (Figure 12.2). This undoubtedly relates to major changes in Icelandic society and material culture, in part stimulated through North American military presence. This, however, is another story.

The documentary data are inevitably patchy, and moreover not very detailed as to the types and sources of the ceramics. Archaeological material is much more informative in this respect. Denmark may have had a trade monopoly with Iceland until the mid-19th century, but obviously this does not mean all the ceramics in Iceland are Danish, even if being imported through Danish merchants. One of the key issues in regard to late 18th and 19th century patterns is the development of industrial ceramic production in northern Europe. England – specifically Staffordshire – pioneered mass-produced, high quality industrial wares in the late 18th century, but it was a while before other North European countries started their own factories. Sweden was the first Scandinavian country to produce industrial whitewares, as early as 1771 with the production of creamwares at

Rörstrand, which also manufactured porcelain and tin-glazed earthenwares (Fredlund 1997). Mass production, however, was mostly centred at Gustavsberg which began production in 1827. At both Rörstrand and Gustavsberg, production was initially set up along German lines, but in 1826 and 1839 respectively, English potters and management systems were adopted, which had a key influence on subsequent designs. In Denmark, by contrast, industrial earthenware production began as late as 1862 with the establishment of the Aluminia factory in Christianshavn. The main output of fine tablewares was in porcelain and faience at Copenhagen, which had been established in 1775 (Mikkelsen 2000).

Essentially then, the domestic production of English style industrial whitewares only began in the northern Europe during the second and third quarters of the 19th century, and before that time, one can assume that almost all imported industrial whitewares in Iceland will be British. Sourcing whitewares with no maker's marks is difficult unless decorative patterns are distinctive, and based on the author's familiarity with whitewares in Iceland, most marked pieces are either English (Staffordshire) or Scottish, rather than Danish – though porcelain appears to follow a rather different and more varied pattern. Archival research would no doubt provide a more fruitful avenue in this question of sourcing.

In this chapter, rather than trade patterns, I want to explore the nature of consumption of pottery, particularly the transition to common ceramic use in Iceland in terms of people's everyday relationships to objects associated with the consumption of food and drink. The focus will be primarily on the hundred years *c.*1850–1950, which is when the majority of the population started to use ceramics in any regular manner. In general, the post-1600 period is the least studied for Icelandic ceramics where greater emphasis has been on the medieval period (see above), and for post-1800 there is effectively no research whatsoever. The discussion in this paper will therefore,

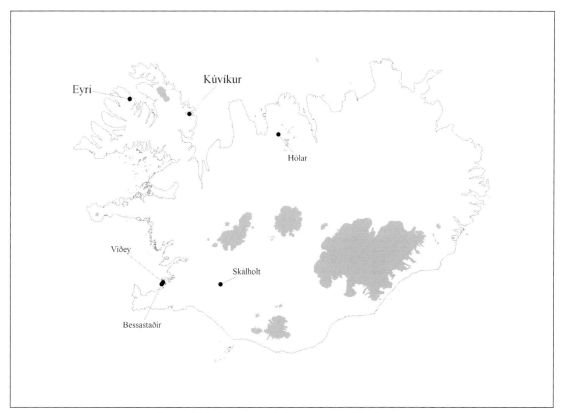

Figure 12.3. Location of sites mentioned in the text.

inevitably be preliminary and based on limited data. The majority of the ceramic evidence for the post-1600 period comes from excavations at high status settlements such as the Governor's residence at Bessastaðir and ecclesiastical centres at Viðey, Hólar and Skálholt. Unfortunately none of this material has been published or even extensively studied, though the latter two sites of Hólar and Skálholt are ongoing projects. Since these are high status sites, they are also likely to be unusual. The discussion here therefore will be based on two midden assemblages from smaller settlements, both located in the northwest of the country and excavated in 2004: a small trading station at Kúvíkur and the farm mound at Eyri (Figure 12.3).

Two Sites and their Ceramic Assemblages

The farm at Eyri was established in the medieval period if not earlier, and was occupied until its abandonment in 1877, by which time the fishing town of Ísafjörður had become established around it (Taylor et al. 2005). The excavated assemblage derives mainly from the upper part of the farm midden and dates broadly to *c*.1800–1877; a minimum number of 221 vessels were recorded from excavations in 2004. The assemblage is dominated by industrial refined whitewares (see Table 12.1), many no doubt from Britain, though of the two identified makers marks, one was Danish

and the other Scottish. One plate was identified to the pottery of J. Marshall and Co. in Bo'ness, West Lothian, which operated between 1860 and 1899, and probably represents one of the latest imports to the site given the known abandonment date. Of the whitewares, the larger proportions were either plain undecorated pieces or with transfer-printed designs of various patterns. Another common type was hand-painted vessels, usually in bright colours and with floral motifs, while the remainder were chiefly spongewares or slipwares (Table 12.2). Bowls, plates, cups and saucers dominated the whiteware assemblage, all in more or less equal proportions (Table 12.3). Porcelain comprised only a small percentage of the assemblage.

The site of Kúvíkur was established as a trading station in 1602, but is unlikely to have had any permanent structures until the late 18th century when the trade monopoly was abolished (Lárusdóttir et al. 2005). It continued in use as a trade port until 1949 when it closed down and the site was abandoned. The excavated assemblage discussed here derives solely from a midden associated with the late 18th century merchant's house and while it may date from as early as the 17th century, most of the material comes from the period *c*.1850–1950. A minimum number of 135 vessels were recorded, the majority tablewares – plates, bowls, cups and saucers (Table 12.4). The composition of the assemblage is dominated by industrial whitewares followed by porcelain

Table 12.1. Summary of wares from Eyri.

Fabric	MNV	%
Refined Industrial Earthenwares		
Creamware	2	0.90
Drabware	1	0.45
Rockingham Glaze	1	0.45
Whiteware	182	82.35
White-slipped glazed redware	2	0.90
Yellow ware	2	0.90
Coarse Earthenwares		
Green-glazed earthenware	3	1.35
Glazed red earthenware	7	3.17
Slipcoated glazed earthenware	1	0.45
Tin-glazed earthenware	1	0.45
Stonewares		
Brown salt-glazed stoneware	5	2.26
Westerwald stoneware	1	0.45
Grey dip-glazed stoneware	1	0.45
Grey salt-glazed stoneware	1	0.45
Frechen stoneware	1	0.45
Other	3	1.36
Porcelain		
Bone China	7	3.17
Total	221	100.00

Table 12.3. Summary of whiteware vessel forms from Eyri

Vessel	MNV	%
Bowl	39	21.43
Cup	29	15.93
Jug	1	0.55
Lid	3	1.65
Mug	1	0.55
Plate	43	23.63
Saucer	33	18.13
Unid.	33	18.13
Total	**182**	**100.00**

Table 12.4. Summary of vessel types from Kúvíkur

Vessel	MNV	%
Bowl	25	18.5
Plate	36	26.7
Cup	17	12.6
Saucer	22	16.3
Drainer	1	0.7
Jug	7	5.2
Basin	1	0.7
Jar	1	0.7
Tripod pot	1	0.7
Other/Unid.	24	17.8
Grand Total	**135**	**100.0**

Table 12.2. Summary of decorative types on whitewares from Eyri.

Decoration	MNV	%
Cut Spongeware	9	4.95
Factory Slipware	4	2.20
Over-glaze painted	2	1.10
Transfer-printed	67	36.81
Undecorated	52	28.57
Under-glaze painted	23	12.64
Other	14	7.70
Unid.	11	6.04
Total	**182**	**100.00**

Table 12.5. Summary of wares from Kúvíkur

Ware	MNV	%
Porcelain	24	17.8
Stonewares		
Brown salt-glazed stoneware	1	0.7
Grey dip-glazed stoneware	1	0.7
Coarse Earthenwares		
Glazed Red Earthenware	1	0.7
Industrial Wares		
Creamware	1	0.7
Whiteware	103	76.3
Majolica	2	1.5
White-slipped glazed redware	1	0.7
Yellow ware	1	0.7
Grand Total	**135**	**100.0**

Table 12.6. Summary of decorative types from Kúvíkur

Decoration	MNV	%
Edge Banded	14	14.1
Cut Spongeware	4	4.0
Factory slipware	4	4.0
Gilt-edge	3	3.0
Lithograph-printed	4	4.0
Lustreware	1	1.0
Over-glaze painted	3	3.0
Transfer-printed	25	25.3
Undecorated	30	30.3
Under-glaze painted	11	11.1
Grand Total	**99**	**100.0**

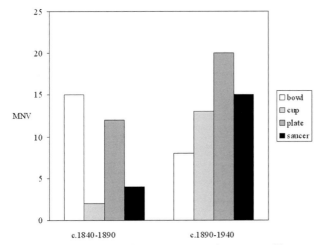

Figure 12.4. Change in the composition of ceramic tablewares at Kúvíkur c.1840–1940.

(Table 12.5). None of the whitewares were marked, but many, if not most, probably derive from Britain. Part of the porcelain, however, is Japanese – two vessels were marked with the Suzuki factory symbol, one of the earliest Japanese companies producing industrial ceramics (Nippon Tokusei Suzuki Co., Japan, founded c.1900–1910). The mark probably dates to the mid 20th century. The larger proportion of the vessels were decorated, mostly either transfer-printed, edge-banded or under-glaze painted (Table 12.6). Transfer-print patterns include 'willow', 'Asiatic pheasant' and possibly 'wild rose'; the edge-banded wares are all similar and on plates – a double blue band along the top of the rim and one along the bottom. A third of the assemblage was undecorated.

Both sites are fairly similar in broad terms, both in the range of wares and vessel forms; even the general decoration types on the whitewares are fairly comparable. However, the

site at Kúvíkur offers more potential for dissecting these figures to explore change within the period, as the midden was well stratified and could be sub-divided into 4 phases. In particular, the largest quantities of ceramics came from phases 2 and 3, which have been dated to c.1840–1890 and 1890–1940. There are two things of particular significance here, when the assemblage is broken down chronologically. The first is that porcelain is relatively rare in phase 2 (2% of the pottery), but increases dramatically to comprise nearly a quarter of all pottery in the next phase (23%). This corresponds well with the small numbers or porcelain at Eyri farm, which was abandoned in 1877, as well as the import data (cf. Figure 12.1). The second pattern concerns the proportions of the four main vessel types – bowls, plates, cups and saucers (Figure 12.4). Generally, plates, and especially cups and saucers increase in phase 3, while bowls decrease. The meaning of these changes needs to be interpreted in the context of a broader understanding of the how ceramics related to other contemporary material culture in the household, especially that pertaining to food and drink.

The Development of Pottery Use in Iceland, 1850–1950

Pottery clearly becomes a major part of the archaeological record in the post-medieval period in Iceland, especially from the mid 19th century, but an important question is how this was adapted to local conditions. In order to start exploring this, we need to understand something of the general background of foodways in Iceland in this period. Throughout Europe, there was a major change in diet from the 16th century towards a greater cereal base; in Iceland, this did not happen. Up until the mid-19th century, the Icelandic diet was dominated by animal products. Typical daily foods included dried fish, butter, *skyr* (a dairy product) and whey. Cereals were used in porridges, but sparingly and bread was a luxury (Jónsson and Magnússon 1997). Other luxuries such as coffee and sugar were only regularly imported after 1776, but their consumption does not become common until after the mid 19th century (Jónasson 1961, 54; Jónsson and Magnússon 1997).

The importation and use of pottery in Iceland clearly needs to be seen in the context of these basic foodways. At least from the late 18th century if not earlier, written and oral sources indicate that eating and drinking utensils in Iceland were wooden, and consisted of personalized bowls and spoons. These bowls, called *askur* (pl. *askar*), were stave-built with usually ornately carved lids (Figure 12.5); spoons were of wood or horn, and people often kept them in pockets or on their person, rather like knives (Jónasson 1961, 51; Finnbogason 1943). People ate from these personal bowls, usually on their lap, and drank a whey drink from a tall, wooden tankard (*kanna*). Eating at tables may have come in during the later 19th century, but then only for

Figure 12.5. Traditional Icelandic food bowl or askur with carved date of 1806 (Drawing by author after a vessel in the National Museum, Iceland).

special occasions such as Christmas. Given the basic diet, a lot of the food was eaten cold. Dairy products and dried fish were made and stored in various stave-built containers, although a cooking pot – usually of iron suspended over a range – would have been used for cooking porridges or soups. Wealthier households tended to use pewter plates and vessels and ate at tables, as among other elites in Europe. In general, ceramics – according to traditional sources – were rarely used, either for food preparation or consumption, because of both cost and fragility.

It is quite clear from both the documentary and archaeological sources that foodways only started to change after the mid 19th century. But how is that ceramics were adopted by households over this period? Is it simply a case that they were cheap and widely available for the first time – along with other goods such as coffee, after the lifting of trade tariffs in 1855? Certainly this played a role, but one should not necessarily assume ceramics were that cheap or regarded as such; one of the most noticeable features of pottery assemblages in Iceland is the amount of repairs one sees on vessels. Although not seemingly in large numbers, compared with assemblages from, for example, England, the differences are evident. At Eyri for example 15 vessels had been repaired (7% of the total), while at Kúvíkur, 4 vessels (2%). There is some suggestion that repair rates drop over the course of the 20th century. Since the numbers are so small from this sample, there is no discernible pattern in the types of vessels which are repaired – plates, bowls, cups and saucer are all more or less equally represented, as are vessels categorized by decoration. It is, therefore, too simplistic to assume the adoption of ceramics was purely driven by external forces; one really needs to understand how Icelanders responded to this new supply of goods in the context of traditional foodways and wooden utensils. Here, the detailed changes

in vessel composition recorded at Kúvíkur provide vital information on this process.

The first pattern to note is the small numbers of cups and saucers before *c*. 1890. This is interesting because, when one considers the role of teawares as the vanguard of industrial ceramics in England in the late 18th century, this in an inverse pattern. At this site at least, teawares seem to be the last addition to the ceramic repertoire of the table, not the first (*e.g.* see Lucas and Regan 2003, 197). This is also related to the later rise in porcelain, since the majority of porcelain vessels were teawares (i.e. cups and saucers). The lateness of teawares at Kúvíkur is partially reflective of the type of site, however; certainly teawares occur in some abundance on late 18th century elite sites in Iceland such as Skálholt (author's data). Furthermore, the use of cups and saucers was probably more for coffee than tea; while tea was popular in the late 18th century, by the mid 19th century, coffee (and chocolate) had become the common hot drinks in Iceland (Gísladóttir 1999, 330); the documented rise in coffee imports after the mid 19th century can probably be linked to the increase in the use of ceramic vessels rather than traditional wooden containers, which would have been poorly suited to hot drinks. However, while cups (and saucers) are perceived as the 'proper' receptacle to use, there is no doubt that bowls were also used for this purpose (Gísladóttir 1999, 331). The small numbers of cups and saucers before 1890 at Kúvíkur may suggest that the bowls were indeed being used instead for this purpose.

The second pattern is related and concerns the changing proportions of bowls and plates. Between the two phases at Kúvíkur, plates increase over time while bowls decrease. The decrease in bowls may relate to the rise in cups and saucers, especially if bowls were used for drinking coffee, but it is also likely something more complex is occurring. Bowls are characteristically multi-functional, and indeed of all the ceramic vessels, are the most similar, functionally, to traditional wooden eating vessels, *askar*. The use of bowls for eating off the lap is easier than plates, which are better suited to tables, especially if using cutlery (Figure 12.6). Ceramic bowls can perhaps be seen as simply replacing the personalized wooden *askur*, though even plates may have been used in combination with bowls for eating dry food with the hand. *Askar* had lids and generally, the bowl was used to hold wet food for eating with a spoon, while the open lid held dry food which could be eaten by hand (Gísladóttir 1999, 21); conceivably a ceramic plate and bowl set could have served the same function. In contrast, the use of plates with cutlery and on tables probably occurred much later and perhaps at first reserved for special dining occasions. The key to differentiating these uses must come from the presence of other tablewares, especially cutlery; it is potentially instructive therefore that no cutlery items were recovered from the earlier site of Eyri, but both a spoon and fork came from the midden at Kúvíkur. Over time, eating

Figure 12.6. Man eating from ceramic bowl, c.1880–1900 (Source: photo by Jón J. Árnason, Akureyri Museum, Iceland).

at tables for everyday dining probably must have become more common, but perhaps not until the early 20th century, though it unquestionably varied according to the location and status of the household (Gísladóttir 1999, 12).

It is a valid question why Icelanders would start to use ceramic over wood after the mid 19th century. While ceramics became cheaper and available as trade tariffs were lifted, there is also a clear suggestion from documentary sources and the archaeology that ordinary people treated them as relatively valuable well into the 20th century. The common presence of repair to vessels suggests that people may have mended broken vessels regularly rather than buy new ones – even if they were available. Given the highly personalized nature of traditional wooden eating vessels, it is possible that similar values were carried over onto ceramics: people may have had their own personal bowls and plates (rather like we may have our own favourite mug

or cup). It was not until the mid 20th century when table dining became the norm that table wares became more impersonal and interchangeable, as they are today.

Mass produced ceramics could not be further removed from the traditional Icelandic *askur*; the one was made abroad, and acquired through commercial exchange, and inherently breakable. The other was locally made, often specifically for an individual and very durable. Given such stark differences, it may seem strange that one could stand in for the other, yet at the same time, without examining closely the process of transition, it is even harder to grasp how ceramics could have been adopted at all. The personalization of ceramics may have been the initial way in which they became incorporated into daily life – especially if they were used in much the same way as traditional wooden vessels. The common repair of ceramic vessels may reflect a level of personal attachment rather than (or as well as) economic necessity, and articulated the contradiction between objects which were inherently fragile and breakable compared to traditional wooden containers. Equally however, it may have been their very fragility that ultimately helped people to learn to de-personalize their relationship to eating and drinking vessels, and facilitate the process of eating at tables rather than on the lap. There is no question that larger processes and changes in the material environment of the home were also at work here, but it seems to me that we should not forget the power of more personal elements in this transition.

Acknowledgements

I would like to thank the following: the late Halldór Bjarnason for supplying the trade data on ceramics; Oscar Aldred for producing the map in Figure 12.3; Mjöll Snæsdóttir for kindly reading over a draft of this paper; and lastly Akureyri Museum for giving permission to use the photograph in Figure 12.6.

References

Finnbogason, G. (1943) Ílátasmíðar, in Finnbogason, G. (ed.) *Iðnsaga Íslands*, Iðnaðarmannafélagið, Reykjavík, 365–375.

Fredlund, J. (1997). *Gammalt porslin. Svenska serviser 1790–1990*, Västerås, ICA Bokförlag.

Gísladóttir, H. (1999) *Íslensk matarhefð*, Reykjavik, Mál og menning.

Taylor, J., Gísladóttir, G., Harðadóttir, A. and Lucas, G. (2005) 'Eyri in Skutulsfjörður'. *Archaeologia Islandica* 4, 68–80

Jónsson, G. and Magnússon, M. S. (eds) (1997) *Hagskinna. Sögulegar hagtölur um Ísland/Icelandic Historical Statistics*, Hagstofa Íslands, Reykjavík.

Jónsson, G. (1997) Changes in Food Consumption in Iceland ca. 1770–1940, in Söderberg, R. J. and Magnusson, L. (eds) *Kultur och Konsumtion i Norden 1750–1950*, 37–60. Historiallinen Arkisto 110:2, Helsingfors.

Jónasson, J. (1961) [1934] *Íslenzkir þjóðhættir*, Ísafoldarprentsmiðja, Reykjavík.

Lárusdóttir, B., Lucas G. Pálsdóttir, L.B. and Ólafsson, S. (2005) 'Kúvíkur. An abandoned trading site', *Archaeologia Islandica* 4, 103–118

Lucas, G. and Regan, R. (2003) The changing vernacular: archaeological excavations at Temple End, High Wycombe, Buckinghamshire. *Post-Medieval Archaeology* 37, 165–206.

Mehler, N. (2000) Die Mittelalterliche Keramik Islands. MA thesis, Otto-Friedrich University, Bamberg, Germany.

Mehler, N. (2004) Die Mittelalterliche Importkeramik Islands, in *Current Issues in Nordic Archaeology. Proceedings of the 21st Conference of Nordic Archaeologists 2001.* pp. 167–70. Félag íslenskra fornleifafræðinga, Reykjavík.

Mikkelsen, L. B. (2000). *Aluminia Fajance 1862–1969*, Viborg, Sesam.

Sveinbjarnardóttir, G. (1993) Vitnisburður leirkera um samband Íslands og. Evrópu á miðöldum. *Árbók hins íslenzka fornleifafélags 92*, 31–49.

Sveinbjarnardóttir, G. (1996). *Leirker á Íslandi/Pottery found in excavations in Iceland*, Hið íslenska fornleifafélag/Þjóðminjasafn Íslands.

13

Gentility: A Historical Context for the Material Culture of the Table in the 'Long 19th Century', 1780–1915

Linda Young

Introduction

The self-control of dining was the goal of a formative psycho-social ordeal at the 19th-century table. The act of dining had become emblematic of the achievement of private refinement and public politesse – or of the failure to achieve them. As described by Agogos, voice of the English-speaking world's most popular etiquette guide in the 1830s, 40s and 50s, *Hints on Etiquette*:

> Nothing indicates a well-bred man more than a proper mode of eating his dinner. A man may pass muster by *dressing well*, and may sustain himself tolerably well in conversation; but if he be not perfectly 'au fait', *dinner* will betray him (Agogos 1834, 18).

Agogos ('teacher') here describes the culture that can be called *gentility*. Gentility was one of a number of terms used in the late 18th–19th century for such a lifestyle; others were respectability, refinement, good taste and good breeding. As used here, gentility is an arbitrary choice of terminology to describe 19th century middle-class culture as read via lifestyle or *habitus*.

The genteel *habitus* frames a historical context for much of the material culture of the table in the 'long 19th century', about 1780–1915, and even beyond. The period can loosely be called 'Victorian' even though it precedes the Queen's reign by about 50 years, for it presents the genteel culture that has long been popularly seen as typical of her era. Additionally, the utility of Victoria's name as a far wider label than her life and role imply shows up in the use of the tag in the United States as well as Britain, referring to the same manifestations of 19th century culture (Howe 1976, 8–9).

The innovation of employing *habitus* as an approach is its cultural framework of lived practice, rather than more conventional analyses by economics or politics; it is specially useful for drawing meaning out of the material remains of the period. Hence this chapter presents the concept of the *habitus* of genteel self-control, with its mutually convertible resources of financial, cultural and symbolic capital as employed via its fundamental mechanisms of etiquette and consumption to generate a new and characteristic middle class that employed a specifically expressive material culture (Young 2003, 69–95). Please take up your table napkin, raise your glass, and enjoy the toast: *bon appetit!*

The Self-Controlled *Habitus* of Gentility

The genteel *habitus* was constructed around a core of self-controlled behaviours buttressed by sustaining values and goods. It peopled the expanding economy created in line with the agricultural, industrial and colonial revolutions of the 18th to 19th centuries with agents who understood how to be responsible, acquired the tools of management, and serviced the growth of capital for a share of the pie. Their self-motivated discipline over mind, body and emotion could be called puritanical, but it was now impelled less by fear of damnation than by a new sensibility of pleasurable satisfaction (Campbell 1987, 100–137). Disciplined comfort might be the essence of smug, which is a more familiar character ascribed to Victorian culture by the modern day. Yet many of its elements are still embedded in today's standards of living, even though others seem fussy and old-fashioned.

The capacity to *dine*, as opposed merely to *feed*, was identified by Norbert Elias, historian of the sociology of self-control, as key in his account of the transition from medieval autocratic power to social control via internalised self-discipline in the modern bourgeois world (Elias 1978, ch. 2). Rules to control personal eating behaviour were codified from the 13th century to teach aristocratic children the manners that would distinguish them from those who lived in more primitive style. They were reinforced by rules for the correct use of a growing battery of material goods which enabled graceful eating, chiefly by separating food from the fingers on its journey to the mouth. Hence Elias's

133

examples focused on the 14th century fork, table napkin and table cloth, all of which reached an apotheosis of influence in the mid-to-late 19th century. (The antithetical seeds of self-expression that then began to be expressed in bohemian practice have since shaped the shift from formal dining to informal 'browsing' as the contemporary style of eating.)

In the quote above, Agogos was making the point that dining was not merely a matter of feeding the inner man but of performing correctly before others by eating and interacting   politely. The context in which he identified dinner as a social performance was the culture of self-control which had informed the lifestyle of educated power in the western world since the middle ages. In the 50 years around the turn of the 19th century and for the next hundred years, once exclusively aristocratic gentle standards infused the burgeoning middle class and the upper reaches of the working class in Britain and the United States, and came to define their domestic and public lifestyle, or at least to inspire their aspirations (Ryan 1981, 231–240; Davidoff and Hall 1987, 319–388).

Such lifestyle, or *habitus* in the terminology of Pierre Bourdieu, constitutes the interplay of cultural practice shaped by values, behaviour and specific material culture (Bourdieu 1984, 1–2, 170). He theorised *habitus* as mediating agency and structure, being subjectively constituted but objectively observable in the positions adopted by categories of people. In his most developed exposition of *habitus*, Bourdieu expanded on its socially constitutive nature as 'the conditionings associated with a particular class of conditions... principles which generate and organise practices and representations', harmonised by material conditions to distil recognisable classes of people (Bourdieu 1990, 58–59). Thus the notion of *habitus* encompasses both the mindset that governs choice and the products of that choice, for example, not only the taste for, but also the expression of, certain spaces, furnishings and equipment in a house, garden, street or town, as well as the variety and mode of lives lived in them and the changes that occur in all these dimensions.

The concept of *habitus* envisages resources as capital in various forms: financial capital or conventional wealth; cultural capital, essentially knowledge gained through education, though not necessarily formal; and symbolic capital, the acknowledgment by others of individual prestige. All are mutually convertible (Bourdieu 1991, 14). Accordingly the field of tastes can be mapped in quadrants defined by financial and cultural capital. The quarter high in both financial and cultural capital contains the wealthy and cultivated and the quarter low in both is the realm of the poor and ignorant. The remaining quarters are occupied by the opposite states of wealth with no learning (the *nouveaux riches*) and learning with no wealth (the genteel poor). Beyond these apexes and nadirs, further permutations of cultivation and money describe all tastes in between.

The important insight given by the theory of *habitus* is to remove taste from the common-sense perception of being either a product of personal idiosyncrasy, or purely a function of wealth. On the contrary, taste is as systematically defined as any of the conventions of social coherence. It is the basis 'whereby one classifies oneself and is classified by others'(Bourdieu 1984, 56). In the long 19th century, acquiring, practising and maintaining the right taste in order to identify and be identified correctly was a matter of exquisite self-control, the defining psyche of the lived and aspiring middle class. The engine of genteel presentation, self-control became a self-perpetuating condition, as cited by an anonymous adviser in 1839:

> Long *self-control* has such composure wrought,
> That *self-control* becomes a thing
> Of which there is no need
> (Anon 1839, 73).

Self-control was practised in expressions such as emotional self-discipline and control of bodily appetites. Eating in public was among the severest tests of bodily self-control. Even today, instinctive greed and the impulse to gobble have to be educated out of every generation of children. The task of training in genteel eating was similar for self-improving adults, who could be highly motivated to learn the sacrifices of politeness. Hence the 19th century genteel *habitus* generated an explosive growth in rules and equipment to govern manners, whose high point to date had been the invention of the fork and the napkin. Far beyond these basics, the Victorian repertoire of table manners and its cast of cutlery simultaneously enabled and required diners to structure their eating into ever more discrete episodes and to ritualise it with many steps. Failure to meet the standards identified and condemned any ignorant imposter. Thus did dining create a hurdle of anxiety on the field of genteel performance.

Despite a common core of self-control, the genteel *habitus* was not a monolithic cultural manifestation. As suggested above, people could practise a somewhat variable span of disciplined behaviours to claim membership in the genteel fold, though the degree to which they would be accepted by others varied with degrees of commitment. Human failing introduced one more condition of variety into the habitus of genteel life, for people did not always live up to the standards they (or their families) set for themselves; as the old adage reminds, the spirit may be willing, but the flesh is weak. Sin might be inadvertent or deliberate, but to manage the reality of both, Victorian gentility raised the art of turning a blind eye to heights that came to seem the essence of hypocrisy.

The range of internal variations set up considerable tension in asserting and maintaining genteel status. In a society in which a constantly increasing number of people became eligible through the acquisition of financial and

Figure 13.1. Controlling food: advice literature presented every vegetable in its place, matching the categories of genteel practice. Beeton's Everyday Cookery and Housekeeping Book, London, Ward, Lock & Co., 1877.

cultural capital to live the genteel *habitus*, a constant struggle ensued to establish a position, protect it from others, and perhaps advance it without opposition. Yet the outcome of this struggle was largely in the hands of others: acknowledgment of one's correctness and acceptability depended on the judgement of those with whom one hoped to affiliate. In Agogos's account, the performance of dining correctly amounted to an index of gentility, the critical evidence by which a subject could express, and a viewer could assess, what kind of person he/she was.

Defining the Middle Class by the Practice of Gentility

Defining the middle class has ever been contentious (Archer and Blau 1993, 19–22). Throughout the 19th century, the gatekeepers of the middle class were its own constituents. This paradox shows that the middle class was not and could never be a homogeneous social bloc. Rather, it was a highly stratified body composed of minutely refined layers of distinction, each stratum distinguishing its own adherents and excluding others. Yet the strata can be seen as unified by the discursive practices of self-control and self-improvement. The range of internal variations set up hurdles of snobbery that generated a tension within the middle class in asserting and maintaining genteel status. Consequently middle-class status was a fluid, dynamic condition, always open for individuals to advance, though risking descent, and constantly contested. One attained middle-class success by acquiescence, through being acknowledged by those whom one sought to join.

Understanding distinctive middle-class culture requires disentangling its apparent adoption of the forms of the aristocracy: its polished manners, refined pleasures and luxurious style. Aristo-imitative elements in the middle-class *habitus* were so frequent that it is easy to assume that the same aristocratic conditions and values underpinned them, but this was not the case. The aristo-imitations contained in middle-class culture point to its essential drive: the urge to aspiration, self-improvement, upward mobility. The dynamic structure of minutely differentiated levels of genteel practice, offering infinite possibilities to move up, was powered by the perception that correct behaviour would achieve the reward of higher status. Very few individuals passed through the barrier to achieve aristocratic status (Stone and Stone 1984, 402–403) But the drive to adopt elegant standards motivated countless aspirants to improve their knowledge, social skills and income and to live ever more comfortable, genteel, middle-class lives in the process of trying.

The values that informed genteel culture simultaneously expressed some of its ambivalences. For though gentility was dedicated to living better and nicer, it was underwritten by a thoroughly unaristocratic respect for the value of work. Where the good life had long been conceived as freedom from labour, the Victorian middle class inverted the relationship to find that labour made the virtuous life (strictly conceived as non-manual labour). Morality replaced pleasure for those who lacked inherited riches, and the work ethic made a virtue out of the necessity to earn an income. And yet the ideal of aristocratic pleasure always represented the peak of elegant lifestyle. This contradiction was resolved by the Victorian middle class in a gendered bifurcation of family responsibility: men worked to make money and women spent it to represent the family honour.

Thus middle-class women became consumers, specialists in knowing what to buy to behave correctly and to create the right environment for social acceptability. In Neil McKendrick's apt phrase, 'luxuries came to be seen as mere "decencies" and "decencies" came to be seen as "necessities" '(McKendrick *et al.* 1982, 1). Spending hard-earned money on goods beyond the necessities of survival could seem like wicked waste, but in the aspirational social economy of the late 18th and 19th centuries, it can instead be viewed as symbolic labour, manufacturing the symbolic capital of honour – which amounted to bourgeois women's work. Still, symbolic labour required the buttress of more apparently productive effort, and thus middle-class women's fancy needlework and decorative parlour crafts were always dignified with the title 'women's work' (except when they were mocked to keep the labour they represented invisible).

In the end, the only solid limits to middle-class status in Britain were, at the top end, the chance of birth that demarcated the aristocracy and, at the bottom, the necessity of manual work that marked the working class. Only the latter barrier existed in the United States, as long as one wasn't a slave. The in-between group was a heterogeneous and endlessly sub-divisible middle class, not united in any public sphere but sharing a body of ideas and behaviours, practised through education, reading, religion, servant management, and kinship connections (Blumin 1989, 11–13; Morris 1990, 318–322). It amounted to perhaps 10–12% of the population in Britain and somewhat more in the United States, but the small number shaped the dreams of many more (Perkin 1989, 28–30; Rorabaugh 1987, 25–26; Pessen 1977, 13). For on both sides of the Atlantic, genteel characteristics joined together a great body of individuals and directed their action and experience in such common ways that it is feasible to call 19th century Britain and the United States bourgeois-inspired societies, led by middle-class values.

Etiquette and Consumption

The self-discipline that constituted the practical-cultural basis of the genteel habitus was expressed in the 'long 19th century' through two regimes: etiquette and consumption. The two shaped the major aspects of the rituals of polite dining, and to the degree they were employed correctly, they underwrote genteel middle-class behaviour and environment. Etiquette and consumption both offered systems of distinction via registers of difference; thus choices among the immense range of possible actions in each system located the practitioner in relation to others. By signifying either inclusion or exclusion from their sector of *habitus* both systems express the agent's command of cultural capital, as well as a certain quantum of economic capital. The practice of both is, as Bourdieu writes, 'an act of deciphering, decoding, which presupposes practical or explicit mastery of a cipher or code' (Bourdieu 1984, 2).

Of the two, etiquette was the purest system of difference. Etiquette had grown out of a 500-year history of courtly courtesy whose original purpose had been the king's control of a potentially subversive aristocracy. But by the turn of the 19th century, etiquette was driven by the individual's internalised commitment to the correct construction of social relations. Not only did etiquette comprise a set of rules, but it also required interpretation of the rules situated in real life. Here clustered the possibilities for variation, in the decisions that directed action the right way or the wrong way. The correctness of the agent's choice could never be certain, being knowable only through its reception by peers (or would-be peers). In this dialectic of actor to audience lay the dynamic of etiquette.

The resource of financial capital was not enough on its own for genteel standing; it had to be conditioned by cultural capital. In fact, cultural capital without wealth could sometimes be accepted as genteel in itself, exemplified by the widowed lady-companion or the orphaned governess, though the extreme difficulty of keeping up standards on a small income was acknowledged with pity. The important thing was that the possibility of buying gentility (and thus fraudulently claiming cultural capital) was sidestepped by the necessity of learning it from scratch, either by childhood up-bringing or determined application by an aspirant adult. But the way for the would-be genteel was anxious: are we performing correctly? Will we be accepted by those we seek as our peers? On the other side of the liminal border of gentility was suspicion: are we being deceived? Is she one of us?

Etiquette: Best Behaviour

Etiquette comprised two distinct fields: the consideration of others that underlies personal good manners and the mastery of the code that governed public intercourse. (Friendship and family relationships were excluded from etiquette, assumed to be governed by affection rather than rules.) Manners constituted the self-disciplined awareness of others in everyday life by controlling the impulse to immediate gratification. The practice was achieved by socialising the child into a civilised adult via education, example and, if necessary, coercion. Once the preserve of the aristocracy,

the growth of good manners trickled to the middling ranks throughout the 18th century, in standards which had been much the same in principle since the late middle ages: physical restraint, personal modesty, and attention to and acknowledgment of others. This continuity is exemplified in the history of *The School of Good Manners*, initially written in French in 1564; translated into English in 1595 and published at least four times; adapted at the turn of the 18th century in New England and reprinted there in at least 30 editions; returned to Britain in 1818 and published in numerous further adaptations until the middle of the century (Vail 1942, 266). Its precepts can be traced in almost every 19th-century compilation on manners, as, for instance, this selection for the table:

> Eat not too fast, or with greedy behaviour.
> Eat not too much, but moderately.
> Eat not so slow as to make others wait for thee.
> Make not a noise with thy tongue, mouth or breath, in eating or drinking (Moody 1818, 7).

Good manners formed the threshold of polite social life and were, by Victorian times, an assumed body of knowledge and practice upon which the formal body of etiquette could be built. Genteel 19th century etiquette descended with persistent aristocratic style from French court etiquette a hundred years before. Ideally, etiquette would be part of adolescent learning in the family, but middle-class aspirants lacking genteel parents turned to the multitude of guides offering to explain the structure of etiquette. Such guides systematised the rules of conduct in public, though small differences indicate that the real nature of etiquette was more subtle, depending on fine understandings of each other by both performer and audience.

Most etiquette books were written for specific demographics. The genre's tradition was overwhelmingly directed to the young in the form of prescriptions for good manners rather than formal etiquette, as in *The School of Good Manners*. Etiquette enters the guides for older children on the threshold of adulthood, usually differentiated by gender, as in *Advice to a Young Gentleman on Entering Society* and *The Young Lady's Friend* (Anon 1839; A Lady 1837). A smaller proportion of etiquette books was addressed to a general audience in a voice that generously assumed the readership needed just a little polish under the guidance of anonymous but allegedly aristocratic authors; *Hints on Etiquette* is in this category. Such books often identifiably re-phrased the prescriptions for good manners from children's guides. Etiquette books were rarely directed explicitly to the working class, other than to enjoin them to be better-behaved within their natural sphere.

As well as advice books, the topic of ritual etiquette was presented to the would-be genteel in the 'silver fork' school of fashionable novels, popular from about 1810–1840, and in short stories in ladies' magazines in the later half of the

19th century. (Adburgham 1983). (The silver fork referred to the emblem of respectable manners, style and income.) Tales of wealthy, fashionable life offered readers vicarious pleasure as well as models of refined behaviour, and authors found they had a voracious market.

Advice books were regularly denounced by the genteel establishment but the demand appeared insatiable, evidence of massive popular faith in self-improvement. Appearing to commodify the cultural capital of the middle class, they were reviled with a jeremiad against upstarts, who were assured it was impossible they could learn anything to assist their ambitions. Reviewing a spate of etiquette guides, a gatekeeper railed against

> the demand for this sort of trash [which] betokened an unworthy and degrading eagerness on the part of a large part of the community to learn how lords and ladies ate, drank, dressed and coquetted (Anon. 1837, 396).

Yet for all the resistance drawn by the etiquette manuals, it is clear that, with some limitations, they helped to produce reality through their discursive presentations. The same writer acknowledged, 'it is undeniable there is a great deal of good sense, with many valuable suggestions regarding manners and conduct, in these books' (Anon. 1837, 398). Yet the inherent limits of codification meant the fine distinctions established in social contact could be recorded only to a degree: a book is a finite piece of reporting on a dynamic process of communication. Nailing it immediately established a canon to be avoided by the empowered, as they re-established boundaries to protect their exclusive interests, even as out-groups vied to fulfil its precepts. But criticism never dampened the market for advice.

The central principle of Victorian etiquette was to understand one's own status in all circumstances, and to act appropriately: 'respectfully open and cheerful with your superiors, warm and animated with your equals, hearty and free with your inferiors', was Lord Chesterfield's mid 18th century advice, which lived on in 19th century manuals (Strachey 1901, v.2, 264). Gauging oneself in relation to others was the crucial step in successful etiquette.

Though never condoned in etiquette guides, the technique of assessing status was small talk, the apparently trivial chat that establishes wealth and social claims through 'incidental' references in polite conversation. Its vital sphere was the ritual of ladies visiting each other at home, making calls and leaving calling cards, in order to establish and maintain relationships – an acknowledged element of etiquette (Young 2003, 140–142). Knowing how to conduct oneself correctly as a visitor and a visitee required the investment of cultural capital for symbolic product. The relationships thus established by women could lead their men to deals and partnerships, which, in an age before business probity could be established institutionally, relied on personal networks of trust. 'Do not imagine these little ceremonies to be insignificant,' urged 'A Lady of Rank', who revised Agogos fifteen years after his first publication, 'they are the customs of society and if you do not conform to them, you will gain the unenviable distinction of being pointed out as an ignorant, ill-bred person' (Agogos and A Lady of Rank 1849, 22).

The further elaboration of etiquette in public encounters such as dinners and balls informed practitioners how to respond correctly, essentially a matter of understanding precedence and having others recognise one's legitimate place in it. The goal at formal events was the ceremony of public identification with one's peers: at a ball, arriving, being announced and greeting the host and hostess; at dinner, moving to the dining room and sitting around the table in acceptable order. In Britain, the nobility defined the only firm rules of precedence, and many etiquette guides contained long discussions of how to treat an earl's son's wife *vis-à-vis* a baronet's lady. But most middle-class people rarely came into contact with titled personages, so the manuals' claim to correct prescriptions was hollow advice.

Instead, people followed a less explicit hierarchy of honour, in which gender, age, learning and wealth constituted the criteria, interpreted rather flexibly according to circumstance. The same characteristics came to define American ideas of polite precedence, which seemed to pose a philosophical challenge: who has precedence in a nation of equals (Hemphill 1999, 130)? But the pragmatic answer, usually defined by wealth, was as powerful in the USA as in commercial Britain. Thus the middle-class motivation to improve its lot sustained the transnational application of the genteel compromise of culture with money. This encapsulates the second great mechanism of middle-class gentility: correct consumption of the right goods.

Consumption: Good Taste

A second system of expressive difference was offered by the consumption of goods. The tremendous variety of goods available in the early 19th century, and their range of material, colour and quality, opened up a field of choices more concrete but not necessarily clearer than that of etiquette. Bourdieu argues that luxury and high culture goods are the most effective for making distinctions among the classes of taste because they require advanced levels of ownership of financial and cultural capital; he finds artworks the surest classifier on account of the range of distinctions they contain (for example, artist, style, genre) (Bourdieu 1984, 16, 226). The new luxuries of the early 19th century fulfil Bourdieu's precept perfectly: in the context of the expanding middle class and the productivity of the Industrial Revolution, the new comforts were closely connected to quantity and innovation.

New capacities to manufacture and to consume developed in Britain in the mid 18th century and in the United States by the early 19th. Factories producing consumer goods multiplied production again and again throughout the 19th century, and goods became less expensive, being made of cheaper materials (such as light cottons instead of heavy wools; veneers instead of solid timbers) and produced with new economies of scale (Shammas 1990, 185). These goods serviced a consumer revolution in demand, expressed by an unprecedented number of people. Their purchasing power steadily improved, admittedly more slowly among the working class than the upper classes, and unevenly in time and location (Taylor 1975, 1). Such consumption recruited working-class people into the enlarging middle-class, powered by social ambition and desire for comfort, while the rise in new middle-class jobs generated a steady and sometimes spectacular increase in prosperity.

The mass availability of domestic goods such as ceramic tablewares, printed cottons for furnishings and clothing, and small metal goods such as cutlery and jewellery, enabled the growing or aspiring middle-class to affiliate with and discriminate among other people, who revealed by their own consumption how they constructed their vision of genteel living. The unprecedented range of goods available made it possible for people with diverse incomes to afford, say, a dinner service: even if the tablewares were a truncated version of the top of the line, each variety of plate and serving vessel was in the same family of goods and presented the same template of genteel characteristics in the practice of their users. The new china constituted a social statement about the values of its consumers.

Aspirants to middle-class status needed to learn how to consume the decencies and luxuries which new values taught them to need and new incomes could sustain. Certain pieces of equipment actively enabled new behaviours; others decorated the person or the environment in conventional but exclusive ways. Owning and using items such as a bath or visiting cards instrumentalised the transformation to genteel status. The individual who washed his body every day had internalised the mental set of valuing a high degree of personal cleanliness; it separated him from the great unwashed and connected him to the refined body of gentility. The person who distributed visiting cards in the card receivers of selected people's halls possessed self-respect and a vision of the middle-class society; if her cards were accepted, she belonged to this society. Without a bath or the pieces of engraved pasteboard, aspirants remained unable to participate in genteel culture. At the same time, possession of the goods without the knowledge to use them correctly constituted not just the absence of gentility but a definition of vulgarity. Exposing oneself to classification by what one consumed could therefore be a tense step for the inexperienced.

The trap for genteel aspirants was that wealth had to be consumed with taste, the mechanism of applying cultural capital to the material world. The fundamental component of genteel taste was restraint, yet another expression of self-control. Restraint applied to all the characteristics of goods: colour, texture, ornament; size, materials and manufacture. This is not to say that middle-class taste was plain and cheap, because correct taste was further qualified by being appropriate to its circumstances. Ostentatious consumption belied taste, yet modesty of expenditure where more could be afforded showed insufficient respect for middle-class propriety. Restraint was invoked to justify the economy of good quality, a judgement that underwrote the new middle-class standard of expensive simplicity, known as 'pure' or 'chaste' taste. (It must be said that Victorian simplicity had a different meaning to the modern concept.) The practised genteel eye could read degrees of taste, noting its propriety and quality in each context, and thus classify self and others. With these standards, *parvenu* incorrectness could be condemned as gaudy, gimcrack, vulgar.

Tasteful goods could be expensive, but were also available in cheaper registers – in either case, the degree of financial investment was evident to spectators who understood the code. At the same time, modest consumption could frame a lifestyle of gentility in simplicity, which in some degree democratised honour by removing the requirement to be pedigreed, rich or famous. Even with relatively limited financial resources, the genteel person could furnish a life with goods that demonstrated genteel standards.

Genteel Material: Etiquette and Consumption at the Table

The forms of etiquette themselves were rituals to be enacted via specific items of material culture, but genteel knowledge was necessary to gather the correct goods, of the right combination, in the precise order, for just the purpose. In the context of polite dining, the exemplary case was the full formal dinner party, practised in reduced forms *en famille* and even, among the truly genteel, alone.

As prescribed in a characteristic later 19th century etiquette manual (Smiley 1889, 167–183), a dinner party was a social occasion for outsiders as well as family, calling for highly controlled performances by the guests, the hosts and the servant(s). Ideally, the hosts would invite guests of similar background, so as not to expose anyone to the discomfort of awkward acquaintances. The pleasure of their company would be requested by formal note, and responded to with an equally polite note. Garbed in best clothes, the guests would arrive on time, to indicate that they were neither hungry for food nor casual about the invitation. Genteel mingling proved that the gathering of ladies and gentlemen were indeed peers – or provoked the first uncomfortable hints of social inadequacy or failure...

By the later 19th century, invitation cards were invented as a specialised genre of ready-made stationery, easing the

Figure 13.2 Producing silverware for all: Reed & Barton's silverplate works at Taunton, Massachusetts, enabled (relatively) cheap table silver for middle class consumption. Scientific American, 41/19, 1879.

pressure on a nervous hostess about getting the style right – but simultaneously drawing a self-defining veil over the real competence of the kind of lady who might use pre-printed cards. Yet the demand for cards and for standard formats of wording provided by helpful etiquette guides constitute clear evidence that people desired the genteel style even if they weren't confident about practising it.

The initial moment of asserting the hosts' standing among their guests occurred when the maid (or butler, if one could be afforded) signalled to the hostess to alert her to that the table was ready, setting off the cascade of precedence in entering the dining room. Partners in the procession would have been mentioned in the introductions beforehand, separating married couples to maximise social interchange. The host led the way to the table with the most important lady on his left arm; the rest of the guests followed in order of honour or seniority; and the hostess brought up the rear with the most important gentleman, to be seated at her right. All took their seats with self-controlled calm, not too close to their neighbours, and began a new round of polite conversation with their neighbours.

The room that the guests had entered was in itself a benchmark of middle-class gentility: to dedicate a room exclusively to dining constituted a claim to refined separation of eating from the kitchen, desirable even at the cost of cold meals. To eat in the kitchen was to acknowledge the production of food, a suitable state for servants and the poor, but not for their betters. Where cultural capital exceeded financial resources, it was a common compromise in the face of necessity to have a dining table in the parlour, but without a dedicated dining room, it was impossible to hold dinner parties, with evident implications for a subject's honour as host. The specialised room required specialised furniture. Domestic advisers recommended substantial goods: a pair of carved mahogany sideboards, a pair of side tables, a handsome dining table with matching chairs, cellarets for wine storage, lamps for the sideboards, a mantel mirror, richly framed pictures on the walls (Loudon 1833, 800; Downing 1850, 404). The correct environment was exemplified by the sideboard, essentially a piece of display furniture for conspicuously housing valuable table plate when not in use and for presenting tableware and food during meals.

Now began the staged drama of the meal, course following course in stately progress. The essentially medieval style of presenting several courses of many dishes on the table simultaneously constructed the major step of polite dining as the self-control to wait for the host to carve the meat and other guests to pass the many dishes. This show of generous plenty was overtaken among the stylish from the 1820s by service *à la Russe*, in which plated meals were presented by servants, thus displaying the host as a lord of men as well as provider of food. Nonetheless, older customs persisted in households of different degrees of wealth and fashion.

The critical practices of dining drew on all the self-controlled resources of the genteel body, beginning with an easy, elegant posture and no abrupt movements, expressions or noises. Appetite was suppressed in a show of small helpings, eaten slowly and quietly in delicate mouthfuls, leaving a discreet bit on the plate as evidence that greed had no place at this plate. The unavoidably animal character of eating was avoided symbolically by touching food as little as possible, thanks to implements that intervened between hand and mouth. Such a high degree of distancing behaviour suggests the power of ritual to control pollution and thus uphold the social order, as understood via the anthropology of social purity (Douglas 1966, 121–122).

Dining was the site of one of the earliest expressions of genteel self-control in the form of table tools; in feudal times, use of a fork had distinguished the gentle person's self-discipline and in the 18th century, fork-use trickled down the ranks of society (Elias 1994, 85–88; Kasson 1987, 130–141). By the early 19th century, matching sets of forks, spoons, and less frequently, knives, occupied the genteel diner's hands. (Knives always retained the potential to be non-matching implements, because they required blades of steel set into handles of many possible materials, not necessarily *en suite* with other implements.) Elaborate sets of cutlery on the table asserted the flattering expectation that all the guests subscribed to high standards of manipulating food, and the generous expectation that the host could satisfy these standards. Even if simpler in style and fewer in number, any multiple of eating utensils communicated the same message to diners. Industrial mass production rose to meet the expanding demand with elegant imitations of rich cutlery and flatware, enabling even the relatively not-rich to participate in the world of genteel dining.

Solid silver tablespoons were the heaviest and hence most expensive items, but it was forks that incarnated genteel significance as the tool of rich, refined eating; Agogos asserted confidently, 'At every respectable table you will find silver forks' (Agogos 1834, 16). Thanks to the new imitation silvers – Sheffield plate, Britannia metal, German silver and electroplating – agents with less income than aspiration could dress their dining tables with the necessary glossy implements. Inventory records show that many middle-class households also possessed a token few items of sterling silver table equipment such as fish slices, sugar tongs and wine coasters, just enough to create an air of luxury to infuse the atmosphere of the imitation goods (Young 2003, 182–183).

The ceramic and glass equipage of the formal dining table constituted further opportunities for the simultaneous display of wealth and of the subtle range of behaviours that marked genteel practice. A standard dinner service comprised 60 or more pieces, mainly sets of different-sized plates, plus a variety of serving dishes, bowls, lidded dishes and sauceboats. The pure white ceramic of Chinese porcelain had defined

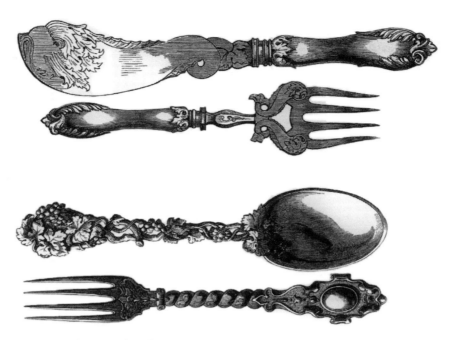

Figure 13.3. Knowing tasteful tableware: silver flatware – here, of virtuosos Exhibition-style – demonstrated not only the wealth to afford it but also the mind to appreciate art. Crystal Palace Exhibition: Illustrated Catalogue, London, 1851, New York, Dover, 1970.

luxurious table-beauty to Europeans since the 17th century and inspired the quest to produce equally white products in local pottery via glazes and new body compositions. White bodies could be decorated with handpainting, linework or transfer-printing in imitation Chinese blue, other oriental colours, local colours and gold, and decorative textures could be applied or moulded or pierced. Combinations of such techniques generated a huge variety of beautiful tablewares at almost every price. Meanwhile, augmenting the oriental imitations and inspirations, the modern 18th to 19th century China trade imported enormous quantities of porcelain, especially to the USA.

Table glass included finger bowls, custard cups, jelly glasses and dishes for preserves, pickles and ginger. Drinking glasses were identified for specific liquids: wine (sherry, claret, hock, champagne), whisky, cider, water and soda water, indicating why an American adviser noted the challenge that 'the fashionable glass for each wine varying so frequently, it is difficult… to give any rules' (Leslie 1841, 258). The decorative layout of the serving dishes, plates and glasses on the table, sketched in many an instruction manual, was ritualised by the elegant repetition of each course, presenting the host's knowledge as well as means. The quantities of differentiated silver, china and glass comprised only one aspect of the genteel mentality in the use of tablewares. For the mass output of the metalworks of the midlands and New England, the potteries of Staffordshire and the Ohio valley, and the glassworks of Stourbridge and Corning, churned out sets available in so many registers of price that the semiotic quality of multiple specific items was

effectively available to anyone possessing the motivation and knowledge to use it.

At the end of the dinner came the withdrawal of the ladies, at the hostess's signal, leaving the gentlemen in the dining room to drink liquor and smoke for a relaxed period of bonding or networking. In terms of strategic business, this could be called the goal of the formal dinner, but it needed the parade of honour and the respectable dining conduct to prove up the standing of potential partners. Meanwhile, the ladies retired for tea or sweet wine in the drawing room, enjoying or enduring each other's company until the men rejoined them 15 or 20 minutes later. Now began the post-prandial entertainment, varying in line with the degree of formality and the hosts' resources. A recital might be given by an engaged artiste or guests might sing, accompanied by the hostess or a daughter at the piano; card tables might be set up; an important guest might hold forth on a topic; earlier conversations could continue, though in public vein only. The point was polite interaction among all, confirming mutual parity; pleasure was incidental, as shown by accounts in Victorian novels of dreary dinner parties.

When dinners had less driven purposes, they could be accordingly less formal, but the highest standards of refined living called for the stages of pre-dinner mingling, entry to the dining room in order of precedence, self-controlled behaviour at table, withdrawal of ladies and subsequent gathering again for entertainment, should still obtain. In reality, few owned the resources or were so driven to perform so fully every night, and hence each family compromised with genteel dinner ritual in its own way. Still, the effective middle class person had to be capable of performing at the highest level as required. As Agogos had written, dinner was indeed the ultimate test.

In sum, in its full-blown use, the dining table was a critical field of the genteel *habitus* that characterised the Victorian middle class and its aspirants. As a private, family site, it was a field of training and rehearsal in the achievement of the self-controlled cultural capital of good manners. It stood as a fulcrum of middle-class social politics in its model of the righteous order of masters, mistresses and servants. As a selectively public site its existence enabled perhaps the prime ritual hospitality of like-seeking people. Its fittings demonstrated the vital mix of cultural and financial capital that framed genteel status in the eyes of beholders. As a public/private interface the table furnished the stage for the genteel performance of introduction, affiliation, connection and validation.

References

Adburgham, A. (1983) *Silver Fork Society: Fashionable life and literature from 1814 to 1840*, London, Constable.

Agogos [William Charles Day] (1834) *Hints on Etiquette and the Usages of Society with a Glance at Bad Habits*, London, Printed for the Booksellers.

Agogos and A Lady of Rank (1849) *Hints on Etiquette and the Usages of Society with a Glance at Bad Habits*, 26th edn, revised (with additions) by A Lady of Rank, London, Orme, Brown, Green and Longmans.

Anon. [Abraham Hayward] (1837) Codes of manners and etiquette. *Quarterly Review*, 59/18.

Anon. (1839) *Advice to a Young Gentleman on Entering Society*, London, A. H. Bailey.

Archer, M. and Blau, J. (1993) Class formation in nineteenth-century America: the case of the middle class. *Annual Review of Sociology* 19, 17–41.

Blumin, S. M. (1989) *The Emergence of the Middle Class: Social Experience in the American City, 1760–1900*, Cambridge, Cambridge University Press.

Bourdieu, P. (1984) *Distinction: A Social Critique of the Judgement of Taste*, London, Routledge and Kegan Paul.

Bourdieu, P. (1990) *The Logic of Practice*, Cambridge, Polity Press.

Bourdieu, P. (1991) *Language and Symbolic Power*, Cambridge, Polity Press.

Bushman, R. (1992) *The Refinement of America: Persons, Houses, Cities*, New York, Knopf.

Campbell, C. (1987) *The Romantic Ethic and the Spirit of Modern Consumerism*, Oxford, Blackwell.

Davidoff, L. and Hall, C. (1987) *Family Fortunes: Men and Women of the English Middle Class, 1750–1850*, London, Hutchison.

Douglas, M. (1966) *Purity and Danger: An Analysis of the Concepts of Pollution and Taboo*, New York, Praeger.

Downing, A. J. (1850) *The Architecture of Country Houses*, New York, Dover, 1969 [facs].

Elias, N. (1978) *The Civilizing Process: The History of Manners*, trans. Edmund Jephcott, Oxford, Blackwell.

Hall, C. (1990) The sweet delights of home, in Perrot, M. (ed.) *From the Fires of Revolution to the Great War*, Cambridge MA, Belknap, 51–102.

Hemphill, C. D. (1999) *Bowing to Necessities: A History of Manners in the United States, 1620–1860*, New York, Oxford University Press.

Howe, D. W. (ed.) (1976) *Victorian America*, Philadelphia, University of Pennsylvania Press.

Kasson, J. F. (1987) Rituals of dining: table manners in Victorian America, in Grover K. (ed.) *Dining in America, 1850–1900*, Amherst MA, University of Massachusetts Press, 114–41.

Lady, A. [Eliza Ware Farrar] (1837) *The Young Lady's Friend*, Boston, American Stationers' Company.

Leslie, Miss (1841) *The House Book, or A Manual of Domestic Economy*, Philadelphia, Carey and Hart.

Loudon, J. C. (1833) *Encyclopedia of Cottage, Farm and Villa Architecture*, London.

McKendrick, N., Brewer, J. and Plumb, J. H. (1982) *The Birth of a Consumer Society: The Commercialisation of Eighteenth-Century England*, London, Europa.

Moody, E. (1818) *The School of Good Manners*, Newburyport, Thomas Whipple.

Morris, R. J. (1990) *Class, Sect and Party: The Making of the British Middle Class, Leeds, 1820–1850*, Manchester, Manchester University Press.

Perkin, H. (1989) *The Rise of Professional Society: England since 1880*, London, Routledge.

Pessen, E. (1977) The egalitarian myth and the American social reality: wealth, mobility and equality in the 'era of the common man', in *The Many-Faceted Jacksonian Era: New Interpretations*, Westport CT, Greenwood.

Rorabaugh, W. J. (1987) Beer, lemonade and propriety in the gilded age, in Grover, K. (ed.) *Dining in America, 1850–1900*, Amherst MA, University of Massachusetts Press, 24–46.

Rosman, D. (1984) *Evangelicals and Culture*, London, Croom Helm.

Ryan, M. (1981) *Cradle of the Middle Class: The Family in Oneida County, New York, 1790–1865*, Cambridge, Cambridge University Press.

Shammas, C. (1990) *The Pre-Industrial Consumer in England and America*, Oxford, Clarendon Press.

Smiley, J. B. (1889) *Modern Manners and Social Forms*, Chicago, James B. Smiley.

Strachey, C. (ed.) (1901) *The Letters of the Earl of Chesterfield to his Son*, London, Methuen.

Stone, L. and Stone, J. F. (1984) *An Open Elite? England 1540–1800*, Oxford, Oxford University Press.

Taylor, A. J. (ed.) (1975) *The Standard of Living in the Industrial Revolution*, London, Methuen.

Vail, R. W. G. (1942) *Moody's School of Good Manners: a study in American Colonial etiquette. In*: American Council of Learned Societies Devoted to Humanistic Studies. Conference of the Secretaries of Constituent Societies, *Studies in the History of Culture*, Menasha WN, ACLS.

Yosifon, D. and Stearns, P. (1998) The rise and fall of American posture. *American Historical Review* 103/4, 1057–62.

Young, L. (2003) *Middle Class Culture in the Nineteenth Century: America, Australia and Britain*, Basingstoke, Palgrave.

14

Feeding Workers:
Food and Drink in Early Colonial Australia

Susan Lawrence

Introduction

Most settlers in the first 50 years of colonial Australia were workers of one kind or another: convicts, soldiers, pastoral workers, farm workers, or, as in this case, maritime workers. For many of these people, their food and drink were provided by their employers as part of their conditions of employment. Some took the provisions supplied and prepared the meals themselves. This was particularly the case with pastoral and agricultural workers, and with convicts in the early years. Others, such as soldiers and maritime workers, often ate communally of food prepared by someone employed as a cook. This system politicised food and created potential for tensions of all sorts: between what was made available and what was acceptable, between what was provided on the ration and what was obtained privately, and most of all between those who supplied and those who consumed. Employers tried to save on cost by providing the bare minimum that their employees would accept. Workers viewed food as a critical component of their working conditions, and withheld their labour if they felt the quantity or quality of food was not adequate. These issues will be explored through the site-specific details of food eaten and dishes used at two shore whaling stations excavated in Tasmania.

During the early colonial period (from first British settlement at Sydney Cove in 1788 to the discovery of gold in 1851), and indeed beyond, the diet of white Australians was heavily influenced by that of their British homelands. Familiar foods such as wheat, oats, barley, mutton, and beef were first imported, then raised locally from imported stock, and prepared in familiar, traditional ways. Although there was some experimentation with local game, native animal and plant species did not appear on the tables of settlers, and, with the exception of local fish and seafood, made no lasting contribution to the settlers' diet. It was not until the late 20th century that the flavours of the bush, or of neighbouring Asia, began to play a significant role in Australian cuisine.

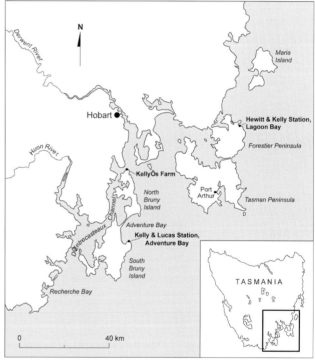

Figure 14.1. Location of the two sites.

The early colonists, like their contemporaries in England, were eating modern, store-bought foods such as tea, sugar, butter, and white bread, rather than the more traditional oatmeal, milk and cheese (Shammas 1990, 144). Both in Britain and in Australia workers were also eating as much meat as they could possibly get, but the colonists, both convict and free, were eating a great deal more meat than those they left behind. It has been calculated that colonial Australians ate as much as 270 pounds of meat annually, compared with the British diet of only 109 pounds per person each year (Gollan 1978, 68). Maize grew better than wheat in the warm coastal settlements, and was adopted by many for bread and porridge, while rice and lentils were imported from India (Gollan 1988, 4; Kingston 1994, 7). Dairies were common on both large and small properties, and butter and cheese were commercially available from an early date (Casey 1999). Fruit and vegetables were also increasingly available, particularly for those living in family groups on farms or on the large urban blocks that prevailed in the early years. Archaeological sites in Sydney have demonstrated that people were growing peas and beans, cabbage, radish, and turnip as early as 1800, and that they were also growing lemon, apple, and peach trees (Karskens 1999, 33). In rural districts and for men, such as shepherds, living alone in the bush, there was little beyond the ration of bread, meat, sugar, and tobacco.

Most of the discussion regarding diet in the early colonies concerns either the ruling elites or the convicts. This reflects both the nature of colonial society, in which free settlers were in the minority until the 1840s, and the nature of the documentary record on which much discussion has been based. To date the best evidence for diet among lower ranked free colonists has come from archaeological sites, and primarily from urban sites in Sydney and Parramatta. Much less is known about those who lived outside these urban centres, or about workers who were free rather than on convict rations. The information obtained from the excavation of the Tasmanian whaling stations constitutes a valuable source of insight into conditions for free workers in the colonies.

Shore Whaling

The whaling industry, which provided the bulk of exports from the Australian colonies until overtaken by wool in the 1840s, was a significant source of employment for colonial-born youths. Unlike most other industries, including agriculture, pastoralism, and construction, where much of the work was done by convict labourers, convicts were forbidden from working in whaling because of the potential danger of escape. Whaling crews were thus exclusively composed of free men, both Australian-born and men from British and American ships, and could include Aboriginal men, African Americans, Azores Islanders, and Polynesians as well as whites. Deep-sea whaling fleets were based in the colonial capitals of Sydney and Hobart, while shore whalers set up seasonal camps or stations in sheltered bays along the whales' migration routes. The stations included facilities for rendering the blubber into oil, storing gear, and living accommodation for the crews. Those employed were generally all male, although in rare cases the manager's wife and children were present.

Onboard ship and at the stations the men worked in teams of six, which made up the crew of a whaleboat. The most skilful and experienced man in each boat was the 'headsman', and the most senior headsman at the station was also the manager. All the workers were employed on a seasonal basis on a system of 'lays'. A lay was a share of the season's catch, and the size of the lay depended on the skill and seniority of the worker. A new crew member might get a 1/100 share, while an experienced boatsteerer might get 1/60th. The size of the lay was fixed at the beginning of each season in the agreements signed by each crew member. Rations were provided as part of the agreement, and during the season the workers could make additional purchases of clothing, tobacco, and other sundries from the stores. The cost of the purchases was then deducted from the amount paid when the season ended.

As skill could be rewarded with promotion, the whaling industry was uniquely a place where an ambitious colonial youth could hope to advance. It was also an industry where those at the top, the owners and managers, had often begun at the bottom. Their ambiguous social lineages made them particularly susceptible to the pressures and tensions experienced by those in the emerging middle classes. The stations themselves became part of the arena in which these tensions were played out, as the material culture of space, buildings, and particularly food became part of the struggle to symbolically differentiate the aristocracy of labour.

Such ambiguities characterise the career of Captain James Kelly. Born of convict parents in New South Wales only three years after the colony was founded, Kelly went to sea at the age of 13. By the 1820s he was a prominent businessman in Hobart with ships, farms, town property, and several shore whaling stations in Tasmania and the mainland. In the late 1990s two of Kelly's Tasmanian stations were excavated, and the results of those excavations has revealed much about the daily lives of the whaling parties. Diet at the stations, and how the food was served, has been reconstructed using a combination of written and archaeological evidence.

The two stations were located at Adventure Bay and Bruny Island. The Adventure Bay site operated from at least 1829 until approximately 1841. Excavations at the site were carried out in 1997, and uncovered the remains of the tryworks, what has been interpreted as the crew barracks, and the quarters of the senior headsman (Lawrence 2006). Artefacts were recovered from shallow scatters of refuse inside and outside the buildings.

The site at Lagoon Bay was established in 1838, then closed by the government in 1842 due to its proximity to the convict settlement of Port Arthur (Evans 1993, 28). A new lease was applied for in 1848, and archaeological evidence indicates that the station was re-occupied for, at least one more season at that time. Excavations were carried out in 1999 and again focussed on the crew barracks and the quarters of the senior headsman, with artefacts recovered from shallow accumulations of refuse in and around the buildings.

The Foods Consumed

Information about the food Kelly provided to his crews is contained in the official agreements between Kelly and individual crewmen that were signed at the start of each season (Evans 1993, 43–44, Chamberlain 1988, 227–233). Each week Kelly was to supply each man with 12 lbs of beef or mutton, or 10 lbs of pork, 12 lbs of flour or bread, two lbs of sugar and 1/3 lb of tea (Tucker 1999, 28). Kelly's meat rations were double those provided to sailors in the British navy at this time, who received only six lbs of salt beef and pork a week (Lloyd 1981, 10). The whalers' allocation also compares favourably with the standard colonial diet of the period, which as has been seen, was itself comfortably more abundant than the diet of the average worker in Britain or Ireland at the time. The generosity of the ration reflects the hard physical labour expected of the men, and the difficult conditions under which the work was performed.

Shore whalers worked outdoors through the cold and rainy winter months and frequently spent whole days at sea in open whale boats, watching for whales. When whales were spotted the men gave chase, rowing the boats at speeds of up to five knots (Nash 2003, 18). Once a whale had been harpooned and killed, the men had to tow the carcass back to the shore station for processing. Depending on how far

out to sea the whale had taken them during the chase, this might involve an arduous journey of many hours, even days, the men rowing all the way. The processing of the whale blubber into oil also required immense physical effort from the men, particularly while the heavy blubber was removed in strips and cut into chunks to go into the trypot. It has been calculated that the Australian male convict's ration provided 28, 381 calories per week, enough for 5.4 calories for each minute of the 56 hour working week (Nicholas 1988, 185). The whalers' rations, and hence caloric intake, was higher than the convict average, but as their working week was much longer, and could involve round-the-clock shifts, their diet was not extravagant to their needs.

While the crew agreements provide a general indication of the diet that was expected, the excavations have filled in the detail, and have also revealed unexpected information about foods not described in the official papers. The excavations recovered bone from many kinds of animals, birds, and fish. Most of the bone excavated was from domestic animals, and probably from Kelly's meat ration (Table 14.1). Of these, the greatest quantity of bone was sheep and cattle. Based on the analysis of the bone it appears that sheep were butchered locally and that beef and pork were butchered elsewhere and probably preserved as salt

Table 14.1. Summary of animal bone recovered.

		Adventure Bay			Lagoon Bay		
Species	**Common name**	**No. of bones**	**Weight (g)**	**No. of animals**	**No. of bones**	**Weight (g)**	**No. of animals**
European species							
Bos taurus	cattle	1238	21756.1	6	150	3340.1	1
Gallus domesticus	chicken	3	2.5	1	1	1.3	1
Ovis aries	sheep	1253	6474.7	13	208	1361.4	5
Oryctolagus cuniculus	rabbit	74	54.2	5	1	3.4	1
Sus scrofa	pig	131	1257.6	5	13	152.5	2
	sub total	**2699**	**29545.1**	**30**	**373**	**4858.7**	**10**
Native mammals							
Arctocephalus pusillus	Australian fur seal	4	9	1	2	13.4	1
Bettongia gaimardi	bettong				23	10.8	1
Dasyurus viverrinus	native cat	1	1.5	1	1	1.2	1
Hydomys chrysogaster	water rat	4	0.9	1			
Muridae	rats and mice	1	0.2	1			
Peramelidae	bandicoot	3	2.3	1	1	0.4	1
Rattus lutreolous	swamp rat	2	1.8	1	3	1.2	1
Thylogale billardierii	pademelon	1	3	1			
Trichosurus vulpecula	brushtail possum	5	4.1	1	9	16.2	2
Vombatus ursinus	wombat	1	1.6	1	1	11.5	1
Pseudocheirus peregrinus	ringtail possum	6	4.8	1	1	0.6	1
Macropus (small 1–8 kg)	kangaroo	46	164.9	2	12	48.1	3
	sub total	**74**	**194.1**	**12**	**53**	**103.4**	**12**

Table 14.1 continued.

Species	Common name	Adventure Bay			Lagoon Bay		
		No. of bones	Weight (g)	No. of animals	No. of bones	Weight (g)	No. of animals
Fish							
Arripis trutta	salmon	21	12.1	1	2	1.4	1
Caesioperca rasor	barber fish	31	0.4	1			
Chrysophrys auratus	snapper	1	0.05	1	3	0.3	1
Dinolestes lewini	pike	217	14.65	3			
Monacanthidae	leatherjacket	5	0.8	1			
Myxus elongatus	mullet	36	3.55	1			
Platycephalus conatus	flathead	39	6.67	2			
Pseudoearanx dentex	trevally	48	7.5	4			
Pseudolabrus tetricus	wrasse	13	4.6	4			
Sarda australis	tuna	1	5.1	1			
large fish (>5 kg)		4	7	1			
medium fish (1–5 kg)		145	38.4	3	4	0.5	1
small fish (<1 kg)		223	18	1	27	1.88	1
unidentified		10	0.65	1			
	sub total	**794**	**119.47**	**25**	**36**	**4.08**	**4**
Birds							
Colluricincla harmonica	grey thrush	3	1	1			
Diomedeidae	albatross	4	12	1			
Dromaieus	emu	9	76.3	2			
Eudyptula minor	fairy penguin	23	13.75	4			
Larus novaehdlandme	silver gull	2	0.6	1			
Puffinus tenuirostris	mutton bird	12	6.9	4	5	2.1	1
Strepera fuliginosa	currawong	9	2.6	3			
large bird (>5 kg)		1	9.4	1			
medium bird (1-5 kg)		12	29.1	1	37	18.6	1
small bird (<1 kg)		27	9.3	1	9	1.8	1
	sub total	**102**	**160.95**	**19**	**51**	**22.5**	**3**
	TOTAL	**3669**	**30019.62**	**86**	**513**	**4988.68**	**29**

meat (Table 14.2). Comparatively few bones from the hooves and skulls of cattle and pigs were recovered, which is consistent with butchering off-site. Both beef and pork were commonly preserved and consumed as salt meat in the colonial period, and excavations of several ships' cargoes containing salt meat have demonstrated that it frequently contained bone (English 1990; Nash 2001; Staniforth 1987; Steele 1995). Both assemblages of sheep bone, in contrast, included hoof and skull segments, indicating that the animals were probably butchered on or near the stations.

The faunal remains suggest that men in the whaling parties were eating more beef than were contemporary working people on shore. Excavated assemblages from the Rocks, a waterfront district in Sydney, consist of around 40 per cent mutton bone and only around 25 per cent of the more

prestigious, and expensive, beef bone (Karskens 1999, 65). At the whaling stations beef and mutton bone made up approximately equal proportions of the identified bone, at roughly 33 per cent each. From this it would seem that while Kelly was taking advantage of the clause in the agreements to provide cheaper mutton when it suited him, his employees were still comparatively better off than other workers.

The men evidently supplemented the rations by hunting and fishing around the stations, but not to a large extent. Wild game forms a small part of the bone assemblage overall (10 % by fragment count) and several of the species, such as the bettongs, paddymelons, and swamp rats, were too small to have been considered a source of food (Lawrence and Tucker 2002; Tucker 1999). Mutton birds were reportedly a favourite with whalers however, so it is not

Table 14.2. Summary of body parts (NISP) for pork, mutton and beef.

Species	Body part	Adventure Bay	Lagoon Bay
S. scrofa	cranial	1	7
	axial	97	2
	girdle	15	
	long bone	18	4
	total	131	13
O. aries	cranial	68	64
	feet	280	16
	axial	647	62
	girdle	41	24
	long bone	216	42
	unidentified	1	
	total	1253	208
B. taurus	cranial	40	22
	feet	21	10
	axial	797	77
	girdle	155	3
	long bone	160	33
	unidentified	65	5
	total	1238	150

surprising that they were taking the birds here (Chamberlain 1988, 122). Kangaroo was also popular with colonial settlers, and they were frequently hunted for their meat as well as for sport. By the 1850s some species of kangaroo, such as *Macropus major* (Forester kangaroo) and *Macropus giganteus* (eastern grey kangaroo) had been hunted almost to extinction in Tasmania (Barker and Caughley 1990).

As maritime workers, it might be expected that whalers would have eaten reasonable amounts of fish, but fish bone was not a large part of the faunal assemblage. Some of the species, including salmon, pike, mullet and wrasse, could have been caught with lines on the beach or rocks. Others, such as snapper, leatherjacket, and trevally, primarily frequent deeper waters and were more likely caught at sea in the whale boats. However, the small amount of fish bone (8.6 % of the bones recovered) in the assemblages may be due in part to taphonomic causes. Both assemblages were recovered from shallow sheet deposits which were highly fragmented, conditions which do not favour the preservation of small elements such as fish bone.

There has been little analysis of faunal assemblages from sites of a similar age in either New South Wales or Victoria. The work which has been done however indicates that the settlers were willing to experiment with native foods on a limited basis, but for the most part continued to rely on

domesticated European species. In Sydney, the bones of native animals are very much in the minority. At the Cumberland/Gloucester Street site in the Rocks, only two of 125, 000 bones catalogued were from native species. Shellfish and fish were much more abundant however, and colonists, like their English counterparts, regularly ate oysters gathered from the nearby shore. Unlike at the whaling stations however, fish species were mainly those such as flathead and bream which could be obtained from the shallow waters along the shore (Karskens 1999, 65–66).

Bread is the other major item in the whalers' rations list, though it is not visible archaeologically. Bread was the largest component of the diet of working people in early 19th-century England, and as little meat was consumed, bread provided the bulk of protein and calories (Shammas 1990, 136–137). The official government ration for convicts in New South Wales in 1831 included 12 lbs of wheat and 7 lbs of meat. Rations for pastoral workers and passengers on migrant ships provided for equal quantities of bread and meat (Walker and Roberts 1988, 5, 19). James Kelly agreed to provide each of his crew members with 12 lbs of flour or bread every week. On board ship the bread would have been hard biscuits stored in wooden casks, and likely to be mouldy, damp, and full of maggots. On the stations fresh bread could have been baked more regularly, and Edward Markham recorded the bread he was given on his visit to one Tasmanian station:

> In the huts of the men I have often got a slice of damper, bread baked in the wood ashes without yeast and very nice it is, I can assure you…As for the [whale] oil, it has no more taste than olive oil would have. I was amused by the men at dinner time, throwing in doughboys, to be boiled in the Fry Pots. I tasted one, the oil does not penetrate more than the water…The difference in whale and olive oil is not perceived in boiling oil (Markham 1852).

Neither the ration list nor the archaeological record mentions vegetables, but other documents suggest that they were probably part of the diet at the stations. At sea sailors relied on stores of potatoes, onions and split peas, supplemented on long voyages by fresh fruit obtained where possible (Chamberlain 1988, 116–124). Potatoes, onions, and pickles are all mentioned in correspondence between Kelly and one of his whaling captains at work along the coast of New South Wales. Account books kept by another Tasmanian station owner show that he agreed to supply his crews with vegetables once a day (Evans 1993a, 45). Colonial farms were sources of produce however, and Kelly used his own farm to supply potatoes to his whaling ships and probably to his stations as well (Bowden 1964, 87).

In contrast to bread and vegetables, condiments do not appear in documentary sources, and yet there is ample archaeological evidence of them. Fragments of broken glass and ceramics recovered from the two sites include pieces of

Table 14.3. Bottles and jars recovered (shown as minimum number of vessels).

	Adventure Bay	Lagoon Bay
condiments	12	5
medicine	-	2
beer/wine (black glass)	12	28
beer/wine (green glass)	8	-
case	3	3
stoneware bottle	1	
stoneware jar	1	2
total	37	40

Figure 14.2. Condiment bottles recovered from the two sites.

Figure 14.3. Cylindrical and case bottles.

bottles and stoneware jars that would have contained pickles, sauces, or other flavourful foods (Table 14.3). Popular pickled foods included olives, walnuts, gherkins, onions, and capers, which may have been sold in the stoneware jars. The wide-mouthed glass jars more likely contained powdered spices such as mustard or cayenne pepper, both of which were commonly mixed with vinegar or water at the table (Jones and Smith 1985, 60–67). Spicy, sugary accompaniments such as these would have done much to enliven the otherwise bland diet of meat and bread, and vinegar and mustard were particularly favoured with salt meats.

There is also some evidence of the beverages consumed. Kelly's ration lists refer to a weekly allowance of one-third of a pound of tea for each man, and tea was certainly well-entrenched as part of both British and colonial diets by this time (Karskens 1999, 66; Shammas 1990, 84). While neither the tea itself nor its packaging has survived archaeologically, numerous teacups were recovered from both sites. As each of Kelly's crewmen were also allotted two pounds of sugar per week, it can be assumed that the tea was sweetened before drinking. Part of the sugar allowance may also have been used by the cook to bake sweet puddings.

Alcohol was certainly consumed at the stations, as indicated by the fragments of at least 54 beer, wine, and case bottles recovered. Determining the quantities and varieties consumed is difficult however. There is some indication that Kelly himself was making alcohol available to his crews. His account books show that in 1834 he purchased 71 gallons of rum and two years later 547 gallons of rum for his whale ship *Marianne*, and in 1841 he held 80 gallons of ale and six gallons of rum in store at a station in New South Wales (Kelly Papers, State Library of Tasmania). However, these beverages cannot be directly linked to the bottles recovered on site because of the practice of re-using and recycling bottles (Boow 1992; Busch 1987; Carney 1999). Before local glass manufacturing began bottles were a valuable commodity, and bottles were even imported empty to be filled locally (Morgan 1991; Peters 1997). If anything, the bottle glass from Adventure Bay and Lagoon Bay probably under-represents the amount of alcohol consumed. Most of the

alcohol on the sites was likely to have been stored in wooden casks rather than in bottles. Kelly's accounts suggest that the alcohol was in casks, and fragments of wrought iron barrel hoops were recovered from the sites.

Serving the Food

Available evidence suggests that the food was prepared and served fairly simply. Standard cooking practice at the time was based on an open fire. Iron pots and kettles would be suspended there, roasting was done on spits over the coals, and baking was done in a Dutch oven. Both sites had suitable fireplaces, and at Lagoon Bay we found fragments of a small iron cooking pot and links of iron chain. No archaeological evidence was found for serving vessels, and it is likely that the meals were dished directly from the cooking pots onto the men's dishes. The dishes could have been either tin or ceramic. Kelly's account books record the goods sold to crews on credit from the slops chest. They indicate that tin

Table 14.4. Glass and china tablewares (shown as minimum number of vessels).

	Adventure Bay*	**Lagoon Bay**
glass		
stemmed glass	2	-
tumbler	4	1
sub total	6	1
china		
plates	11	11
cups	10	3
bowls		4
cup/bowl		3
plate/saucer	2	1
serving dish		1
teapot		1
jug		1
vase		1
sub total	23	26
total	29	27

* a single china chamberpot was also represented in the collection but has not been included here

plates and tin 'pots' could be bought for one shilling and sixpence. However, on at least one occasion Kelly also purchased seven dozen china plates, which seems a lot for his own domestic use and may have been meant for the stations (Kelly Papers, State Library of Tasmania).

Archaeology demonstrates that at least some of the men on the stations chose to use ceramic plates, and many fragments were recovered from the excavations (Table 14.4). It is tempting to speculate that the ceramic plates were used by the officers and that the crew used tin plates, but there is no clear-cut association between ceramics and status. Indeed, the ceramic plates may even have been cheaper than the tin ones. Hobart shops advertised new transfer-printed plates at six shillings per dozen in 1839, less than half what Kelly was charging his men for tin plates. The patterns recovered from the sites were generally older designs such as shell edge, plain creamware, and Chinese export porcelain, and would probably have cost even less, particularly if acquired second-hand (Table 14.5). Some of the plates were in newer and more fashionable transfer-print designs, but none were flow-blue or in colours other than blue. There was no spatial correlation in the distribution of patterns that might hint at status. At Adventure Bay the crew areas were not sufficiently well-preserved to enable comparisons to be made, and at Lagoon Bay the styles were distributed evenly between the two buildings.

A combination of tin, ceramics, glass and other materials were also used for consuming beverages. Men could buy tin 'pots' from the slops chest, but archaeological fragments of ceramic teawares and glass tablewares were also

Table 14.5. Decorative techniques at the two sites (shown as minimum number of vessels).

		Flat ware		**Hollow ware**	
Decoration		**Adventure Bay**	**Lagoon Bay**	**Adventure Bay**	**Lagoon Bay**
Transferprint:	blue	6	10	9	4
	red				1
	green			1	2
	black				2
	brown			1	1
Handpainted					1
Sponged					1
Shelledge		5	2		
Basaltware					1 (teapot)
Banded				1	1
Slipped					1
Moulded					1 (jug)
Plain			1		
Creamware		1			1
Chinese Export Porcelain		1			
total		13	13	12	17

Figure 14.4. A range of tea and tablewares.

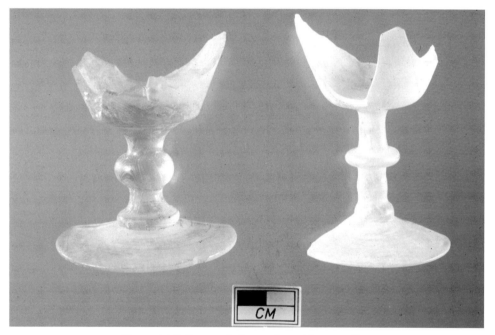

Figure 14.5. Stemmed glasses from Adventure Bay.

recovered. Unlike the plates, the teacup patterns were relatively new and possibly more expensive. Transfer prints predominated, many in the fashionable colours of red, green, black and brown. Comparatively few glassware items were represented, which could suggest a number of things. Tin may have been more acceptable for cold beverages, or teacups may have been used for beverages other than tea. The men may also have been using cups of leather, horn, or wood, or even sharing a 'circling glass' passed around. Two pieces of glassware found at Adventure Bay were stemmed wine glasses, suggesting that someone at that station was keen to maintain some social graces.

Food and Politics

Kelly and the other owners provided most of the goods at the stations, whether as rations or in the stores. They determined the quality, the quantity, and the nature of the goods, and in the case of the stores, the price at which it was sold to the men. What was provided and what was private, individual property was intensely political. Crewmen could avoid the system as much as possible by bringing their own clothing and mess kit with them, and the variety of ceramic plates and cups found in the excavations suggests that they often did. The ceramics are similar in decoration and value to those recovered from contemporary sites in Sydney and Hobart, many of which were in the waterfront districts frequented by whaling men in the off-season. In Hobart's Wapping district archaeological contexts dating from the 1830s and 1840s produced numerous examples of Chinese export porcelain dishes and shell-edged dishes, along with transfer prints in a range of colours (Wilson 1999). Similarly, excavations in Sydney's Rock neighbourhood have produced shell-edged plates and Chinese export porcelain wares as late as the 1860s (Karskens 1999, 95–96). From this it would seem that the men in the whaling parties preferred to take with them the familiar dishes they used at home, rather than be subject to Kelly's tastes and Kelly's prices.

With food however they were forced to be more reliant on the owners, and therefore more vulnerable. There is no record of Kelly's men complaining about the food he provided, but other crews did. Deep-sea whaling voyages occasionally ended early when the crews refused to work because of poor food, and men cited poor food as a reason for absconding (Chamberlain 1988, 120–122). Convict workers protested against meat that was 'too bony' and bread made from grains other than wheat (Karskens 1999, 64). Kelly cut his costs by supplying his stations with vegetables grown on his own farms, and with his own fresh mutton rather than salt beef and pork that he had to pay for. The men may have welcomed the fresh food, but they would also have been instantly suspicious of anything that threatened their entitlements, such as the substitution of mutton for the more prestigious beef. The faunal remains also indicate that whenever their whaling duties allowed it the men tried to supplement Kelly's rations with fresh game and fish that they procured themselves.

Along with tension between the crews and the owners, there may also have been tensions on the stations between the elite headsman and boatsteerers, the 'officers', and the ordinary crew. The officers received higher pay and had greater authority. Although they had once been regular crew themselves, they were now on their way to joining the ranks of the middle class. Something of their aspirations are reflected in a statement made by William Davis, the headsman and manager of the Lagoon Bay station. In 1838 he wrote to the colonial authorities protesting against the use of convict labour on a neighbouring station. Aside from being illegal, the use of these unskilled and unpaid workers threatened to undermine the whalers' access to work and their social position. Davis writes that the convicts were 'prejudicial to the petioners' future welfare', and he described himself and his colleagues as 'whalers and free men, ... a considerable portion of which are married and have families entirely

dependent on their exertions for a subsistence' (Correspondence files, Colonial Secretary's Office, State Library of Tasmania). In a convict colony that was a statement of pride and expectation.

One suspects that it was these men who were using the more expensive coloured teacups and the basaltware found with them, the fashionable transfer-printed plates, and the stemmed glasses. They had the better quarters with more privacy, like the snug apartment at Adventure Bay. There, one end of the large stone building had been walled off from the other. It had a separate entrance and fireplace, and two comfortable rooms, of which the smaller, inner chamber was probably for sleeping and the larger outer chamber for more general use. It was a luxury of private space compared to the shared barracks of the men. However, despite these subtle differences, the officers and the men in their boat crews were mutually dependent once on the water and engaged in the dangerous business of hunting whales. Tension and conflict could not become too overt or lives and profits would be lost. Although the men were not all equal, it was not prudent for distinction and privilege to extend far beyond the subtle differences displayed at meal times.

Conclusions

The assemblage of food-related items from the two whaling stations has contributed new perspectives on diet in colonial Australia. Like other white Australians of the time, men in the whaling parties had access to a more varied, abundant, and nutritious diet than did their contemporaries in Britain. These men also appear to have had more abundant diets than did convict workers, but it is not clear whether this is due to their status as free men or because of the exacting physical demands of the whaling industry. It is almost certain, however, that had the men considered the diet to be substandard, they would have protested by withholding their labour. In comparison with contemporary urban dwellers, the whaling men had relatively more beef in their diet and also more native animals. They were also able to access deep-sea species of fish rather than just the on-shore varieties consumed in Sydney. However, it is likely that the urbanites had greater access to fresh fruit, vegetables, and dairy products than did the whalers. In other respects the meals the whalers ate were familiar to them: food was boiled or roasted in the traditional way, and eaten off the same fragile, decorative ceramics that the men used at home. Other aspects of their pay and conditions were often less than satisfactory, but it appears that with regard to food, at least, the men who worked for James Kelly had grounds to be satisfied.

Acknowledgements

Archaeological investigation was carried out under the auspices of AWSANZ (Archaeology of Whaling in Southern

Australia and New Zealand), a collaborative project between La Trobe and Flinders Universities and heritage management agencies throughout southern Australia. The excavations, in 1997 and 1999, were funded by La Trobe University and an Australian Research Council Industry Collaborative SPIRT grant in partnership with the Department of Parks and Wildlife Tasmania. The support of Tom and Cynthia Dunbabin is also greatly appreciated. In addition to editing the present collection and organising the Table conference at the University of Sheffield, James Symonds kindly arranged for a British Academy grant which enabled me to participate and I am grateful.

References

Barker, R. D. and Caughley, G. (1990) Distribution and abundance of kangaroos (*Marsupialia: Macropodidae)* at the time of European contact: Tasmania. *Australian Mammalogy* 13, 157–166.

Boow, J. (1992) *Early Australian Commercial Glass: Manufacturing Processes*, Sydney, Department of Planning, New South Wales.

Bowden, K. M. (1964) *Captain James Kelly of Hobart Town*, Melbourne, Melbourne University Press.

Busch, J. (1987) Second time around: a look at bottle reuse. *Historical Archaeology* 21, 67–80.

Carney, M. (1999) A cordial factory at Parramatta, New South Wales. *Australasian Historical Archaeology* 16, 80–93.

Casey, M. (1999) Local pottery and dairying at the DMR site, Brickfield Hill, Sydney, New South Wales. *Australasian Historical Archaeology* 17, 3–37.

Chamberlain, S. (1988) The Hobart Whaling Industry 1830–1900, PhD thesis, Melbourne, La Trobe University.

Correspondence files, Colonial Secretary's Office, State Library of Tasmania, Hobart.

English, A. (1990) Salted meats from the wreck of the *William Salthouse*: archaeological analysis of nineteenth-century butchering patterns. *Australian Journal of Historical Archaeology* 8, 63–69.

Evans, K. (1993a) *Shore Based Whaling in Tasmania Historical Research Project.* Volume 1: *A Social and Economic History*, Hobart, Department of Parks and Wildlife Tasmania.

Evans, K. (1993b) *Shore Based Whaling in Tasmania Historical Research Project.* Volume 2: *Site Histories*. Hobart, Department of Parks and Wildlife Tasmania.

Gollan, A. (1978) *The Tradition of Australian Cooking*, Canberra, Australian National University Press.

Gollan, A. (1988) Salt pork to take away, in Burgmann, V. and Lee, J. (eds.) *Making a Life: A People's History of Australia.* Melbourne: PcPhee Gribble with Penguin Australia, pp 1–17.

Jones, O. and Smith, E. A. (1985) *Glass of the British Military ca. 1755–1820*, Ottawa, National Historic Parks and Sites Branch, Parks Canada.

Karskens, G. (1999) *Inside the Rocks: The Archaeology of a Neighbourhood*, Sydney, Hale and Iremonger.

Kelly papers. State Library of Tasmania, Hobart.

Kingston, B. (1994) *Basket, Bag and Trolley: A History of Shopping in Australia*, Melbourne, Oxford University Press.

Lawrence, S. (2006) *Whalers and Free Men: Life on Tasmania's Colonial Whaling Stations*, Melbourne, Australian Scholarly Publishing.

Lawrence, S. and Tucker, C. (2002) Sources of meat in colonial diets: faunal evidence from two nineteenth-century Tasmanian whaling stations. *Environmental Archaeology* 7, 23–34.

Lloyd, C. (1981) Victually of the fleet in the eighteenth and nineteenth centuries, in Watt, J., Freeman, E. J. and Bynum, W. F. (eds) *Starving Sailors: The Influence of Nutrition Upon Naval and Maritime History*. Greenwich: National Maritime Museum, pp. 9–16.

Markham, E. (1852) *Edward Markham's Van Diemen's Land Journal 1833 with Six Historical Essays by K. R. von Stieglitz*, Launceston, Telegraph Printery.

Morgan, P. (1991) Glass Bottles from the *William Salthouse*. BA (Honours) thesis, Archaeology, Melbourne: La Trobe University.

Nash, M. (2001) *Cargo for the Colony: The 1797 Wreck of the Merchant Ship* Sydney Cove, Hobart, Navarine Publishing.

Nash, M. (2003) *The Bay Whalers: Tasmania's Shore-Based Whaling Industry*, Hobart, Navarine Publishing.

Nicholas, S. (ed.) (1988) *Convict Workers: Reinterpreting Australia's Past*, Cambridge, Cambridge University Press.

Peters, S. J. (1997) Archaeological wines: analysis and interpretation of a collection of wines recovered from the *William Salthouse* shipwreck (1841). *Australasian Historical Archaeology* 14, 63–68.

Shammas, C. (1990) *The Pre-Industrial Consumer in England and America*, Oxford, Clarendon Press.

Staniforth, M. (1987) The casks from the wreck of the *William Salthouse*. *Australian Journal of Historical Archaeology* 5, 21–28.

Steele, D. (1995) *The Hungry Years Re-Visited: Dietary Evidence from the Wreck of an 18th Century Merchant Ship En Route to Port Jackson*, Hobart, Tasmanian Parks and Wildlife Service.

Tucker, C. (1999) A Whaler's Ration: A Comparison of the Faunal Remains From Adventure Bay and Lagoon Bay Shore-Based Whaling Stations in Tasmania. BA (Honours) thesis, Archaeology, Melbourne: La Trobe University.

Walker, R. B. and Roberts, D. C. K. (1988) *From Scarcity to Surfeit: A History of Food and Nutrition in New South Wales*, Sydney, New South Wales University Press.

Wilson, G. (1999) *Wapping Parcel 2, Hobart, Tasmania: Archaeological Investigation 1998, Artefact Report, Ceramics*, Sydney, Austral Archaeology.

15

A Not So Useless Beauty – Economy, Status, Function and Meaning in the Interpretation of Transfer-Printed Tablewares

Alasdair Brooks

Introduction

Perhaps no single decorative technique from the industrial era has been subject to more comment and analysis than transfer prints; they have been studied chronologically (Samford 1997), economically (Miller 1991a, 1991b), ideologically (Brooks 1997, 1999), and as art history (Copeland 1990; Coysh and Henrywood 1982, 1986; Kelly 1999) – and this small sample can only provide the smallest hint of the extent of the literature on the subject. The level of decorative detail, combined with definable stylistic chronologies, makes transfer prints an extremely useful decoration for diagnostic purposes. They are more than just a decoration: they are also a potentially valuable tool in helping to interpret a variety of issues often crucial to our understanding of archaeological sites. Finally, they are also extremely common, though subject to important variations in distribution across the English-speaking world in the 19th century; Majewski and O'Brien (1987, 141) have noted that the popularity of printed decorations was one of the more important reasons why potters moved away from marketing by ware, and instead began to market materials by decoration.

The present paper aims to demonstrate the benefits, and potential pitfalls, of using this important ceramic sub-group for a more interpretive archaeological analysis of the more recent past. The goal is not to offer a comprehensive survey of the topic and its literature – something worthy of a full book in itself – but rather to offer an overview of the main issues. The dominant themes within this discussion are economy (how transfer prints arrived at a site), status (how they interacted with hierarchical social relationships relevant to the site), function (how they were used at a site), and meaning (how they were perceived at a site).

While transfer prints are in origin a British technological innovation, the ceramics trade in the 19th century (and readers will hopefully pardon any avoidance of 'Victorian' given the potential for confusion between the Queen's reign and the Australian state) was a global phenomenon. The impact of shifting local contexts on interpretation is an important consideration in any overview of transfer print interpretation. Therefore while Australian examples are prominent in the following discussion, examples from the United Kingdom and North America – and comparisons between all of these regions – feature throughout.

The Technology of Transfer Printing

Before discussion moves to more analytical matters, a brief introduction to the technology of transfer printing may prove useful to those unfamiliar with the subject. This technology was subject to variation according to location and time, but the basic process involves the placement of a transfer paper on an inked and engraved copper plate. The transfer paper is then applied to the vessel, often with the assistance of a felt pad. The ware is then typically immersed in cold water, stiffening the ink and causing the paper to float off – but leaving the design behind.

Transfer printing was a British innovation. The earliest overglazed transfer prints seem to have been developed outside Staffordshire as early as 1750, and some Staffordshire potters indeed sent their wares to Liverpool for decoration by specialists (Coysh and Henrywood 1982, 8). Nonetheless, transfer printing only became common in the wake of the introduction of Josiah Wedgwood's creamware (itself the culmination of earlier Staffordshire experiments in whiter-bodied refined earthenwares) in the early 1760s. The early black or red overglaze prints were, however, problematic as the print was easily damaged. Many examples recovered archaeologically are only identifiable through a remnant 'ghost' image, only visible when light shines on the vessel at a certain angle. This led to the development of more durable underglaze transfer prints, which form the majority of examples in archaeological assemblages dating after 1780 (overglaze printing continued at least into the 1820s on bone china). On underglaze prints, the decoration was applied to

Figure 15.1. Willow pattern transfer-printed plate. Photograph by the author with Rudy Frank and Wei Ming, from the collection of Susan Lawrence.

the vessel in its biscuit state, the glaze was then applied, and a final firing occurred (Coysh and Henrywood 1982, 8; Majewski and O'Brien 1987, 141–142). The first underglaze prints were blue, and while this remained the dominant transfer prints colour, the necessary technology to produce green, red, yellow, and black designs was developed by 1828, and polychrome transfer prints were introduced about 1840 (Majewski and O'Brien 1987, 141–143; Miller 2000, 13).

While hardly comparable in its broader impact on the development of the modern world, within its specific industry, the impact of the arrival of transfer printing was not wholly dissimilar to the impact of the printing of text on book production. Transfer printing's crucial contribution to the technology of ceramics decoration was that for the first time it was possible to mass-produce identical highly detailed images on ceramics. Prior to this, only moulded decorations could be mass-produced; all coloured decorations had to be added by hand. Almost any type of pattern was reproduced, from copies of traditional Chinese landscapes such as the 'Willow' pattern (Copeland 1990; fig. 1) through to romantic reproductions of British (Brooks 1999) and American (Samford 1997, 12) scenes, by way of sheet patterns where a single abstract design was applied across the surface of the vessel. The laxity of contemporary copyright laws further facilitated the copying of images with existing popular associations. The Byron's Views series of patterns by the Copeland and Garrett firm consisted entirely of copies of engravings from Finden's existing *Landscape and Portrait Illustrations to the Life and Works of Lord Byron* (Coysh and Henrywood 1982, 64). It is this multi-faceted decorative content, combined with their near-ubiquitous presence on 19th century archaeological sites, that makes transfer prints so important to archaeological interpretation.

Interpreting the Transfer Prints

With an understanding of the 'how' of transfer printing in place, it is now possible to move on to a consideration of some of the more abstract issues of 'why'. While the present chapter focuses on the interpretive and ideological aspects of the analysis of transfer-printed ceramics, this should not be taken to imply that the basic particularistic identification of transfer prints is somehow considered unimportant. Instead, the present discussion is based on a two-level model for the identification and analysis of industrial period ceramics (Figure 15.2).

A far more detailed discussion of the theoretical and methodological underpinnings of this model may be found elsewhere (Brooks 2005, 15–18). For the present discussion, it is enough to state that the model was designed to help bridge the gap between identification and analysis, and to encourage interaction between these two different levels. At the 'identification' level are those characteristics with which a fragment of pottery is inherently imbued, and which exist objectively outside analysis. In other words, all researchers agree that ceramics are made of something (ware), have a certain shape (form), and have a certain external appearance (decoration) even if they disagree on how to define those categories. Any interpretation here is in essence a matter of boundaries and definition. The topics in the 'analysis' level of the model depend on these basic building blocks of analysis, but are based on an entirely different level of interpretation and subjectivity. In other words, while a ceramic vessel intrinsically has a ware and form type (even if we are sometimes unable to agree on what to call those types), no ceramic vessel is automatically imbued with function, status, meaning, or a specific economic role. These are categories entirely socially constructed by both the original users and/or the archaeologist, and which have no real existence outside of those constructions.

It is thus the themes underlying the second level of the model, 'analysis', that frame the current discussion. At the same time, it is vitally important to acknowledge that interpretation and analysis are impossible without supporting

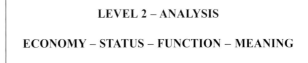

LEVEL 2 – ANALYSIS
ECONOMY – STATUS – FUNCTION – MEANING
LEVEL 1 – IDENTIFICATION
WARE – FORM – DECORATION – DATE

Figure 15.2. The Ceramics Analysis Model (from Brooks 2005: 16).

Figure 15.3. Relative values of three different decorative techniques on 10 inch dishes, 1815–1855 (based on Miller 1991,14).

knowledge of the basic building blocks of identification. It must also be acknowledged that each of the categories at the 'analysis' level are inextricably interlinked. Issues of economy often impact discussions of status; issues of function often impact discussion of meaning. These divisions are not hard and fast absolutes, but rather a loose framework for further interpretation.

Economy

Within 'economy', the present chapter includes not only the issues of trade that have been at the forefront of the study of ceramics from any time period (e.g. Orton *et al.*, 26–28), but also issues of cost and consumer choice. Considerable work has been done in historical archaeology on these topics, of which Miller's examination of price lists to develop the CC index (Miller 1991a, 1991b), which measures the relative costs across time of different refined earthenware decorations, is perhaps the best known internationally. More recently, Ewins' (1997) and Gaimster's (1997, 51–114) research has greatly contributed to the understanding of the mechanics of the international pottery trade on the macro-level. Studies of consumption are also important within this framework, particularly as regards Martin's (1993, 142) definition of one of the central aspects of consumerism as the role of fashion and demand in economic growth and shifts in production. Majewski and Schiffer's (2001) examination of broader consumerist themes in archaeology is of particular relevance here in that its case study was the impact of the fashionability of Japanese-style Aesthetic movement decorations on transfer print design.

As far as the actual price of transfer prints specifically is concerned, much attention has previously been paid to the fact that Miller's index reveals that from their intro-

duction until *c*.1850, transfer prints were the most expensive decorated refined earthenware available (Miller 1991b, 12–22). This has, not unreasonably, often led archaeologists to make interpretations about the presence of transfer prints on sites associated with the poor, arguing, for example, that transfer prints found on a site associated with the 'poor' are influenced by a nearby site associated with a wealthier household, or that the local poor had more purchasing power than originally anticipated. (e.g. Adams and Boling 1991, 84; Heath 1991, 55–70, 1997).

An awareness of some of the specifics of the international ceramics trade, however, demonstrates the importance of local context in the critical application of ceramics values to transfer print analysis. This is particularly true when international differences in taste and fashion are considered. Miller's price indices were developed for North American analysis, and are entirely appropriate within that context; the development of transfer print economy in the United Kingdom and Australia, however, is entirely different.

The raw figures from Miller's most recent index (1991b) can be used to show how the relative value of transfer prints in North America fell over time compared to other decorations (Figure 15.3). It can be seen that the relative value of printed wares fell more rapidly with the introduction of white granite in the 1840s. The latter highly fired semi-vitrified earthenware typically featured no colouring, and relatively light moulded decorations, and became highly fashionable in the United States in the middle of the 19th century; the Staffordshire potters reacted accordingly, producing white granite in large quantities for the American market (Ewins 1997). While transfer prints never disappear from the archaeological record in the US, they are definitely supplanted as the highest-end earthenware for some 30 to 40 years. In Britain,

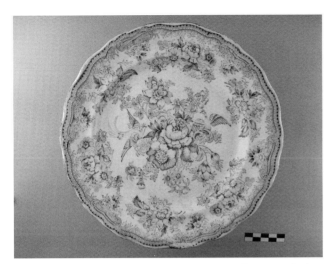

Figure 15.4. Asiatic Pheasant pattern transfer-printed plate Photograph by the author with Rudy Frank and Wei Ming, from the collection of Susan Lawrence.

Figure 15.5. Rhine pattern transfer-printed platter Photograph by the author with Rudy Frank and Wei Ming, from the collection of Peter Davies.

transfer prints do not seem to be replaced in popularity by white granite. Research on 19th century cottage assemblages from Pembrokeshire (Brooks 2003, 132), in fact strongly suggests that as the 19th century progresses, the percentage of transfer prints within assemblages associated with the rural poor of Wales increases as the cost of transfer prints in Britain decreases. White granite is virtually non-existent in these assemblages. Whether this new accessibility of transfer prints in parts of rural Britain is down to the continued decline of transfer print costs (an issue of price) or improved transport links to western Wales (an issue of trade) is unimportant to the immediate discussion. What matters is that the different economics of transfer print availability on different sides of the Atlantic leads to potentially very different archaeological signatures.

Australia presents a different environment entirely. Here transfer prints appear to have been the most important element in most domestic assemblages since almost the very beginning of settlement. Lawrence (2003) has noted that the presence of transfer prints in Australia might well be connected to a British Empire-wide preference for bright, colourful decorations. So common are transfer-printed wares on Australian sites that Wilson has correctly observed that making economic judgements based on the presence of transfer prints on sites associated with the urban Australian poor is essentially impossible (Wilson 1999). Briggs (2005) has demonstrated that local Australian merchants could make specific requests and choices when ordering ceramics from Britain, while Allen's classic study (1978) demonstrated early on that newly fashionable goods could reach Australia almost as quickly as the time required to ship newly manufactured materials from Britain.

Whatever the specifics of individual sites and the requests of individual merchants, the fact remains that the Australian

market was far too small to influence ceramics production in the same way as the United States could and often did. The Australian ceramics market rarely exceeded more than 2% of British ceramic exports during the 19th century (Brooks 2005, 56–57). Furthermore, just four transfer print patterns typically dominate assemblages in south-eastern Australia: the internationally ubiquitous 'Willow', the almost as ubiquitous 'Asiatic Pheasant' (Figure 15.4), 'Rhine' (Figure 15.5), and – in New South Wales and South Australia – 'Albion'. Other designs certainly occur, but where the only 'sets' of vessels in an assemblage are in those four patterns, it seems more likely that the assemblage is reflecting the local availability of commonly available goods as it is much in the way of consumer choice.

This discussion demonstrates the need to consider how the transfer print signature in different regions can not only help us understand the different economic environments of those regions (whether economy is a matter of price, fashion, or other considerations), but is also influenced by those differing economies. Perhaps on one level this seems self-evident, but as historical archaeology becomes an increasingly global discipline, there is a danger that someone engaging in interpretation in one part of the world will use an analytical system or approach that, while entirely appropriate to its own region, is wholly inappropriate to another. The economic importance of an assemblage of 'expensive' transfer prints from a site from 19th century Ohio will usually be entirely different from that of an assemblage of transfer prints from either south Wales or New South Wales.

Status

The crucial difference between status and economy is that while economy deals in cost, acquisition and trade, status refers to the socially constructed conceptual hierarchical role assigned to material culture by producers and consumers. Status is an interpretive issue with a long tradition in the archaeological literature, particularly as regards using Miller's economic data as a means to a more social discussion of status (e.g. Adams and Boling 1991; Spencer-Wood 1987). Yet even in parts of the world were Miller's data may not hold, archaeologists have still used the idea of differences between 'fine' wares and less expensive materials as a means to look at issues of status (e.g. Brooks 2003; Lawrence 1998, 10–13). Yet with many ceramic decorative techniques – and this is very much true of transfer prints – the relationship between vessel cost and vessel status is by no means absolute. It is entirely possible for the cost of vessels to vary both temporally and geographically while nonetheless maintaining the same general social status (and vice versa).

An example related to vessel form and material illustrates how this principle might also apply to vessel decoration. At rural poor sites in Pembrokeshire, there is a strong correlation between teawares and porcelain (including bone china); porcelain teawares are always at least 50 per cent of the assemblage, and more usually 65 to 80 per cent of the assemblage (Brooks 2003, 129, 132). Tea-drinking was originally an activity associated with a highly ritualistic, elite consumption pattern itself associated with both expense and status (Weatherill 1996, 158–159). Yet in the late 18th and early 19th centuries, the industrialisation of ceramic production made mass-produced teawares widely available across the British Isles. That the correlation between teawares and porcelain – the most expensive tableware available – existed demonstrated that the broader status connection between teawares and status remained intact, even while the cost of those teawares was decreasing, and the availability increasing (Brooks 2003, 132).

Similar observations might well be made of transfer prints. The previous discussion of economy has already mentioned Wilson's observation that the presence of transfer prints on Australian sites associated with the urban poor is essentially meaningless when it comes to making judgments on the relative purchasing power of site inhabitants (Wilson 1999). But when analysed in the appropriate context, transfer prints can still maintain a status association, even in Australia where they comprise such a large percentage of most assemblages. The connection between economics and status is perhaps too obvious, too easy a means through which to examine constructions of social hierarchies. Status relationships can also be uncovered through connections with other analytical themes such as function and broader ideological meanings. This point can be demonstrated particularly well through a discussion of vessel display, but to examine this point in detail requires a temporary digression through the complexities of vessel function.

Function

Function – how a vessel was actually used – has previously been described in *Pottery in Archaeology* as the 'least accessible' of ceramics-based interpretive issues to the archaeologist (Orton *et al.* 1993). While this may be true for earlier periods, a strong tradition exists in historical archaeology of looking at functional issues. The influential – though still contentious – work of South (1977) on functional categories and pattern analysis is particularly important in this regard. But even accepting that historical archaeology has a long-standing tradition in this area, the archaeologist studying the more recent past must still be ready to consider the differences between *primary intended function* and *primary intended use*.

One issue of importance to transfer prints that serves to illustrate this distinction is the use of transfer prints as a display element on dressers. The use of dressers as a means to display ceramics on sites associated with the rural poor in both Wales and Scotland is well-attested in the British archaeological literature (Brooks 2000, 88–89, 2003, 132–133; Vincentelli 1992; Webster 1999; see also Mytum this volume). But this issue is hardly of interest only to the Celtic nations of Britain. An example from recent research in Australia demonstrates how this can also be a potentially significant issue elsewhere.

The Lake Innes estate of Archibald Clunes Innes, near Port Macquarie, New South Wales, was the subject of extensive archaeological investigation in the late 1990s and early 2000s (Connah 1998, 2000, 2001, 2002). Archibald Innes was born in Caithness, Scotland in 1799, the sixth son of an army Major and minor landowner. Innes joined the army towards the end of the Napoleonic Wars, and relocated to Australia with his regiment in 1822. In Australia he soon found himself at the forefront of colonial society, and married Margaret Mcleay – the daughter of New South Wales' colonial secretary – in 1829. Innes seems to have had the intentional desire to run a landed estate in keeping with his perceived position in colonial society and moved with his family moved to Lake Innes in 1831. He was eventually financially ruined by the ending of free convict labour, and abandoned the estate in the 1850s (Connah 1998, 9–22). Of particular interest to the present discussion is evidence that came to light during a recent re-evaluation of the estate's ceramics assemblages by the present author, particularly as regards a blacksmith's hut in the servant's village.

One of the more interesting aspects of the blacksmith's hut assemblage is the large number of transfer-printed flat plates and saucers, and a noticeable lack of cups (matching or otherwise) to go with those saucers. Examination of the assemblage as a whole, and comparisons with the other relevant assemblages from the estate, demonstrated that this is a genuine lack of cups rather than an artificial by-product of field or lab methodology. Furthermore, the identified plates and saucers at the hut site comprise a considerably higher percentage compared to most of the other sites. The relevance of these data comes in the interpretation. One possible explanation for these figures is that the blacksmith was acquiring the relevant materials for display purposes. Display is notoriously difficult to prove archaeologically, and the entirely reasonable question of why the best display pieces would then have been discarded must also be asked. The blacksmith nonetheless seems to have acquired vessels in types and numbers that appear to be symbolically meaningful.

Though saucers had a range of potential kitchen functions beyond simply holding cups (Scott 1997), the possibility of some sort of display of the saucers seems more likely given the relative lack of cups. The available evidence thus suggests that even here at this conceptually isolated outpost of the British Empire, the poorer (though not the poorest) estate occupants were able to engage on some level with the construction of 'social gentility', and perhaps even display their finer transfer-printed wares to emphasise that they had a higher status than the other occupants of the servants' village.

This neatly illustrates the original point about the distinction between primary intended use and primary intended function. In this case the primary intended function of transfer-printed vessels at the point of manufacture might well have been for food or liquid consumption, but the primary intended use at the point of acquisition was to use the vessels for display. This display use is neither unusual nor arcane, but in fact common on many sites associated with the poor in different areas of the world. Through this awareness of the functional dichotomy of transfer-printed vessels, and the impact of the latter on other interpretive issues such as status, a more nuanced understanding of the role of vessel function in site interpretation becomes possible. Indeed, this analysis from the Lake Innes blacksmith's cottage was used to support the construction of a social 'hierarchy of servitude' across the site. Not that this functional dichotomy is somehow unique to transfer-printed vessels, but given that the latter are used for display more than perhaps any other vessel (bone china teawares are the only real rival), it remains an important point to consider in transfer print analysis. This example has additionally illustrated the importance of the interconnectedness of conceptual themes. Discussion was not solely about function, but also about how vessel function impacts conceptions of status. Combined analysis of this nature is often both necessary and important when examining socially constructed archaeological concepts.

Meaning

The final interpretive category is meaning, and it is perhaps here that transfer prints truly come into there own. Within this context, 'meaning' specifically refers to the potential wider ideological meaning (beyond status implications) not only of an assemblage, but also of individual vessels. While the preceding sections have focused on transfer-printed vessels, in most cases discussion was not solely relevant to transfer printing. In discussions of meaning, however, the ability of the manufacturer to mass produce complex designs makes transfer printing a uniquely suitable vehicle for a ceramics-based examination of decorative ideology. This is not to say that similar studies are impossible with other decorative techniques – Wall (1991, 78–80), for example, has examined the broader ideological context of the moulded Gothic pattern – simply that the richness of decorative detail on transfer prints makes them particularly important to this type of research.

Martin has previously discussed the analysis of ideological meaning in ceramics in some detail. Her analytical model is somewhat different from that used here, but in noting how 'creative juxtapositions across time, space and cultures raise new questions … structured in a matrix of time, space, technology, use, value and aesthetics' (Martin 2001, 34), the multi-faceted nature of her approach has much to recommend it. As Martin notes,

> ceramics leap and soar through multiple categories of analysis. Just as some wares can be mysterious and elemental, others can be practical. The analysis of meanings may require an understanding of the complex interrelationships between commerce, science and art (Martin 2001, 30).

In the specific realm of transfer prints, Martin briefly offers examples of how Asian-themed designs – however fantastical – could make Europeans believe they could 'travel' to China through their ceramics vessels (Martin 2001, 40), how classical designs were preferred over Asian designs by the 'elite' as a means of communicating their status and wealth (Martin 2001, 39), and the paradox of post-Revolutionary transfer prints made in England representing the mythic apotheosis of George Washington (Martin 2001, 35). The latter two issues, the mythic self-image of a power elite and the emergence of new national ideologies, as expressed on transfer prints, have also been considered within a specifically British context.

For example, attention has previously been paid to the importance of transfer-printed ceramics in both overtly and subconsciously conveying images relevant to both romanticised versions of the Celtic Scottish and Welsh pasts (Brooks 1997) and the formation of a new, unified British identity (Brooks 1999), and the significance of both to the British governing classes. The appearance of modern Celtic myth on transfer prints was part of a wider process in which material culture was simultaneously reflecting the new popularity of the mythic romantic past (as partially represented by the novels of Sir Walter Scott, the popularity of Ossian, and the new Romantic-period landscape ideal) and the appropriation and normalisation of that myth by a governing elite (as represented by the 'Balmoralisation' [Jarvie 1989, 199] of Scottish culture) to the extent that potentially divisive ideologies of the past were rendered symbolically safe (Brooks 1997, 1999, 58–60). This type of transfer print includes kilted Scotsmen, illustrations from the novels of Scott, and 'wild' mountainous Welsh landscapes. In the case of the new British identity, transfer prints can reflect the attempt of the new 'British' ruling class (whether English, Scots, Irish, Welsh or some combination thereof) to project an image of their power over a fictional calm and prosperous Britain and the search for a new national unity during a period of ongoing war (Brooks 1999, 54–58). Transfer prints associated with this theme might include the 'Titled Seats' series of the Careys firm, the 'British History' series of Jones and Son, or individual patterns such as 'Night Sea Battle' and 'Trafalgar' (though the Battle of Waterloo appears to be curiously underrepresented).

Examined as material culture outside of the context of individual archaeological sites, the transfer-printed patterns associated with this theme clearly have great symbolic power. Their presence or absence on archaeological sites might therefore have great symbolic importance. For example, the absence of British-themed transfer prints on sites associated with the rural Welsh poor 'could serve as a further indication of a [local] rejection of Anglicisation' (Brooks 1999, 61–62). But there is a world of problems hiding behind that that '*could*' if this kind of approach is applied uncritically. The absence of British-themed prints might equally be an indicator of nothing more subtle than this type of pattern was unavailable locally – and indeed, the importance of the American market to transfer print exports in the first half of the 19th century (Ewins 1997) is vitally important in this regard. The American market was so valuable that many of these patterns were simply not made for domestic consumption, but rather to export across the Atlantic. Similarly, how to explain that if one were to survey recent studies of relevant assemblages from four sites in North Pembrokeshire, Wales and one site each in Barra, South Uist and St. Kilda, Scotland (Brooks 2000, 2004; Branigan and Foster 1995; Kelly 1996), one would find precisely one transfer print – a black transfer-printed bone china cup showing 'Welch [sic] costumes' – with a Scottish or Welsh theme? Once again, this need not indicate that the various site inhabitants were less Scottish or Welsh – or more 'British' – than anticipated, simply that the relevant materials were unavailable, or that the various locals chose not to acquire them for any number of other reasons.

None of which is to suggest that archaeological analysis should not consider the symbolic power of transfer prints within individual assemblages. But an in-depth under-standing of the issues surrounding that site is necessary. An understanding of what goods were locally available or fashionable in an area – and here we tie back into 'economy'

– is particularly crucial. Otherwise the archaeologist risks believing that every single transfer print in an assemblage is somehow deeply significant ideologically. And if we accept that all material culture is symbolically loaded, then no doubt it is – but there are limits. With apologies to George Orwell, all material culture may be symbolic, but some material culture is more symbolic than others. It would be a foolhardy archaeologist who tried to argue that the presence of 'Willow' or 'Asiatic Pheasant' patterns on any archaeological site somehow automatically indicated an inherent Asian ideological orientation within a household.

When analysing transfer prints on any site – whether associated with the poor, the wealthy, or any points in between – there is a further need to keep in mind an ideological dichotomy as significant in its own way as the functional dichotomy between *primary intended function* and *primary intended use*. Here the distinction is between *ideology of manufacture* and *ideology of acquisition*. Much as the intended function of an object at the point of manufacture may be different from the intended function at the point of acquisition, so might the ideological environment in which a ceramics manufacturer selects decorations for wares may be very different from the environment in which those same vessels are acquired.

Conclusion

Discussion in this chapter has frequently involved the outlining of potentially problematic areas in the analysis of transfer prints, yet this should not be taken as implying a tone of pessimism about the possibility of using this important decorative technique in interpretive analysis. These have merely been cautionary tales, not active discouragement. It is only because transfer prints offer such a useful means for examining all of these issues that caution is necessary. Transfer prints are so common – in Australia, so common so as to sometimes cause local archaeologists to consider discarding any real cataloguing by ware in favour of cataloguing by decoration (Brooks 2005, 26–27) – that they must by necessity form an important part of the analysis of any late 18th and 19th century assemblage. Through the analysis of transfer prints, it is possible to gain valuable insights into issues of economy, status, function, and meaning, and the relationships between these issues. One of the most intriguing aspects of transfer print analysis, one of the implicit themes of this entire chapter, is indeed in seeing how the standardised industrial mass-production of this decorative technique allows for an analysis of the shifting social context of the use of a supposedly more expensive, supposedly higher status decoration by the lower status strata of society across the English-speaking world. Transfer prints may not be the only means of studying these issues through the artefact record, but they are frequently one of the more visible and available, at least on domestic sites, and for that reason will retain a central role in the interpretive analysis of industrial-era sites.

References

Adams, W. H. and Boling, S. J. (1991) Status and ceramics for planters and slaves on three Georgia coastal plantations, in Miller, G. L., Jones, O., Ross, L. and Majewski, T. (eds) *Approaches to Material Culture Research for Historical Archaeologists*, Tucson, Society for Historical Archaeology, 59–86.

Allen, J. (1978) The archaeology of nineteenth-century British imperialism: an Australian case study, in Schuyler, R. (ed.) *Historical Archaeology: A Guide to Substantive and Theoretical Contributions*, Farmingdale, Baywood Publishing Company, 139–148.

Briggs, S. (2005) Portonian respectability: Port Adelaide labourers' attitudes to middle class respectability through material culture, 1860–1900, paper presented at the annual meeting of the Society for Historical Archaeology, York.

Branigan, K. and Foster, P. (1995) *Barra: Archaeological Research on Ben Tangaval*, Sheffield, Sheffield Academic Press.

Brooks, A. (1997) Beyond the fringe: transfer-printed ceramics and the internationalisation of Celtic Myth. *International Journal of Historical Archaeology* 1:1, 39–55.

Brooks, A. (1999) Building Jerusalem: transfer-printed finewares and the creation of British identity, in Tarlow, S. and West, S. (eds) *The Familiar Past? Archaeologies of Later Historical Britain*, London, Routledge, London, 51–65.

Brooks, A. (2000) The Comparative Analysis of Late 18th- and 19th-Century Ceramics – A Trans-Atlantic Perspective, unpublished DPhil Thesis, University of York.

Brooks, A. (2003) Crossing Offa's Dyke: British ideologies and late eighteenth- and nineteenth-century ceramics in Wales, in Lawrence, S. (ed.) *Archaeologies of the British*, London, Routledge, 119–137.

Brooks, A. (2005) *An Archaeological Guide to British Ceramics in Australia, 1788–1901*, Sydney, Australasian Society for Historical Archaeology, and Melbourne, La Trobe University Archaeology Program.

Connah, G. (1998) The archaeology of frustration: an Australian case study. *Historical Archaeology* 32:2, 7–27.

Connah, G. (ed.) (2000) The 1999 Excavations at Lake Innes Estate, Port Macquarie, NSW, preliminary report to the Heritage Council of New South Wales, Sydney.

Connah, G. (ed.) (2001) The 2000 Excavations at Lake Innes Estate, Port Macquarie, NSW, preliminary report to the Heritage Council of New South Wales, Sydney.

Connah, G. (ed.) (2002) The 2001 Excavations at Lake Innes Estate, Port Macquarie, NSW, preliminary report to the Heritage Council of New South Wales, Sydney.

Copeland, R. (1990) *Spode's Willow Pattern and Other Designs after the Chinese*, London, Studio Vista.

Coysh, A. W. and Henrywood, R. K. (1982) *The Dictionary of Blue and White Printed Pottery 1780–1880*, Volume 1, Woodbridge, Antique Collectors' Club.

Coysh, A. W. and Henrywood, R. K. (1986) *The Dictionary of Blue and White Printed Pottery 1780–1880*, Volume 2, Woodbridge, Antique Collectors' Club.

Ewins, N. (1997) 'Supplying the present wants of our Yankee cousins...': Staffordshire ceramics and the American market 1775–1880. *Journal of Ceramic History* 15.

Gaimster, D. (1997). *German Stoneware 1200–1900*, London, British Museum Press.

Heath, B. (1991) A report on the archaeological excavations at Monticello, Charlottesville, Virginia; the Stewart/Watkins house 1989–1990. Mss, on file, Thomas Jefferson Memorial Foundation, Charlottesville.

Heath, B. (1997) Slavery and consumerism: a case study from Central Virginia. *African American Archaeology* 19, 1 and 5–8.

Jarvie, G. (1989) Culture, social development, and the Scottish Highland gatherings, in McCrone, D., Kendrick, S., and Straw, P. (eds) *The Making of Scotland: Nation, Culture and Social Change*, British Sociological Association Vol. 29, Edinburgh, Edinburgh University Press, 189–206.

Kelly, H. (1996) Crockery, in Emery, N., *Excavations on Hirta 1986–90*, 19–20, 68–70, 120–123, 153–154, and 193, Edinburgh, HMSO.

Kelly, H. (1999) *Scottish Ceramics*, Atglen, Schiffer Publishing.

Lawrence, S. (1998) The role of material culture in Australasian archaeology. *Australasian Historical Archaeology* 16, 8–15.

Lawrence, S. (2003) Exporting culture: archaeology and the nineteenth-century British Empire. *Historical Archaeology* 37(1), 20–33.

Majewski, T. and O'Brien, M. J. (1987) The use and misuse of nineteenth-century English and American ceramics in archaeological analysis. *Advances in Archaeological Method and Theory* 11, 97–209.

Majewski, T. and Schiffer, M. B. (2001) Beyond consumption: toward an archaeology of consumption, in Buchli, V. and Lucas, G. (eds) *Archaeologies of the Contemporary Past*, London, Routledge, 26–50.

Martin, A. S. (1993) Makers, buyers, and users: consumerism as a material culture framework. *Winterthur Portfolio* 28, 141–147.

Martin, A. S. (2001) Magical, mythical, practical and sublime: the meanings and uses of ceramics in America, in Hunter, R. (ed.) *Ceramics in America 2001*, London, Chipstone Foundation, 29–46.

Miller, G. L. (1991a) Classification and economic scaling of 19th-century ceramics, in Miller, G. L., Jones, O., Ross, L. and Majewski, T. (eds) *Approaches to Material Culture Research for Historical Archaeologists*, Tucson, Society for Historical Archaeology, 37–58.

Miller, G. L. (1991b) A revised set of CC index values for classification and economic scaling of English ceramics from 1787 to 1880. *Historical Archaeology* 25:1, 1–25.

Miller, G. L. (2000) Telling time for archaeologists. *Northeast Historical Archaeology* 29, 1–22.

Orton, C., Tyers, P. and Vince, A. (1993) *Pottery in Archaeology*, Cambridge, Cambridge University Press.

Samford, P. (1997) Response to a market: dating English underglaze transfer-printed wares. *Historical Archaeology* 31:2, 1–30.

Scott, E. (1997) A little gravy in the dish and onions in a tea cup:

what cookbooks reveal about material culture. *International Journal of Historical Archaeology* 1:2, 131–155.

South, S. (1977) *Method and Theory in Historical Archaeology*, New York, Academic Press.

Spencer-Wood, S. (ed.) (1987) *Consumer Choice in Historical Archaeology*, New York, Plenum Press.

Vincentelli, M. (1992) *Llestri Llafar – Talking Pots*, Aberystwyth, the University College of Wales.

Weatherill, L. (1996) *Consumer Behaviour and Material Culture in Britain 1660–1760*, 2nd edn, London, Routledge.

Webster, J. (1999) Resisting traditions: ceramics, identity and consumer choice in the Outer Hebrides from 1800 to the present. *International Journal of Historical Archaeology* 3:1, 53–73.

Wall, D. D. (1991) Sacred dinners and secular teas: constructing domesticity in mid-19th-century New York. *Historical Archaeology* 25:4, 69–81.

Wilson, G. C. (1999) *Wapping – Parcel 2, Hobart, Tasmania. Archaeological Investigation 1998, Artefact Report – Ceramics*, Adelaide, Austral Archaeology.

16

Postcard from Te Awamutu: Eating and Drinking with the Troops on the New Zealand War Front

Alexy Simmons

Introduction

Much of the data archaeologists and historians obtain informs like postcard snippets or lingering phrases. The abbreviated information is often provocative and commonly leaves substantial space for interpretation. The strength of historic archaeology lies in the restraint and equilibrium afforded by data cross-referencing. The intent in this paper is to explore the consumption patterns and dining style of the private soldiers and officers fighting in the New Zealand War campaigns of 1863–1872 in the Waikato and Bay of Plenty areas (Figure 16.1). Diaries, journals, letters, military records, commissariat reports and archaeological data are used to document how the officers and private soldiers got their daily bread in the field, as well as the cooking equipment and tablewares, what was consumed, the food supply systems, and the 'rum ration'. The differences evident in the archaeological data and written references are delineated.

Military Life

Daily life in an army that has been deployed particularly to a foreign shore and battle front largely revolves around the basics – that is eating, drinking, sleeping, bodily functions, rest and duties. The essence of eating and drinking with the enlisted men/ private soldiers and officers is captured in letters sent to England from New Zealand, like this one from Captain Hugo Light of the 68th Regiment (Durham) Light Infantry.

In March 1864 Captain Light wrote home:

> I hope you got my last all right. I mark all my letters to you so you will know when you miss one – this is No 2… Our rations are very fair. Three of us dine together in one tent. We get fresh bread baked in camp, three quarters pound of meat, potatoes and a good go of rum. And by drawing our servant's rations with us, we manage to get a fair joint now and then. I must finish as the steamer is just off again (undated letter probably 10 March 1864 in Bilcliffe 1995, 134).

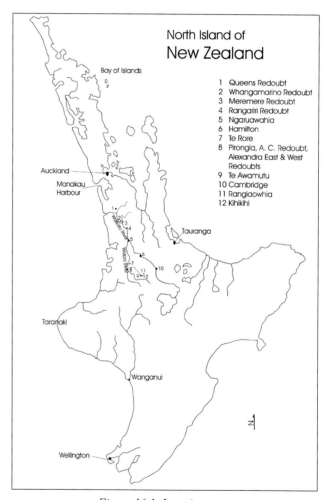

Figure 16.1. Location map.

North Island of **New Zealand**

1 Queens Redoubt
2 Whangamarino Redoubt
3 Meremere Redoubt
4 Rangariri Redoubt
5 Ngaruawahia
6 Hamilton
7 Te Rore
8 Pirongia, A. C. Redoubt, Alexandra East & West Redoubts
9 Te Awamutu
10 Cambridge
11 Rangiaowhia
12 Kihikihi

Woven into the fabric of this investigation of subsistence is the hierarchical structure of the military and the associated horizontal structure of peer bonding and fellowship. Military disciplinary power is overtly incorporated into the rules and regulations that dictate the daily life of a soldier. The apparatus of control is vested in military rank. The military structural hierarchy was reinforced by spatial separation (i.e. officers' mess, officers' quarters, men's barracks, 'men room' etc.), differential treatment (i.e. officers' orderly and officers' rations), control of a private soldiers' time and labour, codified behaviours associated with rank, and rules for advancement/privilege and punishment. The military structure was particularly exemplified in rationing and consumption patterns. Rations were also used for control or maintaining discipline; punishment, for example, frequently included the suspension of a private soldier's rum ration.

The highlight of a day of hard manual labour or a long march in the rain for a private soldier was having a warm meal. The standard ration for a non-commissioned officer or soldier in the British Army in the mid 19th century varied little from day to day. The monotonous diet consisted of approximately 1½ lbs of bread for breakfast with coffee, and a mid-day dinner of boiled beef or mutton accompanied by potatoes and any vegetables the men could contribute. Captain James Stichbury, then a private in the 1st Battalion of the Auckland Militia, noted in his diary in 1863: '24 July – We get, per day 1 gill of rum, 1 lb of meat, 1¼ lb of bread, 1/6 oz tea, 1/6 oz coffee, ¼ oz of sugar, and a grain of pepper and salt' (in Cowan 1983, 461).

The enlisted men's rations in New Zealand were similar to those of their contemporaries in the Union Army in the United States of America fighting in the civil war during approximately the same time period (McCarley 1988, 2). The military diet, while better than that of English and Welsh labourers of the time, was still a focus for complaints.

The dinner venue, a mess or area adjacent to a cookhouse or camp fire, provided a forum for the men to voice aggravation. This included complaints about food, one such complaint was recorded by the commissariat:

> The small pickle ration was a source of constant grumbling, and it was not unusual for a soldier to be seen going about with half a diminutive onion on the point of his fork saying 'look at the ration I'm charged 1½ d for' quite forgetting that he had had (sic), in addition a pound of potatoes for his money (Robertson 1864, Inclosure 1, no. 18, 66).

Complaints about the smallness of the pickle ration related in part to the extra salary, 1½ pence, levied to provide the 'pickle'.

Officers faired better than enlisted men, except on the battle front where traditional markers of 'one's place' were frequently blurred. Rank provided privilege both formal and informal, as well as social constraints. The spatial separation of officers and men was visually evident in the style in which they dined and the rations received. Officers followed unwritten rules relating to who they associated with, including who they 'messed' with. They also had a tradition of organized messes and financial means to collectively supplement the standard ration. The officers' mess was a symbol of rank and also used to construct and reinforce relationships of power.

Context: the New Zealand Land Wars

The campaigns that are referred to as the New Zealand Wars began in 1845 as a series of conflicts between the British and some Maori tribes in the North Island of New Zealand. The New Zealand Wars are part of the 'Revolutionary Wars' that occurred in the British colonies between 1775–1914 and resulted from changes in political systems, the balance of power, and control of resources. The New Zealand campaigns mobilized approximately 12,000 men (some historians suggest 18,000; Belish 1988, 15). Involved in the conflict were Imperial Regulars and a naval brigade. The colonial forces included two permanent corps and the militia. The colonial corps included the Colonial Defence Force (cavalry) and the Forest Rangers. The Rangers were bush fighters used for scouting and rapid strikes. The militia was composed of the Waikato Militia (or Military Settlers) and the Auckland Militia and Volunteers.

Every man in Auckland over 17 years of age was drafted into the Auckland militia, but not all were involved in active service. Enrolled in the Waikato Militia were 2,300 'Australians'. Many brought their families with them from Australia. In addition there were small numbers of Maori 'Queenites', those loyal to Queen Victoria, and a few 'friendlies' (neutrals). These indigenous royalists and supporters of the British and colonial government are relevant to the subject of getting one's daily bread on a war front.

The commander of the force was Lieutenant-General Duncan Cameron. Many of his staff had served in the Crimean War. Cameron and his staff were determined to avoid the repetition of the logistical fiascos associated with the Crimean campaigns. Cameron was an able commander and the calibre of his staff high. In particular D. J. Gamble, the Quartermaster General, was considered: 'the most zealous officer and one of rare business abilities' (Belich 1988, 127).

During the New Zealand Wars the British forces performed three basic tasks to ensure logistic success. The first was the transportation of supplies through the war zone; the second task was protecting the communication system; the third task, and the role associated with war, involved the deployment of the column of attack. The column of attack was the last priority since the supply system had to be manned, mobile and protected before the column of attack could function. The greatest challenge to the supply system and obstacle to movement of a large military force is supplying troops at a distance from the main depot. The military train (baggage train) had to deliver supplies at the right place and the right time.

The Crimean War experience had taught the British that many soldiers can perish due to inadequate rations, food quality and handling. The soldiers involved in the New

Zealand Wars benefited from Alexis Benoist Soyer's work in the area of diet, food preparation and handling during the Crimean War. His work included invention of the 'Soyer field oven' and recipes for the military to use in the field, establishing basic rules of food handling and gaining a commitment from the military for assignment of a regimental cookery sergeant for each regiment (Clement-Lorford 2004 and Rippon Papers 1857).

Supplying the Campaign

Quarter Master General Gamble and H. Stanley Jones, the Commissary-General, were challenged from the start by the landscape of conflict. The campaigns of the New Zealand War took place on unbroken frontier dominated by bush vegetation, forest, and wetlands. There were no railroads or cross-country road systems. The main depot for the supply of the army was at Auckland and the next in importance was at Drury 23 miles south of Auckland. Drury could be reached by water, which proved useful because the road from Papakura to Drury was unfinished. Queen's Redoubt, Lieutenant-General Cameron's headquarters, was 35 miles from Auckland. The road from Drury south to Queen's Redoubt, the main headquarters for the army at the head of the Waikato region, was in tolerable order but passed over three steep hills. Supplies were transported by cart and boat to Queen's Redoubt.

Gamble noted in his report that 100 civilian bush cutters, primarily Nova Scotians and some German colonists, were employed to clear the vegetation along the Great South Road between Auckland and Queen's Redoubt. The work included cutting down all the vegetation 'to a breadth of 220 yards at each side of the road' (Gamble, 4 September 1863, 54).

Twelve types of carriage were used to get the military baggage train and commissariat supplies to campaign posts 100 miles into the interior. Often the supply train was a packhorse train (second class horses or sturdy animals that were lighter then draught horses but not cavalry mounts).

> On Friday the 4th (sic January) as per margin, marched from Esk Redoubt at 5am and reached Paparata at 1.30pm the camp equipage, entrenching tools, supplies, baggage being conveyed on 90 packhorses.
> … We made ti tree fascine roads across all the swamps, bridged one river and improved the crossing at all the rest (Greaves 1863–1864, 4 January 1864, 83).

Bullock and horse carts were obtained from Sydney and shipped across the Tasman Sea along with other supplies. The horses and bullocks were purchased locally from Australia. The difficulty of supplying forage rations for horses and bullocks on the battle front was an on-going problem. Tenders for provision of forage were a regular feature in local newspapers such as the *Waikato Times*.

The field ration of forage consisted of oats and hay; but other articles were permitted to be substituted, such as maize, bran, and green fodder in regulated proportions. Different scales of forage rations were in operation for nearly every different description of animal; officers' chargers, artillery horses, transport, heavy draught and light horses, horse of the Colonial Defence Force, working bullocks, & c. (Robertson 1864 Inclosure 1 no. 18, 67).

The Cape pack saddle previously used in other British campaigns was replaced by a New Zealand-style saddle, the Otago pack saddle, which was used by the gold miners in the South Island of New Zealand. The Otago pack saddle reportedly produced less abrasion.

Shallow draft riverboats and barges were the work horses of the supply system to the Lower Waikato although not always with out problems. On 8 February 1864 the Avon, laden with commissariat supplies and towing a barge that was also laden, struck a snag that sank both the ship and barge. Ten days of rations for the force at Te Rore were lost resulting in the deployment of supplies via alternative arrangements including the use of canoes manned by friendly natives under chief Te Wheoro (Robertson 1864 Inclosure 1 no.18, 62).

> In the month of August the barque 'City of Melbourne' was chartered for the conveyance of commissariat supplies to the Waikato and for the purpose of being used as a depot-ship in the river. It was arranged through the Colonial Government that friendly Maori should convey the supplies from the City of Melbourne to Maugatawhiri creek (Robertson 1864 *Inclosure* 1 no. 13, 20).

Military rations arrived at Whangamarino Redoubt twice a week via river, but carrying the rations up a hundred steep steps from the river to the redoubt was not easy given the supplies arrived in the form of 200 lb sacks of flour and oats. The commissariat Transport Corp was assisted by sailors and Waikato 'Queenites' and others such as local suppliers.

Many supplies had to be requisitioned from overseas since the New Zealand settlements were small and could only supply a fraction of the army's needs. Robertson reported 7 September 1864 (Inclosure 1 no. 13, 18):

> In times of peace considerable quantities of grain were grown by the Maoris themselves and brought into the Auckland market. They also brought to the market onions, potatoes, and pigs. This source of supply was of course completely cut off as soon as the war broke out. There were small numbers of cattle, the property of settlers, at different places in the province, but scarcely sufficient to supply the local market, without taking into consideration the requirements of the army... Almost all the supplies for the army had therefore to be obtained from other countries either directly by the Commissariat or indirectly through contractors.

Australia, New Zealand's nearest neighbour, supplied beef, mutton and flour. Biscuits (also referred to as hard tack, cabin bread, sailors' bread, or sailors' crackers) were obtained from overseas and locally:

> 'The chief supply of biscuits was manufactured in Auckland by Charles Canning the contractor, and was of very fair quality. Some was (sic) obtained from troop ships and some of very superior quality, from Sydney' (Robertson 1864 Inclosure 1 no. 18, 65).

Local contractors for groceries included R. Simpson until 31 March 1864 and after that Mr W. J. Young. The contractors tendered to supply the commissariat's requirements. An advertisement for tender was included in the *Daily Southern Cross*, Auckland NZ (25 February 1864, 1):

> Commissariate (sic) NZ Auckland 16 Feb 1864 Tenders from persons willing to contract for the following:
> Rum, West Indian, 5 percent under proof per gallon.
> Sugar, chocolate, tea, salt pork, salt beef, per lb;
> Split peas, per bushel;
> Flour, suet, raisins, or currants, per lb;
> Oatmeal per bushel;
> Mustard, pepper ground per lb;
> Vinegar, lemon juice per gallon;
> Stearine candles, 8's ditto, 24's per lb;
> Oil sperm, do Olives, per gallon
> Tobacco, soap per lb;
> To be packed in strong iron bound casks or cases, numbered, the tare and net weights clearly scribed and delivered to Commissariate (sic) Store Auckland.
>
> Firewood ti tree or other hardwood-length of 4 ft per 100 lbs
> Lime per bushel. To be delivered into the ships boats.
> Mixed vegetables per lb in about equal portions of onions, carrots, cabbage, turnips and pumpkins, and other vegetables when in season to be delivered into the ships boats included in one tender
> 6- *(casks)* each of salt beef and salt pork to be opened in the presence of a commissariat officer.
> Commissariat 27 May 1864 The Deputy Commissariat General H Stanley Jones" (*Daily Southern Cross*, Auckland NZ newspaper clipping inclosed in the Deputy Commissariat General Report, 1864 WO 107/7)

J. Leslie Robertson, Deputy Assistant Commissary General, wrote lengthy reports (7 Sept 1864, 24–26 and 23 August 1864, 71–73) that contain detailed descriptions of various transport and labour problems including: administrative problems associated with the division of supply and transport responsibilities between the Navy and Land Transport Corps; theft of supplies facilitated by the use of private contractors and the two military organizations; storage and food quality issues associated with stockpiling supplies; and problems with local contractors.

Some of the issues critically described in field reports range from supplying fresh meat to storage and food quality. References were made to controlling the overdriving of cattle by the contract cattle drovers; the potential for dishonesty on the part of the butchers (who were militia men); the loss of cattle through escape from enclosures; as well as costs and supply shortages.

The commissariat used government meat contractors to supply the troops but also encouraged opportunistic acquisition. The meat was usually butchered on site, hung, and boiled. Private Bodell and his friends were not above taking a sheep off the government contractor. In June 1865 he describes dressing a carcass of a sheep stolen from the government contractor's mob and sharing it with mates. He commented, 'Next day mutton was plentiful in camp' (Bodell in Sinclair 1982, 162).

Bodell and many other soldiers were opportunists. Bodell noted in his reminiscences (in Sinclair 1982, 155):

> several fat Bullocks were up the River behind Meremere and any Bullock so seen straying about was considered good loot for the troops and 5 of us went up the River in an old Canoe…. after cutting it into quarters we shipped it… it was soon cut up and hung up in joints. Early the next morning we sent a nice plate of steaks into the officers' Hut, no questions asked.

There are also references in the men's dairies and letters noting that they hunted duck, wild pigs, captured domestic fowl and purchased eels and fish from the 'friendly' natives.

In April 1865 the Commissariat General reported that the Lieutenant General prohibited parties of soldiers from rounding up and driving in roaming cattle and had given orders that one month's consumption of salted meat was to be provided for the whole of the force (Jones 1865).

Beef cured (salted) in New South Wales was obtained at about 3d (3 pence) a pound for the 1863–1864 campaign in the Waikato, although the troops apparently preferred salt pork (Robertson 1864 Inclosure 1 no. 18). Salt pork averaged 6d (6 pence) a pound and was obtained through a local contractor who supplied American, English and New Zealand Brands. Among the supply problems noted were problems with a variety of salted New Zealand pork that was fed on fish and smelled of fish when cooked. Salted meat also proved a storage problem in the summer months due to the expansion of the contents and bursting of one or two of the barrel hoops through corrosion caused by leaking pickle. Among the instructions to commissariat officers were instructions for wines, spirits, salted meat, etc.

> 426. Wines and spirits, and all other wet provisions in store should be under constant observation… 430. Every cask of salt meat coming into store should be examined at the bung…431. During the summer months, the salt meat casks are liable to burst by the expansion of the contents from the heat, and it is necessary to take out a small quantity of the pickle to prevent such accidents (War Office 1864 Appendix 4, 75).

Rations and Allowances

The scale of allowances for field service included:

> Ordinary field ration (general order no. 541 11 July 1863): 1lb fresh or salted meat, 1½ lb bread or 1 lb biscuit, and 1 gill of rum. The Grocery ration (General Order no 1974 February 1862) 1/6th oz of tea, 1/3rd oz of coffee, 2 oz of sugar 1/36th oz of pepper, and ½ oz of salt (War Office 1864, Appendix 4, 75).

The Commissariat Corp supply system was considered successful since no soldiers ever starved and the sick-rate never exceeded five per cent. This is probably a reflection of the good management of the force by the officers and not strictly the supply system. In October 1863 several of the regimental commanding officers requested the nutritional health of the troops be investigated as they were at a distance from many of the posts and in a disturbed country and could not provide themselves with vegetables through the usual sources (vendors or personal gardens). The outcome was a daily vegetable ration under General Order no. 624, dated 6 October 1863.

> The Board recommended a daily ration, consisting of 1 lb of potatoes, ½ oz onions; and when the vegetables were not procurable the substitution of the following articles, 4oz rice, or ⅓ pint of peas, or 1 oz preserved compressed vegetables, and ½ oz pickles, or 1/12oz mustard; and for this ration they proposed to make an additional stoppage of 1½ d. a day from the soldier's pay (Robertson 1864 Inclosure 1 no. 18, 66).

Other nutritional health measures included the issue of lime juice. General Orders No 660 (12 November 1863), no 701 (30 December 1863), and no 741 (13 February 1864) (in War Office 1864 Appendix 4) required that: 'lime juice 1 oz and sugar for lime juice 1 oz to each officer and man when salt meat is issued and on fresh meat days when no vegetables are issued' (War Office 1864 Appendix 4, 76).

Corporal George Brier noted in his diary (in Bilcliffe 1995, 165) the rations allocated in 1865 and how they were supplemented:

> We were allowed 12 ounces of beef or mutton per man a day, 6 days a week. Once a week we had either 12 ounces of salted beef or salted pork. The day we got salted meat we got 1 ounce of lime juice to prevent us from having scurvy. We got a pound and a half of bread a man per day and 1 pound of potatoes. Two or 3 days a week the natives used to bring us eels and fish and we gave them bread for them. They also brought us plenty of peaches and in the honey season, they brought us honey. We spread the honey on our bread instead of butter or treacle... if we gave them tobacco for their peaches and honey, they were well satisfied.

Cooks and Bakers

Each Imperial Regiment had a cookery sergeant (Correspondence to W. E. Gladstone 17/1/1863 in Ripon Papers Vol. XXIII 1857). In most established camps, redoubts and block houses cooking duty was assigned to private soldiers daily along with other rostered duties. At Kihikihiin the 1870s, the Diary of Duty lists the same private as having cooking duty for several months. Cooking duty could also be requested. For example, on 26 November 1863 Private Stichbury noted in his diary he received punishment for disobedience and was assigned two days pack drill and his grog stopped. He got out of the pack drill by offering to go as a cook.

> At larger camps there were several cooks and bakers. Field bakeries were established at many of the main redoubts and bread was supplied to the other posts from these bakeries at least four times a week. By 1865 there were 69 bakers at 26 posts in the North Island. The most productive was at Te Awamutu where 40,600 lbs of flour were issued in May 1865 and 6 bakers, using 6 ovens, produced 55,720 lbs of bread (Jones 1865).

(In 1863):

> When the Lieutenant-General marched from the Queen's Redoubt in November of that year field ovens were in full working order at nearly every post from which the troops were supplied... when the Lieutenant-General reached Ngaruawahia a short time elapsed owing to the difficulty of transport before the field ovens were forwarded to that post; but an excellent substitute was employed by Deputy Assistant Commissary-General Marshall, who supplied the Staff with very good bread baked in holes in the ground (Robertson 1864 *Inclosure* 1 no. 18, 65).

E. Strickland, Deputy Commissary-General, noted in his report 25 March1865 that the iron used in the construction of the Aldershot and Curragh ovens in use in Taranaki is hardly thick enough and does not last well (Strickland 1865 Inclosure 1 no. 15, 38). The iron single-cased ovens were improved over time by the addition of a second metal skin to prevent the oven roof collapsing under the weight of the earth overburden which was placed on top for insulation, but earlier ovens were also in use. Other improvements were made in the door and flue and the New Zealand bread oven evolved. Leslie Robertson included a drawing of the New Zealand bread oven in his 23 August 1864 report (Figure 16.2). He noted the oven with troughs and other implements for baking could be transported in one cart. The New Zealand field ovens were manufactured by Messrs Vickery and Masefield (of Albert Iron Foundry) and ready for the march from Queen's Redoubt into the Waikato in November 1863.

Imperial Officers, Private Soldiers and the Colonial Militia

The army on the New Zealand front on the simplest level was composed of two classes, officers and 'men' (soldiers of private rank / enlisted men). Officers tended to be drawn

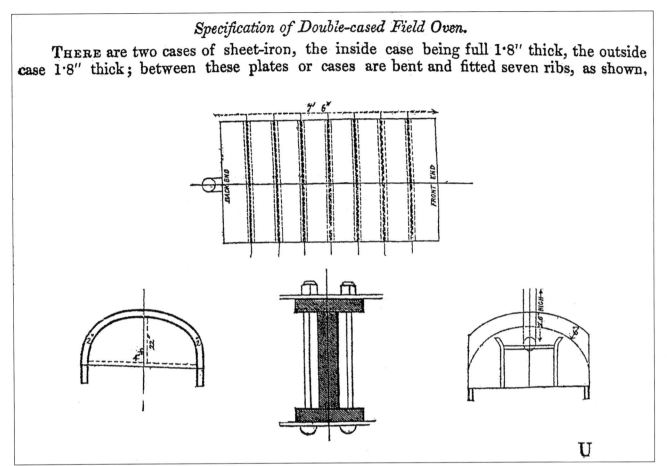

Figure 16.2. New Zealand Land Wars bread oven (Vickery and Masefield 1864).

from the landed aristocracy and gentry. The 'men' in the British army were commonly drawn from the unskilled labouring class. These two general classes were marked by a regulated line of behaviour and differentiated social spheres outside the military institution that found continuity within. While many upper class 'wild lads', younger sons or sons of impoverished gentry built new lives in the military, they did not escape their social class. Food and a regular income attracted unskilled and often illiterate young men to the military.

The formal rules of any military institution are that the disciplinary power increased with rank. In the Colonial Militia many of the pre-existing British class lines did not exist, but military structure relied on officers having definite roles. Positions of power were seldom refused. The informal rules of the battle front differ from the formal and this is particularly evident in the colonial militia. Disobedience was not uncommon nor was intense loyalty to specific officers. The Forest Rangers in particular were often scorned by the Imperial Regulars since they operated outside the standard rules of military engagement and behaviour. Yet the worth and necessity of the Rangers were acknowledged by both the column of attack and the commissariat corp.

The physical separation of officers from men was evident in the type of accommodation provided, mess systems, separate latrines, officers' clubs, and regulated privileges. The men lived in crowded barracks or under canvas and cleaned their kit and commonly ate where they slept. 'One's place' in the military was clearly indicated on a daily basis by the codified segments of hierarchy intrinsic to the military. Spatial arrangements and what may be the physical expression of privilege/status/class is evident in the material culture recovered archaeologically at redoubt sites. Written records clearly identify the separate facilities associated with officers and 'men'. At Hamilton East and West Redoubt the inspection report notes: 'one hut 54 × 18 feet for five officers, and one hut 30 × 20 feet for twenty men' (Unknown author, *Returns of the Blockhouses, Redoubts and Stockades in the North Island*, 1869).

The horses at the Hamilton Redoubts faired better with over double the space allowed the men, i.e. one 60 × 20 foot hut for 14 horses. At Te Awamutu there was an officers club, along with its three redoubts (Figure 16.3).

Shelter in the field also marked differences in rank. The bell tent was essential housing for the field force. In 1862 Quartermaster General Gamble (1864, 2) issued:

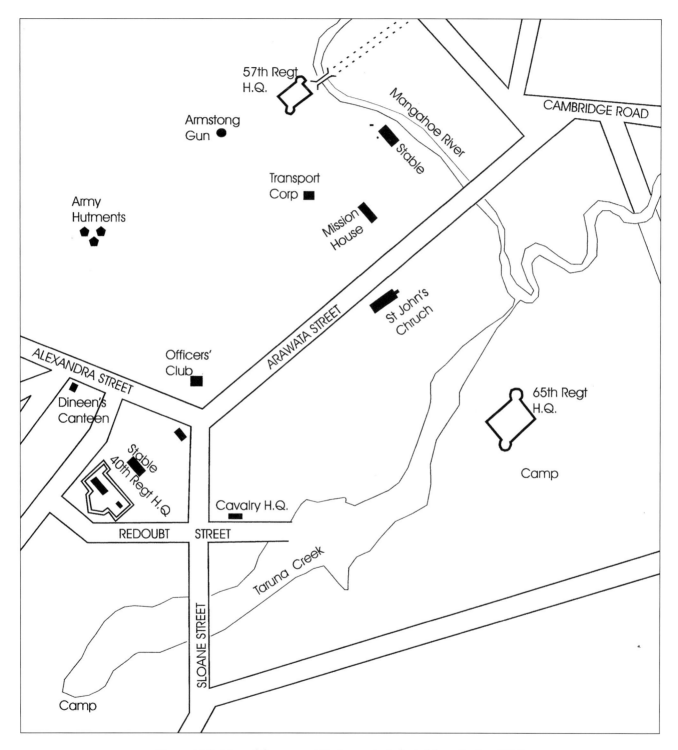

Figure 16.3. Map of the camp at Te Awamutu (adapted from Barber 1984).

one circular tent to each officer. One circular tent to every twelve men. [This was considered a maximum for preservation of health during the summer months in this climate] Two circular tens for temporary hospital puposes. One circular tent for orderly room.

Although 12 private soldiers in a tent was considered the maximum, more in a tent was not unusual. In Tauranga on 21 April 1864 Captain Grace wrote (Biliciffe 1995, 137): 'the men pitched their tents and get in them… . Fifteen men in a tent.'

Dining

British Regimental Mess Chest

British Regimental companies had a mess chest for storing utensils, plates, dishes, tablecloths and cooking frocks for each mess. The mess chest was the property of the company. The cost of the chest was covered by each soldier's annual utensil allowance and the men's weekly mess contribution. The items in the mess chest might include tableware printed with a standard transfer print pattern in the regiments colours (Figure 16.4); marked with the regimental number and/ or insignia; utensils might be inscribed with the company number and the initials O. M. for officers' mess and later S. M. for sergeants' mess. The mess chest of the Imperial Regiment's enlisted men would have contained less expensive ceramics and may not have contained eating utensils. The ceramics in the officers' field mess chests may have differed substantially from the setting found on the officers' table at established posts.

Officers messed together in a style that suited their status. It cannot be emphasised enough; who you ate with and the style in which you ate separated officers from the enlisted men. Officers of lower rank were separated from those of high rank. Sergeants, for example, messed together in a separate mess at many of the redoubts.

Dining with the Officers

When they were at established redoubts officers ate breakfast, lunch, high tea and the main meal of the day, and a supper which would include several courses. Officers messed together and paid for extra rations and drink by contributing a set amount to the mess fund or paying a mess subscription. Dining was a part of the entertainment associated with class and status and not simply subsistence. Within the military, even on the New Zealand frontier, class lines were exemplified at the dining table. The officers' mess was the centre of social activities and became an institution that followed its members wherever they went. The officer's mess had a mess president, as well as waiters and other staff assigned duties necessary to operate the mess.

After Captain Sheffield Grace, 68th Regiment, arrived in Auckland from England on 4 March 1864 and travelled

Figure 16.4. Ceramics from the 58th regiment of foot officers' mess in New Zealand, 'Mason's Patent Ironstone China' (in Godden 1984, 417 mark 2530), Cambridge Museum Collection, New Zealand.

to Tauranga, he noted where he dined in many of his diary entries (in Bilcliffe 1995, 136), for example:

> 5 March – Got up to Barracks and got into a tent. Bolden and I dined in scratch mess at the Barracks [Bloden was Lieutenant Leonard Bolden].
> 7 March – I went early to the stores, got a blue jumper. Had a tooth stopped. Bought a revolver and ammunition. Dined with Bolden at the Club [probably the officers' club].
> 12 March – Paraded at eight. Left with the 12th and 68th drafts for Meremere. Got in by one p.m. Nine miles. My company was in the fort. Dined at the mess at Meremere [Meremere Redoubt].

Major Charles Shuttleworth's diary included the following descriptions of his time in Tauranga.

> 22 Jan 1864 – A very pretty camp close to shore, nice riding ground; a tent to self and plenty of provisions apparently to be bought. Turnor [Lieutenant William Turnor] and I at present mess together and get on very well. Excellent rations; fresh meat and quite as much as one can eat….
> 25 Jan 1864 – Began building redoubt. Lots of fish and fruit came over today. Milkman supplies us regularly.Got a small wooden house put up as a cook house. Turnor and I get on very well together in mess (Bilcliffe 1995, 132).

The officers stationed in Tauranga dined with Reverend Brown and his family at Te Papa Mission Station (also known as The Elms). Colonel Carey's force was encamped for several months outside the mission station gates. When the officers dined with the Browns the meal was prepared and served by the Browns' servant. The menu was probably similar to other meals served at the mission which was the headquarters for Church Missionary Society work in the region. The meal probably included roast mutton, pumpkin and potatoes, rice pudding, apple pie and tart (Vennell 1984). They dined formally at the oval table in the mission house: 'The table setting was described as being covered with spotless linen and shining silver and gleaming glass' (Vennell 1984, 97).

Establishing an Officers' Mess

When constructing a new redoubt at Judea, near Tauranga, in 1864, Major Shuttleworth was intent on having an officers' mess building.

> 27 May – Rode afternoon – getting much better. Busy arranging about getting up a mess. 28 May – Busy about a mess. Settled to have one (Bilcliffe 1995, 147).
>
> 29 May – Very wet morning. No church parade. Fine afternoon. Had a ride out to look at house for mess.
>
> 30 May – Rode out with Colonel. Spoke about Mess house and agreed to have wooden house brought in ….? 5 men working for mess ½ day (Bilcliffe 1995, 148).
>
> 14 June 1864 – Busy with mess. Opening dinner rather a scramble but will do. 'Alexandra' came in with Headquarters Waikato Militia. Tunks came with it and dined with us (Bilcliffe 1995, 151).
>
> 26 Nov 1864 – Appointed Private Young mess waiter vice Rudman sick (Bilcliffe 1995, 158).
>
> 8 April 1865 – Mess meeting and again to be Mess President. Lovely weather (Bilcliffe 1995, 163).

Dining with the Enlisted Men

Captain James Stichbury (then a private in the 1st Battalion of the Auckland Militia) kept a diary that documented his life in the militia. The contrast between the officers' dining experiences and that of a private soldier is made very apparent by the entries in James Stichbury's 1863 diary.

> 24 July 1863 – Served out with regimental clothes. They were forage cap with topknot, blue-serge shirt, trousers with red stripe down the side, blucher boots, short leggings; also tin plate, pannikin, knife, fork, spoon, haversack, & c. (in Cowan vol. 1 1983, 461).

Unlike the officers the men were responsible for their kit, including their cutlery. At Albert Barracks in Auckland bone-handled cutlery with the initials of the private soldiers inscribed were recovered during an archaeological excavation. The private soldier's metal pannikin probably served as a cup, bowl-plate, and a small cooking pot in the field.

Daily Duty and Private Soldiers' Rations

Private Strichbury's diary records the daily life of an enlisted man (i.e. duty, food and shelter).

> 21 July – At 9 o'clock came off guard duty. At 10 marched from the camp to our destination, Papatoetoe, to build a redoubt. Reached it at 2 o'clock; took our tent and bread and raw meat with us. As soon as we had got our tents pitched – we had not time to dig the trenches round – it came on to rain. We had nothing to eat this night, for the rain would not let the fires burn; and what made it worse, we had no blankets for two days after we arrived here. We had to lie on the wet ground with only our greatcoats and no fern. Dreadful night.
>
> 22 July – Very cold and miserable this morning having to lie in the wet all night. Rain never ceased all day. Had to build some cookhouses as well as we could. Had no grog today, though we were entitled to it as soon as we started from Otahuhu…
>
> 23 July – Got served out to us a blanket and piece of oilskin, which came in very acceptable…
>
> 24 July – Served with regimental clothes …also tin plate, pannikin, knife, fork, spoon, haversack, & c. We get, per day 1 gill of rum, 1 lb of meat, 1¼ bread, 1/6 oz tea, 1/6 oz coffee, ¼ oz of sugar, and a grain of pepper and salt…
>
> 5 August – …Had breakfast – nice dry bread – stale as a brick and coffee without milk and very little sugar…
>
> 8 August – The men were confined last night …(some of the men were put in the guard tent for grumbling at (sic) their meat)…
>
> 22 August – Fine day…Went into the bush and found some bee-hives in the trees. Got two buckets of honey—quite a treat (Stichbury in Cowan 1983 vol 1, 461).
>
> 21 October – Got up at 7, and tried to get some meat for breakfast but could not. Had dry bread and a little drop of milk we managed to buy between us. Formed up at 9 to march…
>
> 10 December – breakfast at 7. The dinner was cooked overnight ready for us….We got grog at 1 – two glasses each… reached the camp at Otahuhu. No tea for us, as the men could not get it till 7. Had some sardines and bread, and went to bed in a hut full of fleas (Stichbury in Cowan vol 1, 462–463).

Stichbury noted the meat they carried was precooked. Cooking meat over night, so it could be carried into the field the next day, was a standard practice. The men were usually sent into the field with two to three days' rations. The soldiers used a white canvas haversack to carry provisions along with other items such as extra rounds of ammunition.

In the Field

The simplicity of the military apparatus of control became more complex on the front and the status quo of privilege and separation was tested by battle conditions. Capt Charles

Grace noted in his diary:

> My company was on in-laying picquet. I had nothing but what I carried up, viz: one blanket, one shirt, one pair of socks, waterproof sheet and coat....All night it rained in heavy showers, no grog, no food and many alarms. I lay wedged between Best (sic Surgeon Major Thomas Best) and Light (Captain Hugo Light) (in Belcliffe 1995, 144–145).

The separation of officers and men continued in the field but particularly in the middle ranks was often blurred by shared adversity. This included relaxation of markers of gentile status or rank such as spatial separation, types and quality of rations, and dining on pottery instead of tin. War Correspondent John Featon noted (1971, 24) that:

> 'for service in the field...The regimental colours were left behind as well as the mess plate of the officers.'

Supply, Power and Discrimination

The commissariat as a military department were installed with power through exercise of their duties, that is, the provision of rations and equipment. The commissariat's role included: selecting contractors; the locations of the field depots, bakeries, and stock yards; accounting for rations charges; and distribution of rations. The effects of the power that the commissariat exercised were felt in the field.

Major General T. J. Galloway (commander of the New Zealand Militia from 1863–1865) noted in August 1863:

> the regulars have far better rations then the Militia and Volunteers. Why this should have been the case is best known to officers at the head of the Colonial Commissariat, who must have had some motive for winking at the inferior quality of the rations served out to the unfortunate Militia and Volunteers (in Lennard 1986, 38).

The Colonial Militia was apparently not fed as well as the regulars and many purchased provisions from the store if they had the money; others were reliant on the generosity of the regular regiments. At one camp, the men of the 65th and 18th regiments shared their rations with the militia and volunteers. Generosity established a relationship of good will as well as obligation between the militia and the 18th and 65th regiments.

The rational for the commissariat's differential treatment of the Colonial Militia is not known. Speculation suggests differential rationing could have been a tactic to maintain regimental loyalty through the creation of 'privilege', at the expense of the colonial forces. The effect was marginalization of the colonial force via nutritional disadvantage.

The levies the commissariat charged the forces also differed. The Forest Rangers, who were paid more then the regular militia as compensation for the hazards associated with their bush and scouting duties, were charged 10 pence a day for rations in contrast to the 3½ pence charged militia men. The Rangers were not issued any special rations despite the extra charge and no changes in the charge were made despite written requests.

Pillage: *'to the Victors Go the Spoils'*

There is some irony in the higher levy for rations charged to the Forest Rangers. The commissariat frequently used the Rangers' skills to supplement the requisitioned food supply through pillage. The results of the Rangers' work were financial savings credited to the commissariat corp. Pillaging supplemented the regular supplies purchased by the commissariat to feed the troops and also filled out the soldiers' diet. While he didn't condone the style of pillage used by some of the troops, the Quartermaster General was practical and aware of potential cost savings gained from the seizure of food supplies. He noted in his report after the taking of Rangiawhia and Kihikihi:

> The loss to the enemy of two such places, with their extensive cultivations is and will be yet still more serious as winter advances. The amount of potatoes alone will, it is estimated, be enough to provide full ration of this vegetable for the whole of the field force during the coming winter (Gamble 4 March 1864, 97).

The Maori were agriculturalists. Their gardens were often located at a distance from pa sites or Maori villages. The major engagements in the Waikato took place during the growing and harvest season for many crops. The commissariat records note that not just kumara (sweet potatoes) and potatoes were recovered but pumpkins, melons, maize, and oats were found by the troops in Maori whares, storehouses and plantations. There were no reports of Maori razing their fields or storehouses when they abandoned a village or garden area. Destruction may have been considered an aberrant practice and difficult in the case of root crops or isolated fruit trees, or impractical when settlements were rapidly abandoned.

Supplementing the Regular Food Supply: Prestige and Power

The Forest Rangers were the regiment of colonial troops most noted for their ability to supplement the regular food supply. Major Gustavus Ferdinand von Tempsky, then an ensign, described a Maori camp the Rangers took in September 1863:

> [We]...revelled in retaken plunder and eating the Maori dinner cooking on the Maori fire. The men found sugar, tea, plated ware, papers, mats, hats, a freshly cooked piece of pork and some jam...We return to Manukau laden with spoil and intoxicated with our victory (Stower 1996, 24).

While there was certainly distain and contempt for the Rangers' frequent misbehaviour the commissariat did not ignore their bush skills and employed the Rangers to their advantage. The commissariat sent the Rangers out scouting for cattle and other food staples like potatoes. On one occasion they found a large canoe near a Maori cultivation of potatoes and peaches and filled the bottom of the canoe with the food and paddled back to camp. When stationed near Te Rore Major Von Tempsky noted:

'No other duty was ours except reconnoitring expeditions into the surrounding locality, as it was the season for water melons and peaches, we were indeed welcomed on our returning for the luscious fruit we brought with us' (Stower 1996, 56).

The Rangers gained prestige and a measure of power (at least temporarily) through resource control, that is, their ability to provide luxury foods. Fresh fruit, like melons and peaches was a welcome change to a soldier's monotonous diet of meat and bread. Following their pillage of food and other items at Rangiaowhia, Major Von Tempsky of the Forest Rangers wrote:

I have since heard that our entry into Te Awamutu created not only admiration but envy; loot being such a scarce article in this war (von Tempsky n.d., 117).

The gardens around Te Awamutu yielded bushels of fine apples to the fruit loving soldier. Peaches we had been surfeited with at Te Rore. Affrighted hens were heard to shriek behind hedges, 'la petite guerre' against property was mildly worming its way against orders, as for the time being these minor moralities could not be attended to; particularly when expert young officers joined and stimulated the men, by the coin of the realm, to the pursuit of the gallinaceous tribes (von Tempsky n.d., 111).

The Rangers' activities some times pushed the bounds and the hierarchy of control was stretched. When they returned from a scouting mission to Wharepapa south of their post at Kihikihi Redoubt they descended on a Maori village near the aukati line (boundary between European controlled land and Maori King country). The village was rapidly abandoned leaving behind pork and potatoes cooking in hangi (in-ground ovens). The Imperial officers in charge of the redoubt ordered the Rangers transferred to Te Awamutu, because of their 'wholly unauthorized' zeal (Cowan 1983, 457).

The pillaging by troops during the war resulted in a substantial number of claims by both colonial settlers and Maori. There were 372 claims to the Compensation Court with a total value of £136,000. This included 40 Maori claimants. Only £71,000 was paid out since the government was short of funds. The Maori claimants received £2,432, about a third of their claim of £7,400.

Discipline and Drink

The ordinary field ration issued under general order number 541, 11 July 1863 included 1 gill of rum. Commissary officer reports frequently noted that transporting rum was inconvenient due to weight as well as theft by those providing transport. Once the barrels of rum reach their destination they were distributed as part of the daily ration. The rum percentage was listed as five per cent proof in the commissariat's tender advertised in the *Daily Southern Cross* on 16 February 1864. Rum when served as the 'grog' ration on board ships was generally watered. Leslie Robertson noted (in 1864 Inclosure 1 no.18, 66): 'the rum obtained by contract, and reduced to the proper strength by custom-house gaugers in Auckland'. The proper strength is not noted in Robertson's report.

Alcohol was issued as a daily ration because it was considered an absolute necessity, due to its nutritional value and its importance to the men as a morale lifter. Forest Ranger Corporal William Johns wrote passionately about the rum ration:

It was the rum that kept us alive. We had so much wet hard work, swimming and fording rivers and creeks and camping out without fires; when we camped in the bush on the enemy's trail it was often unsafe to light a fire for cooking and warmth and we never knew when we might have a volley poured into us, so we just lay down, cold and wet as we were and we'd have been dead but for the rum (in Lennard 1986, 94).

General Cameron ordered an extra ration of rum for the men following the taking of Rangiaowhia to acknowledge the troops efforts. Rangiaowhia was a bloody battle at an agricultural settlement that consisted of two clusters of whares near Rangiaowhia's Catholic and Anglican Churches.

The rationing of rum was also used for control and discipline. Common punishments included having the grog ration stopped for a set number of days, incarceration in the stockade, hair-cropping, and flogging. The punishment most complained about in diary entries is having the grog ration stopped. Officers considered cutting the grog ration an effective punishment. James Stichbury was punished with a sentence of three days 'grog stoppage'. He wrote on 4 August 1863:

was told off to work in the trenches. I got my shovel but did not do any work until I saw the captain; so I went to him and told him I could not work in the trenches without my grog, for it is hard work digging on dry bread and coffee (in Cowan 1983, 461).

Soldiers were allowed to buy alcohol, but private soldiers were not permitted to keep it in the barracks. In contrast, officers, being by definition gentlemen, were allowed to keep alcohol in their private quarters. Common soldiers could be punished for keeping alcohol in their quarters or for drunkenness on duty. Fifty strokes with a cat-o-nine tails was the common punishment.

Private soldiers could afford only a few small luxuries. Alcohol, because it was relatively cheap, accessible and its effects were instantly gratifying, became a significant part of a soldier's life.

Archaeological Findings at Redoubts and Other Military Sites

The details of daily life as recorded in historic records do not necessarily match archaeological findings. Similarly there are gaps in the archaeological record that are filled out by the historical data provided in commissariat records, diaries, etc. Evidence of dining and diet have been recovered from many military occupation sites in New Zealand along with the other artefacts of daily life and military affiliation. These artefacts have been recovered from features such as ditches, gun pits, buildings and tent circles, latrines, and garbage holes. The latter holes are a common feature of military sites.

Garbage disposal holes are usually composed of a mix of drink or food storage bottles, ceramics, bone and miscellaneous other artefacts. Often they are crushed together in a single layer representing a single event. The diary of duty from the Kihikihi Redoubt shows that redoubt clean up was a regularly assigned duty. This may explain the number of often small, less then a cubic metre, size deposits. Deeper holes have also been identified at some sites. The contents of a garbage deposit, 'feature C', (0.86 m × 1.60m × 10–20 cm in depth) at the Te Awamutu military stables is listed in Table 16.1. The stables were near the redoubt used by the 57th regiment and the Transportation Corp headquarters. The percentages of alcohol, food and tablewares shown in Table 16.1 are similar to those recovered from other garbage holes. The dominance of alcohol bottles is typical as are the minimum number of other artefact types.

The tablewares recovered at redoubt sites commonly include large platters, dinner plates, soup plates, cups and saucers, mugs, bowls, and teapots. Transfer-printed earthenwares usually make up about 60% of the ceramic tableware sample or more. Common transfer-print patterns found at most of the redoubts are: 'Asiatic Pheasant', 'Rhine', 'Clyde', 'Blue Willow', 'Cable', 'Gem', 'Rouen', 'Kulat', 'Antique', and 'Foliage'. The popular transfer-print tableware patterns were produced and distributed by several English manufacturers. At redoubt sites popular patterns produced by more then one manufacturer are often recovered. Other tableware designs include blue and red banded wares, sprig decorated porcelain, gilt ware and a small amount of blue bodied ware, as well as embossed and plain white wares.

The ceramics found at redoubts in New Zealand have often been assumed to be associated with the presence of officers, but historic accounts such as those of Corporal George Grier, indicate that even the officers may have dined on metal plates in the field camps and construction phase redoubts. Corporal George Grier of the 68th regiment was stationed at Gate Pa. He noted in his diary:

> We have nothing in the pottery line; all we had was our Mess-tins and a tin flask. We had our coffee in the morning for our breakfast in our Mess-tins, then at 12 o'clock we had a dram of rum in it. At one o'clock we had our broth in it, at 4 o'clock we had another dram of rum in it and at five o'clock we had our tea in it. So you hear that we made very good use of our Mess-tins (in Bilcliffe 1995, 165).

The mess tin Grier refers to was probably a D-shaped (nested) mess tin, first introduced about 1812. The tin flask may have been the half-moon shaped tin flask or the kidney shaped tin flask.

Documentation from overseas forts indicates that the private soldiers' mess, included table services of tin plates and large meat-serving platters. Barracks regulations in England called for two meat dishes for every 12 men. It is suggested that larger ceramic vessels such as meat plates or large serving platters were not necessarily associated with officers' mess, but may have also been used in the private soldiers' mess, but soup plates and dinner plates may be associated with the officers' mess.

The range of ceramic tablewares recovered from New Zealand war sites are similar to the functional types and stylistic patterns found at sites in South Island gold fields in New Zealand and in Australia. No plates with printed mess numbers, scratched numerals, or personal marks have been recorded. The majority of the wares were probably

Table 16.1. General summary of artefacts by function recovered from Feature C (Garbage hole); Military Stables, Te Awamutu (Simmons 2001).

Function	MN	Associated Dates	General Descriptive Notes
Architecture	4		Nails, Flat glass
Alcohol	43	1860–90	Glass containers – Stout Beer, Beer, Cognac, Brandy
Non-Alcohol Beverage	2	1830–70	Glass containers – Cordial/ Mineral Water
Food	8		Bos taurus, Chine stutchburyi, Pickle, Sauce, Salad oil
Tableware and Kitchen ware	7	1860–80	Ceramics – Transfer pattern tableware ('Kulat', 'Rhine', unidentified patterns; tableware with gilt line on white; brown salt glaze crock fragment); Drinking glass
Medicine	2		Glass bottles (no markings)
Other	1		Metal container fragment/ lapped seam (probably food container)

purchased through local distributors or were simply those popular at the time in the colonies and England. When an officers' mess was established it was not uncommon for the officers to donate their own personal equipment cutlery, plates, bowls, etc.

Ceramic patterns that have not been previously identified at other sites in New Zealand could represent tableware that was part of a regiment's mess chest or equipment belonging to an individual. Two complete plates recovered from the stables site in Te Awamutu featured a brown transfer print 'Maltese Scroll'. Based on a literature review this pattern has not been found at other redoubt or mining sites in New Zealand, including the extensively excavated 40th regiment redoubt, in Te Awamutu. The registration mark matches the registration of 'Maltese' in December 1861 by William Brownfield, Cobridge, Staffordshire Potteries. The other potter registering 'Maltese' was T. Barlow (Cotton and Barlow 1850–1855). The plates could have been produced by either manufacturer. The only other mark on the plate base was an impressed 'B'. An impressed 'BW' was used by Brownfield from 1850–1871 and an impressed 'B' by Thomas Barlow from 1849–1882 (Godden1964; Kowalsky and Kowalsky 1999). These plates were recovered from a privy and may relate to an unauthorised meal.

Drinking ware and Cutlery

Though not mandatory, it is likely each soldier brought to the table some type of drinking vessel. Archaeological finds include cups or mugs, glass tumblers, a wine glass, and a drinking glass made from the base and mid-section of a bottle. Historically, forks and knives were purchased in pairs either from the regiment's quartermaster or a local merchant. Bone-handled tableware is the most common type found at redoubt sites in New Zealand, but this may be a result of the preservation qualities of bone handles and the mounting plate since both are found. At Albert Barracks in Auckland bone-handled cutlery found in a well featured the initials of private soldiers.

Serving the Troops: Other Tableware and Kitchenware

Archaeological evidence of kitchens and serving large numbers of people includes serving platters, teapots, and meat forks, frying pans, metal pot fragments. A fry pan was recovered from the Armed Constabulary (A. C.) Redoubt that has a width of 332mm and a depth of 50mm (Vuletich 2004). Two teapots produced by W. and J. A. Bailey, ALLOA Pottery Scotland were also recovered from the A. C. redoubt.

Other kitchen wares found at military sites includes mixing bowls. Baking dishes are not usually found, although four baking dishes were found at the A. C. Redoubt at Pirongia. Two of the baking dishes were produced by the W. and J.

A. Bailey, ALLOA Pottery Scotland inscribed with 'patent fireproof unbreakable baking dish' and two were produced by Sharpe of Sharpe Brothers and Co, Burton on Trent, Staffordshire (Vuletich 2004). The baking dishes were rectangular in shape and 25×31.75 cm, 25×31.75 cm and 26.67×34.29 cm (Vuletich 2004).

These dishes could have been used inside cast iron camp ovens (Dutch ovens) nested in the coals of an open fire or a cast iron oven with firebox, or used in pits filled with heated stones. The description of bread-making in holes in the ground at Ngaruawahia prior to the establishment of a bakery suggests the possibility that the baking dishes may have been used in this manner.

Equipment that can definitely be associated with the production of the bread ration has not been identified at redoubt sites. It is assumed that the 2.29 m long iron baking ovens were probably sold off as surplus when redoubt buildings and other fittings were sold and may not be evident. Alternatively the sample size or location of many redoubt excavations may account for this deficit. The redoubt bakehouse may have been located outside the redoubt defences in the general camp area. Excavations have commonly been focused on the area inside the redoubt defences and not the surrounding area.

Meat, Fish and Shellfish

Redoubt faunal collections are dominated by beef bones. The meat cuts tend to be rump and shoulder cuts. Mutton and pig are also evident along with small numbers of fowl. Feeding a large number of people with fowl would have presented greater handling and conveyance problems then feeding the troops with livestock such as beef or mutton.

Other high protein foods noted in the diaries included fish and eel. Fish and eel bones have not been recovered at redoubts, but shellfish are commonly found in low numbers and the varieties of shellfish included: oysters (*saxostrea* sp.), cat's eye (*Lunella amaragda*), paua (*haliotis* sp.), *Melgraphia aethiops*, *Neothais scalaris*, *Haustrum haustorium*, and *Perna canaliculus periostracum*. These probably would have been purchased from friendly Maori. The species most commonly found at redoubts is oysters. Also recovered at the Armed Constabulary Redoubt at Pirongia were egg shells from domestic chickens. On at least one march in the rain, 21 January 1866, a horse was killed to supplement provisions that were exhausted, followed by a second horse the next day (Stower 1996, 166). No horse remains with butcher marks have been found at the redoubt sites.

A recent faunal analysis at the A. C. Redoubt suggests that the animals were not slaughtered on site (Watson 2000a). The meat cuts recovered were dominated by beef, particularly rump cuts, mutton leg cuts, and pig head. The meat may have been obtained from a local contract butcher.

Casked brined meat, pork and beef was provided to the troops but has not been identified in faunal collections at redoubt sites. Reanalysis of the A. C. redoubt collection and the Alexandra East collection resulted in the conclusion that no salted meat cuts were evident in the sample (Watson 2004 pers. comm.)

Canned Goods

The only food product can types that have been clearly identified at Land War sites are sardine tins. In several cases these had copper labels. Many fragments of unidentifiable can and metal box have been found in garbage holes but identification of their contents has been hampered by poor preservation. These can fragments could represent biscuit boxes, canned meat, cocoa tins, treacle cans, jam cans, or even dried (preserved) vegetable tins. The commissariat record and the soldiers' diaries reference these products.

Lieutenant Colonel Thomas McDonnell and Major von Tempsky, then junior officers, went on a spying expedition to Paparata and had to lie low during the mission. McDonnell recorded the experience and noted:

> we were in what the Yankees term a 'considerable fix', we determined to make the best of it, and commenced our breakfast of biscuit, two cakes of chocolate and a tin of kippered herring, and prepared for what might happen... (in Ryan and Parham 1986, 64).

This journal entry suggests that some of the fish tins from redoubt excavations may be herring and not sardines. The usual indicator used to differentiate the two types of canned fish is size of the tins, herring tins being larger and ovoid.

Vegetables and Fruits

Potatoes are frequently referenced in the diaries but have not been evident archaeologically. Peach pits are commonly found sometimes in reasonably large quantities, such as 59 peach pits at Omata. The Te Awamutu stable site latrine had one *cucurbitaceae* sp. seed. This was probably a marrow squash seed.

Private Bodell noted (in Sinclair 1982, 149) when he was at Te Rore, not far from Te Awamutu: 'we often got wild pigs and vegetable marrows and other vegetables from deserted Maori Villages'.

The deposits also had buckwheat seeds. The buckwheat might have been a weed seed associated with local wheat growing, an ingredient in bread, biscuits or even animal feed, since the privy was near a stable. Seeds that should be present in archaeological sites that are noted in diaries or letters include apples and cherries. The other seeds recovered from sites have been from native species such as New Zealand harakiki. At the A. C. Redoubt in Pirongia a burned mass of food was recovered that is believed to be

peas (Vuletich *pers. comm.* March 2004). A pea ration of 1/3 pint is mentioned in the commissariat records as an allowed ration, as was rice.

Food Condiments

The majority of the food containers that have been recovered are glass. The products they represent include: salad oil, olive oil, vinegar; pickles produced by Mortons, Mills and Ledge, Stowers and Crosse and Blackwell; Olson's tomato sauce; Goodall Backhouse Yorkshire Relish, and the ubiquitous Lea and Perrin's Worcestershire sauce.

Other types of food bottles recovered include caper and curry bottles. A particularly high number of curry bottles were recovered from Alexandra East Redoubt. This may suggest something about the quality of the meat at the redoubt or the preference of the troops (many of the British troops came to New Zealand from posts in India). The commissariat records document the purchase of olive oil and vinegar, and pickled onions. The other sauces noted – curry powder, capers, jars of pickles – are not listed in the commissariat records. These condiments may have been purchased by the mess or by individual soldiers pooling their money.

Soft Drinks and Ginger Beer

Only a few soft drink bottles have been recovered from military sites. These would have been individual purchases by the men or possibly mess purchases. Those with labels indicate they were bottled by New Zealand or Australian drink manufacturers. A few ginger beer bottles have also been recovered, but may only represent a small amount of the actual ginger beer consumed. Private Bodell noted (in Sinclair 1982, 164): 'we found Hamilton a fine station, good barracks accommodation... remained for 14 months. I was carpentering, making ginger beer for the hotels and as usual making money and spending it as fast.'

Ginger beer that was made by the men, like Bodell, was probably bottled in recycled bottles and not the traditional stoneware bottles or the large ceramic jugs.

Alcohol

Rum was distributed in hogs and decanted into bottles and other containers for the daily rum ration James Bodell noted (in Sinclair 1982, 155) that in Nov 1863:

> a hog of Rum had to be got up the cliff (at Whangamarino) and I stood watching the men get this up the Cliff. ...the rum was soon at the top... (It had to go around a small gully) the cask took a wrong turn...it busted in to ...ran in rivulets... down goes a lot of men on the same errand and there they lay as thick as herrings in a barrel sucking the rum into their mouths.

No rum hogs have been recovered, but barrel hoops have been found at most of the military sites investigated. Hog-sized barrels also had other uses including storage of salted meat, pickled onions, nails, and packing and transporting goods as was evident in the commissariat tender notice for local suppliers. Bodell describes cask ale and notes that it was bottled at the redoubts. He brewed ale during his duty in Tauranga and sold it for one shilling and sixpence a bottle.

Beers are the dominate alcohol bottle type found at New Zealand War sites. A few beer bottles have been recovered with labels. For example, at the military stable site in Te Awamutu there were several bottles of Barclay and Company's Stout, bottled by J. E. Lambard, Wapping, London (Simmons 2001). At the 40th regiment redoubt, also in Te Awamutu, Indian Pale Ale and Allsopp's Red Hand Brand were recovered (Ritchie and Gumbley 1992). Other bottles with labels indicating they contained French-made cognac have been found at most redoubt sites. Bottles that are believed to have contained brandy have also been recovered. One of the labels explains the confusion: Cognac technically is simply high quality brandy from Cognac in France. Private Bodell noted he made friends with a clerk of works and drank pale brandy with him while at Whangamarino Redoubt.

Bottle finishes/ tops with corks and foil still attached and bottles with sheered off necks are commonly found in the New Zealand Land War sites. This type of bottle opening behaviour pattern has also found in New Zealand (South Island) gold field sites. Breaking off a bottle's corked section to open the vessel apparently was not a behaviour restricted to the military. Bottles with sheered necks still feature sufficient neck in most case so they could be stoppered and recycled.

Case gin and schnapps which are common in archaeological sites that date from the 1860–1880s in New Zealand are found in minimal numbers at redoubt sites. By the mid 19th century gin was a respectable drink in British high society; prior to that it was the drink of the working-class and regulated in the 1700s (BBC 2004). Whisky is also found in low percentages in redoubt sites.

Bitters, including quart-sized bottles of bitters produced in Germany. Bitters may have been consumed as an alcohol or in combination with other alcohols or used as a remedy for the effects of alcohol. Bitters are alcohol based and are associated with alcohol consumption. Historically bitters were used to treat stomach complaints, dyspepsia, colic, gas, diarrhoea. Some bitters were also used for constipation. The bitters found in sites might be associated less with food and drink consumption and more with medical treatment. Medicinal products were not included in this paper but are often found at redoubt sites, albeit in small quantities. Although illness is mentioned in at least one diary no medicinal product was noted.

High numbers of alcohol bottles are recovered from Land War sites. The percentage of alcohol bottles is far higher than any other artefact type recovered. The alcohol bottles may represent only a fraction of the alcohol actually consumed because of cask decanting. The officers' diaries and letters contain very few references to alcohol. In contrast the diaries of the 'men' do reference alcohol.

Comparative Differences: Historical Records and the Archaeological Record

Many of the differences in the data available from the historical records and the archaeological record are based on issues such as preservation. The slice of daily life represented by the archaeological record is animated by the historical records. The lively monologues of the diaries and correspondence, and often very opinionated reports of the commissariat officers breath a life into the material culture of food consumption at the New Zealand War sites. The historical records have some information overlaps and provide a measure of the information deficits apparent in the archaeological record. The archaeological record fills information gaps in the historical records, including the use of dinner wares, glass and ceramic drinking vessels, eating utensils.

Table 16.2 summarizes and compares the food items referenced in commissariat documents; the personal papers of soldiers; items recovered from archaeological sites; and provides a list of items that have not been recovered archaeologically. What is apparent and not unexpected is the lack of representation in archaeological sites of perishable foods. The chances of finding perishable organic foods such as potatoes, onions, turnips, milk, sugar etc. is considered extremely low. Foods associated with seeds, for example, apples, cherries, and wholegrain in bread or biscuits or dried pulses like peas/ split peas, have a potential for representation in the archaeological record. At the Armed Constabulary Redoubt what are believed to be peas have been found and seeds like marrow squash and buckwheat have been recovered from a privy matrix. The information obtained from the privy suggests the need for more soil sampling and more focus on sampling this type of feature.

Many fragments of tinned cans have been recovered from sites but with the notable exception of sardine tins these are usually not identifiable. In analysing tin can fragments the range of product identified in Table 16.2 may be useful. Careful analysis of fish tins may shed light on the lack of herring tins represented. What is interesting about the fish tins is the comment by several men concerning the purchase of sardines. Sardines were listed as part of the rations. The purchase of items not issued as a ration or listed on commissariat tender documents may include the many sauces found at archaeological sites: for example, Worcestershire, tomato sauce, Yorkshire relish. Were the sauces like alcohol

Table 16.2. Food products referenced in commissariat documents, personal papers of soldiers, and archaeological site reports in the Waikato, Bay of Plenty, and Taranaki.

Commissariat Purchases	Commissariat Obtained off the land	Officers and Privates	Archaeological Sites	Food Types not Identified in Archaeological Sites
beef (*bos*)	beef	beef	beef	
mutton/sheep		mutton/sheep	mutton/sheep	
pork (*sus*)		pork	pork	
salt beef (*bos*)		salt beef		salt beef
salt pork (*sus*)		salt pork		salt pork
			rabbit	
		duck	duck	
			chicken eggs	
			chicken	
		fish		fish
		eels (*anguilla sp*)		eels
		sardines (tinned)	sardines (tinned) – Albert & Cie of Lorient, B Basset of La Rochelle, R Balestrie of Concarneau	
		herring (tinned)		herring (tinned)
			oysters (*saxostrea sp*)	
			cat's eye (*Lunella amaragda*)	
			Melagraphia aethiops	
			paua (*haliotis sp*)	
			Neothais scalaris	
			Haustrum haustorium	
			Perna canaliculus periostracum	
sugar		sugar		sugar
flour/bread		flour/		flour/bread
		bread		
			buckwheat seed (bread?, biscuits ? or gruel?)	
biscuits		biscuits		biscuits
suet				suet
		butter		butter
raisins				raisins
currants				currants
rice				rice
oatmeal				oatmeal
peas			peas ?	pea ?
dried preserved vegetable				dried preserved vegetable
olive oil			olive oil – Mortons	
			salad oil – Geo Whybrow's	
vinegar			vinegar – Whybrow's, Waters	
lemon juice				
lime juice		lime juice	lime juice ?	lime juice ?
pepper		pepper		pepper
salt		salt	salt – Weston and Weston	
mustard			mustard barrel ?	mustard ?
		milk		milk

Table 16.2 continued.

Commissariat Purchases	Commissariat Obtained off the land	Officers and Privates	Archaeological Sites	Food Types not Identified in Archaeological Sites
coffee		coffee		coffee
tea		tea		tea
chocolate		chocolate		chocolate
		jam		jam
		treacle		treacle
		honey		honey
		water-		watermelon
		melon		
		peaches	peaches	
		cherries		cherries
		apples		apples
preserved compressed vegetables				preserved compressed vegetables
turnip				turnip
carrots				
pumpkin				
		marrow squash	marrow squash	
potatoes	potatoes	potatoes		potatoes
	Indian corn			corn
onions				onions
pickled onions in cask		'pickle ration'		Pickled onions
			mixed pickles – Morton's, Mills and Ledge, Stower's Pure Pickles, Crosse and Blackwell, Geo Wynbrow	
			relish – Goodall Backhouse Yorkshire relish	
			Worcestershire sauce – Lea and Perrins	
			tomato sauce – Olson's tomato sauce	
			capers	
			herb bottle ?	
			curry powder – Mortons	
			essence (flavour)	
rum – hog		rum – cask		rum – cask
		beer – cask	beer – stout, ale porter	
		brandy	brandy	
			cognac	
			gin	
			schnapps	
			whiskey	
			bitters – Dr Soules Hop Bitters, JJW Peters (Hamburg), J von Pein (Hamburg), Conr... Stoll of Hamburg,	
		ginger beer	ginger beer	
			aerated water	

and sardines a personal purchase or a purchase by an organized mess? The jars of mixed pickles or pure pickles might also be a personal purchase or mess purchase since the pickle ration was associated with pickled onions in a cask.

While it is acknowledged in written records that there was a difference in the rations available to officers, private soldiers of the regiments, and militia, an indication of the hierarchy and differential treatment has yet to be identified in the archaeological record. This situation will probably be rectified once more redoubt sites are sampled and compared. The style in which men and officers ate is only suggested by the archaeological record. The historical records provide details like the separation of rank, separate messes, officers' clubs, etc.

Summary

The establishment of supply systems and depots, kitchens, and bakeries was built into the infra structure of fortification, advancement of the line of attack, and later guarding the frontier. Feeding the troops and for a soldier getting their daily bread was a focus of daily life on the front. The combined information from archaeological sites and historical records provides a fuller picture of subsistence during the New Zealand Wars since both types of data provide different information.

The archaeological record of the diet of soldiers and officers during the New Zealand Land Wars suggests that while grog was a staple of soldiering and probably still is, the diet of many of the soldiers was reasonable good. Some of the daily excerpts from private soldiers' and officers' diaries and letters give an impression of the opportunities taken to fill one's belly, or exploit a situation where food resources were at hand. The opportunities taken by the officers and men to supplement their military ration with local produce and fresh meat probably increased their nutritional health and fitness as soldiers. The military rations for private soldiers were better and included more protein than the food ration of a labourer during the same period.

The separation of officers from men was an intrinsic part of the military institution they operated within (i.e. part of Foucault's 'terrain of power'; McHoul and Grace 1993). While campaigning the formal mess rarely existed but based on historical records separation of the officers and the enlisted men was still standard practice. For most of the officers and enlisted men in the regiments and militia the links between food and drink and power were simplistic and intrinsic to the military regime they participated in.

Control of rations, including rum, instilled power in the commissariat and officers. This power along with other controls exercised over their daily lives was recognized by the men. Differential treatment was also evident in the rationing. The Colonial Militia were one of the main targets for differential treatment through rationing. The motive behind the treatment is a point of speculation. The intent may have been to increase separation between the colonials and the British regiments.

The Forest Rangers frequently pushed the edges of disciplinary power. The Rangers paid higher ration costs, but were paid more then the troops because of the risk associated with their duty. They pillaged on behalf of the commissariat and thus maintained the status quo and disciplinary power of the commissariat – while challenging the status quo of the commanders of the attack column with unauthorised behaviour that was admired by other soldiers and partially sanctioned. Their tactic for gaining power through discursive methods was successful and often provided a level of freedom not afforded the other colonial forces or the Imperial regiments.

The campaigns in New Zealand were fought over land and English settler demand for productive land. Imperial and colonial troops benefited from the agricultural acumen of the Maori. The fruits (quite literally) of Maori labour fed the force that sought to conquer them.

References

Armed Constabulary Force (1870–1872) Diary of duty, Kikikihi Station, manuscript, Hamilton Public Library, Hamilton.

Barber, L. (1984) *Frontier Town: A History of Te Awamutu 1884–1984*, Hong Kong, Ray Richards Publishers and Te Awamutu Borough Council.

Barton, L. (1979) *Australians in the Waikato War 1863–1864*, Marrickville, NSW, Southwood Press.

Belich, J. (1988) *The New Zealand Wars*, Penguin Books, Hong Kong.

Bilcliffe, J. (1995) *Well Done the 68th*, Chippenham, England, Picton Publishing.

British Broadcasting Corporation (2004) The History of Gin (and Tonic), 22 June 2004, www.bbc.co.uk.

Cowan, J. (1983) *The New Zealand Wars: A History of the Maori Campaigns and the Pioneering Period*, Volume I *1845–1864*, Wellington, New Zealand, Government Printer.

Clement-Lorford, F. (2004) Alexis Benoist Soyer. www.soyer.co.uk.

Daily Southern Cross, Auckland NZ (1864), Commissariate (sic) NZ Auckland 16 Feb 1864 Tenders, no. 2066 Vol. XX 25 February 1864, 1, Auckland, New Zealand.

Featon, J. (1971) *The Waikato War, 1863–1864*, Christchurch, New Zealand, Capper Press.

Gamble, D. J. (1864) *Journals of the Deputy Quartermaster General in New Zealand From 24 December 1861 To 7 September 1864*, London, War Office. (Copy held at Department of Conservation, Hamilton, New Zealand.)

Gladstone, W. E and Defery, Lord (1863) Correspondence 17/1/1863, Ripon Papers Vol. XXIII (MS 43513) 1857, British Library, London.

Godden, G. A. (1984) *Encyclopedia of British Pottery and Porcelain Marks*, London, Barrie and Jenkins.

Greaves, G. W. (1863–1864) Deputy Commissariat General Report

December 5, 1863 to January 4, 1864. War Office 107/77, Public Records Office, London.

Greaves, G. W. (1864) *Journals of the Deputy Quartermaster General in New Zealand From 24 December 1861 To 7 September 1864*, London, War Office. (Copy held at Department of Conservation, Hamilton, New Zealand.)

Jones, H. S. (1865) Report Showing the Quantities of Flour Issued, Inclosure 6 no. 6, War Office 33/17A, Public Records Office, London.

Kowalsky, A. A. and Kowalsky, D. (1999) *Enclyclopedia of Marks on American, English, and European Earthenware, Ironstone, and Stoneware (1780–1980)*, Schiffer Publishing Ltd., Atglen, PA, USA.

Lennard, M. (1986) *The Road to War*, Whakatane, New Zealand, Whakatane and District Historical Society.

McHoul, A. and Grace, W. (1993) *A Foucault Primer: Discourse, Power and the Subject*, Dunedin, New Zealand, University of Otago Press.

McCarley, J. B. (1988) Feeding Billy Yank: Union rations between 1861 and 1865. *Quartermaster Professional Bulletin, December 1988*, 1–6, www.qmfound.com/feed_billy_yank.htm.

McGibbon, I. (2000) *The Oxford Companion to New Zealand Military History*, Oxford, Oxford University Press.

Morgan, B. H. (1986) Report on Archaeological Work Carried Out For Waipa County by Morgan Leatherby Associates at the Ohaupo Cemetery Reserve, unpublished New Zealand Archaeological Association Site File S15/11, Department of Conservation, Hamilton New Zealand.

Nicholls, B. (1988) *The Colonial Volunteers: The Defence Force of the Australian Colonies 1836–1901*, Sydney, Australia, Allen and Urwin.

Parker, E. (2004) Notes from the Buckland Family History on the Buckland's 58th Regiment China, unpublished, Cambridge Museum, Cambridge New Zealand.

Prickett, N. (1981) The Archaeology of a Military Frontier: Taranaki, New Zealand 1860–1881, unpublished PhD Thesis, University of Auckland, New Zealand.

Prickett, N. (2003) The history and archaeology of Queen's Redoubt, South Auckland. *Record of the Auckland Museum* 40, 5–37.

Rippon Papers (1857) Correspondence to W. E. Gladstone from Lord de Frey. Vol XXIII Addit. Manuscript 43513, 14 and 24, British Library, London.

Ritchie, N. A. and Gumbley, W. (1992) The 40th Regiment Redoubt Site Te Awamutu S15/173 Archaeological Excavations 1991, unpublished, Department of Conservation, Hamilton.

Robertson, J. L. (1863) Report on War in New Zealand from May 1863, Closing with the Termination for the Campaigns in the Waikato. War Office 33/16, Public Records Office, London.

Robertson, J. L. (1864) Inclosure 1 in No. 13, 7 September, Report on War in New Zealand, 5–26, War Office 33/17A, Public Records Office, London.

Robertson, J. L. (1864) Inclosure 1 no 18, 23 August 1864, Continuation of Narrative of the Campaign in the Waikato Country, Auckland New Zealand 1863–1864, 59–73, War Office 33/17A, Public Records Office, London.

Ryan, T. and Parham, B. (1986) *The Colonial New Zealand Wars*, Wellington, New Zealand, Gratham House.

Simmons, A. (1990) Historical Research on the Hamilton West Redoubt, unpublished New Zealand Archaeological Association Site File, Department of Conservation, Hamilton, New Zealand.

Simmons, A. (2001) Te Awamutu Events Centre and Swimming Pool, Report on Archaeological Monitoring, unpublished New Zealand Archaeological Association Site File, Department of Conservation, Hamilton, New Zealand.

Sinclair, K. (ed.) (1982) *A Soldier's View of the Empire: The Reminiscences of James Bodell 1831–1892*, London, Bodley Head.

Strickland, E. (1865) Report 25 March 1865, Inclosure 1 no. 15, 36–38, War Office 33/17A, Public Records Office, London.

Stower, R. (1996) *Forest Rangers*, Hamilton, New Zealand, Print House.

unknown (1869) Returns of the Blockhouses, Redoubts and Stockades in the North Island 10/9/1869. T61/6 National Archives, Wellington.

Vennell, C. W. (1984) *Brown and the Elms*, Tauranga, New Zealand, Publicity Printing.

Vickery, W. and Masefield, J. (1864) Appendix 1, Inclosure 2 no 18; Specification of a Double Cased Field Oven. Continuation of Narrative of the Campaign in the Waikato Country, Auckland New Zealand 1863–1864, 73–74, War Office 33/17A, Public Records Office, London.

von Tempsky, G. F. (n.d.) Memoranda of the New Zealand Campaign in 1863 and 1864, manuscript, Hamilton Public Library, Hamilton, New Zealand.

Vuletich, L. (2004) Artefact Catalogue Armed Constabulary Redoubt Pirongia, unpublished draft catalogue, available from Les Vuletich, Hamilton New Zealand.

War Office (1864) Appendix 4, Instructions to Commissariat Officers and Others in Field Service in New Zealand. Inclosure 3 no. 18, 75, War Office 33/17A, Public Records Office, London.

Watson, K. (2000a) Armed Constabulary Redoubt (faunal analysis), unpublished paper.

Watson, K. (2000b) Alexandra East Redoubt (faunal analysis), unpublished paper.

Young, R., Curwnow, H. and King, M. (1981) *G. F. von Tempsky: Artist and Adventurer*, Martinborough, New Zealand, Alister Taylor Publishers.